COMPETING FOR
INFLUENCE

THE ROLE OF THE PUBLIC SERVICE IN
BETTER GOVERNMENT IN AUSTRALIA

COMPETING FOR
INFLUENCE

THE ROLE OF THE PUBLIC SERVICE IN
BETTER GOVERNMENT IN AUSTRALIA

BARRY FERGUSON

Australian
National
University

PRESS

Published by ANU Press
The Australian National University
Acton ACT 2601, Australia
Email: anupress@anu.edu.au

Available to download for free at press.anu.edu.au

ISBN (print): 9781760462765
ISBN (online): 9781760462772

WorldCat (print): 1103671031
WorldCat (online): 1103671281

DOI: 10.22459/CI.2019

Cover design and layout by ANU Press

Contents

List of illustrations

Boxes

Figures

Tables

Abbreviations

ACCC	Australian Competition and Consumer Commission
APRA	Australian Prudential Regulation Authority
APS	Australian Public Service
APSC	Australian Public Service Commission
ASIC	Australian Securities and Investments Commission
ASX	Australian Stock Exchange
CBO	community-based organisation
CPD	Centre for Policy Development
ERP	Enterprise Resource Planning
HIP	(Royal Commission into the) Home Insulation Program
JCPAA	Joint Committee of Public Accounts and Audit
NCOA	National Commission of Audit
NPM	New Public Management
NPV	net present value
OECD	Organisation for Economic Co-operation and Development
PGPA Act	*Public Governance, Performance and Accountability Act 2013*
PISA	Programme for International Student Assessment
UNDP	United Nations Development Programme
VAGO	Victorian Auditor-General's Office
WEF	World Economic Forum

Foreword

Good policy, transparency of decision-making and accountability for results are key foundations on which the community at large might reasonably expect government to be built and delivered. This should come together through sound public sector governance accompanied by demonstration of able custodianship of community resources and respectful ministerial and parliamentary behaviour. Nonetheless, while political parties in opposition see these foundations as a good idea, this ideal slips out of sight once they come into office.

On any reasonable comparison with private sector governance, the public sector lags a long way behind – by perhaps an order of magnitude – and, somewhat ironically, well behind the government's own regulatory standards set for private sector governance. The government's own performance is sliding, with a public sector landscape dominated by growing political and administrative fragmentation and regulatory capture.

This seems to be part of a race to the bottom, given the accumulating evidence of private sector and not-for-profit institutional and governance failure (for example, banks and financial services, religious institutions and the aged-care sector). The combined evidence of institutional failure across all major sectors indicates a broad-based downward moral spiral that is desperately in need of a circuit breaker.

Some three years ago and following some initial academic research, I decided to build on my previous involvement with the public sector and write a book examining issues surrounding government accountability and performance in Australia. As such, this book presents a determinedly public service perspective on the challenges of good government, seeing the public service both as a (desirably) well-managed organisation in its own right and an important instrument of public policy.

The content of this book is focused on the role of the public service in addressing the difficult project of establishing and maintaining good government, beginning with a discussion of the key shortcomings of government today, then viewing the role of the public service in three parts – its present role, the role prescribed in the *Public Service Act 1999*, and the role it *could* play in the public interest. It is not a book about politics or government, but much of the detailed discussion revolves around the nature of the interface between the political and administrative arms of government, which is a necessary tent of any model of public administration. The aim in writing this book was to put forward a clear alternative to the destructive path of subordination and replacement of the public service that is inherent in the present path of government today.

The discussion of the role that the public service might play in the public interest draws heavily on private sector management literature – perhaps ironically given the criticism that can be levelled at the application of private sector management reforms to the public sector over the last 30 or so years. The resolution of this apparent difficulty for the reader can be found in an accompanying discussion of the merit of these 'managerialist' reforms, their selective nature, the accompanying motivation, the success of their implementation and their impacts. The book is essentially an Australian case study but it grapples with problems that are global in origin. This is a book written *to* policy leaders and public servants in Australia, and *for* the Australian public. Its simple message is that the public service has lost touch with the community it should serve and needs to be re-imagined as a custodian of the public interest. Seven prime ministers in the last 10 years is a ready starting point in making this case.

The focus and content of this book has been heavily shaped by a lengthy involvement with government. I joined the Victorian Public Service in 1985 after a decade with Shell Australia, and the apparent management chaos I observed contrasted heavily with the order of a well-managed and led Shell Australia. Contrary to textbook views, self-interest motivates most individuals in the political and bureaucratic system, no less so than with Shell. In the case of the latter, this pursuit was clearly channelled into a framework of fulfilment of corporate goals.

My interest in public sector management was piqued in 1992 by the introduction of the New Public Management (NPM) reforms to the Victorian public sector by an incoming Liberal–Country Party government and the subsequent attempts a decade or so later by a Labor government to undo some of the damage. This interest has also been shaped by earlier academic study of corporate behaviour and, in particular, in organisational management of relationships with the external environment. Notions of organisational strategy, structure and adjustment to change figure prominently in what follows.

I would like to thank Janine O'Flynn of the University of Melbourne and John Wanna from ANU for encouragement at important stages of this project. I would also like to thank Sam Vincent at ANU for his skilful and enthusiastic management of the publication process and my son Brett for technical advice and support. Above all, I would like to thank Anthony Arundel at UNU-MERIT Maastricht University for his encouragement to embark on this project.

Barry Ferguson
September 2018[1]

---

1   Facts and figures in this book were accurate at the time of writing. However, circumstances change; where possible, attempts have been made to ensure data is up-to-date.

1

Introduction

1.1 A global problem

Evidence is mounting that governments around the world are failing their communities. The causes of this global failure of government are manifold and interrelated, ranging from the rise of a political class, the associated growth of lobby groups, a growing plurality of voters, a mismatch between the length of the electoral cycle and today's wicked public policy problems, subordination of the public service and, quite simply, governments that are lost in pursuit of self-interest. Poor government is accompanied by the addition to its structures of a growing number of task forces, royal commissions, government 'coordinators', tsars, commissioners, ombudsmen and standing committees. These various ad hoc additions to the fabric of government are placed on top of structures that are already marked by poor governance. This is underpinned by the absence of a discernible political or moral compass or courage. Good public policy today has few friends in conception and execution.

For decades, government structures have grown in a higgledy-piggledy manner, driven in part by common economic imperatives but following the ideological fashions of the day and without proper regard to the impact on their operational efficiency or their ability to measure and deliver results. For nearly 40 years, fads in government style have been incompletely grafted onto an evolving environment that is not always receptive to their charms and while the previous fad is still in the process of being bedded down. The associated poor governance is manifested by an obsession with the aggregate financial dimensions of government;

the near impossibility of assessing outcomes at program, policy and departmental levels; and a failure to identify, evaluate, and address root causes in a systematic manner.

At the same time, most of today's 'new' problems already have a home. The majority of the government-appointed task forces, royal commissions, standing committees and advisory boards are products of governments wanting to be seen to be in control, but rarely does any such body have a mandate to resolve problems. Worse still, each new examination invariably identifies a failure of successive governments to implement the recommendations of previous such bodies, which might have diminished the need for the latest round of band-aids. These layers of coordination, administration and investigation dilute the accountability of those already charged with addressing the real problems. Consider, for example, the impact of over 35 separate 'significant' and supplementary reviews into the Australian Government's Department of Defence since 1973. A 2015 report identifies a long and unfortunate history of gaming the system, lack of integration, lack of accountability, substitution of process for outcome, underpinned by an absence of leadership (Peever 2015). The publication of the committee's final report under the title *Creating one Defence* points clearly to the core problem.

Major political parties have been seduced by the increasing number of electronic targeting and marketing tools that enable them to focus on the swinging voter rather than the community at large, and have lost sight of the big policy picture and their communities along the way.[1] The demise of good government has been aided by broad-based societal and technological changes that have added to the challenges. Voters around the globe have withdrawn their support from the major parties, encouraging minor parties and the growth of new political splinter groups, both within and without the major parties themselves. Governments have become self-serving custodians in residence, window-dressing and pursuing containment strategies rather than solving problems, whilst rewarding themselves handsomely for their failure.

---

1   Press reports following the victory of Donald Trump in the 2016 US election suggested that the company supporting the Trump election campaign, Cambridge Analytica, amassed up to 5,000 data points on every American adult as part of a program to pinpoint Trump voters. See Fergus Hunter, 'Cambridge Analytica, the "psychographic" data firm behind Donald Trump, eyes Australian move', *Sydney Morning Herald*, 12 January 2017, www.smh.com.au/politics/federal/cambridge-analytica-the-psychographic-data-firm-behind-donald-trump-eyes-australian-move-20161212-gt926e.html.

Box 1.1 A 'First principles review of Defence'

In August 2014, the Minister for Defence appointed a team to undertake a 'First principles review of Defence', the team being led by a former managing director of Rio Tinto, David Peever. The Peever review team was tasked by the Australian Government to ensure that the Department of Defence was 'fit for purpose' and 'able to deliver against its strategy': their findings were published in 2015. Some extracts from this final report make interesting reading:

> There is general agreement about the nature of the problem. The current organisational model and processes are complicated, slow and inefficient in an environment which requires simplicity, greater agility and timely delivery. Waste, inefficiency and rework are palpable …

> Defence is suffering from a proliferation of structures, processes and systems with unclear accountabilities. These in turn cause institutionalised waste, delayed decisions, flawed execution, duplication, a change-resistant bureaucracy, over-escalation of issues for decision and low engagement levels amongst employees …

> Previous reviews and interviews with stakeholders indicate Defence operates as a loose federation where the individual parts from the highest levels, then down and across the organisation, are strongly protective of their turf and see themselves meriting more favour than other parts of the department. The centre is weak and not sufficiently strategic. (Peever 2015, p 13)

As the subject of such regular 'significant' reviews (over 35 since 1973) and many more supplementary reviews, according to the Peever review team, Defence has established destructive opportunities to game the system and resist change. The core recommendation of the Peever review was to integrate departmental operations and establish one integrated system, termed 'the One Defence approach'. In turn, the review team recommended the establishment of a new 'One Defence business model', comprising seven 'first principles' and 76 accompanying recommendations. The first principle, embracing 19 of the 76 recommendations, was to establish a strong, strategic centre to strengthen accountability and top-level decision-making.

Defence is the most complex and technically challenging department from a leadership and management perspective within the government of Australia, and most other governments for that matter.[1] It involves the determination, equipping and maintenance of both individual and integrated land, sea and air capabilities; it is geographically dispersed and also requires the integration of the two major – public service and military – employee streams; it must implement a strategy that makes long-term capability commitments but simultaneously maintains an agility to meet rapidly changing international circumstances; and it must maintain an intelligence capability that supports its planning horizons of 30 or 40 years as well as emerging situations.

In its breadth and complexity it can be viewed as a microcosm of the broader public sector challenge embracing some of the more complex strategic and management issues across this sector and needing 'transformational' change in structures, capabilities, systems, culture and alignment to become fit for purpose. Complex organisations require strong leadership, a point that the Peever report makes in many different ways by highlighting the existing organisational shortcomings, and envisaging integration of operations running from strategy through enhanced control of resources to monitoring of organisational performance. Indeed, the 76 recommendations were put forward as an integrated whole, not to be cherry-picked (and they were not with 75 of the 76 being accepted 'in principle' despite a change of government in the meantime). The reader should have no difficulty aligning these and other recommendations in the Peever report with the broad thrust of this book and its arguments for change across the broader public service.

[1] It is presently being overtaken in this regard by the establishment of the Department of Homeland Security, which was announced in July 2017.
Source: Peever 2015.

Solutions to this failure can be found with those who would wish to, indeed claim to, govern – namely our politicians. I focus, however, on the public service and the role that it plays, rather than on 'the government'. I do not suggest that the public service holds the solution in its hands, far from it. But I do believe that, with judicious changes to public policy, combined with a public service that grasps the competitive nettle, it can be an important part of the solution to the poor government being experienced today.

Underpinning such a view is one that the public service must become a *public* service. Today it receives very little attention in the public domain outside of the reported cases of maladministration and inappropriate personal behaviour. This position should be addressed, in the public interest, and the Australian Public Service (APS) should be encouraged to actively build its brand both within and outside of government. Redressing this invisibility is part of the broader solution from a public policy perspective. Because the public service has not recovered from losing its way, and all sense of self, over 30 years ago, learning lessons from history so as to understand the antecedents of our present problems, avoid repeating the mistakes of the past, and be better able to determine the way ahead should be the starting point for change.

International academic researchers have observed that there was a stable style of government in many countries for much of the 20th century, but that a turning point occurred from the late 1970s with the arrival of the New Public Management (NPM) reforms, led by governments in the United Kingdom and New Zealand, paving the way for private sector inspired change to sweep the democratic world. This 'revolution' followed growing fiscal pressures on governments and a long period in which the public service was a partner in government around the globe. The revolution was encouraged by the emergence of wicked problems and materially aided by the development of cost-accounting techniques in the private sector in the latter decades of the 20th century, thereby enabling the more effective allocation of overhead and joint service delivery costs to programs in the public sector (matching costs with 'outputs'). State and national governments imported this 'revolution' to Australia through the mid-1980s and the early 1990s.[2]

The NPM reforms reflected prevailing practices in the private sector. Its two phases were characterised by the terms managerialism and marketisation: the former focused on the management of the public sector's underlying belief in the universal applicability of professional management and the latter on the use of markets for the delivery of services.[3] Government departments were held to account for 'outputs', not just sound process and good financial accounting; authority within the public service was decentralised; and accountability was pushed down to lower (departmental) levels. As a consequence of these changes, one public service became many in culture, employment and focus. The placement of the department at the apex of public service activity occurred at the expense of the collective ('the centre') and established service to minister(s) as the primary focus of departmental activity. This opening-up of traditional public service activities to competition, and the consequent development of competitive markets in policy advice and service delivery, led the public service to relinquish its pre-eminent position in both fields.

These reforms have enabled the development of a broad-based political class in which community activists, elected representatives, ministerial staffers, consultants, public servants and lobbyists move seamlessly around the public and private sectors. The growing influence of the political class over the formation of policy has been matched by the growing influence of private for-profit and not-for-profit organisations over the

---

2   I speculate on what triggered this 'revolution' in Chapter 10.

3   'Managerialism' can also be viewed in terms of a theory of state where the organisation replaces the individual as the dominant social unit, and in associated political terms as a set of beliefs that both links good government with 'rational' management, viewing it as a form of governance. What is important is the underlying valuation of generic managerial skills in application to the public service, and the conclusions that might be drawn from this global 'managerialist' experiment.

implementation of policy. This has been accompanied by the evolution of government philosophies from the 1980s version of 'the private sector does it better' (e.g. outsourcing and executive employment contracts), to concepts of partnering and networking with a wide variety of commercial and community-based organisations that are already involved in the delivery of government projects and services.

Unfortunately, the development of a more distributed form of government has not been matched by governance frameworks, and a lack of political will to properly account to the Australian public for resource use has undermined the capacity of the public service to contribute to accountable government. Arguably, when the overarching duty of government through the public service was a responsibility to deliver due process and sound financial accounting, then it was ably acquitted. But since the purported focus on performance measurement has moved on from accounting for financial inputs (under old/traditional administration) to outputs (under NPM) to outcomes (under joined-up and networked government), the public service has failed to deliver.

National auditor-general reports from a range of countries, including Canada, the United Kingdom, Australia and New Zealand, attest to this conclusion.[4] Today, the public service in these countries is stalled somewhere between the phases of effective financial accounting and the development of meaningful output and activity measures. This is despite the last 30 years of progressive complementation of financial audits with performance audits as the primary public administration performance assessment tool of state and national auditors-general.[5] Most importantly, what has been lost in all of these changes is strategic oversight of government policy across its conception, implementation and consequent performance. The current position is of public policy for sale, mounting electoral cynicism and, confronted with this, voters expressing

---

4   See, for example, a speech by then retiring Auditor-General Ian McPhee in May 2015 in which he identified 'performance measurement for programs, and outcomes, particularly assessing impact' as one of four remaining 'soft' areas in government administration in Australia. The other three were: risk management, taking a narrow view of responsibilities and implementation under pressure. Interestingly he identified companion strengths to include governance frameworks, public sector reform and values, and collegiality/accountability. What emerges is the picture of a public service that is good at the bigger picture management dimensions but not so good at converting it to effective operations on the ground (McPhee 2015). This issue is discussed in some detail in Chapter 3.
5   Hehir (2016) catalogues the Australian evolution from financial to performance accounting.

their discontent by increasingly turning away from the major parties to independents and the minor parties, and regularly electing single-term governments.

The failure in regard to governance – across the spectrum, from policy formation through to effectiveness – is symptomatic of a broader failure: the fragmentation of our system of government accompanied by political lack of interest in the bigger (policy) picture. For example, governments today see their policies in terms of impacts on the swinging voters in marginal electorates: long gone are the days when a vision for the country and a small and stable set of high-level policies would win a succession of elections. Today voters are presented with fragmentation of government service delivery, brought about by increasing use of external service providers and reliance on markets; fragmentation of our political parties; and the ongoing organisational fragmentation of the public service.[6] Each of these has important implications for the operations of the public service, especially at a time when our system of government needs a large injection of cohesion. The unifying focus must be the final consumer and the broader public value created around the act of final consumption of government services. Considering the role of government as the primary customer of the public service is a useful perspective from which to view the different standpoints of good public policy and public service strategy.

1.2 The position today in Australia

While this is a generalised global description of events and problems, it applies directly to Australia, which has actively participated in the global evolution of the various styles of government over the last 30 years. Indeed, not only has the southern hemisphere not been left behind by these international developments, but our neighbours in New Zealand have been at the forefront of change over recent decades, and have dragged Australia along. Those public servants in the mid-1980s to the mid-1990s who were actively involved in implementing changes to the public

---

6   In *The next government of the United States*, Donald Kettl paints a disturbing picture of one 'logical' outgrowth of this fragmentation, namely of the US public health system's reliance on external providers, such that patients are handed from one contractor to another, never coming into contact with anyone from 'the government', and with no one in charge of their case (Kettl 2008).

service at state and federal levels within Australia will readily recall the appointment of New Zealanders to bring their intellectually impoverished cousins the message of reform with an almost religious fervour.

In her 2015 essay 'Political amnesia: how we forgot how to govern', Laura Tingle points to the damage done to the quality of government in Australia by the reforms of the 1980s, specifically the loss of institutional memory and the consequent political amnesia. Tingle also points to a contributing cause associated with the election of a Labor government under Gough Whitlam in the early 1970s, when distrust of the public service ushered a new class of player into the political game – the ministerial adviser (Tingle 2015).

While the Whitlam government might have started the slide, subsequent bipartisan support for the market-based reforms of the 1980s indicated the strength of the global movement and of its enthusiastic local adoption.[7] Indeed, the Liberal-led Coalition government elected in 1996 enshrined a number of Labor's earlier changes in a new public service Act in 1999, and these have remained largely untouched to this day. Tingle observes the consequences of these changes as,

> We have not just lost frank and fearless advice; we have lost the memory of how policy has been made before, of the history of the groups and issues with which government must interact every day. Government in the broader sense of the word, therefore has lost much of its capacity to remember and thus learn from past mistakes. (Tingle 2015, p 17)

Philosopher Simon Longstaff has considered the impact of these changes with regard to the realignment of public service and government interests, suggesting that the quality of democratic government took a turn for the worse in Australia in the 1980s, which has materially impacted on community trust in, and regard for, the legitimacy of our parliamentary institutions (Longstaff 2015). Chapter 2 incorporates the legacies of these changes with a sketch of the evolving government styles and their impacts over the last 40 years. This sets the scene for a more detailed examination of the sorts of management capabilities and tools that might be employed to improve public service and government performance today.

---

7   Indeed, a focus on the concept of achieving private sector productive efficiency levels, arguably at the ongoing expense of effectiveness, has been present in political debate on public service performance since well back into the 20th century. See, for example, APSC (2004).

Governments might be failing their constituents around the globe, but a threshold question is, where does Australia stand today in the performance tables, and how deep are our problems? Data embracing a global perspective on the performance of the Australian Government and a voter perspective, point to some important questions regarding the 'structural' – institutional and organisational – foundations of good performance (the necessary pre-conditions for such performance), as well as the available activity-based evidence.

Few sources for a view of the current Australian position are more important than information regarding the impact of government on competitiveness, as wealth creation provides the resources that enable a country to pursue its social and environmental objectives. At the highest level of country performance – as evidenced by the World Economic Forum's *Global competitiveness report 2016–2017* – Australia ranks in the low 20s (of 138 countries), ranking 21 in 2015–16 and 22 in 2016–17, with our overall performance noted as 'remarkably consistent but never stellar' (WEF 2016).

When it comes to the specific contributions of government, Australia ranks reasonably well, with its highest ranking for judicial independence (10), diversion of public funds (15), irregular payments and bribes (17), favouritism in decisions of government officials (22), transparency of government decision-making (23) and public trust in politicians (23). Australia performs poorly, however, in important administrative areas, including wastefulness of government spending (52), business costs of terrorism (55) and the burden of government regulation (77). Australia also performs poorly in some policy areas, including incentives to work and invest (effects of taxation on incentives to work (111), and invest (96)), and business start-ups (105th in days taken to start a business).

When considered as a whole, the 114 separate indices paint the picture of a country that has clean processes and is reasonably well governed, but is perhaps over-governed and, in some areas, poorly governed (weak policy and administrative waste). Part of this assessment can be attributed to the burden of three tiers of government and the overheads carried by a small and fragmented economy. There is little reason on the surface, however, why Australia should rank so poorly in terms of the wastefulness of government spending, and the lack of incentives to work and invest. One would expect that, given Australia's distance and scale handicaps, these would be areas of government policy and practice in which it needed to be better than the rest, rather than worse than most. Whilst the processes of government might be clean – 'stellar' even – this data raises questions about the quality of government policies and the efficiency of their administration.

Data published by Transparency International in the form of the 'Corruption Perceptions Index 2016' provides some insight. This index is taken from a somewhat larger collection (168) of countries and is largely compatible with the *Global competitiveness report* indices on a broad measure of public corruption (13). The data suggest that the quality of Australia's public institutions underpin this ranking, but with a key gap in the absence of a national anti-corruption body, leaving Australia as a middling performer on the global stage within the group of developed countries.

Table 1.1 Transparency International: 'Corruption Perceptions Index 2016'

Country	2012	2013	2014	2015	2016
Denmark	1 (90)	1 (91)	1 (92)	1 (91)	1 (90)
New Zealand	1 (90)	1 (91)	2 (91)	4 (88)	1 (90)
Australia	7 (85)	9 (81)	11 (80)	13 (79)	13 (79)
Canada	9 (84)	9 (81)	10 (81)	9 (83)	9 (82)
United Kingdom	17 (74)	14 (76)	14 (78)	10 (81)	10 (81)

The first number in each row represents that country's global ranking, while the bracketed number is their score on a scale from 0 (highly corrupt), to 100 (very clean).

Indeed, this 'middling performance' is associated with a steady four-year slide in Australia's ranking (from 7 to 13), including against a small group of countries – the United Kingdom, New Zealand and Canada – with whom it shares a common style of government and history, and measured against whom it is now worst in class. Other evidence to support a view that the performance of the Australian Government is declining can be found in the PISA rankings, which report the OECD's 'Programme for International Student Assessment'. The last published (2015) results (published three-yearly) point to a steady and continuing decline in the performance of Australia's national secondary education system, with results in mathematics, science and reading continuing the decline from 2000.

Nonetheless, a close examination of these different indices points to the need for careful interpretation of any of these comparative international measures, as some are absolute while others are relative. In the case of the PISA results, the scores are absolute and the published results show that Australia's absolute scores declined as well as its ranking(s). The Transparency International scores are also absolutes (and Australia's absolute scores have declined there as well).

In the case of the WEF, the scores are relative to the best rather than absolutes. This difference is important because absolutes and the trend in absolutes is often more important to the political performance of governments than the relative rankings. Thus, the public will regard Australia's rise or fall in ranking as irrelevant if government waste is seen to be on the rise. What may, therefore, be most important is a country's current, relative to its historical, performance. This dimension is especially important when it comes to the Australian public's perceptions of the broader functioning of our society as well as of the performance of the government of the day – which shape the environment within which public servants work.

A rising tide of community cynicism towards government performance is observable in Australia. This is most likely associated with growing public concern about incompetence and, perhaps, corruption, in key public and private institutions. This cynicism has been fuelled by a flow of media stories over the last three years about the lack of accountability of political parties for the donations received; politicians living and travelling lavishly at the taxpayers' expense; corruption in government departments; government interference in the management of its 'independent' entities; systematic underpayment of workers in the hospitality and related industries; private sector abuse of market power, international bribery, deceptive and misleading conduct by large corporations; cynical government attempts to claw back revenue; abuse of the vulnerable by religious (and charitable) institutions; and regular government reports (e.g. parliamentary committees, royal commissions, expert committees) indicating basic failings in public administration. Banks (and other financial institutions), property developers, convenience stores, supermarket chains, religious institutions, charitable institutions, political parties, individual state and national politicians, governments, government departments, and manufacturers all take a hit in this blame game.

Perhaps the biggest hit to community trust in Australia's institutions was delivered by the Royal Commission into Institutional Responses to Child Sexual Abuse, with the commission receiving written and oral submissions over a period of nearly five years and presenting its final report to the Australian Government in November 2017. Moved from state to state, the commission heard repeated harrowing tales of abuse, with over 8,000 personal stories being told in private sessions and with over 4,000 individual institutions being reported as places where abuse occurred. The commission subsequently made some 2,575 referrals to authorities (including police). In its final report, the commission determined that institutional abuse had occurred for generations and described this as heartbreaking and a national tragedy.

The commission's activities were accompanied by extensive local and national media coverage, from its inception on 12 January 2012, the appointment of commissioners on 11 January 2013, through to the completion of the final report. This coverage reflected the widespread geographic and institutional reporting of cases of abuse and the concomitant failure of state instrumentalities to protect vulnerable children. The commission's final report noted this failure to include police, child protection agencies, and the criminal justice system (both the civil law itself and investigation processes). No corner of Australia was left untouched by the widespread media coverage of the commission's reporting on this widespread failure to protect the vulnerable. The commission's activities also heightened national and local interest in some high-profile cases initiated outside of the royal commission's processes.

In the private sector, cases of the systematic underpayment of employees in the hospitality and services sector, often migrants or those employed on short-term visas, continued to emerge through 2016 and 2017. A joint ABC and Fairfax investigation found that a variety of franchisees had systematically underpaid their workers, thereby raising questions about the effectiveness of Australia's employment law and the Australian community's willingness and capacity to protect those least able to protect themselves.[8] It also raised questions about the sustainability of the business model(s) employed by a number of franchisors, and their

---

8   See, for example, Liz Hobday, '7-Eleven wage underpayment claims taking too long: Allan Fels', *ABC News*, 31 Aug 2016, www.abc.net.au/news/2016-08-31/7-eleven-wage-claims-taking-too-long-allan-fels/7803008. See also Anna Patty, '7-Eleven compensation bill climbs over $110 million', *Sydney Morning Herald*, 13 June 2017, www.smh.com.au/business/workplace/7eleven-compensation-bill-climbs-over-110-million-20170612-gwpdfx.html.

business ethics in implementing franchise models that were unlikely to yield a satisfactory income for franchisees, who thereby barely met minimum award conditions for their employees.

The banking and financial services industry has also received an ongoing stream of poor media. Media reports of questionable practices and individual employee misbehaviour resulted in the prime minister and treasurer jointly announcing a royal commission into 'the alleged misconduct of Australia's banks and other financial services entities' on 30 November 2017.[9] This followed community, whistleblower, Opposition, and media pressure on the Australian Government to establish such a commission, and was preceded by the Australian Banking Association releasing research showing 'low levels of trust, confidence and transparency in the banking industry', and the heads of the big four banks (ANZ, Commonwealth Bank, NAB and Westpac) writing to the treasurer to acknowledge the desirability of an inquiry.[10] The operations of the banking, insurance, superannuation and financial services industry are of national relevance and the royal commission's phase of public hearings, beginning in March 2018, generated widespread media attention.[11]

The third area that has received much adverse publicity for its performance over the last few years is that of 'government'. Whether it has been state or federal government ministers resigning over their expenses claims (the Victorian Government managed to lose both its speaker and deputy speaker), their foreign connections, or the suitability of federal politicians to sit in federal parliament, 2017 was a year in which Australia's state and national politicians hit the headlines for the wrong reasons.[12] The impact of these events was added to by reports from the Australia Institute and the Australian Public Service Commission (APSC) on issues of corruption in the public service. This gave rise to the headline in the *Sydney Morning*

---

9   See Malcolm Turnbull, 'Royal Commission – Banks and Financial Services', media release, 30 Nov 2017, pmtranscripts.pmc.gov.au/release/transcript-41355. See also 'Here's what we know about the banking royal commission', *ABC News*, 4 Dec 2017, www.abc.net.au/news/2017-12-04/banking-royal-commission-heres-what-we-know/9210214.

10   See Australian Banking Association, 'Banks set trust benchmarks', media release, 28 Aug 2017, www.ausbanking.org.au/media/media-releases/media-release-2017/banks-set-trust-benchmarks.

11   The royal commission directed its final report on 4 February 2019.

12   See, for example, Paul Karp, 'Sussan Ley quits as health minister as Turnbull outlines reforms to expenses', *Guardian*, 13 Jan 2017, www.theguardian.com/australia-news/2017/jan/13/sussan-ley-quits-health-minister-turnbull-outlines-reform-expenses. See also Lucy Sweeney, 'Sam Dastyari resigns from Parliament, says he is "detracting from Labor's mission" amid questions over Chinese links', *ABC News*, 13 Dec 2017, www.abc.net.au/news/2017-12-12/sam-dastyari-resigns-from-parliament/9247390.

Herald on 11 January 2018, 'Perceived public service corruption sapped $72.3b from GDP: Australia Institute' and, in *Government News* on 12 January 'Significant corruption revealed in Australian Public Service'.[13] And, whilst the APSC played down the results of the 2017 employee census, reporting that '*only* 5 per cent of respondents reported having witnessed corrupt behaviour' (my italics), the Australian public might be forgiven for thinking that one employee would be one too many.

In sum, it is reasonable to conclude that Australia has a broad-based problem of ethics that is marked by large institutions' single-minded pursuit of self-interest at the expense of their congregations, members and customers (especially the weak and vulnerable), matched only by the rampant opportunism shown by our elected officials. Whilst many of the publicised human and systems abuses are not directly attributable to the public service, or government, the community at large will, more generally, hold government accountable for the totality of what goes wrong in our community, and is certainly entitled to hold governments directly responsible where there are clear failures of enforcement of laws. The community is also likely to hold their elected representatives responsible where the rules and laws themselves do not meet community expectations: communities are entitled to be especially angry with their politicians when, instead of foreseeing challenges ahead, they apply a band-aid to the latest disaster.

Indeed, the years 2016 and 2017 confirmed declining community regard for politics and politicians, as reflected in the post-election Australian Electoral Study published in December 2016 (Cameron & McAllister 2016). The study interviewed some 2,800 people in the three months following the July 2016 Federal election and found declining levels of interest in elections (only 30 per cent took a detailed interest). This was associated with a long-term declining trend in the proportion of voters who always vote for the same party (now 40 per cent, down from 72 per cent in 1967), diminishing trust in our politicians (only 26 per cent expressed confidence in the government), and sharply rising numbers who believe that politicians only look after themselves (74 per cent). These conclusions are broadly supported by data from the 2017 Edelman global Trust Barometer and a 2017 Australian Centre for Policy Development (CPD)

---

13   See Hannah Aulby and Rod Campbell, 'The cost of corruption', The Australia Institute, Jan 2018, www.tai.org.au/sites/default/files/P381%20Costs%20of%20corruption%20FINAL_0.pdf; and 'APS values and the code of conduct', in APSC (2017b).

report. The Edelman barometer pointed to a continuing loss of faith in politics, business and media (in Australia, trust in government fell sharply from above to below the global average obtained from 28 countries), and the CPD report pointed to serious fault lines in Australia's democracy and an accompanying, encouraging, community appetite for reform.[14]

The most interesting conclusion from these studies is that, despite the recorded diminishing trust in democracy, our government and politicians – and despite continuing community disengagement from a lifetime of one-party voters – the electorate is increasingly interested in policy issues and reform. In the 2016 election, 59 per cent of voters made their decision based on policy issues (a strong upward trend) compared with 23 per cent on parties as a whole (trending down slowly), 9 per cent on leaders (trending down), and 9 per cent on the local candidates (slowly trending upwards). This growing preference was associated with a developing view that it makes little difference who is in power, and with a steadily rising share of voters who determine their voting decisions during the election campaign. One interpretation of these results envisages a direct link between the electorate's growing interest in policy matters and the rise of the minor parties, with the latter being used as a vehicle through which to reward political parties that focus on matters of importance to the electorate.

This evident cynicism towards politicians brings with it direct costs, as government activities are increasingly resisted by well-organised public campaigns, which extend decision-making processes; increasingly subject to the risk of class actions, which incur substantial legal costs; and face a balanced mix of judicial and community-based processes that diminish political output. This cynicism grows in the face of taxpayer funds being used to defend ill-considered government actions, particularly those that developed out of party political matters and should have been defended with party political funds.

Community cynicism also has an impact on the quality of government that is delivered, due to a reduction in the amount of time in any term of office that governments and the public service are able to focus on

---

14   See Edelman Holdings, '2017 Edelman Trust Barometer', www.edelman.com/research/2017-edelman-trust-barometer, and Michael Koziol, 'Distrustful nation: Australians lose faith in politics, media and business', *Sydney Morning Herald*, 21 Jan 2017, www.smh.com.au/politics/federal/distrustful-nation-australians-lose-faith-in-politics-media-and-business-20170118-gttmpd.html.   See also CPD (2017a, 2017b).

delivering valuable outcomes. A rearrangement of the public service also affects delivery of quality government.[15] Just how costly these changes to public service structures are is evident in the reorganisation that followed the election of the Liberal–National government under Tony Abbott in September 2013. The APSC's *State of the service report 2013–14*, reported on the public service–wide employee census conducted during 2014 (APSC 2014a). This survey followed the announcement in September 2013 of wide-ranging machinery of government changes to the structure and functions of a number of APS departments and agencies.

The report's examination of the incidence of 'major change' found high levels of impact on employees. For example, 80 per cent of the senior executive service (and 73 per cent of next-level employees) reported recent experience of 'major change', with the most commonly reported types of change being decreases in staff numbers (67 per cent of all employees surveyed) and structural changes (57 per cent). After excluding smaller agencies from the survey, the report noted that the proportion of employees in each agency experiencing some form of major change ranged up to 98 per cent. Moreover, only 35 per cent of all employees perceived that change in their agency was well managed, further compounding the negative impacts of the changes themselves. In these circumstances, the tendency of individuals to look inwards to defend their territory, rather than upward and outward to their political masters and customers, impacts output levels and effectiveness.

The consequent lost productivity was the focus of a 2016 Victorian parliamentary committee report examining the rationale for, and execution of, the machinery of government changes in Victoria that followed the 2014 election of the Labor government under Daniel Andrews, pointing to the likely substantial nature of these costs (Parliament of Victoria 2016a). A UK National Audit Office report on the impacts of machinery of government changes noted that structural change in the public service was rarely associated with substantial activity change and almost never underpinned by a business case for change and an ex-post review (NAO UK 2014). Publication of such reports, along with examples of political and public service maladministration, can only diminish a community's confidence in its government.

---

15   The associated challenge at election time in Australia pales into insignificance with that in the United States at the time of a presidential election as over 4,000 positions may change incumbents, with such change accounting for much of the top three layers of a new administration.

Some of the issues identified so far – the rebalancing of the political parties, the diminishing trust in our politicians, and government's capacity to do the right thing by the community – have important implications for the role that the public service plays. It is equally important to note, however, that the APS is far from proactive in acknowledging and adapting to the rapidly changing political landscape – as a number of official observers and past officials have admitted. For example, in the *State of the service report 2013–14*, then APS commissioner Stephen Sedgwick highlighted the 1980's antecedents but pointed to a public service that, in his words, 'may have become too reactive, too focused on the short term and the delivery of tasks, and unable to generate the range of new ideas that it might have liked'. In doing so, he identified the need for 'transformational change' to meet the productivity imperative, supported by change in the culture, processes and practices of the APS to address 'systemic issues across the public service' (APSC 2014a). APS Commissioner John Lloyd later reinforced these comments in 2015 when he referred several times to the reality that the public service endures beyond individual governments and the consequent need for the public service to look over the horizon (APSC 2015a).

Since leaving the role of secretary of the Department of the Prime Minister and Cabinet in 2011, Terry Moran has also made a number of speeches covering a handful of common themes – of confusion over ministerial and departmental responsibilities, loss of public service capabilities, the omnipresent role of economists, and the need to explore new organisational forms in public administration. For example, in a May 2015 speech to Queensland public servants as president of the Institute of Public Administration, Moran asked 'How is our sector going?'. His observation was that, though Australia had one of the best performing public services in the world, it could be better. Moran highlighted the actions required to improve public sector performance in three ways:

1. rethinking accountabilities and responsibilities
2. rebuilding some core capabilities that the sector has lost or is losing
3. restructuring the sector organisationally.

In the discussion that followed, he noted the pressure placed on Australia's system of government by a political class with an unsteady grasp of the strengths of Australia's Westminster system; the need to rebuild core capability in engineering; the loss of ability in broad strategic planning and its replacement with the economist's view that the answer to every policy challenge is the development of a well-structured market and the application of a price to everything; and slow progress in restructuring the public sector through the use of special-purpose vehicles, such as statutory authorities and companies with a degree of independence from government departments, appropriately matched to circumstance (Moran 2015).

Public sector performance can be understood by attending to the motivation and goals of Australia's political class and public service. Instead of simply believing that politicians do (or should) work only for the public good and not their own self-interest, the focus ought to be on how they behave.[16] Not that the general public these days buys the notion of an altruistic political class: a recent ANU (The Australian National University) poll found the public regarded self-interest as the primary political motive (Cameron & McAllister 2016), with only 12 per cent of respondents believing the government is run for 'all the people'. These findings are supported by the findings in a recent discussion paper that declares, 'The survey reveals almost three-quarters of Australians think politics is fixated on short-term gains and not addressing long-term challenges' (CPD 2017a). This community view is consistent with Longstaff's reminder that political parties are above all private associations formed and run to further the interests of their members, and given a public face by the election of some of their members to the houses of parliament (Longstaff 2015).

For analytical purposes, the validity of the assumption that elected representatives serve themselves and not the public good at both individual and collective levels is given impetus at a macro level in a major, recent study of the impacts on the cost and quality of government in the United Kingdom, focusing on the private sector–driven reforms of the 1970s and 1980s. The study raises the possibility that these reforms were not so much a product of politicians wanting to bring private sector management techniques to public sector performance to improve the cost and quality of government, but rather simply rent-seeking behaviour on their part.

---

16 An example of the naïve view that politicians ought to put the public interest ahead of their own is contained in the editorial 'How to restore faith in politics and democracy' (*Age* (Melbourne), 7 Jan 2017), which refers to politicians' 'duty to be honest and altruistic'. This contrasts with the sentiment embodied in the often used quotation attributed to former NSW premier JT Lang, and popularised by former prime minister Paul Keating, 'In the race of life always back self-interest; at least you know it is trying'.

The authors find an absence of evidence to support the argument that the reforms were designed to improve public sector performance (Hood & Dixon 2015).[17]

In Samuel Furphy's edited volume *The seven dwarfs and the age of the mandarins*, Nicholas Brown supports the argument that the major objective of these reforms in Australia was the transfer of power from the bureaucracy to the political class (Brown 2015).[18] Brown points to the inherent conservatism of the mandarins, the diminishing disparity in education levels between ministers and public servants, and a range of pressures coalescing around the 1972 change to a Labor government after some 23 years of conservative rule. Brown suggests that together these factors placed the 'land of the dwarfs' under siege in the 1970s and comprehensive challenge in the 1980s. It is further arguable that, at the very least, the global-market driven public service reforms of the time provided a ready vehicle, if not impetus, for reform.

Viewed in this context, the assumption that political parties and their elected members will act just like any other private organisation might make a better starting point than an assumption of the pursuit of public good. As they are members of private organisations, politicians and their associates need to be recognised for what they are and carefully incentivised and regulated in a manner reflecting today's community standards.

The public service should not be excluded from a discussion of motivation, even though, and by contrast with the government of the day, it is entirely a creature of the public sector, established by an act of parliament (*Public Service Act 1999* in Australia's case). Just as the assumption of self-interest should be made for politicians, public servants cannot be regarded as entirely altruistic. The challenge in both cases is to embed in

---

17   There is a vast literature on the subject of the overall impact of the reforms on government, described by Hood and Dixon as 'relatively evidence free', 'surprisingly ideological in practice', with the bottom-line question 'barely answered at all'. My interest is in the motivation for the changes being an explanation for the downsides to some of them.

18   There is some debate about who exactly were the mandarins who are the subject of the title, but Brown's discernment of the most likely list is of a group reportedly ranging in height from 150 to 160 centimetres.

the processes of government a system of rules and incentives with suitable rewards and punishments that achieve a commonality of interest of each with the public good (and each other).[19]

This matter of actor motivation is important because some of the changes proposed in this book – in the interests of good public policy – would involve a return (certainly a perceived transfer) of some power to the public service from the government. It is not entirely a zero-sum game, however, as the set of changes are proposed in the interests of improving government performance with both the government and the public service arguably net beneficiaries in the longer term. The issue from the point of view of achieving change is the short-term (single term of office) focus of our politicians and their required short-term payback.

Nonetheless, this short-term horizon need not be a problem if the argument can be won in the court of public opinion, and the independents and minor parties continue to act as leverage against the major parties, much as occurred with Prime Minister Malcolm Turnbull's 2017 announcement of changes to the management of politicians' 'work expenses'.[20] Indeed, the ongoing scrutiny in the court of public opinion is becoming more important to our politicians as they are forced to make budget choices in the face of slowing revenue growth, and explain why it is, for example, that they continue to promote corporate tax cuts, retain negative gearing, and maintain superannuation and capital gains tax concessions, while reducing old age pension payments and child care subsidies, and deny the public funding levels achieved by the richer schools to the poorer schools.[21]

---

19   Caution should be used in assuming that individual motivation within organisations can be readily assigned to the organisations within which they work: Alford and O'Flynn (2012) reflect that a number of organisational, indeed contextual, factors, may intercede. This issue is more important in the case of the public service than for private organisations because the manner in which governments impact on public service activities is an important public policy issue. On the other hand, academic research supports the argument that public servants, along with other members of the community, are importantly driven by self-interest: see, for example, Halvorsen et al. (2005) on the motivation for senior and middle-level public service managers to innovate. This latter accords with my own experience – I am yet to meet that mythical public servant whose actions are dominated by the public good. The actions of some may be mistaken for this but their commitment is invariably to either or both of a discipline and/or an ideology.

20   Malcolm Turnbull, *PM Transcripts*, press conference, Sydney, 13 Jan 2017, pmtranscripts.pmc. gov.au/release/transcript-40682.

21   Much of this scrutiny is, of course, encouraged by the politicians' obsession with the 24-hour news cycle. One of the better ministers I worked with gave out publicly very little about what he and his department were doing. His view was 'to give the b*****ds nothing', because more questions would result. He preferred to get on with it rather than spend time with the media.

This matter of actor motivation is especially important in any discussion of governance because the content and effectiveness of governance regimes varies with the motivation of the participants. Moreover, governance is commonly thought of simply as an ex post, after the event, activity. Yet the primary foundation on which an effective governance system is built involves the incentives put in place in the operating system to create a commonality of interest between the participating parties. On this basis alone it should be clear that a robust form of governance must be built on such a system of incentives for reasons both of effectiveness and cost – the better aligned the actors are the better will be the outcomes and the less will need to be spent on publicly funded watchdog and integrity bodies to audit and encourage compliance.

This balance between ex ante incentives and ex post governance is a matter to which I return, noting that demonstration of transparency in the conduct of the business of government, however achieved, is an important component in achieving community trust and confidence in government. This transparency is notionally achieved through formation of 'a contract' with the electorate at election time, delivery of this contract, and confirmation of its delivery through suitable reporting processes. But there is also an ongoing, cumulative, impact from government activities. Specifying only the 'winners' in the contract with the electorate, and not identifying the losers, is destructive of this trust.

In recent years, the shortcomings of the Westminster system of government, along with the evolved public management system, have been the subject of much analysis.[22] In Australia's case, recent examples include the ANZSOG conference 'Hyper-government: managing and thriving in turbulent times'; and the dedicated volume of *Griffith Review* 51, *Fixing the system*, edited by Julianne Schultz and Anne Tiernan (Pfeffer 2016; Schultz & Tiernan 2016). Tingle's *Quarterly Essay* (2015) is another interesting commentary on these problems. In addition, many Australia-based think tanks and research institutes have conducted forums focused around the short-termism and hyper nature of government. A number also have ongoing programs in effective government.

---

22   The much-used term 'public management' means different things to different people. I use the term as applied by Ryan and Gill, 'Public management ultimately is the organisation and conduct of everyday processes of governing, of how systems, resources and policies are brought together in ways intended to improve the collective well-being of citizens' (2011, p 311). Underpinning this are the legislative and institutional frameworks in place.

This activity has been complemented by privately funded research programs focused on individual policy blocs, which are sometimes ideologically flavoured but are nonetheless contributing to the debate about the role of government and its proper execution. Indeed, the rise of policy-focused think tanks has been a major feature of Australia's policy formation landscape since governments decided to encourage contestability of policy advice as part of its implementation of the NPM reforms over 30 years ago.[23]

There has, however, been very little broad-ranging public discussion of the respective roles and responsibilities of government and public service in Australia. Some political discussion of these respective roles and the manner in which the APS should be organised and led were put forward in 2014 by the Coalition's National Commission of Audit, chaired by president of the Business Council of Australia Jim Shepherd (NCOA, 'the Shepherd'), but the government was disinclined to accept most of the commission's recommendations, especially those relating to the leadership of the APS (NCOA 2014).[24] While the inaccessibility of this issue to the public at large makes it difficult to envisage how change might occur,[25] this should not, however, prevent an examination of what is in the public interest.

1.3 The search for a solution

1.3.1 The foundations of good government

Consideration of what 'good government' might look like in Australia identifies the establishment of a national anti-crime and corruption commission, the extension of all terms of government at state and federal

---

23   There is a broad-based literature, both popular and academic, addressing the role, rise and influence of think tanks in democratic societies. See, for example, James M McGann with Erik C Johnson, *Comparative think tanks, politics, and public policy*, Edward Elgar Publishing Limited, Cheltenham, UK, 2005. For an Australian perspective, see Sharon Beder, *Free market missionaries: the corporate manipulation of community values*, Bath Press, UK, 2006. Finally, Carol Weiss has written extensively on the subject of the relationship between policy and research and the role of evidence; see her informative article 'Research for policy's sake: the enlightenment function of social research', *Policy Analysis*, vol 3, no 4, 1977, pp 532–45.

24   The major changes that appear to have followed from the NCOA report in regard to the APS have involved a reduction in the number of non-principal (Commonwealth) bodies, and the introduction of a contestability program for departmental functions.

25   As noted earlier, however, there does appear to be a latent appetite for change in the community. See CPD (2017a).

level to five years, greater transparency and immediacy in the disclosure of political donations, and the banning of political office holders from participating in their industry for at least five years. Other desirable changes could result from the broadening of the political gene pool and a reduction of the influence of lobbyists on the direction of national policy.

These changes have been canvassed from time to time and would most likely contribute to better government, and certainly to the perceived cleanliness of government processes in Australia. The relative weakness in the quality of government in Australia, however, lies not with the cleanliness of decision-making processes but with the quantity of government and the content of the decisions themselves – the policy choices. Good government requires sound and transparent decision-making processes free of undue influence applied to making and implementing well-constructed policy choices. It also requires an enabling set of institutions, and organisational and actor relationships that enable these policy options to be canvassed and assessed. Failure in any of these areas can lead to substandard performance.

Governance determines where the policy end of the spectrum of good government – its formation and implementation – meets the cleanliness of the processes. This should attest both to the meeting of stakeholder objectives through robust activity choices and the cleanliness of the systems, which achieve the associated objectives. When looked at through the lens of governance, there are substantial shortcomings both in the architecture and execution of the business of government, and that governance has invariably been treated as an afterthought, to be built onto the new structures, rather than into their design.[26]

---

26   While I do not define the term 'good government', the Executive Summary of the 2014 NCOA does, however, provide a reasonable such definition. The NCOA examined the scope, efficiency and sustainability of the Commonwealth government and its programs and developed a set of 10 'common sense' principles to guide its deliberations, which it designated the 'Principles of good government'. My focus determinedly lies with the efficiency, effectiveness, transparency and accountability dimensions of the principles outlined (NCOA 2014). The following references are useful in understanding the foundations and history of government: SE Finer, *The history of government from the earliest times*, Oxford University Press, 1999; WI Jennings, *Cabinet government*, Cambridge University Press, 1965 (1936); AV Dicey, *The law of the constitution*, Oxford University Press, 2013 (1889).

1.3.2 The analytical framework

One of the challenges of analysing the business of government is to establish a framework through which one might take a systemic view of the business. The most popular way is to view 'government' as a whole: an agglomeration of the activities of the political and administrative arms of government shaped by the voters. This is a convenient means of looking at overall government performance, but is of little use for the analysis of the contribution of the public service. Ideally, the public service should be analysed by its contribution to 'good government', independent of the government of the day. This is made difficult of course by the conception of a dominant master–servant relationship, which is embedded in the Public Service Act: some servants perform better than others.

As is made clear in Chapter 3, the available evidence, however assessed, is piecemeal. The global academic literature, reports from government committees, and auditor-general reports certainly point to an under-performing public sector around the globe, and Australian Government equivalents paint a similar picture. While some of this evidence is systemic, most of it comes from specific case studies – auditor-general program-level performance audit reports, for example – without any accompanying advice about public service-wide implications. Only sometimes are these 'case studies' followed by annual reports from the relevant reporting bodies providing a systemic view. The question that arises is how best to assemble a picture of performance in the absence of systematic evidence: what framework to use to try to knit together some pieces?

In an investigative sense, then, the most useful way to view the contribution of the public service to good government is from the vantage point of governance: it can provide a systemic framework within which to view performance, but also, when considered in terms of models of governance, enable conclusions to be drawn about capability and performance from the governing structures; in other words, to supplement the more hard-edged performance data.[27] The latter point – regarding the relationship between

---

27   There is a large literature on governance covering private and public sectors. The focus of discussion in this book lies primarily with the relationship between governing structures, organisational performance, and performance measurement. The following background reading provides an Australian perspective: Janine O'Flynn and John Wanna, eds, *Collaborative governance: a new era of public policy in Australia?*, ANU Press, 2008; Edwards et al. (2012); ANAO (2014a); Australian Public Service Commission, *Foundations of governance*, 2013, www.apsc.gov.au/foundations-governance; and, for a discussion of governing, governance and governing by networks, see a survey by Christian Lo, 'Between government and governance: opening the black box of the transformation thesis', *International Journal of Public Administration*, vol 41, no 8, 2017, doi.org/10.1080/01900692.2017.1295261.

structures and performance – is especially important for this book. Much discussion of public sector performance focuses on operational matters, especially the relationships between the actors, and with the immediate operating environment.

In interpreting such performance, this focus tends to ignore the broader organisational and institutional context that sets the scene for it. An organisation without a risk management committee might reasonably be expected to perform worse on this front than one that does have such a committee and one that has external representation on this committee might be assumed more likely to perform better than one that does not. Similarly, one that has a 12-month work plan incorporating external presentations and regular briefing papers on important audit topics might be assumed to perform better than one that does not. There are many such important 'structures' and associated processes in any organisation that can give strong pointers to performance short of any 'bottom line' itself.[28]

The Public Service Act is a useful starting point in providing a structural view of the public service and a set of operating guidelines. The designated role of the APS as established in the 1999 Public Service Act has evolved through its 1902 and 1922 predecessors. A central feature of the changes made in the 1999 Act, and one that plays a major part in this book, is the move away from one of centralised control of APS operations and administration to one of primary responsibility allocated to individual departments and agencies (Nethercote 2003, especially Chapter 2).

When viewed from a private sector and corporate perspective, it seems odd that such a large organisation – there are over 150,000 people employed in the APS – would not have an overarching authority, nor an annual report. A lot of useful information about public administration in Australia can, however, be derived from the Productivity Commission's annual *Report on government services*, and also the annual *State of the service report* prepared by the APSC – which together present data about the services delivered and the workforce characteristics of those responsible. But no performance-based information of a systemic nature about the APS as a self-managed entity is available.

---

28   A central such structure and related process for this book is the relationship between a board (structure) and a strategy (process).

The focus on a department-led public service, and the absence of an effective public service board, denies the public service and the Australian community access to many of the benefits of public service corporate leadership and management, particularly those accruing from a real sense of self.[29][30] Moreover, when considered in an historical context and taken together, the 1999 Act and associated government policies towards the public service were selective about the private sector approaches and management tools chosen. This of itself is interesting because since Federation, the public sector enthusiastically embraced a range of private sector management tools and concepts; however, the embrace of managerialism in the 1980s was less than complete, which raises the question of why some tools and not others?

This led me to do a casual stocktake of which private sector tools and concepts had and which had not been embraced by the public sector: I considered the development of a range of private sector tools dating back to the second half of the 20th century, which made it clear that there was a strong focus on the concept of productive efficiency and the associated tools of operational level management – somewhat at the expense of effectiveness – but that some of the more important developments in strategic management, from what Walter Kiechel has called 'the management century', were ignored by the public service (Kiechel 2010, 2012). In particular, the developments in what was then called business strategy (now corporate strategy), and in organisational design, were not picked up and applied within the public sector.

Certainly, the practice of preparing corporate plans had been legislated for under the *Public Governance, Performance and Accountability Act 2013* (PGPA Act), and such plans are now being prepared by government business undertakings, government departments and their derivatives, including service delivery agencies such as Centrelink and Medicare.[31]

---

29   By *corporate* here I do mean both 'whole of body' and private sector in style.

30   This concern is not alleviated by the presence of a Secretaries Board (the successor to the Management Advisory Committee (MAC)), which is more akin to a management committee than a corporate board (and/or corporate office) in responsibilities and style.

31   For guidelines, see Department of Finance, *Corporate plans for Commonwealth entities*, Resource Management Guide, no 132, Commonwealth of Australia, Jan 2017. It should also be observed that the second report on this matter from the ANAO provided qualified support for agencies in meeting PGPA Act requirements with regard to the publication of annual performance statements. *Formal* requirements to publish were met by agencies examined, with question marks raised over report quality and methodologies. See ANAO, *Implementation of the Annual Performance Statements requirement 2016–17*, report no 33, Commonwealth of Australia, 2017–18.

Such plans (e.g. the Department of the Prime Minister and Cabinet Corporate Plan 2017–21), however, are more in the nature of extended annual business plans and lack strategy content – when considered in private sector terms as the so-called three Cs of strategy: customers, costs, and competitors.

I could not find evidence of the application of the concept of corporate strategy in the public service. Indeed, the last 30 or 40 years of development in organisational design; customer focus ('effectiveness' in public service terms) around notions of value propositions, value chains and value-delivery systems; and the distinction drawn between transactional and relational marketing (and even the tools of brand management), have been missed entirely by the public service. Advances *have* been made on the accounting side with the introduction of accrual accounting and the incorporation of advances in cost accounting (overhead allocation) with the implementation of output budgeting, but even these advances have contributed little to the understanding of the impacts of government policy, and to the ability to determine the economic and social returns delivered by individual government programs. There have been subsequent developments in the concept of public value in the public sector management literature but this concept has not made its way into public service practice.

There is also an absence of recent evidence of improved public service performance. In his introduction to *Future state directions for public management in New Zealand*, Peter Hughes notes many beneficial reforms and advances in human resource management, only to conclude: 'But we have not necessarily seen better results' (Hughes 2011, p 13). Hood and Dixon in their 2015 assessment of the impact of the NPM reforms on the UK central government some 30 years on, conclude: 'that the UK central government "cost a bit more and worked a bit worse"' (2015, p 183).

The broad conclusion one might draw – that democratic governments have not been delivering improved results for their citizens – combined with questions about the selective adoption of private sector tools and notable absence of some of the more widespread advances in private sector strategic management, leads me to ask whether the judicious application of these concepts to the public service could contribute to better government. Part of the answer might be found in an assessment of the contribution of these tools in public service hands to the three important dimensions of public sector performance, pointed to by

Hughes: outcomes, effectiveness, and leadership. Part also might come from a (re)consideration of the applicability of private sector tools to the public service – the in-principle arguments. And part of the answer might be found in the merits of the individual tools.

When I look back at the NPM reforms, and Australia's current position, I see a once-strong centrally led public service much diminished in its capacity to service the Australian people by these reforms, created through an environment of competition for influence and the business of government. Indeed, the pursuit by successive governments of a smaller public service, although not necessarily a smaller public sector, places the whole palette of traditional public service activity on the road to privatisation. In an analytical sense, the only way to respond to this situation is to say, 'righto, let's recognise reality, governments want a smaller and competitive public service, let's envisage the public service as a competitive enterprise and consider whether it could deliver better outcomes for the community when re-imagined in this manner'.

In order to do this, I use Michael Porter's (1985) corporate strategy framework and associated notions of competition. This framework has provided much of the language of business and industry competition, indeed competition amongst nations, for nearly 40 years. In more recent times there has been much discussion about the utility and content of corporate strategy, as well as some companion discussion focused on organisational form. Porter's basic framework is the starting point for my structural analysis asking whether better public service performance could be expected if it matched best private sector practice in organisational design and strategy?

1.3.3 The themes that emerge

To properly research matters of good government within this framework, a number of practical matters required attention. The first of these was to define the business of government in amenable analytical terms as a starting point for an examination of the contribution of the public service. Much of the literature treats 'the public sector' in a holistic way, but much of the real action from a public policy standpoint happens at the interface between the government and the public service – where policy is formed and implementation methods chosen. A second such matter was to consider the growing recognition of the complexity of public policy problems and the difficulties posed for the package of policy formation, implementation, and governance (both government and public service). The third matter requiring attention was the performance measurement of government activities. The fourth was the legacies of the different and evolving models of government governance, especially the reforms implemented under the NPM banner.

In a pragmatic way I found that the ideas that emerged from this research could be consolidated around four basic concepts that populate substantial parts of the management literature: the notion of strategy, which is best observed as corporate (i.e. 'whole-of-body') strategy; the closely related notion of competitive positioning; the notion of organisational design and supporting administrative systems captured by the concept of organisational architecture; and the notion of good governance, captured primarily in the form of government governance but embracing the notion of public service governance. Beyond that, a number of recurrent themes populate the surrounding discussion.

The first of these is the alignment of the administrative and elected arms of government. This theme has both normative and practical dimensions and points to questions of the desirable relationship between the government and public service; for example, should it be one of servant–master or should the two be partners? Should the public service only serve the government of the day or should it serve the Australian public? And if it were to serve the Australian public, how would conflicts that arise in serving both be resolved?

A second and closely related theme is that of a public service sense of self, which seems to be missing, at least in structural terms. Nonetheless, its presence would be represented by a strategically led public service pursuing stated goals and reporting as a collective regularly in a systemic manner (for example, an annual whole-of-public-service business report), and would exhibit a layer of management dedicated to leadership and strategy. In turn, its absence is often most evident in structural terms but may also be observable through organisational performance exhibiting an absence of cohesion. I argue that, in strategic and operational terms, there are many public services not one.

Another theme that emerged strongly is that of the challenges of good governance in a system that is becoming increasingly fragmented in its political system (with the rise of the minor parties and the independents); public service (with the destruction of its centre and the focus placed on individual departments); government policies (with the replacement of a vision for the country and a set of high-level policies by a set of low-level policies/programs); the tools of public sector management (with a more complex environment requiring a more varied toolkit and greater flexibility in its application); and of the whole policy formation and implementation process (involving both the degradation of the public service knowledge base and an ever increasing number of players in the game). In addition and partly as a consequence, much of the surrounding activity – of the political parties with their voters and governments with the public service – could best be described as transactional (rather than relational).

A fourth issue is the need for the public service to move with the times. Both determination of an initial competitive position and recognition of the need for systematic adjustment to changes in the operating environment are necessary components of such a capacity. This book considers extensively the ways of providing the public service with the tools to compete in a dynamic context and, arguably, that structures and processes exist that would better enable it to do so. This must involve not just the tools to adjust organisationally but also the continuing reinvigoration of the core policy advisory capability.

When considered in broad economic terms, government expenditure is increasingly focused on individual acts of consumption rather than investment, reflecting the attitude of the major political parties to government itself: attempting to build a winning coalition around whatever sells at election time, rather than investing in building a long-term voter base around a vision for our country.[32] When considered in the traditional terms of Australia's decaying public infrastructure, this is inexcusable given the passing era of minimal interest rates. But this loss – of notions of 'capital' and of 'investment' at all levels of politics and public policy – is evident and costly, not just in terms of infrastructure and other physical assets but in social policy terms. Moreover, the Australian public deserves to know when second- (and third-) best policies are used to contain rather than resolve problems. More generally, the language of investment should be used to move on from the short-term concept of services to individuals

---

32 This is unfortunately reflective more broadly of a society that wants personal consumption rather than community investment, what social commentator Hugh Mackay describes as 'the me culture'. See Hugh Mackay, 'The state of the nation starts in your street', Gandhi Oration, University of New South Wales, 30 Jan 2017.

(and recipient organisations), that focuses on budgetary containment of policy problems – which encourages repeat use – and on to the language of long-term *solutions*. This requires a long-term view of policy well beyond the purview of today's governments, actively embracing notions of 'capital' and 'investment' across the policy spectrum.[33]

The fifth theme to emerge, and a central issue in public sector administration, is the applicability of private sector management concepts and tools to the public sector. As noted earlier, there are subtle and obvious differences between the public and private sectors in activity and institutional terms, accompanied by a long interest in the public sector in private sector concepts and tools. This is first observable in the development of the concept of productive efficiency nearly a century ago, and is also evident in the corporatisation of public sector businesses in the latter part of last century, and is most evident in the public service through the NPM reforms, which indicated strong faith in private sector human resource management tools and markets to deliver publicly valuable results. It is debatable, however, whether these reforms represented wholehearted endorsement of the philosophy of managerialism, when seen as an expression of faith in the skills of the professional managers to manage anything. Indeed, the absence of key elements of the full managerialist kit would suggest not. Just as the focus of managerial reform in the public service for much of the 20th century was on efficiency, so it appears to have remained with the NPM reforms, whereas the primary focus of business is 'the customer'.

Suffice it to note at this stage that opinions about the validity and success of the application of private sector management tools in the public sector continue to be much debated, with a commonsense view being that principled pragmatism is required in selecting any tools. This pragmatism is based on the observation that there are some key bits missing from the kit of public

---

33 A particularly encouraging example of 'investment' in services is associated with the then minister for social services (now Attorney-General) Christian Porter whose 'priority investment' approach to social services delivery was novel and associated with an objective to equip people to permanently leave the welfare system ('move to self-reliance' in the jargon). This concept is discussed in Chapter 3, but see: 'Australian priority investment approach to welfare', *Review of Australia's welfare system*, Department of Social Services, 25 Jan 2018, www.dss.gov.au/review-of-australias-welfare-system/australian-priority-investment-approach-to-welfare; see also, Peter Whiteford, 'Will an "investment" approach to welfare help the most disadvantaged?', *ABC News*, 21 Sep 2016, www.abc.net.au/news/2016-09-20/will-welfare-investment-approach-help-the-disadvantaged/7862758. The same notion can be employed to provide a rationale for the field of business welfare – both the taxation expenditure and subsidy dimensions of government support – in conjunction with the notion of externalities.

service management tools and that these bits seem to have been somehow 'missed' at the time of the NPM reforms. It can reasonably be argued that these 'bits' were missed in part by design and in part by accident.[34]

A closely related concept, and the next theme, derives from the importance of structures. I pointed earlier to this book's focus on leadership, noting that my interest was not so much the skills of the individual but the organisational structures and processes that enable corporate leadership. In reviewing the content of the highest levels of leadership and management in the private sector and public service, most notably missing in the public service is a real sense of public service strategy, which in private sector terms would focus on where to play (the choice of where to deploy available resources), and how to win (how to outcompete rivals). This absence of strategy can in turn be largely attributed to the absence of the top two organisational layers from the public service, namely a board, and a dedicated corporate CEO and head office.

As is noted in Chapter 4, these missing two layers contribute not just additional resources (quantity) to the organisational leadership pool, but also specialist skills. These latter are whole-of-organisation skills associated with the development (board) and management (CEO/divisional heads) of strategy, and active support (the corporate office). A critical part of the value added by the existence of a whole-of-organisation strategy is pursuit of horizontal strategies through horizontal coordination that is driven by the CEO/corporate office. This is a noted operational weakness in public service management. I argue that these two organisational layers (missing by design), and the organisational strategy, are critical to the performance of the public service and without which the public service will continue to wither away. Structures are especially critical to leadership in both public and private sectors – a further important theme of this book.

The final theme is the two-part cost of governing. The first is the cost of delivering a standardised unit of service that embraces the full cost of public administration, including service delivery costs. This is a difficult issue to corral overall because of the absence of systemic benefit data but there are environmental reasons to believe that this cost is rising in real terms. The externalisation of public sector programs may bring with it a raft of new coordination and transaction costs that need to be accounted

---

34   To achieve clarity in this discussion, it is necessary to distinguish the public service from the broader public sector, as the latter contains a significant proportion of business undertakings directly emulating the private sector and not subject to the constraints of a public service act.

for in the decision-making calculus.[35] Scepticism is also warranted about the impact of the wholesale application of efficiency-seeking private sector tools to a public sector that is different in both structural and operational ways.

The second part of the discussion of the cost of governing involves opportunity costs and is associated with the notion of optimising (i.e. minimising) the costs associated with alternative public service configurations. It lies partly in the unexplored costs of alternative public service organisational configurations. For example, it is not clear that 'super departments' work as an efficient organisational form, nor is there evidence of the impact of organisational size on public sector efficiency, although theoretical academic research should raise concern. More generally, studies by Hood and Dixon (of the UK Government) and Kettl (of the US Government), on which I focus in the public policy discussion in Chapter 10, provide a good reason to suspect that a diminishing proportion of government expenditure directly benefits citizens (Hood & Dixon 2015; Kettl 2008).

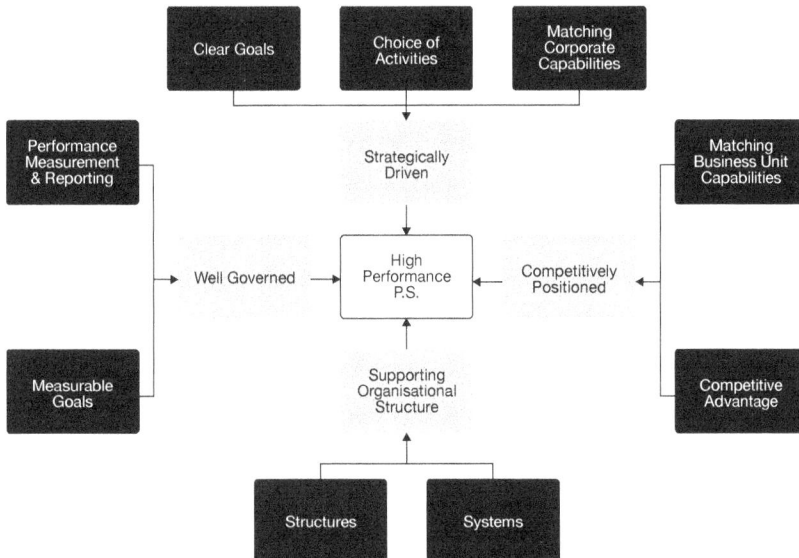

Figure 1.1 The analytical framework

---

35   A valuable discussion of the challenges of working with other parties across public service lines and more broadly with external parties (under the banner of 'externalisation') is provided by Alford and O'Flynn (2012). The authors recommend a pragmatic approach – 'it all depends' – and lay out a cost–benefit framework within which to consider individual cases.

The exploratory framework used throughout this book is set out in Fig. 1.1 as a combination of foundational elements and contributors. The framework comprises four foundational elements: strategy, competitive positioning, organisation, and governance. What characterises this 'model' is the significant overlap between the four foundational elements and between the contributors to each of them. What binds these various elements together is that they are all essential components of a high-performing organisation, ranging from the choice of activities, establishment of matching capabilities, and competition for success, through to the active demonstration of achievement of stakeholder goals.

The first foundational element refers to a strategically driven public service with clear goals, an aligned set of activities and capabilities, and a focus for all activities that is driven by the customer(s) and which binds the organisation together. Stakeholders usually provide clear goals. A starting point in the case of the APS is the notion of service to the collective of government, parliament, and the Australian public, and how this service is to be provided (values and conduct), embodied in the Public Service Act, and internal aspirations for the creation of 'a high-performing public sector', a phrase that occurs regularly in the speeches of the various Australian public service leaders and in the published plans of their organisations.

The next contributor to the first foundational element is the choice of activities. As with the determination of goals, I consider the political and public service dimensions: the framework for this analysis is set by the notion of where to play, in terms of market, product, and customer choice dimensions.[36] This is an important question for governments in straitened financial times and the public service a significant contributor through its provision of the analytical frameworks necessary to determine the prospective and actual budgetary and outcomes dimensions of government choices. But the same question – of where to play – should equally be applied to the business of the public service as it also faces decisions about how best to serve the government in implementing its choices, how best to serve the parliament, and how best to serve the community at large.

---

36   Roger Martin has been one of the leading academic corporate strategists in North America for several decades. His associated work on integrative thinking and design thinking is pioneering. See Martin (2013, 2014) and Lafley and Martin (2013). He reduces the challenge of strategy to two simple questions – where to play, and how to win.

The final contributor is matching corporate capabilities. The APSC is responsible for the determination of the required capabilities for the public service to deliver its mission. My focus here, however, will not be on the full suite but, rather, the missing corporate capabilities of the public service – the capacity to lead and support an integrated public service, viewed most readily in terms of the dedicated board and 'head office' resources through which multi-business companies run their businesses. In the case of the public service the equivalent notion is of a well-resourced and focused 'centre' embodying organisational (i.e. whole-of-public-service) leadership.

The second foundational element for this book is that of competitive positioning with contributing elements for this being the creation of whole-of-public-service competitive advantage and matching business unit (i.e. departmental) capabilities. This element addresses the second overarching strategy question of 'how to win'. The notion that the public service should regard itself as a competitive enterprise may seem alien but, clearly, it is in active competition with third parties for parts of the business of government – through contestability – as well as more broadly competing for influence. Chapter 8 considers public service activities in terms of a number of the markets in which it competes, and the competitive position it occupies in each of these markets. The corporate – that is whole-of-body – dimensions of this 'strategy' determine whether the public service might better deploy its resources. At the same time I observe that a public service strategically led from 'the centre' would actively devote resources to building competitive advantage amongst the operations of the various component parts ('departments/business units'): in corporate strategy terms it would pursue horizontal strategies as well as generating and cascading corporate benefits. This is the focus of discussion on the required capabilities rather than any systematic discussion of skill sets.[37]

---

37   Those writers who might describe the organisational content of the NPM reforms in terms of an unsuccessful application of the corporate multi-divisional business form to the public service focus unnecessarily on the establishment of the departments as separate business units, and miss the critical role of the board and corporate office ('the centre') in unifying the whole organisation, creating economies at the corporate level for the benefit of the operating units, and building cohesion and adding value at the operating level, all by systematically drawing on own, and other, whole-of-organisation experience. See, for example, Head and Alford (2008). A subset of this debate focuses on the respective merits of 'deliberate' and 'emergent' strategy; see Mintzberg and Waters (1985). These critical issues are discussed in Chapter 7 of this book.

The third foundational element is organisational design and architecture. By this I mean the combination of formal organisation structures with the supporting administrative systems. It is important to note here that the conception of 'organisational structure' relates to the whole of the public service, not the whole of the public sector or the structure of individual departments. While I am interested in the manner in which the whole of the public service task is disaggregated and 'works', the primary unit of organisational analysis is the whole public service.

The formal organisational structure is important for a wide variety of reasons including: it is the vehicle through which resources are deployed and managed and activities accounted for; it adjudicates the competing functional claims for organisational leadership; it impacts organisational behaviour; it determines the economies of scale that constituent functions are able to deliver; it determines how organisations will interact with the environment (conduct and boundary conditions); and, most importantly for our purposes, organisational structure is the vehicle through which strategy is executed.

Beyond this, embedded administrative systems should not simply be seen as the poor cousin in this mix because these systems play a number of roles: in the day-to-day management at all levels of the business (the capture and interpretation of 'micro' data); in reporting performance up business and functional lines (the aggregation and interpretation of micro data-based reports); in the generation of additional ('macro') data to determine overall organisational performance (e.g. in meeting corporate social responsibility goals); and, in the satisfaction of stakeholder interest in organisational governance (integrating macro data with aggregated micro data-based reports). It is the capture and aggregation of data through these systems (the micro data) along with the generation of complementary high-level reports (the macro data) that lay the foundations for the fourth foundational element, good governance, embracing clear and measurable goals and performance measurement and reporting. Key supporting elements of good governance include data coverage and quality, and the recording and reporting systems chosen.

Underpinning much of the discussion of government and public service governance in this book is the evolution of models of governance over the last 30 or 40 years, and the accompanying changed focus from measuring program-level inputs (sound financial accounting), to outputs (public administration activities), to outcomes (impacts on recipients of public goods and services and achievement of overall policy objectives), to public value (community valuation of government programs), and 'results' (impact of achievement of policy objectives on community welfare). This evolution in measurement focus has been well documented in the academic literature, but lags behind in practical application, the latter being stuck somewhere in the transition from inputs to outputs and still focused largely on efficiency at the expense of effectiveness. The value of such limited data on the measurement of impacts of government programs can be readily seen to limit the capabilities of governments to make effective policy choices on other than political grounds.

The framework outlined in Fig. 1.1 captures the four dimensions of public service activity developed from observation of the important structural elements necessary in considering public service performance today. In particular, it is determinedly 'structural' in its content and built on the premise that sound strategy and supporting organisational design and administrative systems are necessary foundations for good organisational performance, and that the presence of the former are a sound pointer to the latter. I envisage a notion of 'structure' comprising the formal organisational design, and the embedded management and administrative systems.

Viewed in textbook terms, this approach sees a clear relationship between organisational strategy, structure, and performance, all set in a defined context. While I discuss the contribution of behaviour – of both politicians and public servants – I do so in a structural context. There is also a normative (public policy) component to this framework for, in determining public performance to be substandard, a framework is established to consider how this performance might be improved through the various foundational elements and their contributors identified in Fig. 1.1.

'Substandard' performance could be measured by converting Fig. 1.1 into a chart providing the four foundational elements as a scale (relative or absolute) on which the position of any public service can be charted. Overall performance could be plotted on this chart by connecting the dots. This has been done in an indicative way in Fig. 1.2, which suggests two alternative performance configurations, the one indicating modest (and equal) performance on all four axes, and the other linking the upper boundaries of performance on all four. There is, of course, no necessity for the symmetry presented, however, in so far as good performance on any axis represents a consciousness and practice of the functions of management, some such positive relationship is likely to exist between all four.

Finally, before outlining the structure of the following chapters, I briefly acknowledge three further elements of public service activity that are important to the discussion, but are not directly represented in this model: culture, innovation, and risk. Each of these elements is present in various parts of the discussion across the next 10 chapters. The easiest one to deal with is the last of the three, which has two dimensions to it – the level of risk that is tolerated in the public service, and risk management practices.

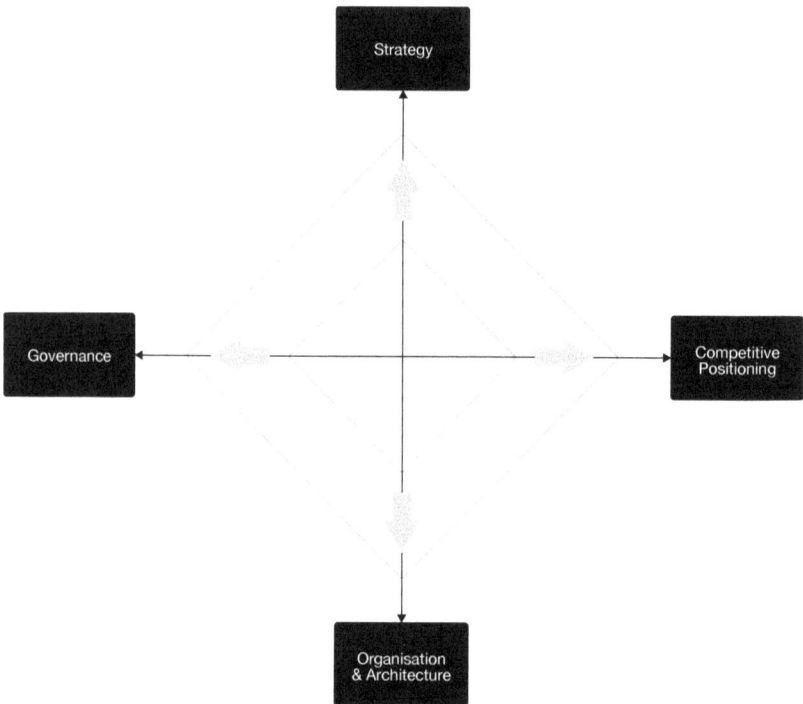

Figure 1.2 A performance measurement framework

All large organisations today should/do have a board committee or committees devoted to risk.[38] This committee takes its lead from its owners/stakeholders in the extent, nature and types of risk it will tolerate

---

38   See, for example, the recommendations of the Australian Stock Exchange Corporate Governance Council for listed entities in ASX (2014).

in determining a framework commensurate with this risk, and then establishing and managing it on an ongoing basis. There are many forms of risk that need to be managed, but political and career risk are especially important to the business of public administration. These may take many and unexpected forms for public servants. Most public servants will know of colleagues whose careers have been cut short, who have been sidelined, or otherwise disciplined, for embarrassing their minister or 'having lost the minister's confidence', often in what may be regarded as 'the normal course of duty'. It is difficult to formulate a set of practices that eliminates political risk entirely from the operations of public administration, and given this, the risk aversion commonly noted of public servants in the academic literature could be reasonably expected. I treat this as a leadership issue and one importantly shaped at the interface between the political and administrative arms of government – a taught rather than innate limitation of the public service. Chapter 4 considers this in the context of the 'frank and honest' provisions of the Public Service Act.

Innovation is important, and its importance in the public sector lies, as it does in any other sector, in the necessity of organisations to change to survive. Whilst the public service has a legislated right to survive, it is facing increasing competition in its traditional markets of policy advice and service delivery, its operating environment is becoming unstable, and it must learn to compete for influence. I view innovation primarily from a public service management perspective, in terms both of its outputs, the (goods) and services that it delivers to its legislated constituencies, along with the manner in which it is organised and delivers these services. Innovation then might be seen to occur across the spectrum of public service activities. It is given particular attention in Chapter 9, having concurrently emerged from the business (strategy) literature as the means of systematically adjusting to a rapidly changing operating environment (and a worthy companion to competitive positioning as the core of corporate strategy), and from the public sector management literature as a worthy addition to the tools of strategic management. The concomitant challenge – of how to balance performance in the present with performance in the future – underpins this interest.

Then there is the third element – culture – 'the way things get done around here'. Every organisation has a culture (internal) and a reputation (external) that is rarely fully manufactured (despite organisational attempts to do so). Rather, both are the result of a series of acts and behaviours 'recorded' in their respective domains – in the case of culture it is the acts (or non-acts) and behaviours of leaders which determine organisational culture and, in the case of reputation, it will usually be driven by the accumulation of interactions that any organisation has with its customers (Lanning (2000) delightfully describes these interactions as 'moments of truth').[39] Values and codes of conduct may be useful but it is behaviours that ultimately determine and are determined by 'the way things get done around here'.

In the case of the APS, some formal intentions are embedded in the Public Service Act: these foreshadow an intention to create a culture of professionalism and service in the APS, as demonstrated in the objects of the Act and in the APS values, code of conduct, and employment principles. But there are additional elements of the Act – such as the placing of the department at the apex of the public service, the limitations on the ministerial directions to agency heads regarding particular individuals, even the content of the formal disciplinary procedures – which importantly also condition individual, departmental and whole-of-public-service organisational behaviour. Another important contributor can be organisational resource-allocation processes. Also very important is the role that the minister *chooses* to play at the interface between the department, government and the community at large. Some ministers may choose the internal (political and/or own department) interface, whilst others may prefer the community interface. The latter, if done well, has the advantage of smoothing the path for departmental implementation of new and/or difficult government policies.

The importance of a consistent 'tone from the top', determines organisational culture as managers (and leaders) importantly shape the culture of their teams.[40] Di Francesco and Eppel point to the profound effect that the minister may have on departmental performance, ranging from driving superior performance to undermining the secretary. They

---

39 It is important to distinguish between 'reputation' and 'brand', which are often used interchangeably but have different uses in this book. Whereas the word 'brand' is used to describe what a company, product, or service has promised to its customers and what that commitment means to them – a customer-centric concept – the word 'reputation' focuses on the credibility and respect that an organisation has amongst a broad set of constituents including its customers, and is a company-centric concept. Brand might then be described as the way a company presents itself to the world, whilst reputation might be described as the way others collectively view the company. See Richard Ettenson and Jonathan Knowles, 'Don't confuse reputation with brand', *MIT Sloan Management Review*, Jan 2008.
40 See, for example, 'Managing integrity risks in the workplace', APSC, Nov 2016, www.apsc.gov. au/managing-integrity-risks-workplace.

also point to the prospect that a *prescribed* ministerial role could alleviate some of these difficulties.[41] In practice, the 'public service culture' is an amalgam of many different departmental cultures and subcultures, ranging from rules to permission cultures, tied very loosely together by the standards – values, code of conduct and employment principles – set out in the Public Service Act.[42] At any point in time, the culture of a department, however mapped, will be a mixture of many such influences with substantial variations existing within and across public service departments.

There are other formal elements that impact on the culture created, such as the policies of the government of the day towards the public service, and departmental remuneration, accountability and reporting systems, but also many informal elements. These include, for example: (a) the role that ministers and their staff choose to play in the release of material under freedom of information legislation; (b) their manner and level of involvement in departmental (public service) appointments; and (c) the manner in which interactions between staffers and public servants play out. A further particularly important contributor to departmental culture – through service delivery – is the impact of information technology infrastructure. This point was highlighted in a 2013 capability review of the Department of Veterans' Affairs, in which the APSC found that an important contributor to cultural problems in the department was an outdated computer network of over 200 individual IT systems, many of which could not communicate with each other.

A government with a clear agenda and set of plans to execute the agenda, which sees the role of the public service primarily in terms of administration (in the sense of administering their plans) and providing advice when requested, will create quite a different environment for the

---

41   Di Francesco and Eppel (2011) suggest formalising the management role in departmental activities by placing the minister as an integral part of departmental managerial and leadership activities.

42   I experienced enormous variation in cultures in my working life across the public and private sectors. In the public sector, the real leader varied greatly from departmental head to minister to premier. Within the public service context, the associated cultures ranged from what I can only describe as an overt permission culture (a great place to work!), through hierarchical/professional (about what public servants expect), and to several stultifying periods with leaders who in differing ways wanted to make sure nothing went wrong (how popular conception sees the public service). I also experienced a wide variety of leadership styles in the private sector but (a) the hierarchical relationships were almost always in play, (b) they all were built on a strong internal expectation of action and, (c) the profit motive was very much in evidence, invariably accompanied by an implicit permission to break the rules if you 'did good' for the business.

public service than one that is more curious about the possibilities of government and open to a breadth of ideas and advice from the public service. The departmental head can also make a substantial difference. Those who see themselves as agents of their ministers generate a different culture to those who actively choose to act as a buffer between the political and administrative arms of government and lead their departments in delivering the government's program.[43] As Hughes (2011) observes, leadership is one of the three principles that must guide public developments as the public sector moves ahead.

1.4 The structure of this book

This book is presented in three parts. The first (Chapters 2, 3, 4, and 5) looks at the business of government and the role of the public service, the second (Chapters 6, 7, 8, and 9) at matters of public service structure and strategy, and the final part (Chapters 10 and 11) looks more broadly at public policy issues and the surrounding context. Chapter 1 provides an overview of the arguments presented in the book. Chapters 2, 3, and 4 are designed to provide some history and context, both global and local, for subsequent discussions of strategy, structure and competitive positioning, using the concept of governance as the prism through which to view public service activities. My first step is to consider the tasks of governments and the services that they deliver. There are many different sorts of services and I start here to explore the interventions governments choose and the execution of these interventions. I try to describe the resultant public sector services in an analytically useful manner for our later discussion of competitive advantage through a 'mapping' of the public sector and its services.

This discussion of 'mapping' canvasses both the production and consumption characteristics of public sector services, and considers the importance of wicked problems and the implications for the role and performance of the public service. An examination of the concept and history of governance follows, including the styles of governance ('models') that government has exhibited over recent decades. These models describe the management focus of government as it has evolved and set the scene

---

43   The requirement in clause 64 of the *Public Service Act 1999* for departmental heads to 'model' desired public service leadership behaviours seems to trivialise the public service leadership role – perhaps deliberately?

within which the role of the public service can be examined. Then I move on to consider government policy formation, considered as the set of policies employed by governments to promote community health and welfare (Chapter 3), and its performance measurement (Chapter 4).

In Chapter 5 I focus on the legislative context within which the APS operates, namely the Public Service Act and the PGPA Act. I consider government policy towards the public service, building the public policy position with a detailed discussion of the first of these acts and a series of recommended changes. Chapter 5 also provides some early pointers to the competitive positioning of the public service, highlighting particular activity areas where the public service both has a current competitive position within the broader 'government' landscape, and related areas where it might make a more active contribution to better government. In regard to the latter I discuss the role of the public service beyond its immediate role of serving the government of the day.

In Chapter 6 I consider what fit-for-purpose organisational architecture looks like. In doing so, I set out the academic antecedents for the study of the role of organisational structures in organisational performance. I look first at the set of characteristics by which organisations may be described, and consider the possibilities in terms of the needs of the public service. This provides a basis to examine organisational structures and boundaries by taking an historical view of the evolution of the dominant organisational forms in private and public sectors. A related important issue is the way in which large organisations successfully adapt to a changing operating environment: an important side issue is balancing organisational needs between exploitation and exploration through formal and informal structures. The discussion of organisational architecture includes the organisation's administrative system's needs, looked at from a governance perspective. Chapter 6 concludes with an application of organisational design principles and practices to the organisational architecture of the APS and the identification of a preferred model.

In Chapters 7, 8, and 9, I establish the strategic management framework through which I view the contribution of the public service to government performance. My earlier commentary suggested that the notion of strategy, particularly in the sense of corporate strategy, is typically absent from both the general and academic discussion of public service activities. In Chapter 7, I set out a standard corporate strategy framework that could (and should) apply to any organisation whether in public or private sectors, and then ask how differently the public service would behave if it conceived of itself as an integrated entity using private sector strategic management tools. What stands out when considering public service activities from a strategic management and organisational design perspective is the diversity of activities (products, services, and relationships) across the public service (by comparison with the private sector), the asset specificity often required, the underlying process commonalities, and the overlaps in customers/consumers and services.

These structural features of the business of government point to a preferred organisational structure built around a core set of business units (departments) with a strong centre orchestrating the required collaborations across business unit lines, all supported by a set of flexible arrangements to cope with the evolving shape of government and its important collaborative activities. How these changing collaborations can be successfully combined with organisational structures and embedded governance systems remains unresolved in the academic literature. A necessary precondition should be a strong centre that drives the public service through dedicated leadership and a support team that delivers leadership for the whole of the public service, the development of service-wide collaborative management tools and competitive strategies, informed by global market intelligence and the capture of service-wide operational intelligence. Moreover, the centre should actively seek to create synergies amongst departments in addition to addressing the more obvious overlaps.

If Chapter 7 establishes a general framework within which an organisation might develop, implement, and manage a strategic approach to its business, then in Chapter 8 I move to outline the nub of any such public service strategy – the establishment of a competitive position in its 'chosen' markets. Competition is all around the public service – for influence, reputation, advice, service delivery, turf and dollars – and from for-profit and not-for-profit organisations, as well as, arguably, from those independent officers of parliament heading up the watchdog and integrity bodies. My goal in this chapter is to develop a framework for analysis of the markets and players in Australia in which the public service competes, and construct a 'winning' strategy for the public service. I spend the early part of this chapter examining the notions of industry attractiveness, competitive positioning and the delineation of markets; I then discuss the development of a corporate strategy for the public service based on a discussion of mainstream private sector strategies.

Chapter 9 was the most difficult chapter in the book to write, and only became necessary after I had written all other chapters. What emerged from the private sector literature on strategy and organisation were some common developments around the notions of successfully competing for business today, whilst building competitive businesses for 'tomorrow', and successfully integrating the two. Chapters 5 to 8 noted notions of marrying (managerial) exploitation and exploration, (organisational) stability and agility (through the creation of ambidextrous organisations), and developing capabilities in continuous resource allocation and transition management. The evolving literature on strategy continues to embrace the static notion of competitive positioning whilst maintaining belief in design thinking and innovation as the means of continuous adjustment and maintenance of growth. Meantime, the literature on public sector management is evolving from a focus on innovation as process to innovation as strategy. Extracting the wisdom for public service management from this mix became the challenge for what became a new Chapter 9.

In Chapter 10 I discuss public policy considerations, distinguishing between (a) public policy (what ought to be) and government policy (what is and likely to be), and (b) public service strategy, while acknowledging that what might be good for government or the public service may not necessarily be in the public interest. I pull together the various recommendations for change to the public service that have emerged in the earlier chapters and consider some of the important issues of implementation. This discussion of public policy is complemented in Chapter 11 by integrated reflections on the underlying themes and recommendations for change that have emerged through the study.

1.5 Some concepts and definitions

The field that I cover is marked by the contribution of a number of academic disciplines as well as by both academic and popular usage of key terms. Clarity of definition is absolutely central to much of what follows. It is important therefore to be clear on the definition and usage of simple concepts such as 'customer', 'public sector' and 'public service', even 'public interest'. Some terms have already been defined, or boundaries proposed, and I define other terms here. It is important to keep these definitions in mind through the book so as to be clear about the actors, the actions, and the domain that are its focus.

1.5.1 The actors

What is commonly described as 'the public sector' can be divided into its political and administrative wings. The political wing comprises the elected representatives and the houses of parliament, whilst the administrative wing comprises the government departments, advisory bodies, derivative agencies, statutory authorities, and government-owned business undertakings with the unifying factor being their accountability to a minister: at the heart of the administrative arm of government lies 'the public service'. Sitting as something of a hybrid alongside the public service are independent bodies, such as auditors-general, ombudsmen, and anti-corruption bodies, that form part of the ongoing administrative apparatus of government but report directly to the parliament.[44]

I use the term 'public sector' to refer to the political and administrative wings taken together with the hybrids. Conceptually this term includes the plethora of agencies and other entities engaged in the business of government, although my primary interest lies with the public service and its departments. I regularly refer to the political wing as 'the government' (a structural definition), although I occasionally use the term 'government' to refer to the act of governing, involving as it does both the political and administrative arms of government, and its consequent impact on the community, as in 'good government' (i.e. a behavioural/performance definition). I use the terms 'administrative wing' and 'public service' interchangeably but my primary interest lies with that element of the administrative arm described in the *Public Service Act 1999* as 'departments'. It is the policymaking, policy implementation, service delivery, and governance roles of this group of public servants, in concert with their ministers, that is the focus of this study.

1.5.2 The domain

It is necessary to have a 'map' to describe the activity domain within which the various public institutions, organisations and players operate. This is important as the locus of change over the last three or four decades has shifted. The map I use was developed by Paul Windrum as a taxonomy of public sector innovation but serves equally well to describe the full spectrum of operations of government (Windrum 2008). This taxonomy

---

44 An informative discussion of the institutional arrangements of the democratic system of government in Australia is set out in Funnell, Cooper and Lee (2012). See also Edwards et al. (2012).

identifies six categories of public sector activity – the underpinning ideological foundations and political beliefs (the conceptual foundations), the derived policy frameworks, the services, the delivery of services, the supporting organisational and administrative systems, and the level of third party/external interaction ('systemic innovation') across the whole organisation.

This taxonomy can be regarded equally as a snapshot of public service activity or, in a linear and causative manner, as the underlying conceptual and belief systems and associated world views that give rise to policy frameworks and services which necessitate organisation and administrative systems in support of service delivery, and which then is delivered (in part) through third party engagement. In doing this latter, I recognise that some linkages are stronger than others and that, whilst the primary line of causation runs from the conceptual foundations through to performance, there are feedback loops in this system, some stronger than others. I also recognise that what Windrum describes as systemic innovation, involving the interaction of the organisation at all levels with third parties, is not so much a separate activity category but one that cuts right across the whole organisation (as depicted in Fig. 1.3).

In addition to providing a map to locate discussions within the broad flow of public service activities – for example, in discussions of outsourcing service delivery or policy advice or the underlying political belief system – the Windrum taxonomy also enables a useful comparison of the models of governance that I explore as their respective emphases vary across the Windrum map. Moreover, in structure it is similar to the standard corporate strategy model, a point that has considerable value later in this volume because it enables discussion to move relatively easily between public and private sectors in consideration of alternative organisational structures and their impacts.

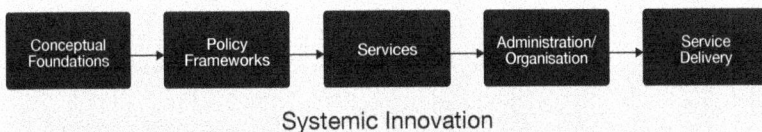

Figure 1.3 The Windrum map of public sector activity

1.5.3 The customer

In considering the beneficiaries of the chosen activities, I define terms in relation to the use of the term 'customer'. It is easy to use private sector terminology to describe organisational purpose in terms of 'creating the customer' and/or 'meeting customer needs' but, for different organisations, there may be many different sorts of 'customers'. I also note that, in public sector parlance, end consumers are typically referred to as 'clients'. Starting from a position that the purpose of an organisation is to create value for 'customers' then, in the case of the public service, 'the government' – with whom the public service has its primary relationship – can reasonably be included within this grouping as an external entity through which public services are delivered from time to time – and the final consumer of the product or service.

For analytical purposes, all such parties may be enjoined under the umbrella term of 'customers', and I use the term generically on occasion. For specific purposes, however, disaggregation is required. Porter draws a distinction between customers and consumers, distinguishing the final consumer of a good or service from the intermediate customers through whom these goods and services may be sold (Porter 1985). Lanning, in his discussion of the value-delivery chain, describes this as incorporating a wide range of customers, customers of customers, and offline entities – such as regulators and standards-setting bodies – and describes this as a chain of customers, each delivering value propositions to the next (Lanning 2000). Alford and O'Flynn discuss the externalisation of public sector service delivery, distinguishing between various classes of external partnerships and the classes of benefits (and costs) generated both for the partners and the broader community (Alford & O'Flynn 2012).

Lanning's approach is useful in this study because it (a) recognises a plurality of customers, (b) orders them, (c) recognises that sometimes trade-offs need to be made, and (d) looks beyond purely financial relationships. This framework is useful with regard to the Public Service Act, which provides for the APS to serve all of the government, parliament and the Australian public, but establishes neither hierarchy nor any mechanism(s) to reconcile conflicts that arise. With regard to the latter, Lanning asks the analyst to identify the customer entity (or entities) at some level in the chain who will determine (contribute most to) the business's success: this is the most essential customer entity for the organisation to understand,

and he designates it as the primary entity. But it is in the holistic nature of the value-delivery system that its value lies in asking the analyst to recognise all of the links in the chain where value can be added.

Applying the notion of the value-delivery system to the business of the government leaves little doubt that it would see the general public as the primary entity, and the public service as but one of a number of entities in its delivery system. In the case of the value-delivery system of the public service, it is reasonable to propose that its primary entity is the government, the entity that funds and empowers the public service, but one could mount a case for its primary entity also to be the Australian public. Nonetheless, viewed in terms of relationships between primary, secondary, customer-to-customer, and offline entitites, it is important to recognise that the value the public service is capable of creating in its business extends through its day-to-day contact with the government, its capacity to successfully implement government policies and manage programs, the establishment of collaborative arrangements in the development of services, the delivery of services to end users, the relationships with outsourced service providers, and more broadly with the Australian Parliament and public in the conduct of its business.

All of these are sources of value that can be created for the government by the public service in the conduct of its business. This approach is consistent with the public sector management notion of public value as the measure of value added through delivery of government services, normally defined to include both the private value generated by end users in the consumption of public services, and the value placed by the broader community on the delivery of particular policies (which, for example, might take the form of citizen approval of drug and alcohol rehabilitation programs provided to other citizens); it could also take the form of improved citizen trust in government as a consequence of professional service delivery and management by the public service.[45]

There are some differences between the public value concept as generally described – a perception of value created for the community in the conduct of the business of government – and the value that the public service should want to create in its own interests. These may be differences at the margin

---

45   The term 'public value' was coined by Mark Moore (1995), who saw it as the public sector equivalent of shareholder value and which has become the standard-bearer for 'bottom-line' discussions of government programs over the last 20 years. I discuss the utility of this concept, as a private sector bottom-line equivalent, in Chapter 4.

but the notion of public service value, the bottom-line equivalent for the public service, does point to some interesting possibilities for the creation and management of the elements of community value. In delineating the roles of public service and government, it is necessary to ask who the value is created by and for whom.

I use the terms citizens, citizenry, and community at large as alternatives for what the Public Service Act calls 'the Australian public'. Following Lanning, I use the term 'customer' generically to apply to a variety of direct and indirect relationships, some complementary and others conflicting, that exist within the value-delivery system. I acknowledge the common use of the term 'client' in the public service context, having the same connotation as the term 'consumer' as used by Porter to describe the final customer, and I sometimes use the term 'end consumer' equivalently. And, in the context of the operations of the government, I use the term public value to describe the total of the private valuations of final consumers of consumption of any government-provided good or service, along with the additional value created for (all) citizens, and the conduct of the business of government.[46]

The role of the APS might be broadly described as performing desired services as determined by the government of the day. However, the Public Service Act also requires the public service to serve Parliament and the Australian public, and I argue in Chapter 5 that, in the spirit of serving these three communities individually and collectively within the terms of the Act and in the public interest, the APS should be accorded a role in creating public value directly with the Australian public as well as through service to the government and Parliament. This role recognises the inverse relationship between community perceptions of the legitimacy of government (an operational rather than legal view) and the cost of governing. Whilst some distrust of government may be healthy, beyond a point the costs will outweigh the benefits.

1.5.4 The concept of winning

A central concept in this book is that of 'winning'. This concept lies at the heart of the discussion of strategy. All organisations should have objectives (goals and targets), a plan to achieve these objectives (a *strategy*), and a body responsible for delivery of the results. To achieve targeted

---

46   Importantly, public value may be created (indeed destroyed) by private entities.

results can be described as 'winning' and the means by which 'winning' is achieved is through the strategy employed. Lafley and Martin contrast the notion of 'playing to win' with that of 'playing to play', around the need to make *choices* (Lafley & Martin 2013). My discussion of these concepts is focused on the public service – its goals, its structures and its strategy – noting in passing that the concept of 'playing to play' may well be a more apt description of public service activity than 'playing to win'.

My objective here is to develop a competitive strategy for the public service and the supporting organisational structures that would enable it to 'win'. As noted earlier, I draw heavily on leading strategist Michael Porter's work in this field, including his notions of *competitive advantage* and *competitive positioning* (Porter 1985). I also regularly use the Martin (and Lafley) terminology of *where to play* and *how to win* to describe critical questions that need to be addressed in this process. And I use the issues raised by Martin (2009), and McGrath (2013), in the strategy literature, March (1991) and O'Reilly and Tushman (2013) in the organisational literature, and Bason (2010) in the public sector management literature, to examine some of the challenges of winning in a changing public sector environment, particularly the appropriate structuring of business to meet the challenges of today and tomorrow. The concluding chapters of the book focus on how the community at large might 'win' from changes to the public service model.

2

Government and governance

2.1 Introduction

The business of government is big business in most economies, commonly dwarfing in size and reach of even the largest of the private sector entities. Viewed as a business within its own domain, government has a monopoly over many activities, although viewed in international terms it is invariably one of many competitors seeking to attract capital and build a competitive economy. As a large administrative organisation and consumer of resources it is important for the nation's competitiveness that the government's choice of activities, and the execution of these choices, meet community needs in a cost-effective manner. For democratic governments today, that means mixing monopoly and competitive elements in the administration and delivery of its chosen activities.

For some of its purchasing activities, probity and security interests mean that the government establishes and purchases requirements from a single supplier. But for the bulk of its requirements, where no such concerns arise, governments willingly purchase in competitive markets, either at home or offshore, where government or citizens are the end consumers of the products. I am interested in how, in the business of government, boundary lines are drawn, activity choices made, and resources allocated.

This chapter focuses on the various high-level choices that political parties make between policy frameworks, programs and services, and the mix of public service and third-party involvement settled on in the implementation of government programs. In particular, I focus on the way in which the various characteristics of government goods and services and the markets into which they are supplied shape these choices. These same elements – product and market characteristics – are also important in the determination of the competitive positioning of the public service and organisational structures that can be employed to manage and deliver the chosen services. I am therefore interested both in the contribution that the public service makes to these choices at the 'in-principle' level, ranging down to the program and services levels, as well as being interested in the competitive environment that this establishes for the public service.

My starting point is a description of the activities of government. There are some 'in-principle' matters to consider here about the role of government and the institutional framework, along with product and market characteristics, which contribute to the role allocated to the public service. These structural elements of the government business marketplace have been largely unchanging for decades, although the context in which they play out has changed substantially. In the second part of the chapter I look at the way in which the strategic management focus of governments has shifted over the last 30 or so years and the consequences that has had for the business of government. I do this through an examination of the evolving governance models employed by governments over this period.

2.2 The public sector and its services

2.2.1 The public sector task

A critical part of this analysis is to consider the nature of the public sector task and the consequent notion of 'public services'. The challenge chosen by government and the nature of the consequent services undoubtedly shapes their optimal organisational form, the strategies employed in their effective delivery, and government performance.[1] Budget size can be readily accommodated as a central measure of the public sector task, but one feature of the public sector task that makes it different to that of many

---

1   'Performance' – for both government and the public service – should be conceived not simply in outcome terms but also relative to the size of the challenge embraced. It may be useful then to distinguish between 'performance' and 'contribution', where the former is conceived of as relative to the chosen task, and the latter is conceived of as independent of this task. Thus a government that sets itself modest targets may perform well but contribute little, whilst a government setting itself stretch targets may perform diffidently but contribute a lot.

private sector multi-business entities is the necessary common linkages that exist between service offerings, both within and across business unit lines, in the provision of services and solutions to end consumers.[2]

Ideally, quantitative tools can measure the complexity of the aggregate task of government to enable a full discussion of the key features of 'the contract' between the government and the public service (and the public), both in terms of the challenge taken on and broader perceptions of the challenge of government. The academic literature shows that there have been attempts to provide guidance here; for example, Head and Alford have created a two-dimensional scale of complexity and diversity that might lend itself to quantification of the public sector task (Head & Alford 2008). In the absence of any broad-based measures of the diversity and internal complexity of the public sector task, however, it is necessary to rely on structural dimensions of the public sector, such as its institutional arrangements, and the chosen mix of strategy, structure and activities – supported by case studies – for insights into the challenges and performance of the public service.

2.2.2 The nature of public services

There are many different ways of describing the set of public services delivered by government departments. They might be described in terms of the attributes of services; the policy/program/service/client hierarchy; the structures used to deliver them; the various classes of recipients; the objectives of the interventions; and the economic and social foundations on which governments choose to intervene in the economy. Arguments about natural monopolies, public goods, and externalities generally fill the economic space, whilst efficiency, effectiveness and equity considerations are commonly the focus of public sector management discussions around policy/program settings and the choice of service delivery methods. More recently, interest has turned to greater community engagement in the processes of government, the collaborative methods (both internal and external) that could be used to deliver better services, and to the companion valuation of the benefits of these interventions through

---

2   These dependencies do commonly arise within the private sector where, for example, a multinational company will use a country-based structure to organise its global activities but overlay this with a matrix management structure to manage its individual business lines at a global level. What the multinational and the public administration have in common is the uniting of their activities across core business unit lines to serve the customer.

the notion of public value. The focus of this attention has been on the effectiveness of government services after over a century-long focus on private sector notions of efficiency.

The hierarchy of public service activities is services, programs, policies, portfolios, departments and whole-of-public-service activities. Several practical examples illustrate the nature of public sector services and the aggregation difficulties. These examples also point to organisational demands that diverse services create individually and collectively. The first is indicative of intra-department public sector coordination difficulties, whilst the second illustrates the breadth of one of the more complex social and economic problems facing the Australian Government: the need for cross-department coordination. I look briefly at public services through the lens of transaction-cost economics, providing a further perspective and insights that are useful when I come to discuss the competitive positioning of the public service.

Consider the following media release from Tasmanian Minister for Human Services Jacquie Petrusma on 19 June 2014:

> The current human services support system has many strengths, however, there are some parts that remain fragmented, uncoordinated and difficult to access. It is not uncommon for a family to have 10 different case workers across government and the community sector. Our election commitment was to deliver a new, joined-up support system in partnership with the community sector. This approach will deliver: a shared entry point and assessment for government and community delivered services; a lead worker for complex cases to build networks of support around individuals and families; and, a system with an outcome-based focus, working with families and individuals on their strengths and goals and getting results.

An even more lucid reflection of the challenge is presented in the 2014 report into Indigenous disadvantage in Australia prepared by the Productivity Commission for the Steering Committee for the Review of Government Service Provision, which presents a sobering picture of the complexity of the problems, one might say labyrinthine, being addressed in this field. This complexity is evidenced by the 12 'headline indicators' underpinned by some 40 lower-level indicators grouped under the seven headings: governance, leadership, and culture; early childhood development; education and training; healthy lives; economic participation; home environment; and, safe and supportive communities. These seven strategic areas are complex problems of considerable magnitude in their own right, spanning many of the government's major portfolio and departmental activities (Productivity Commission 2014b).

There are many further ways in which services might be classified. They might be considered as tangible or intangible, even visible and invisible; they might be classified according to their demand characteristics (e.g. available on demand or targeted), their consumption characteristics (the experiences they deliver), and their mode of service delivery (e.g. electronically or in person); they might be 'co-produced' and created at the point of consumption or predetermined; or they might be classified according to their underlying technology type and intensity. Of special relevance is a distinction made by Miles (2005, p 441) regarding innovation in services in the *Oxford handbook of innovation*. Miles examines services diversity and highlights the extent to which services are standardised or specialised to individuals, further noting opportunities for individuals to participate in the design and production of services in the latter cases.

The simplest case of public services is of a single, clearly defined service, delivered by a single service provider to a clearly identifiable customer, in a single location. This might be a financial counselling service delivered to a small business owner; delivery of a letter by Australia Post; the payment of a subsidy to an aged care facility for an eligible resident; an income tax assessment prepared by the Australian Taxation Office for an individual; or the renewal of an Australian citizen's passport. As should be clear, however, many variations are possible around this simple service design and delivery model: they may be tailored to the individual (e.g. in the field of law and order); there may be several organisations involved in the design of a single service (e.g. placing children with foster parents where police checks are required); there may be multiple services (and organisations) involved in delivering services to citizens (e.g. those threatened by domestic violence); there may be multiple physical and electronic locations involved (in, for example, addressing criminal activity); and there may be a multiplicity of customers (e.g. 'the Australian community' who are the focus of defence, border control, and counter terrorism 'services').

Of particular interest is the degree of difficulty added to this mix through the participation of multiple government departments and agencies, culminating in the delivery of services to multiple individuals. A succession of local and international auditor-general reports continues to note the increasingly required level of this interaction, and the growing need to maintain effective governance over third-party and joint service delivery.[3] Multiple examples of the complexity of public sector service provision are provided by the Productivity Commission's reports on government services (ROGS) that are prepared annually for the Council of Australian Governments. The primary purpose of the report is to provide government with information about the equity, effectiveness and efficiency of government services (with a secondary purpose being to promote public accountability). The current focus of the report is on social services, which account for some 67.9 per cent of budget expenditure (Productivity Commission 2016b).

In its 2016 report, the Productivity Commission noted the growing emphasis on the management of policy issues that cover more than one service sector, service area, or ministerial portfolio. The commission identified 16 broad service areas held together by common or similar objectives across jurisdictions grouped together into six sectors (childcare, education and training; justice; energy management; health; community services; housing and homelessness). Having grouped the 16 broad service areas together into these six sectors, the commission noted the existence of 'cross-cutting and interface issues' at three levels: within individual service areas placed in a sector, across the service areas placed in each of the six sectors, and across the boundaries of the six sectors.

The magnitude of the challenge of linking public services and providers across service, program, policy, even portfolio and sectoral lines, and establishing effective governance, is a distinguishing feature of public sector activities. Careful consideration of the respective distinguishing characteristics of public and private sector activities would today most likely place such streamlining as *the* distinguishing feature of public administration operations. Although, as I argue in Chapter 5, it has almost certainly become a bigger problem than it needs to be because of the fragmentation of the public service and the missing strategy and structure linkages. It is a feature that, given today's structures, is extremely difficult to address from the optimal position of a whole-of-public-service level, given that it is the department, not the whole of public service, that is the decision-making unit vested with greatest authority. And, as Michael Porter points out, in such circumstances in a private sector

3   See, for example, Hehir (2016).

setting, unless otherwise motivated or mandated, it is to be expected that individual business units will pursue their own goals rather than whole of organisation goals (Porter 1985).

Some of the practical challenges for public service management include problem definition, the joining up of services, the generation of solutions (not just services), organisational structures, and performance measurement and management. Clearly, the organisational challenges of delivering services to end consumers of public services can be complex, especially when multiple work units are involved in delivering programs and services, even within single government departments, let alone across government and sectoral boundaries with external parties. Finding ways to systematically address the breadth and depth of the management challenges organisationally is important whether through the use of matrix management, project-based teams, traditional public service cooperation, collaboration, or even super departments and flexible organisational structures. Any such organisational tool must, however, address interrelated sharing and accountability issues: service/ program management, resourcing, internal communication, performance measurement, and reporting – including the sharing of results.

It is difficult to foresee the implications of the product characteristics of public services for the respective roles of the government and the public service, without understanding how they play out in service delivery; that is, in the meeting of end consumer needs. Oliver Williamson's work on transaction costs provides further insight into the challenges associated with the nature of public sector services. This work is of interest because it links service characteristics with the choice of an efficient organisational form to approach these challenges (Williamson 1999).

In an article examining the role of public bureaucracies, Williamson considers how an organisational form that is so widely used can also be regarded as inefficient? (Williamson 1999, p 306). To address this question, Williamson assesses the public agency's suitability for particular transactions. He proceeds to compare the efficiency of public and private sector bureaucracies, first noting the diversity of public sector transactions, and then considering the question in the context of the class of sovereign transactions and the particular case of foreign affairs. Making this choice, he argues that the study of extremes highlights the essence of the situation, and points out that almost no one recommends that these (foreign affairs) transactions be privatised; Williamson asks why is this so? His multi-layered argument in response is as follows.

Williamson argues that the basic unit for analysis of alternative organisational structures should be a transaction: that the key attributes of transactions are asset specificity, uncertainty, and frequency, and that a comparison of the efficiency of organisational forms can be made for any class of transactions from a comparison of public and private sector bureau attributes. Underpinning this analysis is Williamson's focus on the ability of the parties to enter into a contract that suitably encompasses any arrangement to outsource service delivery of any sort, whether of sovereign transactions, human services, or even transport services. The more routinised is the service, the more capable of entering into a complete contract are the parties concerned (although Williamson argues that all contracts are incomplete to some degree). The more diverse and unpredictable are the services required, the more difficult it is for the public agency to enter into a binding contract because of an inability to specify the quantity of services and any sort of standard rate; in extreme cases, this uncertainty so dominates any prospective contractual relationship that the details of any such arrangement can only be readily determined ex post, thereby exhibiting very poor cost control properties, which leave the public sector little choice but to deliver such services in-house.

Having laid out these concepts, Williamson next argues that the skills required to conduct and maintain the foreign affairs activities of any government are necessarily specific to the task, and cannot readily be found and replicated (in the quantities required) in the private sector. He argues that highly specific asset investments, such as are required in the case of foreign affairs – both by the individuals who pursue careers within this specialised field and the government that similarly invests in the function – give rise to a high degree of dependence between the government and the public service, and strongly favours the delivery of such services from within. Moreover, the case in favour of the public bureau as service deliverer is further strengthened by (a) the presence of incomplete contracting in the face of uncertainty about the task, (b) the requirements for a dedicated governance regime, and (c) the need for both privacy and probity in foreign affairs transactions (and the governance regime).

It can be seen from Miles' survey of the field of services, and Williamson's description of the key attributes that might best enable a choice of organisational form for the delivery of public services, that there are a number of dimensions that should determine this choice once the nature of the government intervention is decided. In the case of standardised transactions and services delivered to clearly identified customers, the basis of choice is relatively straightforward. But once there are multiple and overlapping services (to one or more customers) involved, multiple agencies/sectors, and customised services, the challenges of effective service delivery multiply, and along with it the challenges of specifying a contract that enables successful contracting out of the delivery of such services. All of these characteristics are exhibited by the foreign affairs case studied by Williamson.

When considered in these terms, the characteristics of public services, both in production and consumption, are critically important to their effective delivery and it is not difficult to develop a picture of the complexity of public sector production and delivery of services through the successive application of Williamson's approach to the various activities/interventions chosen by governments. In the absence of hard data on which to base an analysis, and companion data about the extent of contracting out, it is possible only to speculate on the extent to which public services might be regarded as routinised rather than customised in practice. What is clear is that it is the dominance of social services on the expenditure side of government budgets where complexity is most likely to occur. But complexity is present in a broad range of service types. An important source of this occurs because of the simple requirement for departments to share information. Examples may include:

- the Department of Human Services and the Treasury (Australian Taxation Office) sharing information in the determination of age pension entitlements
- the corporate regulatory agency sharing information with the industry department about the eligibility of applicants for business grants (e.g. records on disqualified directors)
- Human Services wanting to check the police record of parents for their foster care program
- counterterrorism authorities wanting to check both other national authority records (e.g. Australian Border Force, the Australian Federal Police), and state authority (e.g. Police) records in regard to individuals who have come to their attention.

The need for day-to-day accumulation and sharing of information across government boundaries has no parallel in the organisation of private sector business, and is an important example of the need for departments to cooperate in the design and delivery of public sector services and solutions.

2.2.3 Government today

I will make some brief comments here about how governments go about structuring the business of government into departments. The first point to note is that the 18 departments listed below service 30 ministers, 12 assistant ministers, 37 ministries, and 16 portfolios. Each portfolio is a set of related ministerial responsibilities usually serviced from within one department; ministers often hold more than one portfolio and may be serviced by more than one department.

Table 2.1 Australian Government departments

Attorney-General's Department	Services Australia
Department of Agriculture and Water Resources	Department of Industry, Innovation and Science
Department of Communications and the Arts	Department of Infrastructure, Transport, Cities and Regional Development of Social Services
Department of Defence	Department of Social Services
Department of Education and Training	Department of the Environment and Energy
Department of Finance	Department of the Prime Minister and Cabinet
Department of Foreign Affairs and Trade	Department of Veterans' Affairs
Department of Health	Treasury
Department of Home Affairs	Department of Employment, Skills, Small and Family Business

In practice, a number of principles compete in the determination of the overarching departmental structure (number of departments, number of portfolios, and portfolio allocation). This includes: the number of suitable ministerial candidates; the number of separable portfolios; the respective emphases the government wishes to place on particular whole-of-government activities, portfolios (and ministers); the matching of prospective departmental heads with departments and ministers; the perceived need to add new functions to the role of government; the desire and appetite for change; and identified opportunities to improve the efficiency and/or effectiveness of government. The ongoing application of this set of principles is likely to be reflected in little change for some departments for decades, regular and substantial change for others, with some portfolios and parts thereof almost guaranteed a change of department at each change of government, if not election.

The activities of the individual departments vary enormously in scale and scope and, consequently, in terms of their contribution to the business of government. A common core of outputs includes policy advice to ministers, the delivery of services to citizens, advice to ministers about portfolio matters and whole-of-government responsibilities, and supporting departmental administration; there may be a number of executive agencies attached to portfolios focused on service delivery. Additionally, there are stakeholder management responsibilities that may be of any or all of a portfolio, ministerial, and whole-of-government nature. Within this common set of functions, however, there are significant differences in the balance of the internal management tasks depending on the policy/regulatory/service delivery balance of the portfolios, along with associated differences in the external interface with customers and stakeholders.

The 18 Australian Government departments cover a broad sweep of fields, ranging from schools, hospitals, prisons, public transport through to national parks and highways, national security, border protection and international affairs, child protection, domestic violence, economic policy, budgetary management, export market advice, small business advice, and tourism marketing. Public services may be visible and delivered directly to individuals and non-government organisations; they might involve services to ministers, other departments, and the community at large; they might be standard or customised to the needs of the individual; interactive and co-produced. They may be personal or IT-based in their delivery; they may be largely indivisible (and invisible), such as in national security and defence. But they are all 'public services'.

Importantly, there are many different administrative/organisational arrangements accompanying the delivery of public services, whether delivered by or through departments or other government agencies. Whilst many services will be delivered under policies for which the individual department is wholly responsible, many others will be delivered as part of a broader whole-of-government policy, both in conjunction with other government entities and across sectoral boundaries. In addition, services may be delivered directly to individual end users – an export subsidy to a small business, for example – while others may be delivered to the community at large; for example, 'the services' from government advisory and regulatory bodies such as the Australian Competition and Consumer Commission. These can be regarded as indirect services.

Governments may also deliver services directly through departments or associated executive agencies, fund external providers, form partnerships, and/or use other mechanisms including subsidising users, impose community service obligations, and provide incentives to users and/or providers. These separate choices and their aggregate are important for their implications for the departmental capabilities and organisational structures needed both to identify policy options, make choices, and then give effect to them. For example, the individual choices made about outsourcing services (or functions) impact the aggregate balance of capabilities required between customer interface and contract management skills.

Table 2.2 Recipients of public service outputs

Customer group	Public service 'outputs'
Ministers	• provision of policy advice (individual policies and overview) • management of service delivery • stakeholder consultation • assistance in fulfilling ministerial accountability obligations to parliament • government governance
End consumers and the community at large	• direct goods and services, and indirect services, delivered on behalf of the government • community consultation and involvement • provision of frank and honest advice to the government. Protection of the national interest • taking a long-term view ('enduring beyond individual governments') • 'seeing' all Australians
Parliament	• provision of information to parliament consistent with ministerial responsibilities and committee processes

Table 2.2 addresses the consequent matter of public service 'outputs'. Key public service outputs include services delivered to citizens and advice to ministers on policy and service delivery matters: this advice may span departmental and whole-of-government activities. It is particularly important to recognise that, whilst an output such as 'policy advice to ministers' may be no more than a single line entry in most departmental

annual reports – amongst pages devoted to program outputs – it lies at the heart of the public service role and underlines the public service's capacity to properly serve its political masters across the full spectrum of public service activities. It is the public service's ability to see each of its activities within the broader spectrum of its whole task that is the basis of its competitive advantage.[4] Departmental activities also include implementation of portfolio policies, advice on the achievement of particular policy objectives, consideration of the impact on the department of implementation of policies in other portfolios, and the overall monitoring of outputs and impacts of ministerial/portfolio policies.

All of these activities are directed by the public service to the government (ministers) in its role as final arbiter of the portfolio of policies directed to enhance community health and welfare. With regard to the dictates of the Public Service Act, however, caution must be used in arguing that the Australian public is served by the Australian Public Service (APS) through service to the government. The Act suggests recognition of a direct relationship between the public service and the Australian public, not simply one conducted through the government as an intermediary.[5] This interpretation makes more sense the longer the time frame of the analysis, and the desirability of the public service playing a role in the protection of the national interest – namely, taking a long-term view, enduring beyond individual governments, and, 'seeing' all Australians. Finally, 'Parliament' is added to Table 2.2 as a public service customer in recognition of the public service responsibility in Section 3(a) of the Public Service Act to 'serve' the Parliament, as well as the government and the Australian public.

4   I also argue that attempting to outsource the activities of public administration may weaken the capacity of the public service to provide valuable advice to ministers across the full range of advisory, service delivery, governance, and consultative activities. I discuss this concept in Chapter 8 in terms of the economies of scope.

5   In Chapter 10 of his book *Delivering profitable value*, Lanning establishes a framework that recognises multiple customers, levels of contributions to organisational 'profit', and the benefit of developing separate value propositions for each participant in any value-delivery chain (Lanning 2000).

2.3 Governance, accountability and responsibility

2.3.1 The concept of governance

The term 'governance' is broad and flexible: it can refer to all manner of organisations and activities: it may be associated with a particular type of organisation (e.g. public, private, corporate, community-based, philanthropic); it may be associated with a 'field' (e.g. environmental, internet or information technology). And it is used in a range of different disciplines and contexts including finance, political science, public administration, business and sociology, with each of these disciplines tacitly relying on different assumptions. As Bovaird and Loffler point out:

> There are few terms which are as vague in social science and in practice as governance. Yet this vagueness may also be the source of its current popularity as different institutions and individuals all ascribe their own meaning to the term. (Bovaird & Loffler 2003, p 316)

Bovaird and Loffler go on to make the point that any useful definition of governance must be context specific. Nonetheless, what these many uses have in common is the underlying concept of the administrative and process-oriented elements of governing. There are three general situations in the context of this book in which this term is used. The first involves its use in the expression 'models of governance', which is commonly used in the public sector literature. The second is that of corporate governance in the government sector, or more simply, government governance. The third involves the concept of governance of the public service, or public service governance. This is an important clarification because there are distinct differences between the practice of governance in public and private sectors and the capacity of the parties concerned to reasonably acquit their responsibilities to their stakeholders in this regard.

In the field of public sector management, interest in the term 'models of governance' arises substantially from the changes associated with, and following, the New Public Management (NPM) reforms to government around the world in the latter 1970s and 1980s; until then, there was only the traditional hierarchical model that had prevailed for much of the 20th century. Following these reforms, there have been a small number of evolutions in the style of government that have led to the whole period – from the foundations of traditional public administration in place at the commencement of these reforms to today's increasingly networked style of government – being described in terms of a number of 'models of governance'.

They are described as 'models of governance' because their chief elements relate to the central processes of government, both internal and external, emphasising governance as structural and process accountability, rather than governance as performance. Indeed little, if any, real progress has been made on the latter front in the presence of much discussion on the evolution of the former. In effect, there is far greater emphasis on the formalities of governance than the provision of substantive effect to their intent.[6]

The second concept of governance is that of corporate governance in the government sector, or more simply, government governance. The meaning of this term can best be understood in relation to the origin of the term corporate governance, which can be traced back several hundred years to the establishment of companies in which ownership was separated from control. The concept developed out of the separation of management from ownership, and the need for the former to actively account to the latter for its stewardship of owners' capital. Just as there is no universally accepted definition of the word 'governance', however, there does not appear to be a universally accepted definition of the concept of corporate governance, although its essence should be clear from the above and, furthermore,

- As described by Bob Tricker, it is the way that power is exercised over corporate entities covering the activities of the board and incorporating its relationships with management, the shareholders, the external auditors and regulators and other legitimate stakeholders (Tricker 2015).
- As described by the Netherlands Ministry of Finance, it focuses on the achievement of an organisation's objectives on behalf of its stakeholders and the role of governance in creating incentives and safeguards to enable these objectives to be met (Netherlands Ministry of Finance 2000).

---

6   I remind the reader that my focus in making these comments lies with government departments and is not intended to embrace a broader range of entities, particularly the commercially orientated government business undertakings.

- In turn, the Australian Stock Exchange Corporate Governance Council emphasises the underlying systems and processes defining corporate governance as the 'framework of rules, relationships, systems, and processes within and by which authority is exercised and controlled within corporations. It encompasses the mechanisms by which companies and those in control are held to account' (ASX 2014).

Taken together, these definitions acknowledge the central role of holding to account those who exercise power in meeting an organisation's stakeholder objectives. This concept is readily adaptable to the business of government, especially in regard to the various public sector corporations and statutory authorities. It is, perhaps, less obvious that this concept should be applied to that part of the business of government delivered through the set of government departments by ministers and the public service. Nonetheless, as the Netherlands Ministry of Finance working paper points out, the concept is potentially applicable to every organisation as all entities (should) acknowledge the basic ingredients of objectives and stakeholders, and a designated group responsible for delivering the one to the other. The question I consider is what, if any, differences there are between the concepts of public sector or government governance, and corporate governance?

A good place to start with this question is a definition of public sector (or government) governance. Former APS commissioner Lynelle Briggs's definition of public sector governance is as follows: 'the set of responsibilities, practices, policies and procedures, exercised by an agency's executive, to provide strategic direction, ensure objectives achieved, manage risks, and use resources responsibly and with accountability' (APSC 2007). Commissioner Ian Hanger adopted an almost identical definition in his 2014 royal commission report into the home insulation program (Hanger 2014). This (shared) definition is similar to those of corporate governance combining, as it does, the core elements of the exercise of power, the meeting of stakeholder objectives, and accountability. Content for this definition in the Australian public sector context can be provided through an examination of the primary acts under which the public service operates, namely the Public Service Act and the *Public Governance, Performance and Accountability Act 2013* (PGPA Act). Whereas the Public Service Act avoids using the word 'governance', the PGPA Act goes into some detail.

Together, these Acts assign primary operational responsibility and accountability within the public service to secretaries as head of departments ('agencies' within the meaning intended by the Briggs definition, and 'entities' within the meaning of the PGPA Act). The Public Service Act assigns specific responsibility to departmental secretaries for delivery of government programs, compliance with the law, engaging with stakeholders, assisting the agency minister to fulfil his/her accountability obligations for factual information to parliament, and (joint) stewardship of the APS. Under the PGPA Act, both general responsibilities are assigned (e.g. to govern in a manner that is financially sustainable, promotes the proper use of resources and the achievement of entity purposes), as well as specific responsibilities (including to prepare a budget and corporate plans; measure and assess the performance of the entity, including preparation of an annual performance statement; establish and maintain systems relating to risk and control; and prepare annual financial statements and an annual report).

Accountability for governance of the core business of government lies with individual departmental secretaries. There is, however, one fundamental difference between corporate and government governance in this regard, and it is central to the broader thrust of this book. For analytical purposes the core of government business, represented by activities of the set of departments and the public service, could easily be viewed as any other business with multiple divisions, not dissimilar to a large diversified corporation. This is not unreasonable given that (a) APS employees are seen to be part of one body established by an Act of parliament, and (b) the same legislation established a 'governing body' comprising the secretaries of the various government departments, meeting as the Secretaries Board, to oversight the activities of the public service.

The fundamental difference between the two is that private sector responsibility for governance in any multi-business unit organisation is seen to lie squarely with the board, not with the individual business units. Certainly, the individual entities in any multi-business corporation retain responsibility for governance within their own domain(s), but this responsibility clearly rests within a corporate framework of governance and reporting within which it is subservient. Clearly, prime responsibility for delivering governance of the activities of the public service conducted on behalf of the government is intended to lie with the individual secretaries, rather than with some overarching 'corporate' entity or 'centre' such as the Secretaries Board, which does not have systemic responsibility for governance assigned to it and is a 'board' in name only on any reasonably comparative basis with private sector boards. This conclusion has major implications for the future operations of the public service, for its strategic direction, its cohesion, and its ability to serve all stakeholder groups nominated in the Public Service Act.

The consequences of an absence of corporate governance in public administration, leaving it largely to the individual departments, can be seen in a 2010 UK National Audit Office (NAO UK) report focused on the costs of reorganising 90 government departments in four years. The audit office found that most government departments did not prepare a business case for change, that they were weak at identifying benefits of change, that there was no standard approach for preparing and assessing business cases, and that they could not demonstrate value for money. In addition, the NAO UK found that the costs were 'far from negligible' (costing around 200 million pounds per year before accounting for lost productivity), that reasons for change were poorly articulated, and that the reorganisations inevitably involved the disruption and loss of service, partly because they were often announced before plans were in place necessitating simultaneous planning and implementation (NAO UK 2010).

Richard Norman and Derek Gill reached not dissimilar conclusions with regard to restructuring in New Zealand's state sector, determining that restructuring: (a) was mainly initiated by public servants rather than governments, (b) had become 'almost an addiction' and a tool to be used to be seen to be 'taking charge', (c) treated organisations as mechanical objects with interchangeable parts rather than as living systems (unfortunately encouraged by the use of the term 'machinery of government changes'), and (d) could be a barrier to more effective inter-agency working. Their recommendations include a 'pause for thought' and assessment of whole-of-system impacts, treating any such proposal on a whole-of-system capital expenditure basis, and having regard to the full set of human resources implications of restructuring. The authors also draw some perspectives from the literature on restructuring, noting in passing that structure was seen as a means of aligning organisations with strategy (Norman & Gill 2011, pp 262–78).

A joint Parliament of Victoria – Legislative Council committee made similar findings. Reporting in May 2016, the Legal and Social Issues Committee investigated the costs of the substantial 2014 machinery of government changes: 9 departments reduced to 7; 17 new portfolios, 25 extinct or merged, and 26 unchanged. The committee regarded these costs as substantial, and found that there was no formal requirement for departments to track these costs, which resulted in inconsistent and incomplete reporting; and that indirect costs were neither recorded nor accounted for. The central recommendations were that either or both of the Department of Premier and Cabinet and the Department of Treasury and Finance work with the auditor-general of Victoria to develop and implement an integrated reporting model.[7] While such a model was subsequently developed and released, it is primarily an implementation manual for public servants and will not address any of the important governance concerns raised by the Victorian Government parliamentary committee and the NAO UK.[8] Clearly, the Victorian Government does not wish to be accountable for public service restructuring and, in the light of the conclusions from the above noted studies, with good reason.[9]

There are several observations to be made in the comparison of corporate and public sector governance before moving on to discuss the public sector's models of governance. The first is a consequence of viewing responsibility for public sector governance as the simple aggregate of individual departmental responsibilities, as it ignores the governance implications of the major problem of public administration today, which is identified in the academic literature and multiple auditor-general reports as management of the set of vertical and horizontal coordination challenges that cross agency and sectoral boundaries.

7   Parliament of Victoria, *Inquiry into machinery of government changes*, Legal and Social Issues Committee, 2016.

8   Department of Treasury and Finance, *Victorian public sector operating manual on machinery of government changes*, State of Victoria, 2016.

9   My own experience of 'restructuring' covers both private and public sectors. My early introduction to it was at a manufacturing company ACI – a large listed Australian company that, in the early 1970s, expanded its product range and market coverage in the face of competition at home as it changed from a functional to a divisional structure, as was fashionable at the time. In the public sector I experienced departmental realignments resulting from machinery of government changes, and individual departmental restructuring initiated by departmental heads. The former were usually initiated to signal a change in government priorities, differing ministerial interests/capabilities, and to address cross-agency coordination issues (the super-department is the latest antidote for the latter). In the case of departmentally lead restructuring, the motive was usually to change the executive team (by restructuring out those who did not have the confidence of minister/head, and restructuring in those who might at least start with it), or be seen to be 'doing something'. In the case of departmentally led restructuring, the focus seemed always on people rather than strategy.

The second observation goes to the requirement of the Public Service Act that the public service serve a triad of stakeholders comprising the government, parliament and the Australian public. Most discussions of public sector governance only address government governance and the role of the public service in this. The public service in Australia, however, has equal responsibilities to these two communities, and without closer examination it would be rash to assume that a public service acquitting its governance responsibilities to the government of the day will consequently acquit its responsibilities to the parliament and the community at large.

Indeed, conflict between the three is regularly publicly observed in Australia in the form of: government reticence to publish business cases for major infrastructure decisions; the poor performance under state and national freedom of information Acts (gross failure to meet response-time targets); and in the determination of governments to label as many documents as possible 'commercial-in-confidence', thereby limiting parliamentary and public access to their contents. Given the importance of good governance to effective government, and the need to actively build trust in government, it would be reasonable to expect the public service to have a plan to acquit its responsibilities to the parliament and to the Australian public, sitting alongside a plan to acquit its responsibilities to the government of the day.

The third observation relates to the ambit of good governance in the public sector. Much of today's discussion around government governance tends to concentrate on the act of governing, the structures, the actors and the relationships to the exclusion of performance measurement. As a consequence, public administration is still struggling to deal with the development of effective output measures let alone impact, outcome, whole-of-policy, or public value measures. Yet, even in regard to performance measurement, a typically narrow view of its importance is taken with a focus on the various dimensions of service delivery. A Netherlands Ministry of Finance paper points to interest in improving public sector governance in an increasingly broader context: raising their sights from the traditional focus on operations to include the very important policymaking functions of government. The paper then develops a framework for the governance of policymaking areas. This is of course a major area of conformance that has substantial performance implications, and is an important reminder that the major benefits that governments dispense are invariably dispensed not through the contracts for asset purchase and service delivery, nor indeed to end consumers, but through the policy decisions made, and which should demand the same level of scrutiny (more perhaps) as any other purchasing activity (Netherlands Ministry of Finance 2000, p 8).

The final set of observations concerns the organisational dimension of governance. The particular importance of whole-of-government governance in this context goes to the observation by the Australian National Audit Office (ANAO) that government policies transcend the activities of individual operating units (e.g. departments), and increasingly necessitate the involvement of a range of government and non-government participants to deliver targeted policy outcomes (ANAO 2014a). This is reflected in the fact that a primary objective of many public sector reforms over the last two decades or more around the globe has been to 'join-up' government program design and service-delivery activities and network with a range of external and internal players in their design, development, and execution. As the public service has a major contribution to make to good government governance in the design and execution of policy and program management across organisational boundaries, along with complementary administrative systems, it is important that it actively and holistically manages itself in this regard. I argue that the public service should see itself as an entity separate from government, as an integrated organisation rather than as a loose federation of departments, requiring established objectives, strategy and governance procedures, just as any other large organisation should do. I also assert that the Public Service Act establishes the APS as a separate organisation, that the matter of alignment of government and public service activities is something to be scrutinised from a public policy perspective, and that it is in the public interest for the APS to look beyond the prevailing master–servant relationship that underlines today's relationship.

I also argue that this position – of a separate public service – is absolutely necessary in the face of widespread contestability of public administration activities and is made all the more necessary by the greater diffusion of authority across the business of government. My final observation, then, in regard to public sector governance, goes to the concept of public service governance and the need for the public service to behave as any other organisation would, in setting its own objectives, developing its own strategy, preparing an annual business plan, and putting in place governance arrangements to secure performance against its plans.[10] This is critical to meet the growing challenge of managing and accounting for these cross-boundary, cross-sectoral collaborative arrangements.

By providing a number of pointers to the effective execution of such arrangements – including managing shared risks, aligning the vertical, horizontal and whole-of-government accountabilities, the sharing of resources and accountabilities and the necessity of entering into written agreements to formalise such arrangements – the ANAO guide highlights the difficulties of successful collaborative management in the public sector. It is also critical if the public service is to grow. If the government has made the APS a competitive enterprise, it will continue to wither unless it also enables the public service to compete.

2.3.2 Accountability and responsibility

Accountability and responsibility are terms that are often confused in discussions of governance. The distinction between them is best drawn in terms of the person who is ultimately answerable for an activity (accountability), and the individual(s) who actually undertakes a task (responsibility). Thus, someone who is answerable for the completion of a task (i.e. accountable) may allocate the completion of this task to another, who is responsible. Grasping this distinction is important to an understanding of the relationship between the public service and the elected government. Thus, whilst governments are ultimately answerable to the electorate for their choice and implementation of policies, and individual politicians to the prime minister, the public service is invariably responsible for service delivery and, within the confines of government, senior public servants are held accountable for the quality of their endeavours.

A particular feature of government in Australia is evidence of responsibility without accountability. In government inquiries into failed programs, it is often possible for the inquirers to identify the individual or individuals responsible for undertaking the failed endeavours but invariably much harder to find someone to hold accountable, either because of blurred and/or crossed lines of authority, or because a committee exercised the

---

10   Even if the public service did not see itself as in competition with any other organisation it should want to compete (a) with its own history, and (b) through demonstrated competence, with taxpayers for a larger slice of their funds.

yes/no authority. As a consequence, committee and judicial findings in such cases invariably lay the blame for failure on 'the system', effectively not allocating accountability at all.

One example is the Parliament of Victoria's Environment, Natural Resources and Regional Development Committee inquiry into the Country Fire Authority (CFA) Training College at Fiskville (Parliament of Victoria 2016a). This parliamentary inquiry into the health effects over a number of years of activities at the CFA training college was established due to serious health concerns. Despite having enabling terms of reference and finding serious discrepancies between the documented knowledge of events and the executive management's claimed knowledge, the committee was unable to recommend disciplinary action against any of the identified executive management group.

This is explicable in part by findings of crossed lines of authority and by inadequate governance practices regulating the operation of the Fiskville facility. The committee did, however, identify a failure of executive management to act on information brought to their attention. This report is unfortunately also notable for the observation of the committee chair that many of the members of the committee were either current members of the CFA – the body being investigated – or had a longtime association with the body, seemingly indicating that this made them all the more suitable for the review task! It is unsurprising that a body set up without regard to appropriate governance was unable to deal effectively with the failed governance of the body it was investigating.

A more interesting commentary on the quality of public sector governance is contained in the Australian Government's *Report of the Royal Commission into the Home Insulation Program* (HIP) (Hanger 2014). This program was commissioned as part of the government's hasty response to the 2007–08 global financial crisis, and resulted directly in four deaths. The royal commission report identified 'seven significant failings in the design and implementation of the HIP'. These included: that the responsible department was ill equipped to undertake the allocated task; that there was an absence of a robust audit and compliance program; that there was substantial reliance by the Commonwealth on the states and territories without advising them accordingly; and that there was predictable conflict or tension between the twin aims of the HIP, namely to insulate 2.2 million households and stimulate the economy. Failures of governance identified applied both to the Australian Government and the public service with

Commissioner Hanger regularly using such phrases as 'it ought to have been obvious to any competent administration', and 'it ought to have been obvious to the Australian Government'.

In a media release dated 5 February 2016, the minister for the environment provided 'the final update' on the government's response to the royal commission, the government having committed to six actions in September 2014. The six included reviews of government and public service processes. The 'final update' noted a finding by the APS commissioner that there was an insufficient basis for formal investigation of individual public servants, but makes no reference to any response regarding government processes. One could conclude that the responsible parties were excused from accountability by way of incompetence (or rat cunning?) because competent parties would have established appropriate accountability and governance mechanisms.

One of the dimensions of accountability – the application of the concept of ministerial accountability – goes to the heart of the question of government accountability and is an important contributor to the declining community trust in government. There is no formal ministerial accountability required other than that voluntarily enforced by the prime minister and inevitably, once questions of ministerial accountability are raised, the game becomes one of politics rather than justice.[11] Ministerial accountability rarely extends in practice beyond activities that a minister is personally responsible for, which often flies in the face of the day-to-day levels of involvement in departmental matters that some ministers and their staff practice.

Perhaps the most destructive cases of public trust in government are those where ministers clearly are responsible, acknowledge so publicly ('Yes I am responsible') but then do nothing about it. These cases are closely followed by those where ministers do things claimed to be within their parliamentary guidelines but are so misaligned with community standards that there is public outrage. And, in those rare cases where ministers are actually held to account for their mistakes, it is the media and public response that invariably produces accountability, rather than

---

11   The focus of the oath and affirmation of allegiance for federal members of parliament and the oath of office for ministers, is primarily one of allegiance to the British monarch, although the latter does include the words 'I will well and truly serve the people of Australia'. Since 1996 there has been a ministerial code of conduct in place but one enforced only at the prime minister's whim.

the nature of the misdemeanour itself; and even then, redemption is usually not far away. Governments must expect that community trust in government will continue to decrease under such circumstances.

Consider two further examples. The first is the failure of the Australian Bureau of Statistics' (ABS) website on 9 August 2016, the night of the Census. The website either crashed or was taken down, depending on which interpretation one accepts, and the relevant minister, Michael McCormack, who was responsible (but apparently not accountable) lined up with the prime minister to shoot either (or both) the head of the ABS, which was conducting the survey, and IBM, which was the service provider. ('Heads will roll', said the prime minister, well before any formal determination of the cause of the problem.) While there may well have been substantive failures by either or both IBM and the ABS, what stood out in the run up to the five-yearly Census and the immediate aftermath was the naïve assurances by the prime minister and the minister 'responsible' that nothing could go wrong, merely compounding the government's culpability with the problem that emerged.

The second example arises from the Australian Government's establishment of an asylum-seeker detention facility on Manus Island following negotiations with the government of Papua New Guinea. There have been regular media reports of maltreatment of the detainees with a standard response of government ministers being that is a matter for the PNG Government. This response represents a fundamental abrogation of accountability. Clearly the government has outsourced a service to a third-party provider using Australian taxpayer funds: as such, it is answerable to the Australian public for the conduct of the contractor just as surely as if the APS were itself the service provider.

A common problem when both the elected and administrative arms of government are involved in maladministration is a lack of effective formal communication between the government and the public service and between levels of government, thereby enabling both parties to avoid accountability in the event of bungling. In the HIP case, a failure by the Commonwealth to advise the states that they were expecting the latter to assume quality control for insulation suppliers and installers was found by Commissioner Hanger to have contributed to both the installation of faulty product, and its installation in a risky manner, thereby contributing directly to the subsequent deaths.

This lack of formal communication may be due to a lack of understanding of the problem itself, or the necessary governance requirements for such activities, and it may be compounded by a desire on government's part to distance itself from problems that may arise, whether resulting from public service delivery or outsourced delivery. Indeed, it would seem that the politicians' risk aversion and apparent lack of confidence in the public service may well lie behind much outsourcing activity. Either way, this is an insidious problem where politicians who do not want to be accountable enable public servants to behave similarly, and it is destructive because poor governance can be expected to lead to poor performance. It should not be so. Our democratic system can only work in a way that extends beyond the ballot box when governments are accountable to the community, both in their own right and for the public service. Were appropriate governance mechanisms in place, accountability would more readily follow but this requires a willingness to be held accountable, both for the outcomes that an organisation delivers (performance) and compliance with the organisation's systems and procedures (conformance).

Figure 2.1 Delivering accountability

Fig. 2.1 describes the key relationships in which the logic chain starts with the choices made about governance – the what and the how – based on the preparedness to be held accountable. There are then two streams of information gathered, the first relating to the objectives of the organisation and capturing its performance, whilst the second stream relates to its observance of the laws of the land and compliance with the organisation's key board and management policies, this stream being best described as conformance. When combined with a commitment to transparency, the information gathered in these two streams enables an organisation to deliver accountability. My focus lies with the good governance that flows from the choices made and the two streams of data captured, and with the accountability enabled by these flows from the accompanying transparency.

The central concept is that of accountability. The notion of accountability in the public sector relates to its stewardship of resource use and the notion that 'the stewards' should account to the stakeholders for this role. In this case, the stewards are the collective of the elected and administrative arms of government and the key stakeholders are the community at large but, as noted earlier, within this collective the elected arm of government (the politicians) must be seen as answerable to the community at large whilst the administrative arm (the public servants) are held to account by the elected arm. As ministerial accountability is interwoven with that of public service responsibility, until the former is clarified – essentially leaving the latter ambiguous – difficulties of 'government' accountability remain.

Accounting to stakeholders should be built on the demonstrated effective and efficient implementation of the incumbent government's policy platform, including sound financial record keeping and management and the demonstration of impacts and outcomes in keeping with policy goals. This should be accompanied by demonstration of the meeting of the required standards of due process and probity expected of government. This is the primary definition of external accountability. The concept of external accountability is essentially a high-level one generally best considered in terms of the communication of organisational performance to owners and (other) stakeholders and incorporates the standard meaning of accountability. Within the boundaries of accountability defined by the government of the day, it is the public service that has prime responsibility for its documentation. The public service must set up and manage the administrative systems that generate the data required – for both conformance and performance – to populate the reports consistent with the governance choices and level of transparency chosen by governments.[12]

One of the more interesting ideas for dealing with ministerial accountability is to provide ministers with additional and clear responsibility through a prescribed, managerial role in their respective departments. The promoters of this idea – Di Francesco and Eppel – propose exploration of this as part of the 'professionalisation' of ministers, improving their competency in line with community expectations, suggesting that this ministerial role is a 'missing link' in the design of public sector governance practices. The authors scope the challenge and identify a number of barriers, including achieving adequate levels of competence in any such role and the enforcement of such responsibilities, but do not venture into the territory of the content of this role, concluding that their

---

12 Internal accountability is also important in this context. From an organisational behaviour and performance point of view, the visibility and certainty of the contribution of the different parts of an organisation to each other is an especially important issue in the performance of collaborative teams built across organisational boundaries.

work is 'exploratory'. The idea has merit, but much work is required to develop it into something that would work on the ground.[13] For better ministers, such a process could formalise what they already do in playing the role of a one-person board to the departmental CEO. The major challenge would, however, be to bring the ministerial team to a common and adequate competency base.

There are two final outstanding issues to address. The first is the possibility that the various structural elements may be in place to deliver accountability but that, unknowingly, the administrative systems associated with service delivery may be failing. Secondly, there is the question of the prospective downside of too much accountability, and an argument that there can be healthy and unhealthy accountability.

When considered as a combination of processes and outcomes, healthy accountability within the public service can be described in terms of a primary focus on the outcomes of these activities, whereas unhealthy accountability can be seen as equal focus on the steps along the way: the processes and the outcomes. Indeed, unhealthy accountability focuses primarily, sometimes solely, on the former. A substantial focus on the processes – both through prescription and transparency – it can be argued, leaves little room for innovation and thereby impedes performance. The alternative is to strengthen the measurement of outcomes, thereby diminishing the need for process prescription and step-by-step transparency.[14]

2.4 Models of governance

2.4.1 An overview

An important concept of governance in the public sector, and especially with regard to public administration, is of it as a set of models that offer alternative frameworks through which to view the oversight of these activities. They are not formal models in the manner that describes corporate governance, but they incorporate different processes that set boundaries around the practice of government governance. These models of governance have emerged and evolved over a number of decades to

---

13   See Di Francesco and Eppel (2011).
14   See Bason's discussion of 'the glass bowl' effect (2010, p 60).

the point where they may now be viewed either in a linear manner, as an evolutionary description of public sector governance, or as a set of alternative management tools that can be mixed and matched to circumstances.

This discussion of models of governance acknowledges that there are few formal beginning and end points, globally or indeed for individual countries, for the various models of governance. Our chosen starting point is the late 1970s because it was then that changes to century-long public administration practices started to occur around the globe. Subsequent evolutions are, however, more difficult to date because the changes have emerged and been blended with one another rather than being announced. As a consequence, there are differing views about the choice of labels applied to the subsequent evolutions. Most observers would agree with the designation of the phases of 'traditional public administration' and 'New Public Management' (NPM).

Moreover, most are agreed that what has followed the NPM revolution of the 1980s has been a more collaborative approach to the business of government. Where the disagreement lies is in how this latter period should be described. Some have described it as an integrated period, identifying it in whole-of-government terms, with others describing it as the New Public Governance; yet others have taken an alternative approach describing successive evolutions as 'joined-up government' followed by 'networked government'. I have chosen the latter two, because they are more descriptive of the evolving challenges for the public service. I have also added a further designation, 'anarchic government', which I shall explain shortly.

When formally considered as models, the key elements of the models of governance should be their theoretical foundations (if any), their management and market-based tools, the service-delivery mechanisms, and the associated performance measures. The core of these 'models' is the common administrative and process-oriented elements of government, embodying one or more of three commonly identified public sector governing structures, namely hierarchies, markets, and the hybrids/networks. Under hierarchies, resources are allocated by administrative decree (as in traditional public administration); under markets, resources may be allocated according to competitive processes (as in NPM); and under hybrids/networks, a range of government and non-government players may participate in the allocation and management of public sector resources (as in joined-up and networked government).

When seen in these terms, perhaps only NPM might reasonably be seen as approaching a 'model', with subsequent evolutions representing more a shift of emphasis of part of the system rather than of the whole model. But even then, the foundations of traditional public administration have remained intact, with efficiency-driven changes largely grafted onto the traditional model. Nonetheless, these models of governance and their underlying governing structures are important because they frame the manner in which governments may be held to account. When properly implemented, progression from accounting for inputs (traditional public administration), through outputs (NPM), to outcomes (joined-up and networked government), provides for increasing scrutiny and accountability.

At one level these models are the management approach brought to the business of government by the government of the day. They may be seen in a linear historical context, or as a suite of management models to be mixed and matched by the public service and government of the day depending on the context; indeed, the various governance models can and do comfortably co-exist with one another today in different parts of government. This reality is reflected in the fact that, even today, the traditional public administration model, which was unchallenged for the first three-quarters of the 20th century, continues to dominate the structures of government in most democratic countries.

The sketch of each of the models that follows, with a summary presented in Table 2.3, sets the scene for issues that are addressed throughout the book. Nonetheless, NPM dominates the discussion because: (a) this was much more broad-based in its intent and impact than the subsequently emerging governance styles; (b) it has left a legacy from which most governments have not escaped (with negative consequences for the public service); (c) the subsequent models have developed in part as a response to the negative impacts of the NPM; and (d) the NPM legacy provides unsound foundations on which to graft the later models, especially for governance (an important issue as networked governance takes hold).

Table 2.3 Models of governance

Dimensions	Traditional public administration	New Public Management	Joined-up government	Networked government	Anarchic governance
Needs/problems addressed by model	Paternalistic Determined by professionals	Wants, expressed through the market	Customer-centred solutions determined by professionals	Community and business engagement	'Local' Issue-based Negotiated
Strategy	Producer-centred Service-driven	Engage markets Public choice	Join-up services Build solutions	Multi-actor-centred program design and service delivery	De-institutionalise government Enable local decision-making
Rationale	Market failure Public goods	Government failure (efficiency)	Government failure (effectiveness)	Access multi-actor knowledge to improve effectiveness	Democratise
Performance measurement	Focus on inputs	Focus on outputs	Focus on outcomes	Focus on public value	Focus on community engagement
Key actors	Public servants 'The centre'	Customers Contractors	Public servants The department	Community Business Public servants	Individuals Local interests The plurality of publics
Governing structures	Hierarchies	Markets	Horizontal coordination between departments	Networks and partnerships	Shifting coalitions of 'local' interest Fragmented
Characterisation of public service management	Technocratic Collegiate	Efficiency-seeking	Effectiveness-seeking	Collaborative	Facilitative

Sources: The primary sources of material for this table include Hartley 2005; Christensen and Lægreid 2007; Sørensen and Torfing 2011, 2012; and Hartley, Sørensen and Torfing 2013.

2.4.2 Traditional public administration

A modern history of democratic government should start with an acknowledgement that 'traditional' public service management structures were in place through much of the 20th century. These embodied a strong centre ('one public service'), a hierarchical style of management, a career public service, strong financial management, a focus on due process, and a de facto responsibility for protecting the national interest.

The limitations of this model for the more unsettled final decades of the 20th century were seen to be its inhibition of innovation, its inward-looking operating style, limited focus on performance measurement and efficiency, and little acknowledgement of the role of the customer. These were encapsulated in the limitations of the notion of a prescient public service applying scientific methods to the determination of the nation's needs and the allocation of resources, which was attacked in the early literature on wicked problems in the 1970s (Rittel & Webber 1973).

2.4.3 New Public Management

The established structure survived for three-quarters of the 20th century but, under the mounting fiscal pressures facing governments during the 1970s, it was confronted by an ideological revolution adopted from the private sector under the banner of the 'New Public Management'. Led by New Zealand and the United Kingdom, a number of governments then looked to the private sector for tools to achieve a more efficient public sector. Authority was devolved from the centre to the departments, private sector managerial tools such as employment contracts and performance bonuses were introduced, whilst contestability, competitive tendering, outsourcing, and privatisation (so-called 'marketisation') were widely utilised to generate service-delivery efficiencies. In addition, new performance measures designed to move the focus down the program logic chain from inputs to outputs were introduced. The dominant features of this movement have been described by Christopher Hood as the lessening or removal of differences with the private sector: a shift from process accountability to accountability in results, and the introduction of a new conception of accountability reflecting high trust in the market and private business methods and low trust in public servants and professionals (Hood 1991).

The way in which the new market-driven system was expected to work can be seen in the focus on performance measurement. If traditional accounting techniques focused on accounting for financial inputs, then the new market-driven philosophy focused on outputs, with departmental secretaries (commonly called 'chief executives') being held to account for the delivery of the specified quantity, quality, timeliness and cost of outputs. The voting public was assumed to hold the minister and government as a whole accountable for outcomes and the selection of outputs to achieve those outcomes. In turn, departmental chiefs were encouraged by incentives to produce outputs of value to ministers in achieving ministerial whole-of-portfolio/whole-of-government objectives. Accounting for these 'outputs' was accommodated by private sector developments in cost accounting facilitating the allocation of overheads more effectively to individual business (program/service) lines.

Much has been written about the impacts of the NPM reforms on various jurisdictions, and many assessments have been made from an ideological position, thereby enabling the various proponents to promote cases right along the spectrum with equal enthusiasm. In a 2009 assessment, Geoff Mulgan observed:

> In their milder versions the reforms helped to improve public services – making them more focussed and responsive … But overall results of the many 'new public management' reforms fell far short of their promise. (Mulgan 2009, p 59)

Mulgan reserves his harshest criticism for the marketisation phase:

> Bold claims were made for the potential of markets to transform public services and other areas of public action during the 1980s and 1990s … those countries which went furthest in marketization served as a warning to the rest. (p 60)

And:

> Markets have many virtues, and they have played an important role in making public sectors richer in information, and in feedback. But the assumption that they are a natural phenomenon, the default option for social organisations, is wrong. (p 61)

The assessment of the contribution of NPM reforms – of producing some significant localised efficiency gains but at the expense of overall government effectiveness – is one commonly made by researchers from many countries. In a 2012 article, Eva Sørensen and Jacob Torfing described its contribution as delivering 'some welcome transformations', 'a number of unfulfilled promises' and 'a large number of unintended negative effects', concluding also that, since the introduction of the NPM reforms, a new set of serious challenges had arisen that the NPM had no answers to. These were identified as dire fiscal constraints, the ongoing processes of globalisation, the growing number of wicked problems, and the need for innovative solutions to break policy deadlocks (Sørensen & Torfing 2012; see also Bommert 2010).

Perhaps the most comprehensive assessment of the impacts of the NPM reforms has been made by Hood and Dixon for the UK economy. They noted the evidence-free nature of the debate and spent several years assembling and assessing evidence of the impacts. Their conclusion, that government probably cost a bit more and worked a bit worse, adds a quantitative dimension to our evidence of the impacts of these reforms but, most interesting, is their attempt to disassemble the reasons for this conclusion, the motivation that drove the reforms, and the public policy implications of this analysis (Hood & Dixon 2015).

It is clear from the literature on the NPM reforms that emerging downsides from the introduction of the reforms were observed, in addition to the more obvious and front-end benefits. Indeed, the accumulation of experience with NPM reforms highlights the fact that the strengthened focus on departmental performance was achieved at the expense of the whole-of-government capabilities necessary to deal with the emerging complex public policy problems. Moreover, the shift to a more decentralised system of public sector management, together with the heightened focus on vertical accountabilities (e.g. between 'chief executives' and ministers) laid bare a number of operating problems, namely: a perceived lack of coordination amongst the central agencies, horizontal coordination between service-delivery agencies, the collective interests of the government, and cross-sectoral coordination. By the beginning of the 1990s, a more collegiate 'whole-of-government' style was already starting to emerge in some countries, initially focused on joining-up departmental service delivery but subsequently evolving into a more externally orientated networked style of government (Pallot 1996; Christensen & Lægreid 2007; Naschold 1996).

2.4.4 Joined-up government

The experience with NPM pointed to the need for a new paradigm that saw societal complexity, and the persistence of public administration silos with discrete, autonomous units as the key challenge rather than public service inefficiency, and the development of interactive forms of governance that cut across organisational and institutional boundaries as the appropriate response. The response sought to address the difficulties created by NPM, in the form of a shift from a predominantly management and performance measurement framework to one in which financial management issues were subsumed within an overall whole-of-government management service-delivery framework (Sørensen & Torfing 2012, p 7).

Joined-up government retained many of the features of NPM but aimed to address the limitations of departmental silos by 'joining-up' services delivered from the different parts of government. Its focus was on coordination processes complemented by some formal and informal organisational change; for example, the establishment of super-ministries (to internalise key coordination problems), the adoption of the matrix management technique from the private sector, and the use of standing committees and task forces across departmental boundaries. The concept of coordination across government was given new emphasis as part of the collegiality sought from departmental chief executives, although some observers saw this as nothing more than the recreation of whole-of-government coordination that was a tenet under the traditional public administration model, albeit one that had been discarded (McGuire 2006; Hood 1991).

An Australian perspective on the challenges of providing more integrated, whole-of-government responses to the increasingly complex and diverse problems confronting governments was provided by the committee of department heads known as the Management Advisory Committee (MAC) in its 2004 report, 'Connecting government'.[15] In seeing whole-of-government collegiality as a strength of Australian public administration, the MAC warned against the injudicious use of the whole-of-government approach, observing that the real challenge was not high-level multilateral exercises, so much as the day-to-day realities of working across boundaries

---

15   See Management Advisory Committee, 'Connecting government: whole of government responses to Australia's priority challenges', Commonwealth of Australia, 2004, www.apsc.gov.au/ connecting-government-whole-government-responses-australias-priority-challenges.

to achieve outcomes. The strength of this report as a document that might lead to changes in the practice of public administration lies in the framework it outlines, including noting a succession of individual challenges such as development of a supportive culture and skills base, instituting appropriate governance, and building community engagement.

Its weakness lies in the fact that it is a guide that agencies consider at will. Given the emphasis in the report's preface to the day-to-day, operational, rather than (high-level) project-based nature of the challenge for public administration in Australia, there is far too little attention paid in the report to (a) changing the culture, and (b) dealing with the challenges of joint working and accountability, with the former being the organisational bedrock of collegiate behaviour and the latter the necessary operational processes.[16] One might also observe a note of unwarranted optimism in the MAC's assessment that the outcomes and output budgeting framework provided a strong base for monitoring Australian government activity. This optimism is part of a pattern of public administration in Australia that sees attention paid to the high-level dimensions of governance with a distinct lack of follow through at the operating level.

The scorecard for the impact of joined-up government across a range of countries in Europe, as well as in Australia, Canada and New Zealand, like its predecessor, is mixed at best. A stocktake of progress in implementing this new approach to UK government, eight years after its formal introduction in 1997, saw it described as 'still in its infancy' (Bogdanor 2005, Chapter 1). A 2013 study by Per Lægried, Åsta Dyrnes Nordø and Lise Rykkja of the quality of coordination in the Norwegian Government found that, whilst collaboration and coordination were an important reform trend in the previous years, it was difficult to discern its impact on policy coherence and coordination. These authors further found that the landscape was a mixture of traditional public administration and post-NPM instruments, illustrated by the fact that hierarchy was still a strong coordinating mechanism alongside cross-cutting partnerships. They concluded that 'overall coordination is assessed as rather poor, particularly between horizontal bodies in different policy areas' (Lægried et al. 2013). The view that the global influence of joined-up government had peaked

---

16   In their chapter 'Working across organisational boundaries: the challenges for accountability', Jonathan Boston and Derek Gill lay out six questions that require attention in this context namely: (1) Who will be held to account? (2) Who will hold them to account? (3) How and when will they be held to account? (4) For what will they be held to account? (5) What is the required performance standard? And (6) What are the available rewards or sanctions? (Boston & Gill 2011).

without achieving its potential was proposed in another 2013 article, this one by Philip Marcel Karre, Martijn van der Steen and Mark van Twist (Karre et al. 2013). Similarly, authors commenting on the progress of implementing joined-up government in Australia delivered a mixed report card that more often than not found the glass half-empty rather than half-full and research has cast serious doubts over the efficacy of the model of joined-up government practised in Australia (Hyde 2008; O'Flynn et al. 2011).

While there seems to have been a penchant for reform following the unfulfilled promises and unintended consequences of NPM, there is limited evidence of the success of the subsequent joining-up of government. Most government departments in the countries noted above are still arranged in a hierarchical structure with joined-up government successes taking place in its shadows. The triumvirate of closely related problems noted by June Pallot with the introduction of NPM – comprising horizontal coordination between government agencies, the collective interests of the government, and the lack of coordination amongst the central agencies – remained an elusive challenge (Pallot 1996).

Studies of the performance of joined-up government highlight the difficulties of successfully allocating responsibility with accompanying accountability across organisational boundaries, and its limitations as a model of governance. Coordinated service delivery and the bundling of services into solutions across governmental (and non-governmental) boundaries require enhanced management and accounting processes to be effective. And, while there has been an accompanying discussion in the academic literature of strengthening the focus on outcome measurement and accountability, this has not been delivered in practice despite the added stimulus provided by a refocusing of national auditor-general office activities over the last 30 years away from traditional financial audits to 'performance audits'. That this should be the position with joined-up government some two decades on from its first broad-scale implementation in the United Kingdom by the government under Tony Blair is disappointing from both academic and community viewpoints, but unsurprising in consideration of the scale and complexity of the challenge and the tools used to address it.

NPM reforms were accompanied by some organisational change with the establishment of executive agencies and larger departments. Indeed, the bulk of the private sector–derived changes were largely of a technical and 'turn key' nature, and could be readily imposed on an organisation on a top-down basis. In contrast, the challenge of achieving effective joined-up government required a more subtle and difficult change to the operating style of public administration necessitating a significant change in culture.[17] This does not happen by administrative decree and requires people at all levels across the organisation to contribute – those with market knowledge, those with policy knowledge, and those with administrative systems knowledge, all under coordinated leadership across departmental boundaries.[18] Moreover, the taskforces, inter-departmental committees, and various steering committees commonly used to 'coordinate' intra-governmental, intergovernmental, and extra-governmental activities have, in the past, been best used to scope problems rather than deliver solutions to long-term problems. The various tsars, commissioners, and ombudsmen that continue to be appointed to deal with operating-level failures of service delivery are unfortunately invariably a costly symptom of this failure rather than a harbinger of success.

As with NPM, it is arguable that the promise of change under joined-up government has not been delivered. Achieving systemic change is a sizeable challenge with the self-interests of ministers and departments all too capable of undermining good intentions. Such failure as has occurred – more unfulfilled promise than unintended consequences in my view – resulted from a combination of underestimation of the task and lack of commitment at the highest levels. There was/is a serious organisational impediment to such change, and changing organisational culture is most unlikely to be achieved by leaving it to the component parts (the departments): success in changing organisational direction is much more likely when a corporate, that is, whole-of-organisation, approach is taken.

In the absence of a corporate headquarters to mandate and support change and broker agreement between the parts – with individual departments having to negotiate their own cross-boundary agreements with their peers – it is most likely that the interests of individual units will prevail. Indeed, Porter (1985) argues that this corporate role has been central to the success of 'phase two' of the life of the multi-divisional corporate form on

---

17 I do not wish to imply by this comment that the NPM reforms were somehow a ready-made success. They were not.
18 Indeed, one might describe the task of implementing the NPM reforms as a management task, whilst the one of implementing the necessary organisational adjustments to achieve joined-up government as one of leadership.

which the organisational form of NPM was loosely based. Nonetheless, as the MAC's 2004 *Connecting government* report demonstrates in its final chapter and case studies, significant change can be achieved in the APS, albeit in the face of a crisis, pointing to the opportunity to learn from these crises not just the formula to avoid them, but how to scale successful change up to whole-of-organisation change. The consequent challenge is to put these 'learnings' into practice (MAC 2004).

2.4.5 Networked government

During the 1990s, and alongside attempts to better 'join-up' their departmental activities, many governments built collaborative processes and networks with external parties (Rhodes 1996; Peters & Pierre 1998; Börzel & Risse 2010; Pryor 2014). Networked government represented a more pragmatic change but of a much deeper sort, being a challenge to the structures and systems that deliver solutions to public policy problems. Whereas the focus of joining-up government was primarily aimed at achieving a whole-of-government approach with improvements in both efficiency (non-overlapping services) and effectiveness (customer-based solutions), the primary focus of networked government has been squarely on effectiveness through the involvement of a range of players in policy and program design and the delivery of the resultant services.

These third-party players – private sector, community-based organisations, and philanthropic groups – are presumed to be able to add value through their existing involvement in the marketplace into which government services are to be delivered. The subsequent incorporation of yet more players in the development and delivery of services through various forms of networking and oversight has brought more market-based knowledge to the provision of services but has exacerbated the underlying performance and accountability problems of decentralised and distributed government.

The apex of support for networking as the governing structure has been reached in the United States, where the role of government has traditionally been seen as a partnership with the private sector rather than as the dominant central player – as it has been, for example, in the United Kingdom and Australia. Stephen Goldsmith and William D. Eggers argue that fundamental change was occurring in the way public services were being delivered in the United States. They applied the phrase 'governing by network' to their conclusion that government executives were redefining their core responsibilities away from managing workers and providing services directly, to orchestrating networks of public, private, and non-profit organisations to deliver the services that government once did itself, and maintained that the new approach was a dramatically different type of endeavour than simply managing divisions of employees (Goldsmith & Eggers 2004).

In a subsequent (2013) book co-authored with Paul Macmillan, Eggers developed this theme further to argue not only that the US Government had become just one of the players in the public policy space designing and delivering solutions to public problems, but that its role as lead player had been superseded. The authors described a new economic paradigm involving a more collaborative system with business, philanthropy, government and social enterprise coming together to solve big problems and create public value. As presented, this new paradigm was underpinned by the creation of a market for solutions to social problems through the internet supported by the profit motive and thereby creating a more productive means of addressing community problems (Eggers & Macmillan 2013). Early signs of this sort of activity in Australia can be seen in the use of citizens' juries to resolve local issues, along with the crowdfunding of a range of new ventures replacing, in part, government grants and bringing new sources of venture capital to the market.

When viewed as a model for community involvement, and in the face of a lack of leadership from our politicians – with citizens, politicians, business and community members together determining needs and accessing public funds – it is likely that this form of networked government will gain popularity. Moreover, the pull of having both those who understand the market and the production and consumption phases of any service may well prove (politically) irresistible. At the same time, the more developed form involving external funding is likely to emerge more slowly. This is because the range of solutions to community problems that are amenable to this form of 'government', relying on the existence (or prospective existence) of a market transaction (creating both in the hands of the provider and the recipient), will be significantly limited. Instead, these sorts of productive community-driven collaborations will almost certainly (continue to) find their most productive use in addressing local issues.

Additionally, those issues of a state or national nature, especially involving public goods, do not seem amenable to this sort of solution. But even the more benign form of networked government has had its critics from its inception. An early problem noted in its development was the challenges presented for the management of the emerging intergovernmental networks by the rigidity of the 18th- and 19th-century public administration organisational structures on which it was built (Provan & Milward 2001). The earlier unresolved challenges of control, resources, and results sharing that emerged with attempts to join-up services were seen as being compounded by the addition of external parties to the supply mix.

Eggers and Macmillan recognised this challenge to good governance in the management and governance difficulties posed by a network of partnerships and relationships, including skill-set issues (managing contracts); technology issues (incompatible information systems); communications issues (one partner in the network, for example, might possess more information than another); and cultural issues (how interplay among varied public, private, and non-profit sector cultures can create unproductive dissonance). Critics of the unresolved accountability difficulties that have dogged joined-up government have described the distributed style of government as 'governance without government' and called for a new theory of accountability (see, for example, Peters & Pierre 1998).

2.4.6 Anarchic governance

In rounding out this discussion of models of government, I note the existence of one further 'model' in common use, which I call 'anarchic governance'. Presented in Table 2.3, it is commonly found at local government levels where various forms of issue-based local democracy are practised. What these various activities have in common is the level of local community involvement in agenda formation, evaluation and resolution of issues, and sometimes funding, and the back-seat, facilitative, role played by politicians and public servants. In this model, a key performance measure that needs to be added to the usual mix is that of community engagement: indeed in some circumstances this might be the prime measure (i.e. the process is the outcome).

There are two strands to this model. The first envisages problem and policy determination led by ever-changing coalitions of community members with the public service playing a facilitation role and, with political consent, providing access to public funds. The second envisages public policy determination and resolution by a variety of non-government players funded by the private sector and utilising methods such as crowd funding (Wacchaus 2014; McGuire 2006)). This broadening engagement of the community directly in the daily processes of government could see important parts of the roles of both the elected officials and the public service acquired by the community on an issues basis and will have important implications both for skills required and the public service management structures of the future.

Both strands are already in play, with the latter having been actively employed at regional and local levels of government for some decades. An Australian national and state government version of this would be 'summits' to address a variety of economic and social problems, such as has occurred in Australia over the last decade in the cases of innovation, homelessness, industrial relations, domestic violence and early childhood learning.

2.5 Some unresolved issues

Any discussion of models of governance must acknowledge the importance of the traditional model of public administration, which prevailed unchallenged for much of the 20th century and remains the foundation of most public service activity. NPM reforms built on this model in important ways. By placing cost-efficiency at the centre of the challenge of government and acknowledging a role for the customer in this system, it opened up the development of public policy to the injection of new influences all the way along the logic chain of government activity, from the conceptual foundations of government policy through to the measurement of its impacts.

This revolution has generated two consequences of particular interest. The first is the loss of a holistic view of the role of the public service, driven by the devolution of authority from the centre to the departments. It was the devaluation of this role, the fragmentation of public service operations that followed, and the loss of associated public service capabilities, which together encouraged the joining-up of services and the refocusing on a whole-of-government approach in order to recover some of the lost effectiveness of public administration it caused. Where Hood and Dixon have cast doubt on the stated (efficiency-driven) motives for these reforms in the United Kingdom, in Australia's case, the substantial weakening of the public service was unlikely to have been an unintended consequence. The more interesting question is whether it was the main game.

The second and closely associated consequence goes to the refocusing of the performance measurement of government activities. The change from inputs to outputs was undoubtedly a step in the right direction, but provided little information about impacts or outcomes and contributed little to the overall budgetary resource-allocation process. It certainly enabled politicians to form a better view of what revenues were 'buying' from the public service. But it provided no ready means for the government to compare the economic impacts (program and policy impacts and outcomes) either of existing programs or of alternatives.

While government policy and program choices will always ultimately be made on political grounds, it is arguable that the role of the public service is to inform government in the formation and detail of these choices, to advise the government of their economic impacts, and to take every opportunity to pursue the goal of better resource allocation. If there is any room for those twins, frank and fearless, in government, it must surely be in regard to the allocation of resources and the means of achieving the best outcomes, especially when one considers that ministers often evaluate smaller expenditure activities more closely than the bigger 'blue sky' and 'nation-building' activities. A day-to-day focus on this issue of sound resource allocation is especially important because the measurement of impacts and outcomes of government activity becomes more critical in a world of joined-up and networked government activity and cross-boundary and cross-sectoral program delivery. Networked government, in particular, adds another layer of complexity to already weak resource-allocation foundations.[19]

The issue of resource allocation also comes to the fore when we consider how organisations can best balance ongoing investment in the present and future.

In turn, the evolution of models of governance has brought to the fore a further consequence of interest to us, and that is the illusion that somehow these models have a connection with the quality of governance delivered. The nomenclature may well point to alternative modes of governance underpinning these 'models of governance' – hierarchies,

---

19   The Australian Public Service Commission has previously examined how accountability and performance management arrangements deal with new modes of policy implementation (e.g. risk-taking, community engagement and innovation). They concluded that not only accountability gaps have emerged but that current arrangements were constraining innovation. See APSC, 'Delivering performance and accountability', 2014b, www.apsc.gov.au/delivering-performance-and-accountability.

markets, networks/hybrids – but it gives no indication of the underlying resource-use accounting and quality of governance that ensues. This latter is as much a matter of commitment to implementation as it is the embedded measurement regime, and it can be observed that, as the models themselves have evolved over the last 30 or so years with progressive improvement in the underlying measures, there appears to have been little real effort since the introduction of output budgeting to implement the embedded changes. With the measurement task becoming progressively more difficult whilst the performance measurement framework has stagnated, the obvious consequence has been a deteriorating standard of government governance. Meanwhile the measurement of public value waits in the wings to be called into action.

In taking a whole-of-government view of this evolution of public sector governance in Australia, Meredith Edwards, John Halligan, Bryan Corrigan and Geoffrey Nicoll noted a number of continuing and emerging tensions and discussed three in some detail: vertical and horizontal governance, central coordination, and agency and board governance. In looking to the future the authors placed the vertical/horizontal dimension at the heart of this challenge in the presence of the growing numbers of actors and inter-dependencies involved, identifying the fundamentals for successful future public governance as leadership, accountability, and shared outcomes and accountabilities (Edwards et al. 2012).

In a presentation to the Institute of Public Administration New Zealand (IPANZ) in March 2012, Bill Ryan commented:

> Assuming a learning orientation, an outcomes focus, particularly in relation to complex policy, leads people on a journey back to everything else I have discussed. As they try to figure out and make sense of their goals and objectives and evaluate their efforts to date in the light of the context, with backwards-mapping, *everything else falls into place* [my italics].

This might be regarded as a substantial concession from someone who brings an historical and sociopolitical perspective to bear on questions of governing, and who is a self-confessed critic of what he describes as 'the excessive influence of certain economic theories on public management'. My underlying premise is that measuring the right things is a necessary condition for good performance and, in Chapter 4, I draw together theoretical argument and observed performance making use of Ludwig von Mises' argument of the necessity of what he calls 'the economic calculation' to underpin sound government (von Mises 1944).

There is one final dimension of governance that has not been systematically addressed but which has received much attention in the private sector literature: the matter of board effectiveness and governance. I have pointed to the importance of leadership and the role of 'the centre' as described in the public sector management literature. In practice the missing public service 'centre', when viewed in private sector terms, comprises two management layers and skill sets, namely an independent board, and a dedicated CEO and corporate office. Their absence denies the public service access to the skills, experience, and processes – ultimately the leadership – associated with the proper functioning of these organisational levels in the private sector. To argue this, I will draw heavily from Bob Garratt's aptly titled book, *The fish rots from the head* (2010).

3

The problem of policy formation

3.1 Introduction

This chapter begins with a focus on the nature of the policy challenge. Is it necessary to examine the performance of a public sector in which the design and execution of its business is straightforward, or one in which the degree of difficulty is high? And how wicked really is the policy environment? A case study in homelessness is used to illustrate some of the critical dimensions of 'wicked problems' and the difficulties involved in delivering beneficial outcomes. The second part of the chapter considers what might reasonably be regarded as a 'tame' problem involving an important piece of government policy, namely contestability, whose importance is both as a piece of government policy in its own right, but also as a major plank in government policy towards its management of the public service. Is it producing the efficiency dividends intended, and what is its impact on the public service?

3.2 The policy environment

3.2.1 The policy framework

If the core business of government is to put in place policies to improve community welfare – expand the 'goods' and shrink the 'bads' as described by Geoff Mulgan – then it is through the processes of policy formation and (successful) implementation that governments achieve this goal. 'Good policy', as seen from a community perspective, can be characterised in process terms from its formation through to the satisfaction of the end consumers, as well as its achievement of broader societal goals, and in terms of the relationship of costs incurred to benefits generated (that is in outcome terms).

'Good policy' in process terms includes a clear policy objective, canvassing of the alternative policy instruments available for achieving the specified objective, along with the options for service delivery, stakeholder (including internal government) consultation as required, followed by the formal documentation (business case) and government approval (usually Cabinet) processes. The business case should incorporate the extent and outcomes from this process, including the costs and benefits of the options considered, and establishes how the policy/program is to be implemented and managed and how its performance is to be assessed. Ideally any such proposal would incorporate whole-of-policy/program life costing and benefits, and not simply be a proposal limited to the time frame of the government's forward financial estimates.

In any particular set of circumstances, the best case scenario from a departmental management and whole-of-government governance point of view is that 'good policy' is possible, that the problem is clearly defined, there are feasible options to be compared, that a solution can be envisaged as arising within a defined time frame, and there is both sufficient political consensus and social support to enable effective implementation. Many problems, however, do not fit this pattern – be they 'bads' such as crime, substance abuse, and pollution, along with 'goods' such as public health, trade and foreign investment, and education. They may not fit this profile because of any or all of: the policy problem is difficult to define, its causes may be difficult to determine, its full impacts may as yet be unknown, new policy instruments may be required to address the problem, 'success' may be hard to define, and the problem as defined may significantly overlap with existing policies and programs. Moreover, there may also be sharply divided political and societal views about the benefits of investment of public funds in pursuit of any 'solution'.

Then there is the issue that containment may be an expensive path to a solution, where the latter is seen as possible only in the longer term. The problem may be even more complicated where some measure of containment is necessary to reduce collateral damage whilst the major problem is tackled. No issue in our community has engendered more heated debate in this latter regard than proposals to provide publicly funded, safe drug-injecting facilities to minimise risks to individual health from drug injection whilst the bigger problem of drug supply is tackled. And this debate takes place in the context of a broader argument about legalisation of (some further) drug use (in addition to cigarettes and alcohol) on the twin foundations (a) that it cannot be stopped and might better be regulated, and (b) that it is a matter of personal choice anyway. Counter arguments about 'not giving up' (with regard to (a)), and the impact of drug consumption on others (the economists' argument about externalities with regard to (b)) also deserve consideration.

The class of difficult public policy problems – where the problem is difficult to define, where the ultimate solution is difficult to discern, and where there might be a range of political and societal views clouding the prospects of achieving any implementation consensus – has received much attention in the academic literature for some decades in discussions of wicked problems. Indeed, over the last four decades or so the concept of wicked problems has come to dominate academic discussion of public policy formation, whilst the policymakers and managers have been largely left to manage an increasingly difficult raft of public policy problems and programs with little advance on the traditional ('rational', 'scientific') toolkit.

3.2.2 Wicked problems

The origin of the term 'wicked problem' is usually traced back to the work of design theorist Horst Rittel in the latter 1960s. Rittel formalised the term in a 1973 article co-authored with urban designer Melvin Webber and published in *Policy Sciences* in which they proposed using 'wicked' in regard to the problems of governmental planning 'especially social or policy planning' (Rittel & Webber 1973). The authors defined 'wicked' problems of governmental planning by contrasting them with the 'tame' or 'benign' ones of the natural sciences, such as solving an equation in mathematics. For the latter, the mission is clear, just as it is evident when the equation has been solved. Wicked problems have neither of these clarifying traits and, according to Rittel and Webber, include nearly all of the (then) public policy issues. The authors went on to identify 10 distinguishing characteristics of these 'planning-type problems':

1. There is no definitive formulation of a wicked problem.
2. Wicked problems have no stopping rule.
3. Solutions to wicked problems are not true or false, but good–bad.

4. There is no immediate and no ultimate test of a solution to a wicked problem.

5. Every solution to a wicked problem is a 'one-shot operation'; because there is no opportunity to learn by trial and error, every attempt counts significantly.

6. Wicked problems do not have an enumerable (or an exhaustively desirable) set of potential solutions, nor is there a well-described set of permissible operations that may be incorporated into the plan.

7. Every wicked problem is essentially unique.

8. Every wicked problem can be considered a symptom of another problem.

9. The existence of a discrepancy representing a wicked problem can be explained in numerous ways. The choice of explanation determines the nature of the problem's resolution.

10. The planner has no right to be wrong.

Since publication of Rittel and Webber's article, the term wicked problem has been widely applied across the social sciences to major problems of public policy such as obesity, land degradation, Indigenous disadvantage, and climate change (see, for example, APSC (2012)). Domestic violence, drug and alcohol abuse, homelessness, overcrowding in prisons, and international terrorism, none of which can be seen to have a 'simple' (for example, a unique single policy instrument/single jurisdiction/solution), could be added to this list.

Indeed, Rittel and Webber saw wicked problems in nearly all public policy issues at the time, not simply because of the physical interdependencies but because of the growing plurality of American society involving the existence of multiple stakeholders with divergent sets of values, and the impossibility of specifying broadly acceptable goals around which optimal solutions might be built. They saw this latter development as rendering redundant the traditional rational scientific approach to public policy determination embedded in public sector management practices of collecting and analysing (more) technical data to determine optimal solutions (as would be done for road networks and public transport routes).

In their view, this long-standing approach might have had some merit in dealing with the postwar infrastructure developments required, but it was seen as not meeting the community's needs for resolution of the growing social problems. Whilst the emergence of this concept in the United

States in the latter 1960s and early 1970s occurred during a particularly turbulent time in American politics in the face of growing ethnic and cultural diversity and income inequality, it effectively foreshadowed an acceleration in the growth and complexity of wicked problems in developed countries around the globe.

The early literature on wicked problems in planning and policy has been followed by research that has generalised the concept and extended it to incorporate super-wicked problems, further developing Rittel and Webber's initial conception of both the social and physical dimensions of wicked problems. The content of this latter literature focuses on the interrelated nature of wicked problems, the existence of multiple stakeholders with sometimes irreconcilable goals, the need for political rather than bureaucratic processes to lead the search for solutions, and the absence of a methodology capable of dealing effectively with these problems (Levin et al. 2009; Roberts 2000; Head & Alford 2008, 2015).

For some decades, discussion of such problems, and the management models developed to address them, have approached the definition of policy problems in a binary manner, treating problems as either wicked or not, without any shades of grey. As a consequence, the academic sphere has made limited progress in developing appropriate management tools to 'solve' such wicked problems. A 2017 article by John Alford and Brian Head criticising such a state of affairs makes a number of useful observations. The first alludes to the absence of data cataloguing wicked problems and the difficulty of determining whether these problems have increased in intensity or not. Second is the essentially binary nature of the discussion – a problem is considered either wicked or not. Third is the consequent, and unnecessarily limited search (by others) for 'one best way' and, fourth, the limitations of the notion of a 'solution' as the success measure in the face of wicked problems. Finally, the authors assert that there is a resulting overuse of the term (Alford & Head 2017).

In response to these problems, they propose a nine-cell typology of policy problems built around what they describe as 'the two irreducible elements of wicked situations' – the actors and the problem – the former described by the number of parties, their values and knowledge levels, and the latter by the clarity of the problem itself and the path to a solution. The cells described are seen as representing a continuum rather than discrete types. The spectrum of problems is then characterised as ranging from tame to very wicked with *degrees* of wickedness applying. With this framework in hand the authors propose to address the shortcomings in scholarship to date by proposing use of a contingency framework built around a combination of the causal factors applicable within any one cell, allowing targeted interventions to make headway.

Guy Peters echoes many of these sentiments and also criticises the binary nature of the discussion, arguing that the concept of wickedness has captured academic imagination beyond its usefulness as a management construct. Peters also emphasises the primary content of wicked problems as being multiple actors and social and political complexity, and notes the emphasis placed on the capacity of leaders and centralised institutional solutions that accompanies such a binary approach. He then points, as Alford and Head do, to varying degrees of wickedness, requiring in prospect, varying management, strategies for success. Peters' particular contribution is to note how little is known about the existence of wicked problems and their management, and he proposes a research program be undertaken to understand more fully which problems policymakers consider wicked; how they conceptualise policy problems, including the wicked and super-wicked; and how policymakers think about addressing these problems (Peters 2017). Several further dimensions of the nature of today's wicked public policy problems can be highlighted before moving on to consider a response to them. One issue that deserves attention is that of problem resolution. The problems addressed by government services are increasingly long term. This creates a political difficulty as the political cycle – whether three, four, or five years – is out of sync with the problem resolution cycle. And, given that problem resolution invariably requires significant front-end investment, effective government in the prevailing political cycle often means budget pain with little electoral gain for a number of years. There is no end game in the standard definition of wicked (and super wicked) problems and, thus, containment rather than resolution becomes the unstated program goal.

Consider the alternative policy formulation for an elimination strategy rather than one of containment – a formulation of the former could involve investigating the level of investment of public resources it would take to eliminate the problem and what inroads the present set of services is making in achieving this solution. These are the questions that demand attention and require a strategic view of the problem if only because elimination strategies may vary from containment strategies at any point in time. And it could further be argued at a philosophical level that accounting for public expenditures should recognise both the actual expenditures on services/problems and the total estimated remaining expenditures required to resolve these problems, much in the way that an electricity generator might be expected to account for the cost of decommissioning an electricity generation plant at the time of its installation, or a petroleum marketing company (selling products through company-owned service stations) might be expected to include the cost of cleaning a distribution site from leaked petroleum contaminants, at the end of its useful life.

Just as the private sector and governments account for the unexpired portion of their assets, and liabilities, so governments could account for the unresolved portion of their key service liabilities. 'Goods' and 'bads' should have equivalent treatment in public sector accounts. If included in the public sector balance sheets then the strength of public sector performance could, in part, be judged over time by the impact on its net liabilities, just as the strength of private sector performance is judged by the impact on a firm's net assets. At the very least, an estimate of the total cost of resolving policy problems should be made at the policy formation stage and regularly revised. And these latter estimates could easily be considered for inclusion in public sector balance sheets, even if only as contingent liabilities.[1]

Other difficulties identified by Rittel and Webber include what they refer to as incrementalism, arguing that if a problem is tackled at too low a level it does not guarantee overall improvement. This advice is consistent with the view that today's governments often seek to contain problems rather than solve them, addressing the symptoms rather than attending to the cause(s). This attitude may lead both to the exclusion of long-term solutions (if there are any) and, ultimately, to the exacerbation of the problem. This is commonly the case in dealing with, for example, community crime primarily through incarceration. Such single-fix 'solutions' reflect a difficulty in tracing problems to their root causes – to what Rittel and Webber refer to as the locus of difficulty – and makes a more collaborative

---

1   It can be argued that much government expenditure is *necessarily* ongoing and, no doubt, this is true for a range of important fields of government expenditure; for example, in health, transport and education. There are, however, other areas of government expenditure – for example, in some business/economic fields (concessions to small business and housing affordability), and the field of law and order and some social policy fields – where there should be an end in sight; two examples would be road deaths and deaths through domestic violence. Focusing on an end point for government services should help to avoid the more obvious conflict between containment and resolution strategies by inviting formal consideration of the trade-offs, and focus policymakers on the need to resolve problems where this is possible.

approach necessary to many of today's policy problems, going hand-in-hand as it does with the advice to address a problem on as high a level as possible.

We are left with some especially difficult challenges in the public policy field. One promising option is to use large quantities of data and computer power to try to map out and estimate the interrelationships between key variables in complex public policy problems to sort out the more important of the drivers and their relationships. This is a promising step in a long journey towards developing methodologies to deal with the more complex public policy problems. There have been some interesting developments in Australia in the use of big data, under the banner of Australian Priority Investment, and some of these are discussed in the case study of homelessness presented in this chapter.

3.2.3 Responding to wicked problems

The identification of wicked problems as lying at the heart of public sector planning challenges in the late 1960s and early 1970s was followed within a decade by the introduction of the New Public Management (NPM) reforms across a range of countries. The attack on the traditional style of public sector management represented by the identification of wicked problems underpinned the introduction of private sector goals and tools to the public sector. This attack was focused on the capacity of the public service to continue to deliver ready-made solutions to public policy problems:

> The streets have been paved, and roads now connect all places; houses now shelter virtually everyone; the dread diseases are virtually gone; clean water is piped into nearly every building; sanitary sewers carry wastes from them; schools and hospitals serve virtually every district. (Rittel & Webber 1973, p 156)

Rittel and Webber argued that the relatively easy public policy problems had by that time been dealt with (at least in the United States), that the traditional tests for efficiency were being challenged by a renewed preoccupation with the consequences for equity, and that the traditional, rational scientific approach to planning as a straightforward process of designing problem solutions was redundant. They argued that the notion of the rational public sector manager assembling all relevant information, defining the range of possible solutions and choosing 'the best' solution should be abandoned. They identified 'the weak strut in the professional's support system' as lying 'at the juncture where goal formulation, problem definition, and equity issues meet' (Rittel & Webber 1973, p 156).

This attack on the pre-eminence of the public sector managers was followed by the introduction of the managerialist phase of the NPM revolution shortly after. There was to be a renewed focus on (technical/cost) efficiency and a new focus on delivering 'outputs'. This was to be a step towards greater accountability for the public service, moving on from simply accounting in financial terms for 'inputs'. Rittel and Webber further cast doubt on the professional capacity of the public service to solve public sector policy and planning problems: this was followed by a significant curtailment in the public service role in this regard, both through the NPM contestability reforms (of both policy and service delivery activities), but also by circumscribing its budgetary freedom through the introduction of 'outputs'.

Ironically, it can be argued that, if anything, the introduction of the NPM reforms to the public sector exacerbated wicked policy management problems through the creation of departmental silos and the fragmentation of public service capacity to respond across departmental and sectoral boundaries.[2] In hindsight, what needed enhancing was the collective capacity of the public service to address these problems, not the capacity of the individual organisational units within it. The consequent emergence of a large number of non-government players in policy development and service delivery, and the growing influence of community groups, has challenged the role of government itself and has led to a re-evaluation of the alternative governing structures, and the practice of public sector management.

In a 2008 conference paper, Head and Alford confirmed that wicked problems sat uncomfortably with the structures and processes of traditional public sector management models and they examined alternative approaches to the conceptualising and mapping of wicked problems, and responses to them. In a later (2015) article they concluded that the role of leadership is critical – through adaptive and collaborative

---

2   It is important to continue to bear in mind that this was the result of the NPM reforms as implemented. This statement makes no judgement about how well the component parts of the NPM reforms were adapted to public sector needs, nor of the effectiveness of their subsequent implementation. These are matters for later consideration and need to be addressed alongside the political motivation for taking this reform route.

leadership models – and that with enabling organisational structures and processes it might be possible to frame partial and provisional courses of action to address these problems.

These enabling processes and structures include more flexibility in organisational structures (e.g. matrix management) associated with targeted project-based interventions, more flexible budgeting and financial systems (e.g. to permit the creation of cross-agency project budgets), acquisition of new skill sets, and a more sophisticated approach to performance measurement. A 2007 Australian Public Service Commission (APSC) publication (updated in 2012) emphasised the role of leadership that focuses on collaborative processes (as opposed to authoritative or competitive) and identifies some of the necessary next steps to establish enabling structures and processes, emphasising adaptive, flexible and innovative leadership (APSC 2007).

Head and Alford's 2015 article is a useful framing of the problem, pointing to the areas requiring attention if even partial solutions are to be found. It is necessary to note the issue of performance measurement and management – acknowledging its challenges and pointing to related accountability issues – especially in the context of cross-boundary public sector collaborations. While they point to a desirable new form of leadership, they do not address the major challenges of (1) defining the detail of these enabling structures and processes; (2) identifying the (new?) organisational source of leadership that will 'assemble and reassemble project teams as problems emerge, progress and come to some sort of resolution' (Head & Alford 2015, p 21); (3) addressing the central questions of governance and accountability in this flexible new world of public sector management; and, (4) the matching of these requirements with context.

This list of the unresolved matters is of central importance to public sector management. Noting the importance of leadership style and the enabling structures and processes is a first step to progress; the next step is to start to lay out some of the management content and to move on from an argument of the need for flexibility in applying these leadership models – organisations need to be able to assemble and reassemble project teams as problems emerge, progress, and come to some sort of resolution – and understand how this might occur. We need to ask at what level in government departments does this leadership reside? What information do these leaders use to make decisions about such complex matters? What are the information sources that generate the evidence for these decisions, and what are the analytical tools and skill sets required to forge these decisions?[3] What are the supporting governance processes? What is the source and location of this new management capability?

Finding a useful balance between adaptive, flexible and innovative processes and the confines of traditional hierarchical public sector administration whilst establishing suitable governance regimes remains the central challenge, for in the absence of some sort of defined structure and oversight to the consequent management task, which provides clear visibility down the management line, flexibility, adaptation, and innovation could be a prescription for chaos. If we look past the public sector management literature to the organisational literature some insights are provided in terms of the need to balance exploitation and exploration, for the development of so-called 'ambidextrous organisations' coping both with stability and chaos, and with dual structures ('mechanistic' and 'organic') coexisting in the same organisation (see Lam 2005, p 117 ff). More recent literature focuses on the contribution that design thinking can make to the resolution of management problems (Martin 2009).

A further important issue is that of performance measurement. Head and Alford argue that an outcomes focus is a necessary part of a solution to wicked problems, but that it should be placed in the context of a collaborative solutions process or systems approach that pays attention not just to the end results, but to the whole chain of inputs, processes and outputs that lead to them. They argue that a systems approach to outcome measurement should thereby acknowledge the role played by all of the organisations involved in the solution chain.

Head and Alford also see value in the adoption of the tools of corporate strategy in the public sector to widen the horizon of choice from simply how to do things to what to do. In the context of a multiplicity of players involved today in fashioning and delivering solutions to wicked public sector problems, Head and Alford see making choices about what to do through the use of tools such as strategic positioning and determination of core competences as potentially beneficial when applied with flexibility in

---

3   An excellent discussion of these challenges, framed by the question 'what causes what?' is provided by Mulgan in *The art of public strategy* (2009). In Chapter 4 he considers the challenges of policy formation in the presence of wicked problems, laying out the mechanics of 'mapping the system' as an effective front-end to policy formation and implementation, providing examples in the fields of urban regeneration and the influences on obesity.

goal-setting and strategy development. At present, however, the common public sector application of these sorts of tools is limited to internal matters such as processes, capabilities, competences and efficiencies and to the departmental level rather than to the whole-of-public-service activities.

I will pick this point up later and argue that the application of these tools to the public sector is potentially much more valuable than this and points to an integrated and better way to tackle the broader challenges of public administration.

In addition to the structural dimensions of wicked problem management, there are also important behavioural dimensions, especially those of teamwork. In circumstances where individual work units and entities across the public service do not 'own' the customer for many government interventions, suitable consumer-based outcomes can only be delivered through cooperative activity. Clearly enhanced teamwork is called for as part of the solution, and the academic literature abounds with recommendations of greater public sector collaboration in pursuit of this goal. This can be seen in contradistinction to traditional public service coordination, sight of which was lost in the academic literature within several decades of Rittel and Webber's declaration in 1973 of the passing of the age of scientific public sector management.[4]

In practice, coordination is the bread and butter of collegiate activity expected of the public service and its employees as a matter of course across the range of organisational levels. This is the same expectation that might be held of any organisation, where the failure to coordinate would be seen as a significant personal and collective failure. Unfortunately attempts to 'join-up' (i.e. better coordinate) government services have shown limited only success around the globe. Determining exactly why this should be so is difficult, as researchers have limited access to the internal workings of the public service. It is a global phenomenon, however, and recent national government audit reports point to continuing difficulties, even amongst central agencies, in coordinating their respective activities.

---

4   In a 1991 article, Christopher Hood expressed bemusement at the emergence of this new term of 'collaboration' asking, rather tongue-in-cheek, whatever happened to the concept of coordination in the public service.

Box 3.1 Homelessness

The public policy challenge

One of the more intractable social problems in Australia is that of homelessness. The 2011 Census found some 105,237 people were reported as 'homeless', or 0.5 per cent of the population. At an Australian Government level, homelessness is managed by the minister for social services within the portfolio of Housing and Homelessness Programme. It is one of a number of portfolios serviced by the Department of Social Services.

For the purposes of data collection, homelessness is defined to include all of the following: current living arrangements in inadequate or overcrowded dwellings, accommodation with little or no tenure, living in supported accommodation, and living in improvised dwellings (this latter being the common understanding of homelessness). During 2014–15, living in severely crowded dwellings accounted for 39 per cent of all homeless people, people staying temporarily in other households accounted for 17 per cent, and those in boarding houses accounted for a further 17 per cent, with some 6 per cent living in improvised dwellings.

The Commonwealth, state and territory governments jointly fund a program to alleviate the difficulties of people who are homeless or at risk of homelessness. Under agreements signed in 2009 and extended to 2017, the states and territories are responsible for day-to-day delivery of services. In the latest year for which consolidated information is available (2014–15), recurrent government expenditure was $707.2 million delivered through partnerships with business, the not-for-profit sector, and the community sector to fund over 800 homelessness services around Australia.

The program performance indicator framework – built around the standard equity/efficiency/effectiveness elements – envisages key program outcomes to include independent housing through financial independence. During 2014–15, the total number of clients addressed by the system amounted to 255,657, with accommodation provided to some 33.3 per cent of clients, assistance to obtain housing to 27.8 per cent, and 23.1 per cent of clients accessed domestic violence services. Annual expenditure and client numbers have been steadily rising over the three-year reporting period in the presence of significant unmet demand for services (primarily accommodation) (Productivity Commission 2016).

Specialist homelessness services

The list of services set out below is of interest because of its extensive nature, the diversity and depth of skills required to deliver the individual services, and the case management skills required both in the diagnostic and management phases of client management. We can also note many other wicked problems present amongst both the specialised and general support services including child abuse; mental health; gambling, drug and alcohol abuse; domestic/family violence; and, inadequate employment skills.

Housing/accommodation services: short-term or emergency accommodation, medium-term/transitional housing, long-term housing, assistance to sustain tenancy or prevent tenancy failure or eviction, assistance to prevent foreclosures or for mortgage arrears.

Specialised services: child protection services, parenting skills education, child-specific specialist counselling services, psychological services, psychiatric services, mental health services, pregnancy assistance, family planning support, physical disability services, intellectual disability services, health/medical services, professional legal services, financial advice and counselling, counselling for problem gambling, drug/alcohol counselling, specialist counselling services, interpreter services, assistance with immigration services, culturally specific services, assistance to connect culturally, other specialised services.

General assistance and support services: assertive outreach, assistance to obtain/maintain government allowance, employment assistance, training assistance, educational assistance, financial information, material aid/brokerage, assistance for incest/sexual, assistance for domestic/family violence, family/relationship assistance, assistance for trauma, assistance with challenging social/behavioural problems, living skills/personal development, legal information, court support, advice/information, retrieval/storage/removal of personal belongings, advocacy/liaison on behalf of client, school liaison, child care, structured play/skills development, child contact and residence arrangements, meals, laundry/shower facilities, recreation, transport, other basic assistance.

Source: Productivity Commission (2016).

3.2.4 Homelessness is a wicked problem

Homelessness is an interesting case study in wicked problems because of a number of related manifestations, lack of clarity of solutions, the involvement of a large number of constituencies, and a number of intertwined policy problems. On the scale of wickedness, homelessness certainly deserves to be considered one of the more wicked (*very* wicked) problems. Box 3.1 outlines the key elements of the government program to address homelessness.

According to the 2016 Productivity Commission report, homelessness has multiple causes, including a shortage of affordable housing, family and relationship breakdown, unemployment and financial hardship. Specialist homelessness services aim to provide support to people who are homeless or at imminent risk of becoming homeless as a result of a crisis, including women and children escaping domestic and family violence. Government and non-government service providers (including community organisations) deliver over 50 separate homelessness services to clients, including short–medium and long-term housing assistance, education assistance, child care, transport assistance, family planning, drug/alcohol counselling, parenting skills, counselling, advocacy, meals services, and financial and employment assistance. The stated objective of these services is to provide transitional supported accommodation and to help people at risk to achieve the maximum possible degree of self-reliance in regard to income employment and housing.

It is clear that the public policy problem of homelessness is a complex one. If the many specialist services are designed to deal with its causes and consequences, then it is also clear that any number of the so-called specialist services for homelessness could equally be listed as 'the problem' and homelessness listed as a cause/consequence; for example, homelessness could easily swap places in this hierarchy with child abuse, family planning, physical disability, intellectual disability, drug and alcohol abuse, and gambling addiction. This reflects a core characteristic of wicked problems – that every wicked problem can be considered a symptom of another problem. The public policy challenge posed by wicked problems is that an attempt to address one of these wicked problems may impact on the state of others, and on the 'solutions' to those wicked problems.

Regarding this latter problem, there are some interesting developments taking place in the Department of Social Services. In a speech to the Family and Relationship Services Australia Senior Executive Service on 24 February 2016, the minister for social services, Christian Porter, outlined his plans for tracking over 1,600 grants to 800 family and community service organisations with the aim of better assessing and improving the services offered and focusing on outcomes. The minister discussed the frontline data collection tool Data Exchange (or DEX), which it was anticipated would enable a shift from outputs to outcomes by standardising data collection from service delivery and putting in place the capacity to amass and manipulate data to measure how services contribute to the immediate, intermediate, and long-term outcomes of clients. He predicted that it would revolutionise service offering over the next decade (Porter 2016).

In the context of a discussion of homelessness, this is a promising prospect that should enable the government to identify risk factors and characteristics of groups and thereby address their specific barriers to independence and employment. It should enable case management plans for individuals to be tailored from their group-based risks and circumstance characteristics. It offers something akin to the provision of small business support based around detailed analysis of individual business's financial statements (enabling comparison with industry norms).

If this project enables the approximation of relative contributions of key causal factors to policy outcomes in a world of complex interrelationships, it will allow better targeting of policies, programs and services to clients, and more efficient use of public dollars to achieve targeted outcomes for the homeless. It might also provide a first step towards unravelling the links between causes and consequences in wicked problems and their interrelated impacts. Those steps forward are, however, some years away. Meanwhile, policymakers must live with 'what is', not 'what might be', and that is a world of complex social problems with interrelated causes and consequences.

3.3 Contestability and outsourcing: Good policy or bad policy?

3.3.1 Contestability is a tame problem

The discussion of wicked problems indicates that there are inherent difficulties in public sector management not likely to be present to the same extent in private sector management. That is not to say that, in the face of growing shareholder and community activism, private sector management is not becoming more difficult also, although the same underlying societal forces are also at work in further challenging the public sector. What it does mean, however, is that the bar is set higher for the public than the private sector in achieving and demonstrating success in its day-to-day operations.

In this section of the book I consider a contrasting 'tame' problem, namely outsourcing. I have chosen this as a case study of government policy for a number of reasons:

- there are few tamer public sector 'problems', given the largely internal nature of the policy challenge
- it is a test of government governance because, with all parties involved under direct or contractual control, the government should be able, through the public service, to manage this program tightly
- whilst essentially a tame problem, there are a number of complexities that arise
- it is an important case study in the application of private sector tools to the public sector

- it provides further pointers to the challenges of strategic management and governance in the public sector.

In the discussion that follows I address the general set of issues that relate to government contestability and outsourcing activities and consider their application to the Australian Government's Efficiency through Contestability Programme.

3.3.2 The challenges of outsourcing

The discussion of homelessness is a useful lead-in to a discussion of outsourcing because of the mixture of public service and external delivery of services, combined with public service program management that the government's approach to the problem of homelessness represents. One of the more important issues in the management of such a large program involves the integration of a number of services for individual clients and a mixture of public service and outsourced service delivery, managed at the pointy end by case officers. In such a world of multiple services and service providers, it can be complicated to maintain a clear line of sight from policy formation to customer for effective service delivery management and governance.

Successful outsourcing of service delivery, which is a critical element in the delivery of a large and geographically dispersed program, is dependent on the contract between the purchaser and the provider addressing and costing the major duties to be performed under the contract, and building reliable and capable sources of supply. Oliver Williamson pointed to some of the challenges in his 1999 discussion of public and private bureaucracy transaction costs, noting that public sector outsourcing may be relatively straightforward where services are standardised, impacts are relatively easy to anticipate, and quantities relatively easy to control (Williamson 1999). But this is not the world of wicked problems. Outsourcing becomes more difficult and less attractive when services are not standardised and it is difficult to define the services to be delivered to clients, and when multiple players and services are involved at either or both of the client and service provider ends.

Wicked problems across the spectrum have elements of complexity and routinisation from the point of view of transaction cost. Problem definition and management can be characterised by a difficulty with the former in defining solutions and, with the latter, in managing the many overlapping services in an integrated manner designed to address the problem. In the case of homelessness, many individual services are sufficiently routinised to allow contracting out. This is the model followed by the Department of Social Services, which has over 50 separate services available and some 800 separate service providers meeting the needs of program clients around Australia.

Outsourcing was one of the central features of the NPM revolution and, arguably, the key feature designed to deliver private sector–style cost efficiency and cost savings to the public sector. Contracting externally for the provision of goods and services in the form of government procurement has a long history in the public sector, but outsourcing the policy advice that underpins the development of services, and the delivery of the services themselves, was far less common as the public sector entered the 1980s. Alford and O'Flynn point to the explosion of outsourcing in the 1980s and 1990s, built around the cost-cutting promise, the methodology of which offers clearly identifiable short-term cost savings but less certain long-term costs. They also point to mixed experiences with outsourcing and a recent subsequent partial reversal of this activity based on a more considered evaluation of its merits and shortcomings (Alford & O'Flynn 2012, Chapter 4, esp pp 87, 102).

Alford and O'Flynn identify three types of costs and benefits associated with managing with external partners: first there are those relating to the service itself (effectiveness, efficiency, equity and quality); second there are the costs and benefits of establishing and managing the relationship; and third there are the impacts on the strategic positioning, power or capabilities of the organisation itself. They also identify the costs of transition. In establishing a cost–benefit framework and considering a variety of relationships between external service providers and end users, their conclusion regarding the merits of 'externalisation' as the preferred course of action, is the pragmatic response that 'it all depends'.[5]

On the credit side of the ledger, the involvement of governments with customer-focused and community-based organisations as outsourcing contractors and as partners in service delivery provides a number

---

5   Alford and O'Flynn (2012) introduce the term 'externalisation' to embrace all arrangements in which one or more external providers produce all or part of a service. As defined it includes outsourcing, contracting out, partnering, volunteering and co-production. I do not propose to go into this detail using 'outsourcing' as a generic descriptor as is commonly done in the business literature and much public sector management literature. (See Alford & O'Flynn 2012, pp 23, 24).

of prospective benefits. Many of these organisations have a long history of serving their communities from their own resources as well as through delivery of government programs and have accumulated practical experience to bring to bear in meeting targeted customer needs. Creating joint entry points, common service offerings, and shared staff training programs provides the foundations for mutual cooperative advantage.

The challenge of properly assessing any such externalisation option is, however, that the service delivery cost savings are immediate and real; the transition and relationship management costs are less visible and ongoing; and the longer-term organisational opportunity costs – in terms of strategic capabilities/de-skilling/loss of career opportunities, foregone productivity gains, market intelligence and institutional memory – are largely invisible and continue past any service delivery contract.

There is also good reason to believe that, whilst a generic approach to outsourcing and externalisation is warranted in the case of service delivery to 'citizen–clients' (the focus of this discussion thus far), there may be important differences between the outsourcing of such services and of policy advice where the 'client' is the government. While it can be argued that outsourcing 'routine' activities is likely be more successful than non-routine, policy advice rarely is 'routine', being the strategic foundation on which the business of the public service is built. As I argue later, policy capability enables the public service to take an overview of government activities and this should be the focus of its competitive positioning. Whilst the public service needs to maintain sufficient service delivery capability to 'keep its hand in', only policy capability enables it to take the necessary strategic and operational overview of government activities that creates real public value.

On the debit side of the ledger, ceding any core organisational capability to other parties carries risk in any institutional setting. Ceding such a critical organisational capability as the ability to think strategically about the business it is in, is likely to come at a high cost to its stakeholders in any business. An organisation that does not have such a capability wired throughout its structures becomes a captive of its past and a ready victim of changes in its environment (see Kiechel 2012). In addition, external organisations providing policy advice invariably 'sell' such advice to other such organisations, thereby substantially diminishing its value.

In looking back over the last 40 years of government in Australia, journalist and author Laura Tingle notes the loss of the public service policy capability, emphasising the legacies of this period as loss of institutional memory, loss of a career-driven public service, and the broad-based loss of policy capability (Tingle 2015). One consequence of this loss of policy capability – made possible by governments determined to make both policy advice and service delivery contestable – has been an increase in the numbers of think tanks, lobbyists, and other third-party organisations. Successive governments have reinforced the initial loss of capability by choosing to bypass their own expert government advisory organisations.

Most of these external groups have the resources to undertake sufficient research to provide credible policy options and then lobby effectively for their solutions. But, those that choose to work with governments are often free to organise 'evidence' around what they presume to be the government's preferred solutions, and not address the associated implementation challenges, opportunity and transition costs. These are organisations attuned to providing policies and solutions to governments to meet their own organisational charters. These policies may meet the political needs of governments, but not necessarily any reasonable community-wide test of net benefit.[6] The rise of such organisations has removed from the administrative arm of the government (and, to a lesser extent, the political arm), the necessity to think at higher strategic levels – what might be called 'strategic policy' at a departmental level where there are individual policy responsibilities with whole-of-government implications, or systemic policy best described as 'whole of public service'. The remaining public service capability is fragmented and not highly valued as a consequence.

At the systemic policy level, this ability is required by the public service to scan the horizon to identify emerging trends, connect the dots, and formulate responses for government consideration; that is, to enhance the effectiveness of the business of government. But it is equally required today to focus on the future of the public service itself, including government policy towards the public service. The public service should not allow itself to be a passive recipient of this policy. At the strategic policy level, individual departments must be able to perceive the effective implementation of an agency minister's policies not just in terms of their

---

6   See, for example, Milliken (2015).

department's role but also in terms of the involvement of, and impacts on, other departments and external organisations. A higher public service level should guide this advice.

The decline in public service capability has occurred at a time – due to the complexity and multiplicity of problems facing government – that an enhanced rather than diminished whole-of-organisation thinking capability is required. Think tanks may well be capable of articulating new political belief systems and accompanying policy frameworks, but there is a huge implementation gulf between this level of strategic thought and effective service delivery on the ground. The very notion that problem/policy formulation could be successfully split from implementation (the policy–provider split), a notion lying at the heart of the NPM revolution of the 1980s, continues to deserve serious questioning.

What is missing from this notion is an understanding of how the public service adds value through a whole-of-process view underpinned by ongoing learning on the job. It is harder to identify and capture the lessons that will better shape service delivery in the future through outsourced contracts than it is through internal service delivery. The outsourcing process lacks a dynamic sense and is, rather, a comparatively static comparison of alternatives.[7] In my experience, some of the better policy ideas are likely to come from public servants who are intimately involved in service delivery, who continuously form and reform hypotheses about customer behaviour and the role played by government support, and who can reshape policy 'on the go'. This is not high-level policy, rather what might best be described as 'operational policy', but it is at this level

---

7   The simplicity, elegance, and certainty of comparative static analysis, which is a particular weakness of economists, is alluring. In an adjunct to *Griffith Review* 51, Jonathan West and Tom Bentley point to some of the public policy dangers of ignoring the dynamic implications of such analysis. West and Bentley use the example of the application of the economists' conception of comparative advantage as a framework used to shape government policies towards industrial development. They make the point that, as a guide to the economic future, static comparative advantage theory is fatally flawed, ignoring as it does three vital dimensions of economic development, namely differential industry growth rates, technological improvement, and the social consequences of concentration in different types of economic activity. The authors use historical examples to argue that what is required is a shift from an industrial development policy based on static one-off comparative advantage, to one of cumulative dynamic advantage. See West and Bentley (2016).

of policy where substantial gains in program effectiveness and service delivery efficiency can be confidently expected over time. This observation applies to outsourcing in both public and private sectors.[8]

A further and growing risk associated with the outsourcing of both policy advice and service delivery is that political processes are delivering 'solutions' to the administrative arm of government without due regard to their ability to be implemented or their contribution to the resolution of the more complex problems of which they are but part. Depending on associated political motives this may not be accidental. Another risk, and one that should be particularly concerning to the public at large, is that these external bodies have the capacity to handsomely reward those in public office for their support – and many 'public officials' choose to further their careers in the subsequent employ of a variety of industry-based and professional lobby groups. The decision-making processes for both service delivery and policymaking deserve to be scrutinised in the public interest, and the former regularly are by auditors-general, with occasional involvement of state-based anti-corruption bodies.[9] Given the potentially substantial impact of policy decisions and their ongoing nature, major policy decisions should come under the greatest scrutiny, and this is where our system of government is at its weakest (see Netherlands Ministry of Finance 2000).

It is difficult to make evidence-based judgements about the costs and benefits of outsourcing as it has been applied in public administration in Australia; certainly there is international evidence that the enthusiastic application of the principles of contracting out in the 1980s and 1990s did not fulfil their promise (Hood & Dixon 2015, pp 84, 91, and esp p 178; Alford & O'Flynn 2012, pp 86–88). In addition, Donald Kettl tells a cautionary tale about the limits to which contracting out might go before it starts to incur additional costs in terms of effectiveness, and requires substantial organisational change to accommodate it. Indeed, Kettl paints a disturbing picture of the US public health system, where

---

8   The policy–provider split, as practised in the public sector, whether merely practised in-house or involving outsourcing, may well produce unintended consequences by placing the service deliverer in a policy straightjacket that removes the incentive and opportunity to continuously improve the service. The emphasis on this split of ownership of policy and operations is much greater in the public than private sectors and may lead to policy advisers (who do not have ready access to the lived experience) and operators following different paths.

9   See, for example, the Independent Broad-based Anti-Corruption Commission (IBAC) press release 'IBAC lays charges in relation to "banker schools" corruption', 10 Jan 2017.

outsourcing has resulted in patients never coming into contact with anyone from 'the government', and no one from the administration has responsibility for the patient (Kettl 2008).[10]

A suitable evaluation of the impacts of the efficiency-driven contestability and outsourcing program that is present today in the public administration arm of government would consider its roots in the NPM reforms and over 30 years of history. It would also consider the three types of costs and benefits identified by Alford and O'Flynn that have been variously incurred and generated by the public service over this period (those relating to the performance of the service, relationship management costs, and strategic positioning), and be founded on a dynamic view of the process embracing whole-of-organisation impacts on productivity, effectiveness, and the capacity of the public service to learn from its activities.

3.3.3 The Efficiency through Contestability Programme

The Efficiency through Contestability Programme was announced with the 2014–15 Commonwealth budget, piloted in 2014 and implemented in 2015. It was established as a three-year program and duly ceased on 30 June 2017. The program sought to determine on a case-by-case basis whether and how the government should deliver particular functions, programs or services, with the primary emphasis on the government's desired outcome. It had four interrelated parts – portfolio stocktake, function review, efficiency review, and contestability review – with potential actions to include cessation of performance of an activity, its provision under commercial arrangements, allowing other government providers to participate, or even modifying governance or organisational structures to improve efficiency.

The program guidelines contained directions to consider a wide range of issues including risk, market maturity, legal, treaties, security and culture, along with an invitation to set the analysis in a dynamic environment involving the sustainability of the options generated within both medium and long-term time frames. And, at the more detailed level of costs and

---

10   Indeed, Kettl's analysis leads one to ask whether there is an optimal (maximum) level of outsourcing well short of the 100 per cent that seems to be the long-term direction of outsourcing in the United States. The problem is that, whilst an ongoing series of individual decisions to outsource may be separately 'justifiable', there are accumulating systems costs not considered, which may render further individual decisions costly.

benefits, matters to be considered included all monetary costs and their form, transition costs, ongoing management costs, and environmental costs. Further instructions included the need to have regard to accountability and governance, the risks associated with inflexible contracts in a dynamic policy environment, and the implementation challenges arising post a contestability review, including accurate specification of outcomes and ensuring that the requisite public service skills were available.

Most of the key elements identified by Alford and O'Flynn for externalisation programs were incorporated in the program guidelines including the efficiency/effectiveness/equity dimensions of performance, the management relationship costs, transition costs, and the broader organisational implications of change. The guidelines also addressed the dynamic consequences of outsourcing, along with inter-organisational consequences and with the costs and benefits to be considered in different time frames as required. Initial estimates of program savings of over $5 billion for the period 2013–14 to 2020–21 and $14 billion for 2021–22 to 2026–27 were projected by the Department of Finance in their 2016–17 annual report and confirmed in the 2017–18 annual report. The ANAO end project performance audit was completed and published in May 2018 (ANAO 2018a).

In this audit report, the ANAO considered the effectiveness of the Efficiency through Contestability Programme in supporting entities to improve the efficient delivery of government functions. The participating entities considered a large number of recommendations from the functional and efficiency reviews, and from the contestability reviews, accepting most and rejecting few outright. The performance audit concluded that the program was effective in supporting activities to review the efficient and effective delivery of government functions and supported Finance's view of budget repair in excess of $5 billion over the forward estimates. In these broad terms, the program might be deemed a success.

However, whilst providing a generally supportive review of program processes, the ANAO report pointed to a number of side issues of concern. These issues included:

- review reports did not generally include benchmarks to demonstrate efficiencies or assessments to evaluate the benefits of implementation
- relatively few recommendations were made to cease functions or identify opportunities for alternative providers

- most projected savings outlays derived from reduction in budget outlays without directly linking these reductions to efficiency
- entities reporting on implementation of recommendations focused on milestones and deliverables and rarely on outcomes
- Finance's implementation of the program and the accountable entities fell short of the ANAO's expectations.

The ANAO report further notes that the majority of the substantial savings were identified in efficiency reviews, which are commonly of organisational administrative processes, rather than through reviews of functions and contractor services. The audit report gives the impression that Finance arranged the exercise to review the externalisation activities of an important part of the public sector and, while it could have delivered substantial one-off savings and ongoing efficiency gains, it was essentially treated as a low-level budget-saving program. This view is supported by the ANAO observation of the relatively low level of projected budget savings of a *total* of a little over $5 billion in the first seven years of the program (less than an average of $1 billion per year) considered against total Australian Government budget expenditure of some $419 billion per year in 2013–14, which was the first year of the program.

The report's key learnings for all Australian Government entities embraced program design, governance and risk management, and performance and impact measurement with specific learnings including:

- the need to prepare an implementation plan and provide advice on implementation risks
- the need for policy design advice to government and program implementation to be informed by sound analysis and a strong evidence base
- the need for the key actions required to meet program responsibilities to be documented, assigned and monitored
- the need for cost savings and benefits to be identified in the design phase along with review and evaluation arrangements.

Either by design or default, a major opportunity seems to have been let slip.

This brief review of the Efficiency through Contestability Programme leads to some general pointers about 'good policy' and, in particular, its implementation. We might reasonably conclude that in this case a seemingly well-designed program was let down by poor implementation primarily in the affected agencies as well as by less-than-wholehearted oversight by the originating agency.

While public service efficiency has a history of government focus extending well back into the last century in Australia, it is arguable that it has typically been delivered in 'hits' or projects by political intervention rather than seen and encouraged as an important and ongoing public service management responsibility. The NPM reforms, for example, were seen as a means of shocking the public service around the world into private sector levels of efficiency but there are mixed views about the effectiveness of these reforms. Indeed, the most comprehensive applied study of the impacts – Hood and Dixon's study of some 30 years of UK experience – points to a likely negative outcome on this count (Hood & Dixon 2015). Later chapters explore the means and benefits of the public service treating efficiency and effectiveness as an ongoing management responsibility in place of regular but somewhat random government interventions in public service operations.

A further general concern arises from the design of the Efficiency through Contestability Programme. Whilst the program guidelines noted the need for governments to adopt 'hybrid delivery models' with greater involvement of other service providers across and outside government and to adopt a new role as 'co-designer and regulator of a transaction environment between clients, government, and service providers', there is little recognition of the overall governance challenges posed by this intended shift, either in the guidelines' preamble or its detail. The few references to governance are primarily concerned with the governance of the program, with the only reference to the challenges of governance of a more distributed form of government being the need to consider possible improvements in governance where they might improve efficiency. And, whilst the word 'effectiveness' is used a number of times, it is clear that generation of client benefits is seen largely as those consequential from securing targeted efficiency gains (rather than being a focus in their own right). The challenges of governance in a world of collaborative and networked government must be placed at the front of considerations of such a mode of service delivery, not tacked on at the end of the design and implementation processes.

Finally, the dominant and easiest component to calculate in the cost–benefit equation for any externalisation exercise is monetary cost savings, which is a readily identifiable benefit. The *costs* of externalisation, beyond contractual costs, however, are dispersed in the form of transition costs, new management relationship costs, and whole-of-organisation costs relating to lost capability and the loss of flexibility in a dynamic environment arising from contractual arrangements with a new provider. There is also the matter on the benefit side of the equation of capturing contract life efficiency gains and not merely letting them accrue to an external service provider. Moreover the costs that only occur in the medium to long term – such as loss of organisational capability and the risks associated with commitment to long-term contracts in a volatile environment – may well be ignored in public service calculations. Put simply, a number of prospective outsourcing costs are dispersed in time and space and are difficult to estimate. Any externalisation calculation is therefore unlikely to capture all of these costs especially those not associated with immediately identifiable outlays and is therefore likely to exhibit bias against in-house continuation of service delivery.

3.4 Conclusions

This chapter has identified the operations of government from the direction of its core business as the formation and delivery of good policy to the Australian community. Whilst a case study of homelessness has been used to consider the formation and implementation of good policy in an environment of multiple and overlapping problem drivers, the case study of the Efficiency through Contestability Programme takes a primary implementation focus and considers a range of reasons why good design may not result in beneficial program outcomes. Given that a major component of effective delivery of the homelessness program is itself a substantial outsourcing program, the breadth and depth of the total effective policy challenge is significant. Nonetheless, it should be clear that the wickedness of policy problems is only one of a number of challenges in the policy business in practice, and that many reasons may drive substandard policy formation and ineffective delivery, of which problem complexity is just one.

Public administration performance measurement

4.1 Measurement

4.1.1 The challenge

In keeping with the long history of public administration and the focus on due process, the focal point of government accounting for resource use has been on financial reporting. The aggregate performance of the government is commonly conceived of as a net budgetary outcome. More substantial analysis, however, would see the gross budgetary dimensions interpreted for their broad social and economic impacts. In a world of good government, government performance should be viewed in terms of the effective implementation of sound policies delivering targeted impacts and policy outcomes.

The elected government of the day should bear responsibility for both the front and back ends of this process – the expenditure decisions and the policy impacts and outcomes. The administrative arm of government can then reasonably be held to account for program-level design (where sought by government), efficient program administration, the quality of the financial record keeping, due process in managing expenditure, and the measurement of expenditure impacts and policy outcomes.

More generally, if the task of the public service is to convert a government's policy goals into delivered programs, through appropriate advice, structures, programs, strategies, and collaborations, then public service performance measurement should focus on measures of these dimensions, culminating in the effective delivery of a suite of services. Whilst the public service is not responsible for the impacts and associated outcomes of the programs delivered, their capture and measurement through good governance should be.[1]

It is important to distinguish between what is happening on the ground (the government's reporting framework and its application), the commentary on this performance (by the government, the public service, and third parties), and what is occurring in the public sector literature (as an indicator of what should be happening). While I continue to draw on comparisons with private sector activity as a further reference point, the starting point for any discussion of performance and measurement must be a discussion of the accountability framework.

4.1.2 The government accountability framework

Chapter 1 of the 2012 publication *Public sector governance in Australia* discusses a number of different but related concepts of governance, comprising (a) public governance (extending out to the private and community sectors); (b) public sector governance (i.e. governance of public administration and the business of government); and (c) corporate governance (organisational governance; i.e. the governance of particular bodies in particular sectors) (Edwards et al. 2012). The primary focus on measurement in this chapter lies clearly with public sector governance and, in particular, with that part of public sector governance relating to public administration, namely the efficiency and effectiveness dimensions of the outcomes of the role played by the public service in administering the government of the day's program. I am also, however, interested in the corporate governance of the Australian Public Service (APS) taken as a whole.

---

1   Chapter 5 addresses the question of what, exactly, the public service can be held accountable for that is neither predetermined nor substantially constrained by the government. What are the public service's 'degrees of freedom'? Clearly, the public service has some 'administrative degrees of freedom' but what else?

The determining framework for these considerations is embodied in three pieces of legislation. The first is the *Public Service Act 1999*, which assigns responsibilities to the APS and describes the values and conduct to be exhibited in their execution. This legislation places the department or, more correctly, the departmental secretary, at the forefront of the management of these responsibilities, although there are some residual responsibilities assigned to the Secretaries Board. The second piece of legislation is the *Public Governance, Performance, and Accountability Act 2013* (PGPA Act), which establishes a framework of governance and accountability for all Commonwealth entities including government departments (but not the Secretaries Board), focused on a performance reporting framework and requiring the provision of meaningful information to parliament. The third important piece of legislation is the *Auditor-General Act 1997*, which is the Act under which the Auditor-General for Australia operates. The Auditor-General is an important part of setting and influencing the standards for the government's performance reporting framework.[2]

4.1.3 What should be measured?

A discussion of the desirable content of the measurement of the impacts of government programs and services needs to consider the respective roles of the players. Governments are elected by the community to undertake activities on its behalf, and regular visits to the ballot box enable the community to deliver ongoing direction to the politicians.[3] The measurement task should serve the purpose of allowing community assessment of the government's performance in addition to enabling the government to acquit its responsibility to parliament to account for its resource use.

2   The Auditor-General for Australia does not have formal enforcement powers but, as an independent officer of parliament, through private consultation and public reporting, is a critical part of the government's performance reporting framework. The Auditor-General is also the primary source of public reporting of the standards being achieved by public service reporting. These pieces of legislation and the resultant reports published – typically at individual entity level – are complemented at a whole-of-government level by the annual Productivity Commission's report on government services. This report covers the delivery of Australian Government services in six major policy-linked blocs, providing comparative output-based indicators addressing equity, effectiveness and efficiency within each of the six blocs. Some of the more interesting parts of the report – certainly from a public sector management standpoint – are presented in brief discussions of cross-cutting issues for each of the six blocs.

3   This convenient assumption is literally correct in a two-party democracy. But in a world of multiple-party government, the community no longer elects a government with a clear mandate, as negotiations between parties to form a government may move their agreed agenda some way from the separate party agendas under which the individuals forming government were elected.

As the vast majority of government activity and expenditure changes very little from one term of office to the next, this task might be reasonably described as a stable one, affording the public service every opportunity to bring to bear the best available tools – subject, of course, to government acquiescence. The community should want to know and the public service should provide – through its ministers – the costs and benefits of the policies the government has supported and the programs and services the public service has delivered (through annual reports, freedom of information legislation, parliamentary committees, and question time).

The business community and the community at large should also want to make some judgement about whether the expenditure foregone in the process of resource transfer from the community and private sectors for these programs and services was somehow 'worth it'. It can be argued that, as every dollar spent by the government would otherwise have been spent by individuals and businesses, this places a high level of obligation on the incumbent politicians to spend these appropriated dollars at least as wisely as their former owners would have; this obligation should be equally felt by the public service.

In an introductory section to the Productivity Commission's *Report on government services* (2018), it is argued that measuring the performance of government service delivery, and public reporting thereof, creates incentives for better performance by:

- helping to clarify government objectives and responsibilities
- promoting analysis of the relationships between agencies and between programs, enabling governments to coordinate policy within and across agencies
- making performance more transparent through informing the community
- providing governments with indicators of policy and program performance over time
- encouraging ongoing performance improvements in service delivery and effectiveness, by highlighting improvements and innovation. (Productivity Commission 2018, Part A, Chapter 1)

The report goes on to explain that it gives equal weight to three sets of performance indicators – equity, efficiency, and effectiveness – and aims also to provide outcome-based measures for each, noting, however, that outcomes are often difficult to measure. Interestingly, the report observes that the rate at which inputs are used to generate outcomes is referred to as 'cost-effectiveness', further noting that no such measures are included in the report. Equity indicators span access, appropriateness, and quality. The report points to three dimensions of efficiency, namely technical (the production of goods and services at the lowest possible cost), allocative (the production of the set of goods and services that the consumers most value from a given set of resources), and dynamic (the offering of new and better products over time to consumers and the same products at cheaper cost). The report goes on to note the reporting focus on technical efficiency. Several aspects of this framework bear scrutiny before moving on to discuss evolution in public sector performance measurement. It is also important to canvass a fourth dimension of efficiency, namely efficiency of markets.

Firstly, discussion of public sector performance and, in particular, of the delivery of government goods and services, is sometimes at pains to avoid association with the notion of the private sector 'bottom line'. Clearly, however, allocative efficiency requires the calculation of such a bottom line, even if only notionally, if the maximum value of government goods and services is to be produced from any given set of resources. Whilst public sector practice in this regard lags behind academic literature on public sector management, the latter is moving in the direction of an integrated bottom line in the form of public value (where the concept may incorporate the costs as well as the benefits of government service delivery).

The second point is that, in the measurement of the performance of delivery of government services, there has been a long-standing focus on the measurement of technical efficiency. This is partly attributable to the availability of data, which sees costs recorded as part of general financial recording, and physical units of services delivered available in lesser number of programs. The focus on costs and efficiency may also, in part, be explicable by a traditional public service culture that embraces its role as deliverer of government services, but not that of the active management of customer (client) expectations and valuation of the associated satisfaction, as part of the government service delivery charter. In most cases, companion effectiveness data requires separate manufacturing.

Thirdly, a discussion of 'costs' and 'benefits' should consider the economic literature in order to be clear about what those terms mean and how they relate to the public sector performance measurement. This is important in order to be clear about the benefit criterion when discussing 'benefits' and 'public interest'.

The ROGS 2018 sets out, in principle, three separate sets of measures, namely efficiency, effectiveness and equity, although data is invariably unavailable to measure equity.[4] If data in dollar terms is available for efficiency and effectiveness, then cost–benefit calculations can be made (in present value terms) either as a ratio or in net dollar terms. If effectiveness data is not available in dollar terms but is available in physical terms, then an inferior calculation, commonly used to compare alternatives (but which provides no indication of overall net benefit) can be undertaken and expressed in terms of cost effectiveness.

The standard cost–benefit bottom line moves beyond the cash value of both costs and benefits to include external effects, commonly called 'side effects' or, more technically, 'spillovers'. These are the often unintended (or unvalued) effects of the production or consumption of a good or service that has value to the community at large. An example of an unvalued cost is of the environmental effects of plastic bags, which might be banned or matched with a tax to discourage their use. An example of an unintended/unvalued benefit is that of patented inventions that incidentally add to the stock of human knowledge and lead to the development of new products and services.

The use of cost-effectiveness as a decision-making criterion is, as noted by Edward Mishan, a truncated form of cost–benefit analysis drawing on only one side or the other of the cost–benefit equation, typically the cost-only side, and is often expressed in physical units. It might be expressed as the cost-per-unit of delivering a service, or the number of customers who might be serviced at a given unit cost. As such, it leaves the question of the optimal decision untouched. In general, it is most useful when there is more than one way of achieving change and a comparison of the alternative methods might be made; however, this necessarily leads to a ranking of available alternatives and not to a determination

---

4   However, when applied as an additional test of the public interest, it is capable of upsetting a positive cost–benefit assessment. See Mishan (1988, p xxiii). Ideally, equity assessments should use a common data set with efficiency and effectiveness assessments to allow a fully integrated assessment.

as to whether one or other desirable. Political constraints – such as the availability of a fixed sum to increase the number of hospital beds in a community – may enable some optimising behaviour through the choice between alternative methods of supplying these beds, but in the absence of such additional information, the cost-effectiveness criterion does not enable cost and benefit choices to be made and, as such, is incapable of contributing to budgetary resource allocation decisions (Mishan 1988).

The issue of additionality arises with the cost and benefit assessments of many government programs. For example, in the assessment of the benefit side of the cost–benefit equation in a program of tax breaks to grow the number of small business exporters, the counterfactual must be interrogated; that is, how many of the new exporters supported by the program would have succeeded in the absence of government support? This is the question of the additional benefits generated by the program. There are tools available to try to access the answer – for example, running parallel control groups, and ex post market research – but the data provided is invariably imperfect. The pragmatic, and best, way to deal with the issue is to assume that there is leakage from the benefit stream for this reason, and then require that the unadjusted benefit stream must exceed the cost stream – if it does not then, clearly, it fails the cost–benefit test without needing to address the counterfactual. Similar first-stage decision-making processes can be used where externalities are known to be present and the direction is known but the quantity is not. The additionality can be approximately 'valued' in this manner.

A final and equally important measure of efficiency, that of efficient markets, can be used in the context of outsourcing decisions and the evaluation of the extent of competition in any market as a driver of efficient resource allocation and use. It is the notion that competitive markets are more likely to drive efficient resource use than monopolistic public sector resource use that underpinned much of the wave of New Public Management (NPM) reforms of the 1980s, particularly its marketisation phase, and has continued to underpin much public sector 'reform'. Marketisation concepts should be applied on a case-by-case basis. Matters for consideration include the need for the public service to maintain strategic capabilities; to build a service-wide data bank of evidence-based policy, program, and other expenditure activities (to learn, not simply outsource); and to provide for public service capture of a share of the benefits of any productivity-cum-efficiency changes during the life of any outsourcing arrangements.

Nonetheless, the short-sightedness of decision-makers has, in a number of instances, caused the failure of government creation and use of markets and associated privatisations as a substitute for public sector ownership and operation. Terry Moran has been a continuing critic of the capture of Commonwealth policy by economists, and the risks of seeing the solutions to all policy problems in terms of creating markets and competitors: Moran has in particular pointed to the primary healthcare system as an example of this 'solution'.[5] The skyrocketing increases in health insurance premiums, and shrinking coverage of individual procedures and costs, must raise serious questions about the effectiveness of this market and, just as importantly, the accompanying regulatory processes themselves.

For example, the chairman of the Australian Competition and Consumer Commission (ACCC), Australia's competition watchdog and regulator, has expressed serious concern over the privatisation of Australia's ports and lack of appropriate regulatory regimes incorporated in the contracts of sale (thereby inflating the sale prices) (ACCC 2016). And the latest set of problems to emerge in energy markets suggests that, despite Australia's abundance of natural gas and coal electricity, the nation could experience regular blackouts in future.[6] This follows the declaration in a 2014 report commissioned by the Electrical Trades Union that electricity privatisation in Australia had failed.[7] Both residential and business consumers would have little trouble agreeing, noting a shortage of supply and escalating prices.

There are, then, questions that must be asked about the manner in which successive Australian governments have used markets as a substitute for bureaucratic service delivery. These questions concern the inherent capacity of markets to deliver an acceptable solution to the end consumer (for example health), and the manner in which governments have applied the market tool to particular problems, where difficulties in assessing costs (outsourcing) and inadequate regulatory regimes (ports) have almost

---

5   See, for example, Terry Moran, 'If I knew then what I know now', speech, ANZSOG Conference, Canberra, 7 August 2014, and Terry Moran, 'How economists captured the policy process' 2 October 2014, *The Mandarin*, www.themandarin.com.au/5190-terry-moran-economists-capturedaustralias-policy-debate.

6   See press report of Prime Minister Malcolm Turnbull's press release 'Malcolm Turnbull gets gas industry guarantee on domestic supply', *Guardian*, 15 Mar 2017, at www.theguardian.com/Australia-news/2017/mar/15/malcolm-turnbull, on the subject of the roundtable meeting with east-coast gas producers.

7   See John Quiggin, *Electricity privatisation in Australia: a record of failure*, Electrical Trades Union of Australia, 2014.

certainly short-changed the community. The fundamental problem is the short-termism of governments focused on selling off public assets to the highest bidder without putting in place the necessary longer-term consumer-based safeguards. The problem lies not with the concepts and tools – efficiency, use of markets, outsourcing – but rather with the underlying deceit in their use by governments.

This discussion of what (and when) to measure demonstrates that there are reasons for measurement to be undertaken but that the overarching one is to enable the public service to provide ministers with sound advice about matters of resource allocation and, in particular, the allocation of resources that lead to the creation of a maximum (or at least improved) community benefit from an available volume of resources. In order to provide such advice, the public service needs to be able to cost the goods and services provided and generate additional information in regard to the valuation of these individual services by the community and the choices made between in-house and external service delivery. The consequence of this advice should be better program and services decisions by government, greater transparency of government (and public service) activities, service improvements, and more transparent governance.

Finally, in cases where governments are determined to proceed down a path that, on any cost–benefit assessment would be clearly sub-optimal (net non-beneficial or lesser net benefit), it is in the public interest for the public service to undertake the standard cost–benefit assessment. This is simply because it is important that the public service retains a high-level capability to assess and advise on policy options and their implementation. This is a core capability and should neither be outsourced, nor left to languish by governments determined to bypass this assessment process. This is where the public service provides the greatest value-adding role for the Australian public and is a capacity that must be retained and recognised for what it is.

Whether or not, and in what circumstances, public service advice should be made public, is a separate question. But safeguards must be put in place to protect the public service and the public interest in such cases, which at the very least involves preparation and filing of public service advice in cases where it is not sought. The public service should be accorded a right to advise, although not necessarily a right to publish.

4.1.4 The evolution in public sector performance measurement

The transition of government performance measurement from costing inputs to outputs associated with services delivered by departments occurred in a fairly short space of time, given the lengthy history of the public sector and the predominance of the input approach for nearly a century. The refocusing of public sector performance in the 1980s at the operational level on costs and outputs was central to the endeavour of NPM proponents to link the budget with performance, and to strengthen the focus on efficiency. This focus on outputs from public sector programs was accompanied by the development of activity-based costing in the private sector enabling, in prospect, output measures to be matched by activity-based costs. This development should have enabled the public service to take an important step along the path of measuring value for money in government expenditure, albeit a cost-effectiveness path only.[8]

And at one level the introduction of output budgeting provided departments with greater freedom to manage their own budgets, as it was commonly associated with the introduction of program objectives and targets and the certification of all appropriations related to the program objective. It was accompanied by the introduction of a running-costs system applying to non-program expenditure where detailed line items for agency administration costs were replaced by aggregate appropriations allowing agencies to move funds, for example, between salaries and administrative purposes.[9] In the quest to implement this new tool to fill somewhat of a vacuum, the central agencies – Treasury and the Department of Finance – misinterpreted the intent of the reforms, missing the opportunity inherent in the underpinning private sector

---

8   This revolution has no private sector parallel, despite the fact that both the public and private sectors are subject to similar economic and societal pressures over time. Indeed the closest that the private sector has come to any change in its measurement philosophy in the same period is its strengthened focus on cash flow, its limited attempts to measure corporate social responsibility, and the demonstration of green/sustainability credentials. (Although putting these last two together suggests, interestingly, that the private sector is inching towards a measure/measures of public value to complement the private value that has been relied on for centuries: these changes have been accompanied by a broadening of the perception of the relevant stakeholder circle.)

9   For further details see John Nethercote, *The Australian experience of public sector reform*, APSC Occasional Paper 2, Commonwealth of Australia, 2003, esp Chapter 6.

philosophy of determining a bottom line through an accompanying focus on an outcome or consolidated set of outcomes, and instead focused on the development of a growing multiplicity of output measures.[10]

Since this 'revolution', there has been a growing realisation that much of the additional performance information generated may have facilitated government and departmental budgetary control, but has contributed little to the effectiveness of whole-of-government budgetary allocation processes, nor to an understanding of the impact of government activities. Even today, little is understood in a systemic manner about the impact of program expenditures beyond their macroeconomic impact as part of the total budget. This is because the responsibility for value-for-money program expenditure assessment is left to state and national auditors-general to pursue through a program of performance audits. They do this through rolling (often five-year) audit programs, applying the principles of economy (acquisition of resources), efficiency (combination of those resources in program activities), and effectiveness (the activities/impacts measured against program goals).

Today, performance auditing has achieved such prominence that auditors-general are commonly devoting more time and effort to performance audits than to the traditional financial audits. Nonetheless, despite some 30 years of activity in this area, a common theme in state and national auditor-general and public accounts and estimates committee reports remains that departments need to devote more time to the measurement of outcomes and impacts of departmental expenditure. For example, the former Auditor-General for Australia, Ian McPhee, identified this as a soft area of government administration in his introductory comments to the 2013–14 Australian National Audit Office (ANAO) annual report, and repeated the sentiment in his outgoing speech in April 2015 (ANAO 2014b; McPhee 2015). The plethora of low-level, non-aggregatable performance measures dominates departmental performance reporting from which it is: (a) difficult to form any reasonable impression of the

---

10   When I moved from the Department of Management and Budget to the Department of Industry, Technology and Resources in the latter 1980s, the dominant method of performance assessment in place there was a rolling (three- or five-year) schedule of program cost–benefit assessments. This had been put in place by a head of department who was determined to bring a private sector performance measurement discipline to his department, insisting that all costs had to be allocated to programs including head office salaries and operating costs. The department was well ahead of its time (it would even be so today!) and unfortunately took a big step backwards with the change of government in 1992 and the introduction of output budgeting.

impact of individual program level expenditures; (b) invariably impossible to assess the impact of aggregates at any of the outcome, policy, whole-of-department, and whole-of-government levels; and (c) equally impossible for the Australian public to determine how well their resources have been used.

The academic literature and government department reports suggest that little effective progress has been made in this regard globally. Supporting evidence for this at the Australian end lies in: (a) a series of state and federal public accounts and estimates committee reports, (b) national and state auditor-general reports, (c) ombudsman reports, (d) parliamentary committee reports, and (e) the standard audits commissioned by incoming governments at state and federal level. Collectively these reports cast doubt especially on the utility of the plethora of performance (output) indicators published by many government agencies.

While the NPM reforms promised much in terms of a transition from accounting for inputs to accounting for outputs, agencies continue to undertake transactional reporting, and little has been achieved in terms of a sharpened focus on outcomes and results. This gives rise to the problem with the public service's role as arguably the central pillar of good governance and accountability. As a consequence, much of the 'evidence' of public service performance revolves around auditor-general performance audits of government programs, rather than on the publication of departmental and whole-of-public-service data, in annual reports. Despite this being an area of public service under-achievement over the last three decades, there have been interesting developments in measurement over the last decade or so, with the management challenge for the public service continuing to evolve.

Growing community involvement in the processes of government and the development and application of underpinning networking models and processes of governance has further challenged the public service. If joined-up government failed to deliver its promise, then networked government promises a revolution in the responsibilities for, and the processes of, government, impacting negatively on the accompanying performance measurement and governance activities in the absence of any new and determined attempts to address its impacts. Moreover, if the primary outcome to be sought under joined-up and networked government has been improved effectiveness through the impact on individual recipients then, over the last decade (in the academic literature at least), this has evolved to include not just the private value placed on services by individual recipients, but also the broader value placed by the citizenry at large on the delivery of such services to others.

The focus on public value in the early part of the 21st century has followed substantial development in the private sector management literature in the last two decades of the 20th century around the notion of creating customer value, including value propositions, value-delivery systems, and value chains, and the placement of these concepts at the centre of corporate strategy.[11] The related major public sector measurement challenge involves breathing life into the concept of effectiveness, invariably a poor cousin to the dominant notion of efficiency, to enable more systematic assessment of the costs and benefits of government program and service delivery expenditure.[12]

The degree of difficulty in measuring government policy and program performance continues to increase, however, with the goalposts and the game itself continuing to change. If the two important characteristics of anarchic governance, an evolving model of governance discussed in Chapter 2, are the distributed nature of the decision-making processes of government and an associated inability to account to the community for resource use, then it must be observed that Australia is at the very least 'on the way'.

4.1.5 Wicked problems and performance measurement

The complexities of dealing with program management in the context of wicked problems are substantial as it is difficult to determine their root causes. Overlapping causes and consequences beset many problems in the social policy field and create difficulties in determining the relative

---

11   The notion of public value can also be utilised as a (new) paradigm through which to view the role of the public service. While it has received little attention, it makes sense as a new hymn sheet from which the whole public service could sing (together).

12   In *Delivering profitable value*, Michael Lanning is critical of organisations that suddenly look outside their four walls to discover the customer and become 'customer-compelled'. He warns against such a strategy and distinguishes carefully between feeling compelled to do everything that the customer appears to want (being 'customer-compelled') and looking beyond what the customer knows and 'wants', to seeking to add value from an understanding of the experiences that a customer would most value (being 'customer-driven'). Being run by your customers, according to Lanning, is just as much a prescription for failure as being run by the supply side of any business. The analogy with networked government should not be lost in a future in which the customer becomes king (and queen) in the public sector system. See Lanning (2000, pp 6–7, 24–28).

importance of the influencing causes across wicked problems. Determining policy objectives, for example, for a child abuse and protection program requires a set of difficult decisions to be made in the presence of overwhelming need. The drivers for such a program will include drug and alcohol abuse, domestic violence, unemployment and homelessness, and it is necessary to determine the respective contributions of the drivers, the development of an appropriate case management model, and the recruitment and training of suitable staff to deal with complex client management problems.

These wicked policy problems present the most complex program management and service delivery problems for the public service. And the particular (political) difficulty that presents itself is the long-term nature of the commitment required to address them. This presents two further management and measurement problems for ministers and public servants. The first is the (political) temptation to resort to input, output, and activity measures in claiming success for these endeavours in the face of inevitably slow progress with outcomes. This is a challenge for the public service to develop outcome-based measures that capture progress in a manner that encourages successive ministers and governments to 'stay the distance' on outcomes (this is an example of the notion of a public service that should 'endure' in the public interest), and not resort to a short-term focus on activities and outputs.

The second and related temptation is to resort to measures of containment rather than resolution so that the former do not necessarily contribute to the latter. Perhaps the best example of this is 19th-century debtors' prisons in Western Europe. A modern-day version of this is incarceration of people with a variety of addictions for unrelated criminal activities (drugs, alcohol, gambling) without treating the addiction. Both of these problems raise the question of whether governments are willing to acknowledge and invest in long-term solutions or merely consume resources in containing such problems. A forward-looking government might consider preparation of regular estimates of the cost of elimination of individual policy problems and their inclusion in public sector balance sheets if only as contingent liabilities.

4.1.6 Is public value the answer?

In the tome *Bureaucracy*, first published in 1944, the Austrian economist Ludwig von Mises offered an austere view of bureaucratic management in a democracy (in keeping with the school of economists to which he belonged):

> Bureaucratic management is management bound to comply with detailed rules and regulations fixed by the authority of a superior body. The task of the bureaucrat is to perform what these rules and regulations order him to do. His discretion to act according to his own best conviction is seriously restricted by them. (von Mises 2017, p 45)

Nearly 75 years ago, von Mises saw the role of bureaucrats as undertaking activities that the private sector would not, with the unifying factor being that there was no market price, indeed cash value, by which the delivered services could be valued. By contrast, he saw great merit in the capitalist system, the market mechanism, and in what he called 'the economic calculation'. By this he meant the valuation of consumer goods, and the consequent array of market prices that enabled designing and planning in the system – of additional supplies, of new products, of capital investment — to be undertaken outside of government. As he pointed out, the real bosses in the capitalist system are the consumers. Questions for today include whether the customer should be king in the processes of resource allocation within government and, if so, whether public value should be the preferred criterion. Again, a little history is useful here.

At the same time that the public sector was undergoing its NPM revolution in the 1980s and 1990s, there were important developments taking place in the private sector management literature. These focused on delivering customer value, and its companion strategy of refocusing competitive efforts on building value chains and value-delivery systems around customers (rather than resources and competences) (Porter 1985; Golub et al. 2000; Lanning 2000). These developments have been latterly mirrored in the public sector management literature placing the end consumer at the centre of the public service delivery challenge, engaging the concept of customer value, and extending this analysis with the application of the notion of the value chain ('the public-value chain') to provide a focus on the interactions between a wider array of potential contributors to achieving public purposes. The concept of public value lies at the heart of this literature (O'Flynn 2006; Alford & O'Flynn 2012, Chapter 10).

The initial development of the concept of public value in the mid-1990s and its subsequent articulation into three components offered a new paradigm and a different narrative for public sector reform. The three components identified are the services (seen as the vehicle for delivering public value); the outcomes (which includes higher-level aspirations of other citizens); and, trust, legitimacy and confidence in government (even where formal service and outcome targets are met it is argued that a failure of trust may destroy public value). According to O'Flynn, the strength of the public value concept encompasses its inclusion of the citizenry in the choice of services through the electoral process; its redefinition of how to meet the challenges of efficiency, accountability and equity; and a fuller, rounder, vision of humanity. Indeed, with the addition of costs to the estimate of value, the criterion would seem to meet the goal of incorporating all of the key dimensions of efficiency, effectiveness and equity, in one measure (albeit with the last of these three in an approximate manner).[13] At a public sector management level, its prospective contribution lies primarily in its reconceiving of the role of the citizenry in shaping public services and its derived performance measurement framework. At the political and social levels, its value lies in the inclusion of the citizenry directly in government resource-allocation decisions.[14] Table 4.1 describes the evolution in the concept of the customer and performance measurement.

Under the traditional public administration model, citizens were regarded as passive recipients of services whose value was determined by public service professionals acting on a mandate from government. NPM brought a reconceptualising of this relationship: the citizenry was now an aggregate of individual customers who collectively placed a value

---

13   The focus of the majority of the discussion of public value lies with the effectiveness and equity dimensions of the concept, focusing on its democratic nature through the inclusion of the citizenry in the processes of government. It is sometimes unclear whether writers intend also to include the costs of service delivery in the criterion. Matters of externalities and 'additionality' are also rarely specifically attended to. The content of the standard cost–benefit criterion can be extended to be a net-benefit criterion incorporating notions of cost, of externalities, and additionality in the concept. In this form it is an appropriate resource allocation (budgetary) criterion. For background see, for example, Bason's discussion of measuring the value of public sector innovation (Bason 2010).

14   The choice of a cost–benefit criterion and the manner of incorporation of equity into the analysis is a much-vexed question in welfare economics. Mishan devotes an important part of his seminal book on cost–benefit analysis to it (Mishan 1988). For a case study in the practical challenges involved see, for example, VC Nwaneri, 'Equity in cost benefit analysis: a case study of the third London airport', *Journal of Transport Economics And Policy*, vol 4, no 3, 1970, pp 235–54, doi.org/10.1016/S1573-4420(87)80009-5. For a local discussion, see: 'Cost-benefit analysis', guidance note, Office of Best Practice Regulation, Department of Prime Minister and Cabinet, Australian Government, Feb 2016, www.pmc.gov.au/resource-centre/regulation/cost-benefit-analysis-guidance-note.

on the services – services in which the private value (of the service in consumption) was the sole determinant of public value (the aggregate of individual private valuations). In turn, joined-up and networked government together brought a (notional) focus on outcomes, in the case of the former on solutions for clients and, in the latter, on the value placed on these services through the involvement of citizens and a broader range of parties in the design and delivery of these services and solutions. The latter also envisaged an expanded role for the customer including (a) being an active participant in shaping the services delivered (a 'co-producer' even 'co-creator'); and (b) as a partial participant in the evaluation of the services delivered; in addition to, (c) being the consumer of services.

Table 4.1 The changing role of the citizen

Models of governance	Who is the customer?	Role of the citizen	Valuation
Traditional public administration	The recipient	Passive recipient of services.	Input costs
New Public Management	The government The citizen	The government buys outputs (quantity, quality, cost and timeliness) from the public service. The citizen values consumption.	Outputs Aggregate of individual valuations
Joined-up government	The citizen	The citizen consumes services and solutions.	Outcomes
Networked government	The community at large, including citizens and businesses	Individual citizens, the community at large, including businesses of all sorts, may participate in the design and production of these services.	Outcomes and community engagement
Anarchic governance	The community at large	To determine government priorities and participate in their delivery.	Community participation
The public value paradigm	The individual citizen Non-consumers The citizenry in toto	Consumes and values services. Values delivery and outcomes to others. Values effective role of government – trust.	Private value Policy and program outcomes Trust/legitimacy of government

Public value broadens the outcome notion to include both the valuation of services by non-consumers, and their impact on community perceptions of the legitimacy of government. It extends the notion of public sector effectiveness beyond private value. It also raises the possibility of extension of the supplier/customer relationship from a series of unconnected transactions to an ongoing relationship. Much of what happens in the political and public sectors is transactional, with parties being focused on a set of short-term exchanges, to be contrasted with the notion of a relationship built on a sequence of linked transactions.

Whilst not strictly a new 'model of governance', public value embodies a new public administration paradigm and incorporates another step in the performance measurement evolution – at least at the academic level. And, while its potential contribution to the practice of public sector accountability, in particular, is significant, providing as it does an enhanced value-based, outcome-driven model, these developments present new measurement and management challenges for a public service struggling to give proper effect to developments set in train some 30 years ago.

The position reached today is one of transition, with the theory of public value and its outcome-based foundations to the fore in the public sector management literature, but with public sector practice still rooted in the measurement of outputs. The active adoption of this new paradigm may come more slowly than is desirable, if private sector experience is any guide. It remains a common failure of strategic planning and strategy formation in business to focus on the cost side – 'inside the four walls' – at the expense of the customer. As the Canadian business strategist Roger Martin points out, this is comfortable for most organisations because supply and costs are under the control of the organisation, and customers are not (Martin 2014).

An interesting subsidiary question that emerges is what role the public service might play in actively creating public value. The literature on public value clearly envisages a more active role in the political domain for the public service in the realm of stakeholder management and beyond the delivery of services. One avenue for doing this, viewed from within the Public Service Act, is the invitation to departmental secretaries 'to engage with stakeholders'. At the head-of-department level, this might range from regular meet and greets with major ministerial and departmental clients (and suppliers), to forging new political alliances with the minister to break new policy ground.

This could be something of a slippery slope for the public servants concerned, being seen as 'political' and being a (bigger) target with a change of government. Balancing a more active stakeholder leadership and management role (as far as the business of government goes) with the preservation of an apolitical standing in the community requires careful footwork by the public service. Ultimately, this is a question of role.

At the start of this section, I asked whether the customer deserved to be 'king' in government resource-allocation processes and whether the public value criterion was 'the answer' (or at least a plausible answer) to the public service measurement challenge. And the answer to both questions is a qualified 'yes'. Placing effectiveness (and therefore the final customer) at the centre of public service advice to government on resource allocation seems eminently sensible from a public policy standpoint. Public value is also a useful paradigm through which to view the role of the public service and, as such, can become more than simply another measurement tool.

That is not to suggest that public value is always the criterion by which public resources should be valued and allocated. The government must be allowed to override public policy–based rankings of activities and, indeed, the apparent wishes of the broader community. 'Political' decisions are a known phenomenon, but such decisions might also be made in the interests of the broader community, where the government has a breadth of view that the community does not, and/or in circumstances where the community does not have access to the full array of information that the government does. The government must be more than a simple conduit for community preferences, and must be allowed to make independent judgements about matters of community welfare in addition to its political calculations. Placing the consumer at the heart of the resource-allocation process, and in a more public manner, might avoid the worst of those policies largely valued by governments for their narrow political value.

Is public value the right criterion? It is certainly a plausible criterion. In its all-embracing form it would undoubtedly be a more representative criterion of community value and welfare than the output-budgeting framework that presently dominates government performance reporting. The journey from the reporting of outputs through the measurement of private value, and community valuation, is a long one. It is, however, a journey worth committing to. Bureaucratic concerns about the difficulties of achieving satisfyingly precise outcome measures, which seems to inhibit progress in this area, need to be set aside and the journey undertaken in the expectation that a lot will be learned along the way.

It may well be that new goals and concepts of 'outcomes' and accountability need to be developed in a world of collaborative service delivery – where the sharing of power may be an important 'outcome' in itself. Most promising in this regard is the work being undertaken in the Department of Social Services under the banner of Australian Priority Investment with the goal of making service recipients self-sufficient to the degree that they can permanently leave the welfare system. Developing such a long-term investment approach to government support and services would reorient the focus and manner of delivery of government services across the board and would be a useful way of signalling a new focus on measurement. Active support from government for sharper performance measures and better governance would materially assist the public service in this journey.

A strong experience-based case for a more systematic approach to this problem is made in a 2011 McKinsey & Company briefing paper in which the authors assert that an integrated approach should be taken if sustained improvement is the objective. The proposed concept of integration to achieve this outcome has two key elements to it. The first is the recommendation to look at the policy and service delivery supply chain as a whole because of the possibility that major service delivery efficiencies can be secured through minor policy (or program) changes. This is an important reminder for a public service under continuous pressure to deliver efficiency dividends at the service delivery end point. The second is to recognise the associated people dimension, as sustained business improvement requires a culture of performance integrating the personal and business performance management systems (McKinsey & Company 2011).

4.2 Public sector performance

4.2.1 An audit perspective

In its 2014 *Better practice guide*, the ANAO defines governance as a term that would normally be applied to the arrangements and practices which enable an entity to set its direction and manage its operations to achieve expected outcomes and discharge its accountability obligations'

(ANAO 2014a, p 7). In highlighting changes that have taken place since the publication of its 2003 guide, the ANAO notes increased emphasis on public sector performance in the light of fiscal constraints, and an associated increased emphasis on performance monitoring, not just at the program or activity level but in terms of a cost-effective contribution to policy outcomes. The 2014 guide goes on to note both the management and measurement challenges that accompany this increased emphasis in a changing environment in which program delivery has commonly been the responsibility of individual government entities but where, increasingly, the outcomes sought by government depend on the contribution of multiple parties – including public sector entities, other governments, private sector and not-for-profit entities, and citizens.

The guide further notes the importance of leadership working across entity, jurisdictional and sectoral boundaries to collaboratively design and deliver programs and services to enhance policy outcomes. The guide reflects the importance of this emphasis by noting the contemporary challenge of engaging constructively with stakeholders and citizens in this collaboration. Public sector managers face a formidable challenge in leading and managing a moveable feast of collaborative arrangements and it is significant that the academic literature struggles to properly frame the problem and develop suitable management tools.

The ANAO guide goes on to explore the challenges of performance monitoring in the presence of these collaborative arrangements, stressing that the building blocks should include recognition of the three dimensions of accountability – horizontal amongst partners, vertical within an entity, and collectively of all partners to a governing body. The guide emphasises the difficulties of reporting on a whole-of-government basis, given that reporting arrangements are invariably geared towards individual entity reporting. Then there are the compounding difficulties of cross-boundary service delivery, including, as the ANAO points out, establishing aggregate budgets, resource sharing and performance measures, as well as confronting different cultures and information technology platforms. These difficulties are not to be underestimated but it is their size that demands a strategic response, not one that seems limited at best to the department and program level. The depth of this challenge makes it clear that this is not a stand-alone project and should be regarded as core business. It is the sort of activity that should be led by a properly equipped, head office team and should not be left to individual departments to grapple with under central agency direction, with the latter running their own (control) agendas.

One of the common responses is to aggregate such activities in order to more readily place them under one management. This occurred, for example, in September 2013 with the announced co-location within the Department of the Prime Minister and Cabinet (PM&C) of 27 programs comprising 150 administered items, activities, and sub-activities from eight separate departments, incorporating responsibility for the majority of Indigenous-specific policies and programs. In May 2014 the Australian Government announced the Indigenous Advancement Strategy with a commitment of $4.8 billion over four years from 2014–15 and a proposal to save $534.4 million by rationalising programs, grants, and activities. The ANAO commenced an audit in March 2016 within the context of the strategy's aim to improve results for Indigenous Australians (ANAO 2017b).

This was a difficult process to undertake, as evidenced by the large numbers of activities to be aggregated and rationalised. One measure of the challenge is the 2,961 contracts that required formal transitioning to the new arrangements. The audit findings identified a work in progress; these findings included a short planning time frame that affected the department's ability to prioritise Indigenous customer needs; a grants administration process that fell short of Commonwealth standards to manage a billion dollars; and a performance framework and measures that would not enable assessment of progress towards achievement of program outcomes. Achieving success with this aggregation and rationalisation process is a work in progress.

This major task was taken on by the lead department in government and not done well. The ultimate test(s) of the changes will be whether better outcomes are delivered (and demonstrated!) for Indigenous Australians and whether the half-billion dollars of projected savings are captured. Strangely, the audit report was silent on this latter matter, not even commenting on whether processes had been established to capture these savings. Also worth noting is an important issue in public administration, which is associated with the report from the Royal Commission into the Home Insulation Program, namely that there was an observed unwillingness to advise the responsible minister of the risks associated with such a short planning time frame.[15]

Apart from identifying common performance shortcomings, as this report does, it also points to an organisational issue relating to the manner in which the public service is organised – as a set of departments overseen by a board (the Board of Secretaries) where the core of the board members are departmental (divisional) leaders with full time responsibilities.[16] A reference point is of similarly diverse private sector organisations and the structures and resourcing they use and leads to the question of what leadership the public service requires and how it should be provided. Possible answers range from (a) a PM&C that detaches itself from operating responsibilities and takes on the role of the corporate office; to, (b) a public service led by an 'independent' board, with a CEO and supporting corporate headquarters.

4.2.2 'Insider' assessments of public service performance

In looking back on 10 years as Auditor-General for Australia, Ian McPhee identified a number of strengths in government administration – governance frameworks, high profile events, public sector reform and values, culture/collegiality, and accountability. McPhee also identified a number of 'soft areas', including risk identification and management, implementation under pressure, taking a narrow view of responsibilities, and performance measurement for programs and outcomes particularly impact assessment (McPhee 2015). The Auditor-General's assessment points to a government administration with sound high level frameworks but one somewhat let down by execution and the detail required to make these frameworks stick. Reviewing occasional speeches from departmental secretaries, along with other published material from successive APS commissioners is valuable in assessing the performance of the APS. The valedictory speeches of a number of secretaries also provide a rich vein of reflections of both a backward-looking and forward-looking nature.[17]

---

15   This final point was noted in paragraph 16 of the ANAO report (ANAO 2017b).

16   In Chapter 5, I argue that it is a board in name only, lacks the commitment of resources and skills to perform an appropriate set of board functions, and operates much more like an executive committee.

17   See Wanna et al. (2012) and IPAA (2017).

Collectively, this material is a useful perspective on the APS as it is a combination of a mix of observations from those 'on the job' and those post-employment. As APS commissioner, Stephen Sedgwick's 2013–14 state of the service report is a useful starting point for these reflections, as are his comments on retirement (APSC 2014a).

In the 2013–14 report, published in December 2014 at the end of Sedgwick's five-year term as commissioner, he called for transformational change in the APS to meet what he described as 'the productivity imperative'. In his overview, Sedgwick noted that for all of the post–Second World War period to the mid-1980s, the APS was heavily regulated and centrally controlled, but within an environment in which senior public servants were often seen to be very powerful compared with their ministers. By the mid to late 1980s, much had changed, with ministers assuming control of the agenda of government and responsibility for the national interest and the public service seen as being responsible for results. Central control of the public service was dismantled, with the progressive devolution of authority and decentralisation of major decisions by government agencies.

Sedgwick suggested that, almost 30 years on, the pendulum had in some respects swung too far. He suggested that the APS may have become too reactive, too focused on the short term and the delivery of tasks, and unable to generate the range of new ideas that it might have liked. In subsequent passages in the same report he pointed to critics who praised the public service problem-solving and issue management capabilities but questioned whether there was sufficient genuinely 'blue sky' thinking. He further pointed to the consequent need for public service leaders to provide forward-looking, creative contributions to government about what the agenda should be and to their stewardship of an enduring institution that can scan the horizon and think beyond the immediate to the medium and longer term.

On taking up the role of commissioner following Sedgwick's departure, John Lloyd echoed many of the same sentiments. His view of the public service role was that the APS advised the government about policy and program options. The advice was thorough, identified choices, and frankly canvassed implications and options. Then, once the government made a decision, public servants were to implement and administer the policy or program with enthusiasm and flair (APSC 2015b). In the same speech he echoed the longer-term perspective that the public service should take, noting that in discharging these roles the public service must be mindful of the longer-term national interest, and that the APS endures beyond elections and its attention to the national interest is important.

Before resigning in 2018, Lloyd brought new emphasis to the role of commissioner with a focus on modernising the employment framework. He pointed to the need to change the current highly regulated, reactive, and prescriptive employment framework to attract, utilise and retain the best people. He noted that the bulk of the restrictions are self-imposed and do not reside in the Public Service Act, and he referred to resulting problems with performance management, absenteeism, and unnecessarily long recruitment processes. He also referred to an excessive focus on transactions and not enough on workforce strategy, with many people being 'stuck in the system'.

What is particularly interesting given the excesses and lingering impacts of the wave of NPM reforms is the notably private sector emphasis that Lloyd has brought to his role. Whether discussing absenteeism, service delivery efficiency, or performance management, the reference points for Lloyd were always private sector – for example, reference to the manner in which (some) private sector companies avoid having people 'stuck in their systems' by managing out the bottom 10 per cent of performers each year. As noted earlier, it is argued that a pragmatic, evidence-based and context-driven approach needs to be taken to the adoption of private sector practices by the public sector. Perhaps a considered examination of the causes of poor performance, against a background of a career-driven public service, the rate of voluntary departures, and a careful examination of the 10 per cent cut-off might be more beneficial than any arbitrarily embedded private sector departure practice?

Another area where caution is required in the adoption of private sector practices lies with the application of the notion of technical (or productive) efficiency to the operations of the public sector. As president of the Institute of Public Administration Australia, Terry Moran targeted notions of private sector efficiency as the standard by which all public sector activities should be judged. Moran's experience as head of both the Victorian Public Service (as secretary of the Department of Premier and Cabinet) and the APS (as secretary of PM&C) has equipped him with a sanguine view of the application of private sector tools and techniques to the public sector.

In a speech to the 2014 Australia and New Zealand School of Governance conference, Moran (2014a) asserted that there are many private sector techniques that the public sector should know more about – commercial strategy, business planning, project management, IT and systems capability development, and accountability. He argued, however, that due to the preponderance of economic analysis, Canberra's policy establishment missed getting the right balance of economics, and advances in contemporary management and the parallel real-world commercial experience, in thinking through the challenges facing government as a whole.

In a subsequent speech, Moran (2014b) repeated this message in pointing to the perils of pursuing a narrow economic focus over more strategic policy analysis. And, in 2015, he pointed to the loss of important capabilities and skills in the APS – engineering and construction (important in the case of the infrastructure deficit), approaches to the management of large organisations (e.g. how to deliver better government with a smaller public service) and broad strategic planning (central to the achievement of effective whole-of-government responses to today's problems), and their replacement with the economist's world view that the answer to big policy challenges is the development of a well-structured market and putting a price on everything (Moran 2015). Moran gave the example of the primary health care system, arguing that the Commonwealth sees it as an aggregation of fee-for-service traders in healthcare rather than as a system.[18]

Beyond the prevailing difficulties and capability shortfalls, Sedgwick and Lloyd both provide useful comments about the perspective that the APS should bring to its tasks. Moran's comments on capabilities and solutions are equally informative and a complementary view is offered by Patricia Scott who, in her valedictory speech following completion of her term as secretary of the Department of Broadband, Communications and the Digital Economy in 2009, made a strong case for the strengthening of

18   It is a moot point whether to take most notice of speeches by leaders in office, their valedictory speeches, or those post-office, as they have differing motivation. I suggest that the last of the three are most useful as the first are underpinned by some notions of loyalty to one's colleagues (and confidentiality), the second by the warm glow of one's own time well spent, and the third might be regarded as both 'objective' and time for a little payback. This rationalisation differs markedly for the private sector where the process starts with in-office speeches, certainly the early ones, invariably pointing to mismanagement that (only) the incumbent is well suited to fix.

the Cabinet process through the reinstatement of traditional relationships between the departments, ministers and staff, and Cabinet. Her argument pointed to a number of weaknesses in the existing system, including:

- central agency domination of public service advice to Cabinet
- the need for written submissions based on addressing a common set of questions to underpin Cabinet deliberations
- major decisions taken by a few Cabinet ministers to the exclusion of their colleagues
- the undue influence of ministerial staffers associated with the absence of senior public service advisors in ministerial offices.

Taken together, the cumulative effect was a compromised Cabinet process that had been diminished to the role of a rubber stamp (Scott 2012).

Scott's observations are reflected in Laura Tingle's essay 'Political amnesia' (2015) and spell out the accompanying government and public service process dimensions necessary to give effect to a capability that should lie at the heart of the competitive advantage of the APS but which has been progressively diminished over the last 30 or so years.

4.2.3 A view from the 2014 National Commission of Audit

A final view of the performance of the APS is provided by the 2014 National Commission of Audit (NCOA) headed by Tony Shepherd, president of the Business Council of Australia, which yielded a range of interesting views and proposals for government to consider around the notion of good government (NCOA 2014). The report noted that the overall efficiency and effectiveness of government is heavily dependent on the performance of the public service and that, by international standards, Australia had been well served by its public service. Nonetheless, the review went on to make some broad-ranging recommendations to improve public sector performance. The Phase Two report and its focus on public sector performance and accountability is most relevant to this discussion. The commentary and recommendations covered a number of issues of interest, including public service structures, accountability, and performance measurement as well as four overlapping matters: devolution of authority, the organisational structures of the public service, performance measurement and evaluation, and the public policy – service provider split.

The devolution and exercise of authority within the public service was the NCOA's underlying theme, with strong support being expressed for its continuing devolution. The Commission noted the trade-off between centralisation of responsibility for employment matters in agencies like the Australian Public Service Commission (APSC), and the provision of appropriate flexibility to individual agencies to manage their own affairs. The NCOA's view was that departmental heads should be empowered to manage their own organisations, drive productivity, pursue innovation, and better deliver on the government's agenda. The proposed decentralised alternatives to the current arrangements for the APSC involved transferring its responsibilities to other departments so as to enable a stronger role for secretaries, coordinated through the Secretaries Board, and thereby improve the strategic focus on the future needs of the APS. This would replace the APSC's stewardship, strategy, and network management functions, with residual functions transferred to other agencies.

The NCOA further noted the need for better information on the performance of programs, to answer basic questions about such things as what the money was used for, what the policy objective was, and whether the policy objective was achieved. The prospective benefits included improved government capacity to assess the merits of different programs and prioritise expenditure. The NCOA recognised that during the last 25 years of the government's reporting framework there was movement from a narrow focus on reporting financial inputs towards an attempt to provide greater information on results and outcomes. Despite this, the NCOA assessment asserted that most performance information remained focused on financial accountability. Referring to several ANAO assessments of entity performance, the NCOA supported the introduction of the PGPA Act to rebalance the focus of entity reporting towards non-financial reporting as opposed to financial. The Commission recommended that more meaningful key performance indicators be developed for each program and that the Department of Finance maintain a central register of all programs. Noting that there was no systematic evaluation of expenditure programs at the Commonwealth level, nor any linking of evaluation to the budget process, the NCOA recommended that Finance undertake a small number of strategic annual reviews of programs and that a separate process be established to audit portfolio agencies.

Finally, the NCOA commented on the effectiveness of the public policy – service provider split and the need for change and examined the potential for a clearer delineation of responsibilities for policy and service delivery.

The Commission concluded that portfolio departments should undertake policy development while agencies should deliver programs and services, and noted that while much of this had happened, the challenge now (ironically) was how better to connect them. In lauding the results of the split being matched by a supportive budget process, the NCOA reported the gap that existed between policy and service delivery, with the policymakers view of the world often differing substantially from that of 'the frontline'. The dismissive attitude of policymakers in these circumstances was anticipated to result in a tendency to revert to first principles rather than learn from 'lived experience'.

4.2.4 A note on the role of the Auditor-General

One of the issues that flows from the NCOA's final point is the role of the auditor-general. Despite 30 years of evolution of performance measurement and an accompanying audit focus on performance audits, the public service seems little advanced from its focus on financial accounting and the measurement of financial inputs, with measurement of outcomes limited only to those parts of the public service in confined fields where cost–benefit analysis has been used as a matter of course throughout the period. The is little advance from the position 30 years ago, with the government strategy remaining to rely on the auditor-general to lift the game in this regard and the auditors-general adopting a strategy of working cooperatively with senior public servants rather than taking a more aggressive 'naming and shaming' approach. The auditor-general's role, it can be argued, diminishes the public service's accountability for performance measurement and government governance.

An obvious option to address this shortfall would be to provide the auditor-general with enforcement powers. This would not only be at odds with private sector standards, however, but it would also do little for the public service's assumption of responsibility for this important task. Performance measurement would remain a compliance activity and not be accorded the resources needed to develop the analytical tools and data collection systems necessary to generate better management information and capture public value, let alone impacts and outcomes. This should be an area of creativity, not one of compliance for the public service, and little seems likely to change until the public service is made fully responsible and held properly accountable for policy and program performance measurement. The present system does not create the right environment and incentives for the public service to assume responsibility for this important part of their role in effective public administration; it is too heavily balanced towards ex post audit and away from incentives, and along the way provides opportunities for ministers to avoid the transparency necessary to underpin real accountability. Patricia Scott makes this point well:

> It is easy to create a veneer of greater openness by reforming Freedom of Information laws but then have a minister insist that the most sensitive material is never provided in writing or have political advisers inappropriately seek to reprimand departmental officers for committing views to paper that would be 'unhelpful' if they were made public. At the same time, self-censorship by public servants in advising is a dangerous trap that is easy to fall into. (Scott 2012, p 122)

Further, and as noted earlier, the area of government governance that remains as absolute virgin territory is that of the governance surrounding policy formation. This has received little attention in Australia at any of the academic, auditor-general, or public service levels. The case in principle for it to receive a similar level of attention to the financial record keeping and performance-reporting activities of the public service is strong. Indeed, it is the missing link in the public sector audit chain, with auditing of record keeping, expenditure processes and their impacts being undertaken, but not the decisions that give rise to these activities. Simply auditing the end point of the chain – expenditure – suffers from the same logical weakness that focuses primarily on the processes of service delivery to the exclusion of the underlying policy in attempts to improve its efficiency.

In the private sector, auditors can identify the source of high-level decisions by pursuing an existing paper trail. Yet, in the case of government, there is no such trail and scrutiny. Given the size of the benefits conferred by the choice of policy areas for attention, the policies themselves, the choice of policy instruments, and the settings of those policy instruments that determine the beneficiaries, there are multiple stages where influence might be exerted, both from inside and outside of government. This area should not go untouched and is ripe for auditor-general attention. Auditing the consequences of decisions without examining how the decisions themselves are made arguably ignores an important determinant of the impact of the decisions.

A thorough reconsideration of the role of the Auditor-General for Australia is warranted. The financial record keeping practices of the Australian public sector are excellent and, as with private sector accounting, require regular external auditing. This function should continue to reside with the auditor-general. In regard to performance reporting, I believe it is time to assign full responsibility for this to the public service and reduce this responsibility of the auditor-general to one of broadly commenting on progress. A new responsibility should be added to this, namely to develop and advise on the implementation of (then oversight) the public sector accounting and governance procedures to go with policy formation. It is anomalous that of the two central responsibilities accorded to the public service under the Public Service Act – the policy advisory and service delivery management roles – only one is accorded any external scrutiny, and the lesser important of the two. This is poor public sector governance indeed!

4.2.5 The cost of governing

The complexity of the cost of governing lies behind a range of issues. The two primary forms of cost are out-of-pocket expenditures and opportunity costs; the latter involve the costs of poor (i.e. sub-optimal) choices. With regard to the latter, there is little to say of a definitive nature, other than to observe that auditing of government expenditure and associated processes makes it evident that opportunity costs are often likely to be substantial. I again point to improved measurement of policy and program impacts as an important step in improving resource allocation (and reduced opportunity costs), especially when it places a value on the consumption of government services.

While it is no less difficult to be definitive about the unit cost of producing and delivering government services, where this cost is considered in terms of a standard unit of community benefit, there are good reasons to believe that the cost of governing is rising rapidly and has been doing so for some decades. My 'evidence' for this includes the UK-based evidence from Hood and Dixon's 30-year study that shows the rising 'cost of governing' is driven both by rising costs and declining value. It is likely that this research, if repeated in other jurisdictions (such as Australia, New Zealand and Canada), would produce similar results because of a similar set of drivers and evolution of the practice of government. Moreover, in a world of complex problems and diverse stakeholders, where the citizenry is becoming more actively involved in the processes of government, is using legal processes in some cases to frustrate governments and project proponents, and is seeking to replace bureaucratic and legal processes with citizen-based processes in others, the administrative cost of government – of a standardised unit of government-delivered outcome – will almost certainly be rising.

Moreover, at the political level, there is increasing minority party representation and diminishing major party representation in parliament, and an associated greater difficulty in forming governments, and lengthy negotiations amongst the parties to achieve passage of government policies. Continuation along this path is likely to lead to the passage of fewer bills through parliament. The productivity of parliament must be diminishing. Good policy is less likely to emerge from such an environment and it is further likely that such political compromises will diminish the value to be placed on policy outcomes. Therefore, not only is the unit administrative cost likely to be rising because of a less-productive parliament and more time-consuming parliamentary approvals processes, but also the aggregate of delivered benefits is similarly likely to be declining, with the added reasoning of diminishing quality (and quantity) of government policy.[19]

A further dimension to consider in assessing the cost of governing relates to the balance of government's ex ante incentives and ex post governance procedures. As Simon Longstaff (2015) points out, it is costly to maintain an array of watchdog and integrity bodies including anti-corruption bodies, a variety of 'commissioners', ombudsmen and women, regulators and auditors-general.[20] All are deemed necessary by governments determined to ensure that our political and administrative systems are 'clean', or appear to be, on some level, and functioning efficiently and effectively. Few of them bring new skills to government: many are designed to be consumer representatives inside a system that is not working. There has been an explosion of these roles over the last decade at state and federal levels in Australia, itself an indicator of declining political and bureaucratic performance.

One notable aspect of this problem is the growing reliance placed on such ex post governance procedures at the expense of building the right incentives into the related systems. As Longstaff points out, this only

---

19   It would be an interesting exercise to measure the productivity of parliament in a composite quantity and quality measure as part of an exercise in measuring the cost of governing.

20   And it seems likely that the financial cost of these bodies will be added to in the foreseeable future with the addition of a national broad-based anti-corruption body.

adds to the cost of governing. One such example, as already argued, is the use of auditors-general to audit performance reporting. Similarly, the appointment of most of the 'commissioners' at state and national levels are an indication that 'the system' is not working, whether 'the system' involves administration of the *Freedom of Information Act 1982*, transport network operation, fair work, privacy, health, small business, the digital economy, domestic violence, disability services, or child safety. As a particular burden on taxpayers, they should be abolished, externally scrutinised and the underlying systems and incentive problems fixed.[21]

The final cost of governing to highlight is the growing scale (both dollars and issues) of government activities. This is a problem of size, in terms of the difficulties of maintaining effective communication and management focus within large and growing government departments. Oliver Williamson(1970) argued that efficiencies are to be gained through divisionalisation of large, functionally arranged organisations, but mused that even these benefits would diminish if organisations became big enough. The impact of size on organisational efficiency in the public sector is another area for research, including consideration of the costs and benefits of different organisational options – both form and size – for the public service. Such research could review the design options for the public service as a whole (holding company, functional form, divisionalised, ambidextrous, and so on) and the contexts within which various organisational forms and mixtures might prove the most beneficial.[22]

Such research should look at structural options (whole-of-public-service and individual departments); the impacts of size on organisational efficiency (both); and the efficiency dimensions of super-departments, including the demonstrated ability of such departments to capture

---

21 Cataloguing the rise and effectiveness of these bodies would be another useful exercise in measuring the overall cost of governing.

22 In later analysis, Williamson (1991) focuses on the efficiency of organisations and seeks to incorporate the cost of changing the organisational state in his organisational efficiency criterion. This is a reminder that the costs of transition must be included in applying a cost–benefit analysis to organisational change. This reminder is relevant in the context for organisational restructuring in the public sector where not only is there limited accounting for the direct (financial) costs, but virtually no accounting for the costs of lost productivity. It is also tempting to treat such change as instantaneous or timeless but, whereas the direct costs are likely to be incurred quickly, the indirect costs, especially those related to lost productivity, may flow for some time *and* the projected benefits may only occur with a lag. Anything less than a present value-based analysis of such change embracing all of these elements would be misleading.

sufficient net-cost savings to justify the aggregation. Effectiveness should also be captured by this research, as should the notion that organisational structures are aggregates of functions, each with its own minimum efficient scale, and this has an impact on organisational design in both horizontal and vertical terms.

4.2.6 The data requirements for good performance and governance

There are many data-based systems within large organisations that contribute to the effective and efficient management of the total organisation, with each function and division having its own part of an integrated recording and management system, both receiving and generating data on which its own performance might be assessed. The business performance measurement system is only one such system, but a very important one. Nonetheless it is important to remember that business performance measurement is not an end in itself, should not be seen as separable from the other tasks of management, does not have a life of its own, and the data required for performance measurement (and good governance) should naturally fall out of any well-designed management information system. Deficiencies in performance measurement inevitably point to deficiencies in management because good performance-based data, required in the determination of what to do and how to do it at all levels of an organisation, provides not just the results of the business, but must also be the basis for its ongoing improvement. As Bason points out, measurement should drive learning and innovation (Bason 2010).

It should be clear that there is a significant and growing challenge confronting the public service in developing a performance measurement regime that matches the aspirations of the higher levels of government accountability. Moreover, if the arguments about the existence and extent of wickedness inherent in government policy are accepted, then the public service has an unenviable challenge in trying to design solutions; the interrelated nature of problems requires development of a systematic understanding of policy problems and their root causes – how to do this in an analytically useful manner is a complex challenge. Such questions as what sort of linkages exist between the root causes of different complex problems, how strong these linkages are, where the best return on investment would be gained by intervening through one or more of these linkages, how one could be confident that such interventions would not worsen related wicked problems, and what organisational structures and interventions would offer the best chance of success, deserve systematic attention underpinned by measurement.

The systematic application of such a 'model', which mapped wicked problems and their root causes onto public service organisational structures, would be extremely difficult to build but invaluable to public service managers for insights it might generate. Looking at government as a collection of projects to address policy problems would be a similarly valuable exercise. The application of standard systems mapping tools to examine links between system elements, feedback loops and lines of causation outlined by Geoff Mulgan offers promise in this direction (Mulgan 2009, Chapter 4). As he points out, this formal data analysis is only the start, to be followed by policy formation, defining goals, and setting direction. To be useful as a service delivery guide, it needs to be accompanied by the development of accommodating structures, a framework for shared resources and rewards, and risk-sharing arrangements that cross departmental and sectoral boundaries.

Mulgan further points to the extensive nature of data demands of effective policy and strategy, with the need for good analysis as a starting point, suggesting that:

> Around any public policy goal there will be many pieces of potentially relevant knowledge, but these are unlikely to have been synthesized into a comprehensive view of the dynamics of change. (p 90)

And:

> the quality of analysis is often the critical factor behind good strategy because all bureaucracies build up systematically distorted views of the world around them. Analysis helps to peel away false assumptions. (p 88)

It is almost certain that progress in this endeavour will involve not only the mining of large amounts of data, but also integrating this with the recorded history and accumulating experience of field staff. The relationships that the data miners look for must be informed by the practitioners' understanding of what happens in the field.

It also points to the need for a corporate market intelligence system, which most successful organisations possess, but that exists at best in the public service in a piecemeal manner. Tingle has pointed to institutional memory as an important component of this function that plays a critical value-adding role in the interpretation of current events, but market intelligence is more important than that. It should deliver information on competitors, customers, underlying demand and supply trends, the impact of technology, market risks, and marry this to information on its own business(es). At the whole-of-organisation level, this information must enable a regular review of the businesses it is in and individual business unit performance (in public service terms, the individual department), together enabling regular adjustment to its determinations of where to play and how to win.

Market intelligence in a public service context should comprise the information that is collected at individual departments level and at whole-of-public-service level. This may range from 'global' developments in consumer, political, industry, social, and environmental behaviour (the core of corporate market intelligence), through to such behaviour in local markets allied with competitor analysis (the core of business unit market intelligence). Good performance starts with good policy and good policy requires sound market-driven foundations. In the best-performing organisations there will be a clear line of sight from the performance of individual businesses (programs/services) through to the local and international market intelligence collected on which basis each such individual activity is managed and evaluated.

4.3 Conclusions and unresolved issues

When the operating environment is viewed in terms of the challenges it throws up for governance, it is clear that there are important gaps in government governance in Australia. In part these relate to high-level institutional shortcomings in regard to the oversight of the probity and integrity of the operations of government. Below that level, where the public service is responsible for establishing the systems, processes and administrative procedures that capture the required dimensions of good government governance, there are serious deficiencies.

Considering performance from a governance point of view enables a broader discussion of the quality of government and public administration performance, in regards to both structural and operational dimensions. While much of this discussion is structural, focusing on the institutional settings and the organisational processes and systems in place, the broad conclusion is that the quality of government in Australia is almost certainly poor and deteriorating and, when considered in qualitative terms on an equivalent own-benchmark basis, is most likely well below the standard of government delivered three or four decades ago. The limited availability of sound performance data confirms this view, which disappointingly reflects little of the recent academic literature on performance measurement.

It is difficult to discern how much of this deterioration is due to a difficult external environment or to internal management failures, but both are contributing. There is clearly also a behavioural component to consider, as politicians who are substantially focused on their own interests at the expense of the public and national interest clearly invite public servants to behave in the same manner and waste time on unproductive matters. In addition, the practice of government in primarily adversarial terms must impose costs on the practice of public administration. The difficulties experienced today in governing surface repeatedly and in the form of the problems of coordination of public administration activities – vertical within departments, horizontal across departments, and the broader cross-sectoral coordination accompanying more networked government.

A more collegiate attitude within the public service and across participating departments could materially assist in addressing some of these difficulties. This issue of coordination in turn highlights the performance measurement challenge where multiple work units, multiple departments and multiple organisations are involved in conceiving, designing, delivering, and managing government-funded programs. Questions of effective program management, risk and reward sharing, and reporting, are yet to be resolved.

Yet this is only the more visible edge of effective performance measurement, there being a number of dimensions of organisational operations where data and measurement is critical to the management of the business, thereby making an important contribution to the overall performance of the organisation. I argue that, for successful strategic management – driving the organisation from the top – there must be clear linkages between the program-level generation of activity and management information; whole-of-organisation resource allocation, and the consequent performance reporting; and the whole-of-organisation management and direction of its portfolio of activities. Lack of effective information at the operating end of the organisation can only be expected to lead to sub-optimal decisions at the top, whilst lack of effective conception of the whole at the top will most likely be the cause of this failure.

One of this chapter's underlying assumptions could be seen to approximate the epithet usually attributed to Peter Drucker, namely that what gets measured gets managed and what doesn't … doesn't. While this is a useful basis for starting a discussion of what should be measured and in describing how data can be used productively in an organisation, I prefer the approach of Christensen and Raynor because they emphasise the learning dimension of data rather than simply the recording of the past. They describe successful management's ongoing quest for predictability (and therefore manageability) in its operating environment and the journey as a learning process of the continuous formation and testing of theories (both personal and organisational) to refine the ability to predict what actions will cause what results (Christensen & Raynor 2003, p 13). The formation of hypotheses about cause and effect, the quantification of relationships, and the observation of results is the foundation of this learning process and sound long-term management: it is both a mental (individual) and physical (organisational) process. No quantification or testable hypotheses means foregone opportunities to learn about cause and effect, build organisational capital, and secure longer-term benefits.

This, in my view, is where the real gains in organisational performance come from – demanding and developing a culture of measurement that encourages individuals to take responsibility for the performance of public resources within their domain – not from one-off outsourcing that contracts out the opportunity to learn and build organisational capital from the experience gained in designing, building, delivering, and evaluating services. Nowhere is this more evident than in the political pursuit of 'efficiency gains', often simply a euphemism for budget cuts. Unfortunately, short-termism prevails with the documented and short-term efficiency gain being more highly valued than the more important challenges of the harder to document development of a culture of learning and innovation.

There is a raft of reasons why individuals and organisations do not take up the opportunities to learn in the manner described by Christensen and Raynor: they may have no conception of how to quantify relationships, they may come from cultures where such quantification is not the standard modus operandi, their minds may be made up with the risk that any quantification might show up bad (in economic cost–benefit terms) decisions, they might regard quantification a waste of time when ultimately policy and program decisions will be (rightly) made on political grounds, and they may regard the quantification as 'too hard'. And, when viewed from within an organisation, the signals from the top may create and/or compound some of these difficulties.

For the public service as a whole, no such excuses should be allowed. The journey of quantifying the benefits and the costs of all government programs and services should be built into the programs. Moreover, whilst quantification may be alien to some parts of the public service, there are pockets of outstanding capacity within it that could and should be built on. Activity measurement – in the integrated form of management information and impact, outcome, and public value assessments – should be automatic in the public service, rather than the afterthought it is. It is easy to forget the wide range of functions that performance measurement plays and the linkages between these functions. They include: resource allocation, budgeting, governance, policy development, and learning and innovation.

The inevitable consequence of a failure by the public service to take responsibility for measuring program and policy outcomes and connecting costs and benefits will be a continuing slide in the quality of government governance. On the other hand, were it to openly and publicly take on the measurement challenge, publish an annual report on the task and progress, it would, I suspect garner a lot of business and community support. This might be viewed as not only a desirable but necessary step for longer-term survival for the public service as an influencer of government policy, as the trend for increasing participation of community groups in policy formation and service delivery continues to multiply the governance challenges in the absence of an appropriate governance toolkit. In the next chapter, I turn to the issue of the conception and management of the public service as a whole in the public interest. This is the question of public service leadership, what it is empowered to do, and what it should be able to do in the public interest.

5

The role and activities of the public service

5.1 Introduction

Recent speeches made by public service heads point to a need to reskill the public service, to think in terms of systems (rather than piecemeal), to look beyond economics for policy advice, for the public service to acknowledge that it 'endures' beyond governments, that it needs to look 'over the horizon', and, have regard for 'the national interest'. As auditor-general for Australia, Ian McPhee pointed to 'soft spots' including monitoring and responding to change, getting lost in the weeds, and performance measurement for programs and outcomes (McPhee 2015); and his successor points to a continuing need to use a series proxies by which to assess an entity's outcome-based performance in the absence of good quality performance information and data despite three decades of audit and change (Hehir 2016).

In this chapter, I focus on the public service, examining the *Public Service Act 1999*, which established the Australian Public Service (APS) and prescribes its role and conduct. Along with (market) context and the institutional setting, the Public Service Act and how it plays out are the key factors in shaping the contribution of the public service to good government. The impact of the Public Service Act invites consideration of the boundaries to this contribution, in terms of its domain and what it can offer within this predetermined field of play. I draw a distinction between what might be in the interests of the APS (as an effective organisation), and what might be in the public interest.

The drafting of a public service act can impact on the contribution of the public service in a number of important ways. First of these is the description of the field of play and the role to be played by the public service. For example, the Public Service Act prescribes an important part of the role of departmental secretaries as principal official policy adviser to the agency minister. If the field of play envisaged here is policy advice, then the public service (department secretarial) role is limited by the provision for other official and non-official sources of policy advice. The second way in which a public service act can impinge on the public service contribution is through the prescription of its organisation and resourcing. The third way is the manner in which it both provides for, and protects, the provision of sound advice. Fourth is the behaviours of key players enabled by the Act. Further, there is the question of intent that lies behind such an Act and which, in operation, can transcend the impact of individual clauses: this might be considered in both stated and real terms. Finally, any such Act is likely to contain important implications for the processes of government, and the organisational culture that results.

In discussing the contribution of the public service to good government, it is useful to distinguish between public service performance and contribution. Clearly, the framing and drafting of a public service act will determine the limits to the potential contribution of the public service to good government. It does this by (a) circumscribing the field of play; (b) establishing the rules of play within this field; (c) creating mechanisms for enforcement of these rules; and (d) through the underlying 'spirit of the game' embodied in the legislation.[1] The public service then takes this description of 'the game', with its embodied contribution limits, and performs more or less successfully. A more expansive Act might permit a larger contribution, while a less expansive one might limit this contribution further. In any event, the public service should only be held to account for what is within its control. Viewed in this

---

1   The Public Service Act also provides for the APS commissioner to issue a wide range of directives on a whole-of-public-service basis and with the status of legislative instruments in the matters of employment, values and code of conduct breaches, and undertake an equally wide range of investigative activities, in his/her own right, upon request from the prime minster or public service minister, and on referral from departmental secretaries, and make recommendations accordingly. See especially clause 41 of the Act.

way, a high-performing public service could be one making a small or large contribution to good government in Australia depending on the constraints and its performance within those constraints.

The first part of this chapter examines the structure and philosophy of the Public Service Act, the Australian Government's primary legislation towards the APS, and includes a brief discussion of the *Public Governance, Performance and Accountability Act 2013* (PGPA Act). The focus of this chapter is on the former, which is a dedicated Act involving the establishment and management of the APS, whereas the PGPA Act is a whole-of-public-sector piece of legislation establishing public governance requirements for all defined 'entities', including government departments. With regard to the former, the chapter considers its major clauses and the impact of the Act on the performance and contribution of the APS and the changes that could be made in the public interest. These changes can be conceived in three parts: corrections to the inadequate initial drafting of the Act, changes necessitated by the passage of time since the drafting of the last Act, and philosophical changes to the Act. Some could be attributed to a combination of these factors.

It is useful to be mindful of the impact of the Act on the public service as influencing a three-part structure: *leadership* (determining what to do and how to do it), *management* (resourcing and organisation of the business), and *operations* (systems and behaviour). These distinctions are important in the public sector, no less than the private sector, because of the impact on organisational behaviour and performance of the leadership of any organisation and the structures through which this leadership is delivered.[2]

The Public Service Act focuses on the notion of 'serving' the government, the parliament, and the Australian public, describing primarily through its values and code of conduct how this service should be provided, without trying to identify its outcomes. The ultimate outcome – at least in terms of the government's performance – might reasonably be considered as conducted at the electoral ballot box, whilst there are no systemic indicators of the performance of the public service, and few even partial indicators. Those that I have considered, suggest that there may be substantial room for improvement.

---

2   I maintain this typology of organisational activities throughout the book but leave the thorny issue of the distinction between leadership and management until later in Chapter 5.

The relevant question here is: given a clean slate on which to redesign the public service, what would a public service that would best serve community interests look like and how would it change from its present state? This question necessarily raises the question of 'the public interest', what it means and how it can be judged.

The notion of 'the public interest' is another of those rarely defined terms that is used to justify a wide range of actions. There is, of course, the simple view that only 'the public' knows what is in the public interest and that some form of plebiscite should be undertaken on all important matters. And it is arguable that a detailed general definition does not serve any useful purpose – because of great variability in circumstances and that, at best, a framework of matters for consideration on a case-by-case basis is most useful.[3] In applying the concept of public interest to prospective changes to the role and operations of the APS, I propose that, in practice, it requires a balancing of winners and losers. In much of what follows 'the winners' may be seen to be the public service and 'the losers' the politicians. My interest, however, lies primarily with 'the Australian public'. The welfare of either or both of the politicians and public service may be necessary collateral damage in achieving change 'in the public interest'.

5.2 Defining the public service role

5.2.1 The legislated framework

5.2.1.1 The provisions of the *Public Service Act 1999*[4]

A discussion of the role and activities of the APS must start with a clear understanding of its goals. The role of the APS is defined in the Public Service Act and further clarified in the PGPA Act, which focuses on the activities of public sector entities, adding some useful embellishments. The following focuses on the objects of the Public Service Act and primarily the parts of the Act addressing the roles, responsibilities, and functions of departmental secretaries, the Secretaries Board, and the APS commissioner. The key clauses of the Act are set out in Table 5.1.

---

3   Chris Wheeler's discussion of the issues argues for a case-by-case approach built around the distinction between the concept and its application (Wheeler 2013).
4   For a detailed discussion of the tortured path to enactment of the Public Service Act, see APSC (2013a).

Table 5.1 The key clauses of the *Public Service Act 1999*

Clause 3 Objects of the Act	Serve the government Serve parliament Serve the Australian public	Leadership
Clause 64 Functions of Secretaries Board	Stewardship of the APS Works collaboratively Canvasses advice widely	
Clause 57(1) Roles of Secretaries	Advise policy Manage service delivery Whole-of-public-service leadership	Management
Clause 57(2) Responsibilities of Secretaries	Deliver results Comply with the laws of the land Engage with stakeholders	
Clause 3 Objects of the Act	An apolitical public service Efficient Effective	Operations
Clause 10 Values, Clause 10A Employment Principles, Clause 13 Code of Conduct (Selective)	Is prescriptive in providing for five values and a 13-point code of conduct, along with the establishment of a safe and discrimination-free workplace for a career-based public service.	

The Act establishes the objects, a set of values, a set of employment principles (including a commitment to a 'career-based' public service), and a code of conduct to guide behaviours to deliver results consistent with the Act. Clause 3 of the Act is central as it sets out the objects of the Act and includes the directive to establish an apolitical public service that is efficient and effective in serving the government, the parliament and the Australian public. Critical to the establishment of an APS that meets this objective are the values required of the public service. Clause 10, which addresses APS values, is set out in full below.

Table 5.2 Public service values

(1) Committed to service	The APS is professional, objective, innovative and efficient, and works collaboratively to achieve the best results for the Australian community and the Government.
(2) Ethical	The APS demonstrates leadership, is trustworthy, and acts with integrity, in all that it does.
(3) Respectful	The APS respects all people, including their rights and their heritage.
(4) Accountable	The APS is open and accountable to the Australian community under the law and within the framework of Ministerial responsibility.
(5) Impartial	The APS is apolitical and provides the Government with advice that is frank, honest, timely and based on the best available evidence.

Clause 10A provides for a career-based public service, recognises that the usual employment is to be ongoing, incorporates the usual provisions for equity and merit in employment and promotion and provides for a safe, discrimination-free workplace. In turn, clause 13, relating to the Code of Conduct, includes requirements to behave honestly and with integrity, act with care and diligence, show respect, maintain confidentiality, avoid conflict of interest, not provide false or misleading information, and, when overseas, behave in a manner at all times that upholds the good reputation of Australia.

It is clause 57 that offers an understanding of the role the Act requires of the APS. This clause deals with the *role* of secretaries, who head up the government departments – this role comprises that of (a) principal official policy adviser (to the agency minister), (b) manager ensuring delivery of government programs and collaboration within the minister's portfolio and with other secretaries across the whole of government, and (c) leader providing stewardship within the department and in partnership with the Secretaries Board across the APS. The role of secretaries is specifically drafted to be limited to these three functions, although there is a mechanism for change.

The *responsibilities* of secretaries are set out in clause 57(2) (sub clauses (a) to (j)), which spell out the detail of the secretarial role. This detail includes: maintaining clear lines of communication within the agency minister's portfolio, ensuring the agency minister's portfolio has a strong strategic policy capability, and assisting the agency minister to fulfil his/her accountability obligations to parliament. Clause 57 also includes agency stakeholder engagement (which embraces ministerial, departmental, and portfolio activities), and addresses the leadership and management of the department (efficient, effective, economic and ethical); compliance with the laws of the land consistent with Commonwealth policies and the interests of the APS; and provision of strategic direction, leadership, and a focus on results for the department.

The Secretaries Board sits at the top of the public service structure and its functions, set out in clause 64, comprise: (a) stewardship and improvement of the APS; (b) the identification of strategic priorities for the APS; (c) the setting out of an annual work program including the direction of subcommittees; (d) drawing advice from business, government and the community; and (e) modelling leadership and collaborative behaviours. The Board is to comprise the secretary, Department of the Prime Minister and Cabinet (PM&C) (chair), all other secretaries, the APS commissioner, and any other parties nominated by the chair. Notably missing from the list of required activities for the Secretaries Board is a requirement to prepare and have tabled in parliament a whole-of-public-service annual report, a requirement that applies to individual secretaries and the APS commissioner (and merit commissioner) in regard to their respective jurisdictions.

Finally, the Act determines that the APS commissioner has an important role both as a member of the Secretaries Board, but also in his/her own right focusing on the development of the public sector workforce. These functions are broadly cast to include the role of partnering with the secretaries in the stewardship of the APS, ensuring that the APS is ready for future demands, and reviewing any matter relating to the APS. The APS commissioner also upholds high standards of integrity and conduct in the APS and monitors and reports on the service capabilities required to provide high standards of accountability, effectiveness and performance, and to develop APS workforce management policies. The commissioner also participates in the appointment and termination of secretaries along with important powers to undertake public service–wide reviews and issue directives. Moreover, the commissioner is required to report annually 'on the state of the public service during the year'.

5.2.1.2 The *Public Governance, Performance and Accountability Act 2013*

The PGPA Act focuses on the establishment of a coherent system of governance and accountability across Commonwealth entities (including government departments) and an associated 'performance framework'. In view of our earlier discussion of public sector performance measurement, governance and accountability, this Act is important for its aspirations. In particular, it requires departmental secretaries (the 'accountable authority') to (a) measure and assess whether the department is achieving its purpose; (b) prepare an annual corporate plan, and an annual performance statement to be attached to the annual report for tabling in parliament; (c) promote achievement of the entity's purpose and its financial sustainability (the latter is more relevant for Commonwealth corporate entities); (d) establish and maintain appropriate systems of risk oversight, management, and internal control; (e) keep the responsible minister informed of the department's activities, including any 'significant issues' that arise; and, (f) provide meaningful information to the parliament and the Australian public.

There is a strong invitation to departmental secretaries to report systematically on departmental performance through the annual report and an attached performance report, the provision of meaningful information about departmental performance, and to address the contribution of government programs and services to the achievement of agency minister's requirements of the department. There are a number of points to be made about the elements of these Acts that impact on key aspects of the public service role and its execution.

5.2.2 Key impacts of the legislated role

5.2.2.1 The public service is to serve three communities

The first point to note is that the public service is required to serve not just the government, but also parliament, and the Australian public (clause 3(a) of the Public Service Act). This may come as a surprise to many, and whilst overlap is not specifically excluded, a careful reading of the Act indicates that these are intended to be three separate communities. As spelled out in the Act, the most substantial role is that of principal policy adviser and manager of service delivery to the government of the day, and there is limited detail in the Act of public service responsibilities (a) to parliament and (b) the Australian public. There are some, however: reference to the provision of factual information to parliament in support of the agency minister's accountability to parliament; reference to an APS that is open and accountable to the Australian community within the framework of ministerial accountability; and reference to an APS that achieves best results for the Australian community and the government.

There is, nonetheless, no evidence from the drafting of the Act that these references are meant to fully describe or in any way circumscribe the role of the public service in regard to these two additional communities. Most importantly, the reference in the Act to serving both parliament and the Australian public (along with serving the government), lies squarely in the objects of the Act; this is not a throwaway line buried in the text of some detailed clause in the bowels of the Act. I interpret the subsequent references in the Act to any public service role in regard to either, more as examples than boundaries.

It can be reasonably concluded that unqualified service to the government of the day is not envisaged by the guiding Act (even after allowing for full observance of the declared APS values), and the common perception that these other communities are somehow 'served' through effective service to the government of the day has no clear foundation in the Public Service Act. The APS clearly has other responsibilities and the Act does not circumscribe the ability of the secretaries to pursue them. This view is not acknowledged by the APSC in its briefing document *Values and code of conduct in practice*, in which it describes a tight accountability framework in terms of: governments accountable to the Australian people at elections; ministers accountable to the parliament; and public servants accountable to ministers and, through them, to the parliament for delegated authority (APSC 2017).

Public servants do, of course, deal directly with the parliament and with the Australian people. Responding to and briefing parliamentary committees (and briefing non-government members from time to time) forms the relationship with parliament, and delivery of services is the basis of dealing with the Australian people. Both relationships, however, are required to lie within the ambit of ministerial authority and both are required under the Public Service Act to comply with the APS values and code of conduct. There is no suggestion in the APSC briefing document of any direct responsibility (nor accountability for that responsibility) of public servants to the parliament or the Australian public. It is implicit that the APS 'serves' the public (and the parliament) by serving ministers and governments. This matter can also be considered in light of a more expansive interpretation of the public interest.

In interpreting the role of the public service through a distillation of public service values, employment principles, and the code of conduct specified in the Act, and the role and responsibilities for secretaries as heads of the departments and members of the Secretaries Board, a simple picture emerges of the role of the public service, as in Fig. 5.1. This figure acknowledges the three communities that the APS is to serve, and its central role of principal policy adviser and manager of the delivery of government programs. The interesting questions that remain are exactly what the Act intends in defining the different goals and roles envisaged for the public service when interacting with the three communities; what sets of circumstances were anticipated to require the public service to reconcile these differences? and, what criteria might be expected to be used in reconciling differences?

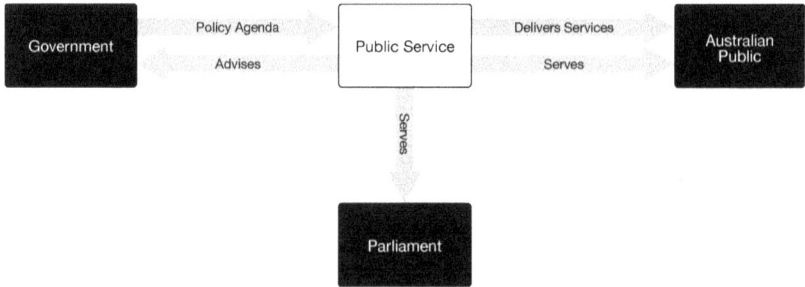

Figure 5.1 The role of the public service: the communities served

5.2.2.2 The role and goals of the public service need to be clearly stated

When it comes to a consideration of the goals of the public service in the context of the Public Service Act, it is difficult to be anything more than trite as the Act is long on processes and values/conduct/behaviours and very short on goals and outcomes (for the public service): the underlying notion is of a public service ready and willing to serve. There is, of course, more to it than that, for a public service ready and willing to serve the government of the day must of necessity take a longer-term view than the electoral cycle requires, and it is here that the presence of parliament and the Australian public in the objects of the Act makes some sense, for arguably to be ready and willing to serve an incumbent government on a day-to-day, even term-of-government basis, the public service must take a longer-term view.

This necessity is most evident in the workforce management and capability development responsibilities assigned to the APS commissioner in clause 41 of the Act, but it is also (arguably) present in clause 10 (A)(1), which states that 'the APS *is* a career-based public service [my italics]'. Clearly, the perspective of public service leaders needs to extend beyond a term of office, even if only in regard to these matters. There are also clear invitations in the Public Service Act to the secretaries and the Secretaries Board to take an integrated view of their activities in regard to the management of individual departments and the public service as a whole, a view that has to extend past the standard three-year term of national governments to be of any value (and thereby meet the requirements of the Act).

Looking beyond the primary policy advisory and service delivery management duties assigned to the public service, to the sorts of outcomes by which the performance of the public service might be judged, the Act contains references to efficiency, effectiveness, and innovation: ultimately, these are not outcomes in themselves but characteristics of services and associated processes that should meet any reasonable resource-use tests designed to deliver targeted outcomes. The corporate plans (for example, 2015–19) of key public service leaders (the secretary of PM&C and the APS commissioner) repeat the standard sentiments about a high-performance public service, but there is also some amplification with the business world introduced as a separate community to be served, along with the notion of a productive public service.

These latter inclusions may well ultimately be a result of advice to the incoming Liberal–National government from the last National Commission of Audit (NCOA 2014), which urged the inclusion of the word 'productive' in the formal requirements of the Public Service Act. This simplification could bring some clarity to the challenge as long as the term 'productive' were not simply seen as a supply-side (efficiency-based) concept and more in line with the notion of 'producing useful things'. I have a fundamental objection, however, with regard to the inclusion of the business community in the set of target communities. This is based on a simple view of the role of the public service and the way in which this perceived need for a better understanding of the business community within government has played out.

As a matter of good practice, the public service must understand the environment and behaviours of the key groups of actors in the policy (and service delivery) space. Alongside this, it must equally be knowledgeable of the various relevant policy frameworks and program options around the globe, and how they might/do impact on the major economic and social actors at home. A plethora of groups within our community who contribute to our economic and social fabric have no less valid cases for inclusion in public service goals, and I have no hesitation permitting them to put their case from time to time. I note further the invitation in the Public Service Act (a) for departmental secretaries to engage with stakeholders and (b) the Secretaries Board to consult with senior leaders in government, business and the community. Properly executed, this aspect of the Act covers the relationships of the public service; making business a special case is both redundant and unnecessary.

Moreover, I cannot support this special engagement with the business community if it is another leg up for those who argue for regular exchanges of staff between public and private sectors. The intention is understandable

– to have more people within government who understand the intricacies of the major social and economic actors, 'representatives', of these communities within government if you like – but this is a naïve and ultimately misguided means to a similarly misguided end. It is akin to the notion that corporate boards should be comprised of 'representatives' of a variety of business stakeholder interests who represent interests without regard to the health of the whole organisation: this denies the common statutory responsibility of directors for the latter. And, as practised, it is certainly destructive of the notion of a career-based public service, which must lie at the heart of an effective, indeed high-performing, public service. This discussion of the content, intent, and limitations of the Public Service Act points to a number of the Act's limitations in serving the public interest. At this juncture, it is useful to reconsider the role of the public service from this vantage point so as to be clear about the switch from what is to what ought to be – and that the frame of reference employed is defined by the question: what changes to the role and operations of the APS can be made in the public interest?

A simple statement about the goals of the public service within the existing legislative framework might start with a comment on its performance in its primary policy advisory and service delivery roles, with the foremost goal of the public service being to discharge these duties effectively, efficiently, and innovatively (or 'productively'). Stated in these narrow terms, it is a role focused on service to the ministers and government. Nonetheless, the requirements of the Act to serve the parliament and the Australian public as well must also be acknowledged. Conflicts arise for the public service in serving all three communities simultaneously with no ready guidance in the Act as to how to resolve them. Moreover, there are other roles that the public service might play, or play better, if the role was framed by a whole-of-community perspective (public policy) rather than a Public Service Act or government one.

The Act's heavy focus on public service conduct can be seen to be a consequence of the absence of recognition of the public service as a cohesive and independent entity driven by its own goals. This absence of role definition expressed in terms of outcomes to produce, and the focus on how to do 'it', is destructive of public service capability to serve the public interest. The perceived need to specify requirements for the departmental secretaries to have regard to whole-of-public-service impacts; the expressed requirement for the Secretaries Board to work collaboratively, even the necessity to establish the roles of APS and merit commissioners; and the manner of creation of the Secretaries Board itself, can be argued to be a consequence of the placement of the department at the apex of public service support for the government, rather than placing a separate board supported by some corporate support functions at this apex.

For example, the specific requirement in clause 64(e) for the board to 'work collaboratively and model leadership behaviours', even the respective requirements of clauses 57(1)(b) and 57(2)(g) for the departmental secretaries to have regard to the whole-of-government and whole-of-APS implications of their activities, would be redundant for a board and head office–led public service, rather than the departmentally led one provided for in the Act. Then there is the set of values designed to steer public service–wide conduct. One might contrast this position with the sort of (public service) organisational behaviour that could be expected if goals (outcomes) were clearly stated in the Act and the APS left to largely determine how it delivered these outcomes. The Act makes the process the outcome, which is at odds with government regulation of other bodies and activities where the thrust of reform moves the regulatory focus from process to outcomes, and leaves the regulatees to determine how best to do this.

In reviewing the content and role of the Public Service Act, and having regard to the passage of time since it was drafted (notwithstanding multiple amendments), I anticipate that the Australian public (and parliament and the government) would be well served by the addition of two further elements to the three already set out in the role of departmental secretaries in clause 57 (i.e. of (a) principal policy adviser, (b) manager service delivery, and, (c) steward APS) with the important change of replacing the word 'stewardship' with 'leadership'. What it is and how it might be delivered underlies much of the discussion of strategy and structure in the subsequent chapters.

The first of these is the inclusion of a clear responsibility for government governance. There are a number of elements to this proposal. The omission of governance from the 1999 Public Service Act remains puzzling, but I argue that it should be included in this Act despite its subsequent (2013) inclusion in the PGPA Act for completeness (of the public service role) because it needs greater prominence to promote better performance today, and because the changing environment within which the public service is operating will only make this challenge more difficult in future.

I also believe that a change to the Public Service Act on this count should be prescriptive about the goals and content of performance measurement to underpin improved governance (and performance). The PGPA Act is directive at a high level – of keeping financial records, of measuring entity performance, and of preparing a corporate plan and annual performance statement. But, in the absence of further detail, it seems unlikely to advance community (perhaps even entity) understanding of public sector performance. The PGPA Act is ultimately focused on the quality of record keeping rather than performance and, whilst it may satisfy the government and public sector leaders that there is a common governance framework in place for all such entities, it is unlikely to contribute to improved performance measurement or to improved performance in public administration.

The final changes I propose to the Public Service Act to improve public service governance of government activities, is the incorporation of a responsibility for the public service to systematically record the policy formation process (in addition to the expenditure processes), with a policy-formation governance module to be developed in conjunction with the Auditor-General for Australia. As argued in Chapter 3, I would propose that the auditor-general be empowered to audit this process through a change to the *Auditor-General Act 1997*.

In addition to these changes to the Public Service Act to enable the public service to deliver an improved package of government governance, I also propose to accord the public service a more active role in developing trust and confidence in government.[5] By government here I do not mean the government, rather the act of governing of which public administration is an important part. The acceptance by the community of the right of any government to govern, built in part on the expected quality of its governing, is an important element in the effective functioning and cost of government. My case for this change is a pragmatic one and is based on three points.

---

5   Words such as 'trust', 'confidence' and 'legitimacy' tend to be used interchangeably. The first two can be distinguished from the latter as being consonant with standard market surveys, while legitimacy relates to legal underpinnings. Available data typically derives from such surveys and is therefore most commonly focused on 'trust'. As there is no need to consider the legal underpinnings of Australian governments, I concentrate on use of the terms 'trust' (mostly), and 'confidence' (occasionally), but note that, simply conceived, trust 'legitimises' the practice of government.

The first is that there is arguably a strong (inverse) link between trust in and the legitimacy of government and its cost, with the latter conceived as the standardised cost of delivering a unit of public value. Democratic (and undemocratic) processes can be used to frustrate governments that do not observe the will of the people, especially in matters where either the prospective costs or benefits are highly concentrated (geographically and socioeconomically). There are, therefore, benefits available to the community at large in improvements in trust and the legitimacy of governments, however achieved. My second argument for action is that not only is the relationship between trust and cost an inverse one but, with levels of such trust declining in Australia (and around the democratic world), the case for some action on this front is intensified.[6] Moreover, I suspect that these additional costs start to rise exponentially when a lack of trust takes hold across a community and reverses the onus of trust from 'I do' to 'I don't'. My final proposition is that levels of public trust in public servants invariably outrank those of politicians, which makes a civil service contribution desirable were public servants enabled to make a more visible contribution.[7]

I therefore include a contribution to trust in, and the legitimisation of government, as a separate element in an expanded public service charter, both for its growing importance and because the APS, properly enabled, has an important contribution to make. The statement should also include a responsibility to capture performance of this duty in line with the broader governance responsibilities of the public service. It should be noted that this is not entirely a new responsibility, underpinning the values and code of conduct, and is clearly stated in clause 57(2)(f) of the Act requiring departmental secretaries to engage with stakeholders.

A third element for inclusion as a formal part of the role derives from Simon Longstaff's (2015) observation that only the public service 'sees all Australians'. There is always the risk with majority rule that minorities and disadvantaged groups will slip out of sight and be left behind: additionally,

---

6   It may be argued that some level of community cynicism surrounding government is healthy in a democracy. Whatever one might think of this argument – and its premises need to be carefully stated in doing so – current levels are well beyond the point at which this argument needs to be considered.

7   The Roy Morgan Image of Professions Survey 2017 shows that health professionals are the most valued by the community (measured in terms of their ethics and honesty), and car salesmen the least; the former scoring 94 per cent (nurses) and 89 per cent (doctors) respectively 'high' or 'very high'. Federal and state MPs each scored 16 per cent, whilst public servants scored 37 per cent. The full survey results can be viewed online at www.roymorgan.com/findings/7244-roy-morgan-image-of-professions-may-2017-201706051543.

in today's world of ethnic and race-based politics, politocracies, and win–lose politics around the globe, there is growing likelihood that the sorts of community safety nets taken for granted in Australia will steadily disappear.[8] It is not enough that community action groups form around the needs of these people; it is important that there is a group within government that has a requirement to 'see' them in the national interest.

Nonetheless, I have not included this as a separate component of an enhanced public service role but have incorporated it in the detail of Table 5.3 below, in which I consider the specified five components and their implications for public service activity across the identified constituencies. Similarly, I treat pursuit of the national interest as a means to an end rather than an end in itself, but I am less concerned about the allocation of items to one category or the other than ensuring all key items are embedded somewhere in the revised role statement. What I propose as the role for the public service through an enhanced clause 57(1) setting out the role of departmental secretaries, would acknowledge the five elements as comprising this role:

- advises governments on policy
- manages service delivery
- provides leadership across the public service*
- delivers government governance**
- enhances the legitimacy of government.**

* Revised
** New

Table 5.3 presents this five-part role with consideration for each component in regard to the three communities to be served. For many of the rest, clearly required improvements have been indicated.

---

8   Apart from matters of equity, the work of French economist Thomas Piketty (2014) and others gives more broad-based policy reasons why minorities and disadvantaged groups should not be allowed to slip out of sight. Recognition of the rising concentration of wealth over the last 250 years has sparked a global debate about the long-term consequences of income inequalities for global economic growth.

Table 5.3 The role of the public service: an expanded view

Function	Serves government	Serves parliament	Serves the Australian public
1. Advises governments on policy	Takes government policy agenda and advises on best policy/program/service delivery combinations to implement. Brokers policy advice amongst political parties and actively manages stakeholders.	Provides meaningful information to Joint Committee of Public Accounts and Audit and other parliamentary committees on policy implementation as required. Briefs all parliamentarians as required.	Provides globally based policy advice to government. Has regard to the national interest and 'sees' all Australians. Actively observes APS values and code of conduct. Actively administers the policy formation process.
2. Manages service delivery	Advises on and implements best service delivery options. Manages contestability program.	Provides meaningful information to Joint Committee of Public Accounts and Audit and other parliamentary committees on service delivery as required.	Delivers services efficiently and effectively to the Australian public. Actively observes APS values and code of conduct. Actively administers the service delivery process.
3. Provides leadership across the public service	Ensures that the public service endures, is ahead of the game, responsive to government needs, and creative in its endeavours. Steps up efforts on performance measurement and cross-boundary collaboration.	Ensures that the public service is responsive to the needs of parliament, particularly in regard to its responsibility to oversight government activities with good data.	Publishes annual report on public service activities.
4. Delivers government governance	Provides government with means of monitoring, assessing and reporting on its activities having regard to its goals. Captures public value.	Ensures that the full reporting requirements under the Public Service Act and the PGPA Act are met. Publishes useful annual and performance reports.	Through published data provides the public with sound information to assess government performance in regard to the authorities vested in it.
5. Enhances the legitimacy of government	Assists the government of the day with 'getting things done' and accounting for the results.	Assists in the preservation of the institution of parliament through support for parliamentary, committee and other processes.	Reduces the cost of governing. Creates and captures public value. Promotes its achievements. Publishes annual report.

5.2.2.3 Operational pre-eminence is accorded to secretaries and departments

In this review of the Act, a critical point to note is the operational pre-eminence accorded to the secretaries and their departments within the public service domain. This is partly observable in the range of duties accorded to the respective key parties – the secretaries, the Secretaries Board, and the APS commissioner – but more particularly noticeable in the way that the secretaries are allocated roles and responsibilities but the Secretaries Board and the APS commissioner are only allocated a long list of functions. This interpretation derives from the definition of the word 'function' as 'a mode of action or activity by which a thing fulfils its purpose' (Moore 1999). On this basis the word 'role' might reasonably be associated with the concept of purpose, where responsibilities and functions are more of the detail of how this purpose is to be achieved. On this interpretation both the Secretaries Board and the APS commissioner might be argued to have a set of duties but not a defined role.

The Public Service Act clearly envisages the principal units within the APS operating framework to be the departments and the leading players to be the individual secretaries, with support provided to the secretaries by the APS and merit commissioners, and the Secretaries Board. The designated functions of the Secretaries Board further appear to indicate a project-based support role to the individual secretaries: the requirement for the secretaries to table annual reports and the absence of any such requirement for the Secretaries Board to do so is instructive in this regard.

In turn, the most important individual in the APS is the secretary to PM&C, who chairs the Secretaries Board and is the notional head of the public service. He/she is appointed by the prime minister following receipt of a recommendation from the APS commissioner, reports to both the prime minister and Cabinet secretary (a political appointee in Australia), and makes recommendations to the prime minister about appointment (and termination) of secretaries to departments other than PM&C and after consultation with the APS commissioner. Whilst there is no formal assignment of central agency status, the other agencies invariably placed in this group are the departments of Treasury, Finance, and the APS Commission (APSC).

In structural terms the APS commissioner is the second-most important person in the operations of the public service being appointed by and reporting to the prime minister, head of a statutory authority (the APSC), advising the prime minister on the appointment (and termination) of the secretary of PM&C (and, through the secretary, PM&C, all other secretaries) being a member of the Secretaries Board, and providing the prime minister with advice about the performance of his departmental head. The commissioner also has wide-ranging responsibilities for the establishment and review of public service employment conditions and conduct. The relationship between the secretary of PM&C and the commissioner might at times be a difficult one given their overlapping oversight responsibilities and individual management responsibilities.

The APS commissioner has an important leadership role – in upholding high standards of integrity and conduct in the APS, monitoring and reporting on the service capabilities required to provide high standards of accountability, effectiveness and performance, and developing APS workforce management policies. But these functions and activities are primarily supportive of the role of secretaries, notwithstanding that, in providing support, the APS commissioner has considerable autonomy in undertaking a range of these duties.

The importance of the pre-eminence of individual secretaries within the public service structure can be found in the Chapter 2 discussions of the models of governance and, specifically, the impacts of the various elements of the New Public Management (NPM) revolution of the 1980s, which are embodied in the Public Service Act. The academic literature pointed to some unintended consequences of these private sector–driven changes and top of the list for these was the impact on public service coordination and service delivery brought about by the fragmentation of the public service into a series of internally driven departments. It is not overstating the position to observe that within the constraints of ministerial direction, the public service has spent the last 30 years trying to undo this damage and build a platform for the sort of enhanced public service coordination necessary to deliver solutions to citizens in an even more challenging contemporary environment. The management philosophy underpinning the Public Service Act is rooted in the past and has become a barrier to effective government.

5.2.2.4 Whole-of-government and public service coordination is required but not enabled

The third point is that, while the Act accords operational pre-eminence to the department, it requires whole-of-government collaboration and consideration by secretaries in the execution of their departmental duties, and collegiate whole-of-public-service stewardship. As noted earlier, this level of interdepartmental cooperation might reasonably be regarded as the distinguishing operational feature of the public service when compared with the private sector. That is not to say that the Secretaries Board is not allocated significant whole-of-public-service functions – it is – but the Public Service Act makes no provision for dedicated resourcing, making it clear that the board's activities are to be project-based. In not requiring the Secretaries Board to publish an annual account of its stewardship of the public service, the Act also makes it clear that the board's role is to support the secretaries rather than provide the sort of systemic strategic leadership and oversight expected from a board in the private sector. Clearly it is a 'board' in name only, being nothing more than an executive management committee and without providing the direction expected of an executive management committee in the private sector.

5.2.2.5 Governance, accountability, and performance measurement

The fourth point focuses on the PGPA Act, which sets out substantial reporting requirements for the public service (departmental secretaries), requiring the preparation of annual reports and performance reports at the departmental level and annual reports for the APS commissioner and Merit Protection commissioner, along with the preparation of corporate plans. It is odd that the Public Service Act does not use the word 'governance' but, despite its absence, significant parts of the Act are concerned with governance – focusing on results and achieving the entity's purpose, compliance with the laws of the land, and providing for protection of whistleblowers. Moreover, the PGPA Act (which followed the Public Service Act by some 14 years) includes a clear governance statement – 'to meet high standards of governance, performance, and accountability' – in its objects.

Nonetheless, it is unclear why there is no specific reference to governance in the Public Service Act and why there are no definitions of this and the two other central terms (accountability and performance) in the title of the PGPA Act. This represents a missed opportunity because the word governance, at least, is a term in such widespread use across a range of disciplines and circumstances that, for the sake of clarity, it actively requires a context-specific definition (Bovaird & Loffler 2003). The absence of a holistic statement of responsibility for governance in the central Public Service Act has arguably been an important contributor to the public service's ongoing underperformance on this count: it was no less an important requirement of public administration in 1999 when the Public Service Act came into effect than in 2013 with the passage of the PGPA Act.

5.2.2.6 Ministerial role in public service appointments

Sections of Part 3, and the whole of Part 4 of the Public Service Act (clauses 20 to 38) deal with APS employment establishing the central role of the APS commissioner in the management of APS employment matters. Additional clauses establish appointment processes for the nominated public service heads – the Merit Protection and APS commissioners, and secretaries of departments. Clauses 58 and 59 set out the appointment and termination process for secretaries. The governor-general appoints the head of PM&C on the recommendation of the prime minister. The appointment of all other secretaries is similarly by the governor-general on recommendation of the prime minister but after receipt of advice from the APS commissioner and the secretary of PM&C. Termination of all is similarly by the governor-general on receipt of advice from the prime minister.

While the application of the termination provisions are subject to notions of procedural fairness, secretaries only occupy their offices with the ongoing support of the prime minister. Should the prime minister determine that a secretary has lost his/her trust, or that of one of the ministers, and should be terminated, then procedural fairness in the termination process is required but is limited to advice as to the grounds of termination and the opportunity to make a case for retention. This leaves secretaries and their staff exposed to political decisions. This latter applies despite the existence of clause 19, which is worded to discourage ministers from providing secretaries with any direction regarding staffing matters. The clause is not enforceable as there are many practical (and practised) ways around it. There are other protections provided for APS employees under the Act in terms of continuity of employment, merit-based promotion, rights to a review, and so on, but the Act's overall impression is that it does little to give effect to these important notions of a career-based public service. Secretaries are employed at the pleasure of the prime minister and all other public employees remain at the pleasure of the departmental secretary and departmental ministers.

Overall, these observations lead one to ask how well one can expect the public service to adhere to the values and code of conduct set out in the Act as well as serve the parliament and the Australian public in these circumstances. Ministers determined to discourage briefing unless requested, and who interfere directly or through intermediaries in public service appointments, discourage public service observation of values and code of conduct, including the provision of frank and honest advice, and discourage the collegiality that is so important to the effective operation of the public service.

5.2.2.7 The role of watchdog and integrity bodies

A simple definition and designated public service role statement in regard to government governance should recognise that the government established a variety of watchdog and integrity bodies that are expected to play an important governance role. These include the financial- and performance-auditing roles of the auditor-general, and the investigatory role(s) of the Commonwealth and other ombudsmen and the various ad hoc 'commissioner' roles (such as transport, health, public safety, telecommunications, and child protection). The impact on the public service of the various bodies and Acts goes well beyond the government's adopted regulatory role in the private sector and intrudes into what should be a self-policing public service role. As a consequence, it thereby diminishes the public service responsibility for good governance in government administration.

This leads me to ask whether the public sector needs dedicated watchdog and integrity bodies and if there are sound institutional reasons for them, or whether the relevant bodies established to oversight related private sector activities could oversight both public and private sectors. A public service with integrated mechanisms to properly account for program-level impacts and their role in achieving policy outcomes, and individual public service heads who are held to account by their ministers for the performance of their departments would not require much of this costly superstructure, and public service responsibility could thereby be placed more closely on a par with that of the private sector.

Whereas the establishment and administration of a suitable governance framework (at least in the sense of government governance), is substantially the responsibility of the public service, accountability in the context of the business of government is primarily the responsibility of governments. Of interest here is the public accountability of governments and the role of the public service. Certainly the Public Service Act (public service value 4 'accountable') makes it clear that members of the public service are accountable to the Australian public ('within the framework of ministerial responsibility'), and that secretaries are accountable to the agency minister for a variety of duties, as noted in clause 57 of the Act.

As demonstrated in Chapter 2, however, the displayed accountability of government has a number of determining factors, including governance choices, the consequent administrative procedures put in place to demonstrate performance and conformance, and the (government) choices made about transparency. Ultimately, the government is in charge of accountability, not the public service. While this is the case with the governance choices made by governments, and the supporting administrative procedures put in place by the public service, the public service has an important enabling role with regard to performance measurement.

It can be argued from the drafting of both the Public Service Act and the PGPA Act that Australian governments want improved measurement of their performance from the public service – consider the references to 'results' and achievement of entity purpose in the Public Service Act and the additional reporting requirements set out in the PGPA Act. It is equally clear from state and national auditors-general reports that this is slow in coming and, together with reports from other jurisdictions, that it is a global problem. Without dwelling on the issue of government willingness to match the words in the Acts with action on the ground, it is noticeable that our politicians have traditionally set very low standards of accountability for themselves – both in terms of measurement and willingness to accept public scrutiny – for example, in regard to political donations and their work-related travel and expenses. It would be easy to argue that this inherent aversion to real accountability extends into the public policy and expenditure domain. It would also be consistent with poll results noted in Chapter 1 that suggest the Australian community see our politicians driven largely by self rather than public interest.

The core of what is missing and required is the measurement of program-level impacts of government programs linked to government policy objectives and the budgetary processes to demonstrate how individual programs contribute to the achievement of government policy objectives and are being consequently resourced.[9] If it could be achieved this would be a major step forward. The second and related part of what is required is the expression of all of these outcomes in dollar terms, which, along with their costs, would enable the return on expenditures in different policy areas to be compared thereby enabling informed choices to be made about resource allocation. Such management information should also enable better decisions about what not to do.

5.2.2.8 The impact on public service behaviour

There is a broad range of elements to consider with regard to conduct of government – management and operations – ranging from how the public service complies with the many behavioural requirements of the Public Service Act, along with the manner in which it manages itself. These elements relate to the Objects of the Act (efficient, effective and apolitical), APS values, responsibilities of the secretaries and the functions of the APS and Merit commissioners and the Secretaries Board. In setting out a framework within which the public service might act in the public interest in pursuit of the goals outlined above, I emphasise the traditional elements (present in the Act) of the APS: giving government apolitical, frank and honest advice; being efficient, effective and innovative; and observing the APS values, code of conduct and employment principles. To these I add the notions of seeing all Australians and observing the national interest as being objectives worthy of recognition by a public service serving the government, parliament and the Australian public.

Some values and elements of the code of conduct are so important to the quality of government delivered that not only do they deserve to be enshrined in legislation but their protection also needs to be provided for in practice. So whilst the Objects of the Act along with the APS values may emphasise notions of an impartial and apolitical public service providing frank and honest advice to ministers, there is little or no effective protection in the Act as it stands for a public service that

---

9   Some of the necessary detail to meet this challenge can be found, for example, in ANAO (2017b).

acts accordingly. The capacity of incoming governments to replace department heads at whim flies in the face of the public conception of 'apolitical'. So, whilst there is arguably no more important value in the Act than that embodied in the terms 'impartial' and 'apolitical', there is no effective protection in the Act for public servants who behave accordingly. The objective 'apolitical' and the value 'impartial', whilst desirable features of public service operations, are not enabled by the Act. The same might be observed for 'frank and honest'.

5.2.2.9 Where is the long view?

Geoff Mulgan argues that long-termism in current governments is made difficult by the day-to-day cut and thrust of politics but that all successful governments establish three horizons of decision-making to create space for learning and reflection. There is the short-term horizon for day-to-day crises and issues, the medium-term horizon consistent with effective implementation of existing policies and programs, and the longer-term horizon that may look out to 50 years (Mulgan 2009; Chapters 1 and 2). Private sector management theorists such as James March describe this challenge as one of balancing exploitation with exploration, whilst strategists Gary Hamel and CK Prahalad frame this challenge around the notion of competition for the future (March 1991; Hamel & Prahalad 1994).

At the level of the Public Service Act, the notion of taking the long view is equally pertinent, whether pertaining to the public service role of principal official policy adviser to agency ministers, or of manager service delivery. Whilst the public service advisory role is rarely visible to citizens (other than perhaps through watchdog and integrity body reports) the advice sought can range from broad policy advice about program-level options to meet a particular policy objective or the detailed planning for public infrastructure, to regular advice to ministers in regard to the 24-hour news cycle and the crises of the day. Concerns may be raised that the allocation of public service resources is too heavily skewed to this latter. In the discussion of the performance of the public sector in Chapter 4, I outlined the views of past and current public service leaders and particularly drew attention to comments by the present (John Lloyd), and most recent past (Stephen Sedgwick), APS commissioners noting that the public service 'endures beyond individual governments', pointing to a duty of the public service to look 'over the horizon', and 'have regard for the national interest', along with the associated suggestion that the public service had perhaps become a little reactive.

These comments point to the way in which advice sought by the government of the day might be framed, but arguably also point to a role whose component parts include an appropriate time frame within which advice is considered and the national interest, and one that moves beyond the simple notion of 'advice' to one of custodianship of the welfare of the Australian public. Longstaff's notion that only the public service can be expected to 'see' all Australians is somewhat akin to the latter (Longstaff 2015). This fits comfortably with a role for the public service in serving the Australian public, and the parliament, in addition to the government of the day, as set out in the Public Service Act. It can be argued that the operational focus of the Act, the heavy emphasis on the government/ public service relationship, and the continuing devaluation of public service policy advisory capability, substantially limit the capacity of the public service 'to look over the horizon' in a productive manner and should be addressed.

5.2.2.10 The philosophical foundations of the Act

Discussions over the content of what became the *Public Service Act 1999* occurred over a number of years before the Act was passed into law. These discussions occurred when implementation of the NPM reforms were in full swing and notions of public service accountability and contestability, along with a focus on public service efficiency, prevailed. It is clear from the structure of the Act that this philosophy is embedded in it. The placement of the department at the apex of public service activity along with the downgrading of the centre, and the strengthening of accountability of departmental heads to agency ministers point to the presence of this philosophy.

As observed by others, this philosophy as practised around the globe quickly outlived its usefulness, with governments moving on to more joined-up, whole-of-government approaches.[10] The NPM's major legacy has arguably been its 'departmentalism', which is fragmentation of the

---

10   For a substantial account of the impacts of the NPM reforms in the United Kingdom, see Hood and Dixon (2015), and for a less detailed view see Mulgan (2009, Chapter 3).

public service by any other name. Yet, in Australia we remain saddled with an Act built on the foundations of an arguably failed philosophy which inhibits such change.[11]

There are many arguments to be made about problems with parts of the Act but, on this argument alone, there should be a substantial rewrite, placing horizontal cooperation – across the public service and external sectors – at the heart of public administration, and properly tasking and equipping the public service to deliver it and measure its impacts. One can only imagine how much different a public service Act drafted with joined-up and networked philosophical underpinnings would be and how much better the APS could be led and managed, and consequently perform and contribute in an alternative context. I next turn to the impact of the Public Service Act on the leadership of the APS, viewed in terms of the roles, structures, and resourcing dimensions of the Act.

5.2.3 The role of 'the centre'

5.2.3.1 Organisation of the business of the public service

There are three critical dimensions of the formal organisation of the business of the public service established by the Public Service Act involving, (a) the manner in which individual departments are structured, (b) the manner in which the departments relate to each other and the whole, and, (c) how the public service relates to the government. In the normal course of both public discussion and academic research, these various elements are commonly subsumed within a whole-of-government framework focused on achieving the government's goals.

---

11   Hood and Dixon (2015) review some 30 years of change from the introduction of the NPM changes in the United Kingdom and conclude, after constructing some purpose-built datasets, that notwithstanding the stated objectives for the NPM reforms, the UK Government seems to have 'cost a bit more and worked a bit worse' (p 183). They conclude, therefore, that the stated objectives for these reforms were apparently not achieved and consider a number of possible explanations as to why. Whilst the subsequent analysis is not conclusive, they leave on the table for further dissection possible explanations, including that the reforms were blunted by a changing social context, that they benefitted the change-makers, that entrenched interests somehow got in the way of change, or that they were only ever about political spin. My recollections of the Victorian Government experience were that (a) the public service was sidelined with the rolling out of the managerialist approach to public administration, and (b) the efficiency mantra was used as the primary justification for changes inside the public service and in the public domain. My interpretation of this experience is that there was strong political belief in the efficiency gains to be secured from the reforms and a strong desire to reconstruct the public service in the image of the private sector, that the timing was politically opportune and the message that could be delivered to the community at large and especially the business community by an incoming conservative government was a strong one. In Victoria the stars aligned.

Any public or indeed academic discussion of these issues would commonly be conducted in terms of the integrated activities of the public service and the government in the management of particular public policy problems, taking the relationship between government and public service as a given (typically involving a delineation of roles) and then working though the coordination issues. In practice, the contribution of the public service to good government and the alignment of the public service and government should not be a given in any analysis of good government but are important variables to be viewed through public policy eyes. These issues can effectively be viewed on a whole-of-public-service basis. Within the public sector management context any such discussion should be focused on the role of 'the centre', which, in this argument, requires an historical context.

5.2.3.2 Some history

In approaching the closing decades of the 20th century, the public service in countries around the globe was strong relative to the elected arm of government and provided much of the policy leadership expected of governments today. In varying degrees, this was a legacy of the major role it necessarily played after the Second World War in the massive physical infrastructure reconstruction and development programs that followed. Through strong departments led by a public service board focused on the development of a workforce fit for the task, it single-mindedly drove and coordinated public service activity to this end.[12] But the NPM revolution, bringing with it the devolution of authority to departments, the upgrading of the role of individual departmental heads, outsourcing of service delivery, and the strengthening of vertical lines of accountability of these 'chief executives' to their ministers, substantially diminished this role.

Laura Tingle provides an Australian perspective on these events, noting that it was the brief period of the government under Gough Whitlam in the early 1970s that started the slide in public service capability and was compounded by the introduction of the principles of NPM by subsequent governments during the 1980s. Tingle describes the initial changes – primarily in the way policy was formed and managed – as resulting from suspicions of public service allegiance. The more extensive changes that were to follow a decade later were foreshadowed by changes to the way

---

12   An account of the Australian experience is provided in Furphy (2015). See also APSC (2013a).

in which ministers and their offices interacted with the public service on policy, to the detriment of public service systemic and strategic policy capability (Tingle 2015).

Brian Head reaches a similar conclusion, determining public service policy capability was decimated by the events that accompanied the outsourcing of policy on the biggest issues (e.g. privatisation of public assets), and left it unable to respond in any other than a piecemeal way to the important subsequent changes in its operating and political environments (Head 2008). Head and Tingle both provide interpretative background to Sedgwick's comments about the 'reactive' state of the public service.

When observed in terms of the flow of history there was clearly a three-part process involved in the degradation of public service authority and independence, and consequently, capability. This involved, firstly, degrading the capacity of central public service leadership through the devolution of authority to departments; secondly, by the diminution in the independence of the department heads; and, thirdly, by the reduction of the number of government departments, which concentrated government management of the public service in considerably fewer (government) hands.[13]

And, as if to confirm the intent of this set of events, in 1996 the appointments of six departmental secretaries were terminated following the election to office of a government under John Howard. Having noted the loss of policy capability as a particular consequence of the changes described above, this was only one dimension – although the most prominent – of the public service capability lost through these changes. The greater problem was the loss of any real systemic central strategic management organisational capability in the form of 'the centre'.

5.2.3.3 Structural models of the centre

Most national government jurisdictions have a virtual public administration 'centre' of some sort. Generally it will be either a 'board' comprising the heads of government departments (the secretaries) chaired by the head of the prime minister's department, or it may be a formal or informal grouping of the so-called 'central agencies' – commonly the departments of prime minister and cabinet, and the treasury (and finance where these

---

13   Another useful chronology of key events has also been published by the APSC (2010).

two are split), along with a 'public service commission'. The head of the prime minister's department may also be formally designated as the head of the public service as part of this leadership structure.

A number of variations may exist around this basic leadership model, reflecting differences, many subtle, about the way in which power is exercised in the oversight and operations of the public service. In the United Kingdom, the most senior civil servant is the Cabinet secretary (a public service appointee) who is also formally designated as head of the civil service. In turn, the Cabinet secretary chairs the Civil Service Board comprising the 11 senior permanent secretaries. The board has general responsibility for the organisational and cultural development of the civil service as well as a number of specific responsibilities, including ensuring that the civil service is successfully implementing the government's program, managing risk, ensuring that national audit office reports are shared and actioned, promoting the civil service as a great place to work, and ensuring that the civil service is well prepared for elections (See NAO UK 2014).

The NZ variation on this model of public service leadership and oversight has a 'corporate centre' through which the three nominated central agencies – the State Services Commission, Treasury, and PM&C – work together. Whilst each has its own responsibilities, these central agencies share responsibility to support each other: in the case of PM&C to ensure that government priorities are addressed (a responsibility also assigned to the State Services Commission); for Treasury, the role is to provide budget context in meeting these priorities and insights into the efficiency and effectiveness of public service activities; and the primary role of the State Services Commission is to ensure that the public service has the capability to deliver the government's program.

The Canadian model is somewhat different again and more complex in terms of the number of players in the public administration field. The department heads are appointed by a similar process as Australia but are known as 'deputy ministers': they are appointed for an indefinite period but with the prime minister able to remove them on a simple unexplained basis. Canada's Public Service Commission is a body similar in mission to our own APSC, with responsibility to promote and safeguard a non-partisan, merit-based and representative public service that serves all Canadians. The most senior public servant and head of the public service is the clerk of the Privy Council.

In Canada, the Cabinet directs the public service in its application and enforcement of current policies and the development of new ones. Cabinet is supported in the coordination of government policies and in the direction and management of the public service by central agencies such as the Privy Council and the Treasury Board, and by departments such as finance, justice and external affairs which have traditionally been major central policy departments. The picture one forms of the Canadian model is of a public service more integrated with the political arm of government than in the United Kingdom and New Zealand, with employment matters the province of an independent body reporting directly to parliament – the Public Service Commission – but with oversight from a number of government bodies that are very much part of the apparatus of government.[14]

As noted earlier, in Australia's case the most senior public service body – 'our centre' – is the Secretaries Board. The Public Service Act establishes the Secretaries Board to be responsible for the stewardship of the APS, its improvement, and the development of strategies to address APS-wide issues. As the most senior public service body, it comprises the heads of all government departments, the APS commissioner and any other appointees recommended by the secretary of PM&C. The Act also empowers the Board to form senior management committees to assist in its duties. Sitting below this board structure are the individual departmental heads (and APS and Merit commissioners) reporting to their respective ministers.

5.2.3.4 The role and structure of the board – a private sector comparison

The standard oversight and management structures of a multi-business corporation in Australia would see a board at the apex and a managing director/chief executive officer reporting to it who chairs an executive committee comprising the heads of the various business units. The board and executive committee would commonly have a number of subcommittees sitting below each of them. The Australian Stock Exchange sets out the role of the board for ASX-listed companies as primarily accounting to shareholders for the performance of the business (ASX 2016).

---

14   For a more detailed outline of the respective roles of government and public service, see Bourgault (2006).

Box 5.1 ASX board charter

a. reviews and approves corporate strategies, the annual budget and financial plans;

b. oversees and monitors organisational performance and the achievement of the ASX Group's strategic goals and objectives;

c. monitors financial performance and liaising with the ASX Group's external auditor;

d. appoints and assesses the performance of the Managing Director and CEO, and oversees succession plans for the senior executive team;

e. oversees the effectiveness of management processes in place and approves major corporate initiatives;

f. enhances and protects the brand and reputation of the ASX Group;

g. reviews and oversees systems of risk management and internal control, and regulatory compliance;

h. oversees the processes for identifying significant risks facing the ASX Group and that appropriate and adequate control, monitoring and reporting mechanisms are in place;

i. monitors the culture of the ASX Group; and,

j. reports to, and communicates with, shareholders.

Some substantial differences can immediately be seen between the governing and management structures for the private sector and the public sector. The first of these is that, whereas the private sector structure clearly separates the oversight (board) role from the role of management, in the case of the public sector there is no such distinction between management and board: the 'board' and 'management' roles for the public service are rolled into one with the heads of the respective business units comprising 'the board'. In large private sector organisations, such a lack of separation would be regarded as a fundamental failure of governance.

The second point is that, even allowing for this structural difference, the content of the respective board roles is substantially different with the private sector board performing an all-embracing role built around accountability to shareholders. The respective ASX guidelines start with phrases like 'reviews and oversees', 'oversees and monitors', 'monitors and oversees', whereas the Secretaries Board focuses on the operations of the public service. Few of the standard (corporate) accountability processes are included in the duties of the Secretaries Board, including approval of corporate strategies, overseeing and monitoring organisational performance, overseeing the effectiveness of management processes, protecting the brand, and overseeing regulatory compliance and risk management and controls. Chapter 6 explores the separation of oversight (board) functions from those of management as an important contributor to the success and growth of corporate enterprise in the second half of the 20th century.

The third point is that the use of the word stewardship in the Public Service Act (which implies a support/service role), along with the establishment of a supporting committee structure to work with the Secretaries Board on a project-by-project basis using departmental resources (rather than the establishment of a dedicated team), both indicate that the Secretaries Board has a part-time, project-based role rather than an on-going leadership role. Oddly, the Public Service Act also 'invites' the Board 'to set an annual work program', 'to work collaboratively', and to 'model leadership behaviours': these are the expected activities and behaviours of a board, performed without the necessity of legislation. And, whilst the APS and Merit commissioners and the Secretaries Board (and the individual secretaries) have stewardship and development responsibilities for the public service under the Public Service Act, the systematic and systemic exercise of these responsibilities does not extend beyond employment and related matters.

Indeed, the watchdog and integrity bodies are the only part of the public sector that provides systematic commentary on levels of governance amongst government departments in Australia. These bodies have an air of independence from government, reporting as they do directly to parliament, but the capacity for, and actual practice of, this 'independence' is often overstated given that the legislation under which they operate is determined by the government and parliament of the day and the appointments to these roles are also made by parliamentary committees chaired by the government of the day. Through the enabling legislation and the accompanying appointments, the activities of these bodies can, within bounds, be constrained to areas that governments are more, rather than less, comfortable with.

A fourth point goes to the role of these watchdog and integrity bodies in both public and private sectors. In the private sector, the Australian Securities and Investments Commission (ASIC), along with other special purpose bodies such as the Australian Prudential Regulation Authority (APRA) and Australian Competition and Consumer Commission (ACCC), play the lead role in regulating corporate behaviour and mixing the roles of ex post governance with levelling the playing field(s). Importantly, however, their roles are designed to complement the governance regimes mandated by the *Corporations Act 2001* and associated legislation for companies and other businesses. In the public sector case, the Auditor-General for Australia and the Commonwealth ombudsman and other watchdogs and integrity bodies are, in part at least, an apparent substitute for a more vigorous public service–led governance regime. This acts to the detriment of a cohesive and strategically led public service, effectively absolving it both from some of its government governance responsibilities, and deterring it from taking responsibility for its own governance. I argue that herein lies a fundamental failing of our system.

In addition, the Secretaries Board does not have dedicated resources nor a budget of its own, publish regular reports, nor more generally account for the stewardship of the public service it has been awarded, certainly not publicly to the Australian public, which is the major stakeholder for whom this stewardship is conducted. Nor does the Secretaries Board account for its role of serving the parliament. Put simply, it is a body of people with limited time to give to the strategic issues that confront the public service and no dedicated resources to do this with. At best it might act as an effective executive committee, but cannot provide the organisational leadership of a private sector board, and dedicated CEO with supporting corporate office. More than simply another two layers of 'management', this latter is the source of additional skills, experience, and tools to lead an organisation.

Bob Garratt makes a strong case for the board role in terms of the skills and experience that it brings to the table, observing the substantial differences between the board and management roles with a board focus on strategy and the necessary governance to deliver stakeholder goals. He argues that the reflective skills (and time) necessary in contributing board members are different from those of the executive team. Oliver Williamson also makes a more general case for a dedicated 'head office' organisational capability, arguing that a threshold requirement for the success of large organisations goes critically to dedicated leadership and support substantially free from operational responsibilities (Garratt 2010; Williamson 1970).

This point is echoed by Mulgan, who writes about the need for governments and other competent and responsible organisations to 'create space' for these activities:

But all successful governments have created spaces for thought, learning, and reflection to resist the tyranny of the immediate, and any government or public agency that takes its responsibilities seriously needs structures and processes to do these things. (Mulgan 2009, p 3)

The question to ask is, what then are the expected sources of and role for leadership in the public service given that it exhibits neither of the structural characteristics of leadership exhibited by similarly large corporations, namely neither resources dedicated to the full range of corporate matters (a corporate headquarters) nor a dedicated board?

5.2.3.5 The concept of leadership

It is important at this juncture to take a step back and think more deeply about the sources and role of leadership in any organisational endeavour: the role of management, the role of the board, and any dividing lines. There are two overlapping parts to this discussion, the first addresses the concept of leadership and its sources, and the second considers the respective roles of board and management. There are also at least two schools of thought with regard to the role and sources of leadership.

The first, which might be described as individualist or American, focuses on 'the leader' as the primary source of leadership in business. In the case of American business, this leader invariably heads the business operations and chairs the board. The second might be described as the organisational or British model, in which the person who heads the business invariably does not chair the board, although he/she may have a seat on the board.[15] These different models represent varying conceptions of organisational governance and leadership with one seeing leadership in an organisation as founded on the skills of individuals and the other seeing leadership in structures and processes underwritten by the law of the land. Garratt has written extensively on this subject and below I draw on the distinctions he makes between the roles of the board and management.

In *The fish rots from the head*, Garratt distinguishes carefully between board and management roles by providing an historical perspective on the evolution of the modern corporation with its division between shareholders (who determine the organisation's fundamental purpose); the board, as the group primarily accountable to shareholders for their

---

15   Here, again, words can confuse because of a multiplicity of meanings. I do not mean by organisational, 'of the organisation', rather I mean related to the organisation of the business.

investment (who choose how the organisation's scarce resources are to be deployed in pursuit of the fundamental purpose); and the management employed by the board to lead the operations designed to give effect to the deployment of the scarce resources to achieve the organisation's fundamental purpose (Garratt 2010, pp 5–6). Garratt is clear that in considering what 'healthy' organisations might look like, the focus should be on the highest organisational levels, where purpose, means, and organisation take place; where the foundations are laid for the successive layers in the organisation to play their part, exercising within their own sphere of influence the levels of leadership and management required to achieve the various cascading business and administrative unit purposes.[16]

The structural leadership limitations of the APS are clearly reflected in *Ahead of the game*, the so-called blueprint for reform of Australian Government administration prepared by an advisory group led by the then secretary of PM&C with a senior and mixed academic, business, and public service advisory group.[17] This group proposed to reform the APS in four areas: the forging of stronger relations with citizens; strengthening the capacity of the public service to provide strategic, big picture, policy and delivery advice; improving workforce capabilities and harmonising conditions across the service; and a stronger focus on efficiency. In their own words: 'The advisory group has put particular weight on the importance of leadership' (Advisory Group 2010).

Consideration of the group's recommendations to improve public service leadership should focus on two proposed sets of reforms. The first is the proposal to strengthen the APSC to unite the APS and lead change. At arm's length, this seems an odd recommendation structurally, with a body sitting outside the business activities of the public service and focused on workforce matters, to lead change. It is also difficult to understand, in the context of the mixed relationships established between the head of PM&C and the APS commissioner in regard to the Secretaries Board, the

---

16   Although not an issue that I take up here, it should be noted that Garratt is especially critical of governments (more so than of the Americans) arguing that they do not understand corporate governance. He argues this following a detailed discussion of the role of the statutory director, the legal background, and the fundamental requirement that such a person has one legally required loyalty only and that is to the health of the whole organisation. He argues this on the basis of the common appointment by governments of 'representatives' to government boards. His criticism of the American approach is that the executive traits required to be a successful executive are not only different but somewhat opposed to those required for a board director. He goes on to argue that an extensive conversion program is needed to convert executives into effective statutory directors (2010, Chapter 1).

17   Oddly, there do not seem to be any published terms of reference for this advisory group.

appointment of the secretary (PM&C) – where the commissioner makes a recommendation to the prime minister; and the performance of the secretary (PM&C) – where the commissioner also prepares a report for the prime minister.

The second set of recommendations focus directly on 'reinvigorating strategic leadership'. These include establishing the Secretaries Board – to replace the Management Advisory Committee (MAC) – and the APS 200 group, to assist the board to discharge its duties. (The recommendations for the establishment of the Secretaries Board and its charter were subsequently enacted in full in amendments to the Public Service Act in 2013.) The criticisms that might be levelled at the reform group on a private sector comparative basis include: its limited vision in this regard, its continuing focus on the skills of individuals as the foundation of leadership, seeing projects involving individuals as the primary answer, and the underlying failure to actively consider (and discard) private sector–style alternative structures for the public service. It may well be that the sort of structural change pointed to by private sector comparisons was off the table but, in the absence of published terms of reference for the advisory group, there is no foundation for this view and the report seems to continue the common pattern of path-dependency in public sector reform.

While the report certainly addressed the issues of effectiveness and outcomes for citizens, which were highlighted as central to the future of NZ citizens (Ryan & Gill 2011), it did not adequately address the hangover from the NPM reforms in the form of managerialism and the question of leadership, the latter highlighted as one of the three principles that should guide developments as the public sector moves ahead. And, whilst it is difficult to argue with the view of the advisory group that it is people not systems who produce excellence and drive change, 'people' must put in place the systems and structures to enable and enhance change.

Graham Allison makes a number of important points in his 1980 article 'Public and private management: are they fundamentally alike in all unimportant respects?'. The first is his answer to the question of how public and private management are different.[18] He begins by

---

18 Allison uses the term 'management' to mean the organisation of resources to produce a desired result with a particular focus on general managers – that is, individuals charged with managing a whole organisation or what he describes as a multi-functional sub-unit.

asking how are they alike and concludes that there is a common set of management functions at general management level – providing a list of eight such functions ranging across three core elements: strategy (establishing objectives and plans to meet these objectives), managing internal components (organisation and staffing, directing personnel, and controlling performance), and managing external components (dealing across the whole organisation, dealing with external organisations, and dealing with the press and public).

Allison concludes by arguing that, whilst the character and relative significance of the various components differ between organisations and over time, there is a common set of functions and the challenge for the general manager 'is to integrate all three elements so as to achieve results'. He asks how public and private management are different and, beyond the observation that public management is harder, he identifies a broad range of differences including in time horizon, authority, media relations, performance measurement and implementation. In putting these two pieces together, Allison concludes 'that public and private management are at least as different as they are similar and that the differences are more important than the similarities' (1980, p 296).

What does this mean for our study? Are there good reasons why the public service cannot or should not be structured along private sector lines? And, what does it tell us about possible gains from the application of private sector concepts to public management?[19] Allison observes, bearing in mind that the study was prepared in 1980 when the nascent NPM had not yet emerged as a global movement, that performance improvement in the public sector is possible in many public management positions: 'perhaps by an order of magnitude, but the notion that there is any significant body of private management practices and skills that can be transferred directly to public management tasks in a way that produces significant improvements is wrong'. And secondly, that improvement will come, 'as it did in the history of private management, from an articulation of the general management function and a self-consciousness about the general public management point of view'. Allison concludes that: 'The single lesson of private management most instructive to public management is the prospect of substantial improvement through recognition of and

---

19   Remember, this discussion is about general management and does not include the role of the board or corporate office.

consciousness about the public management function' (1980, p 296). This is not a conclusion of fundamental differences between the two, rather one of context, and emphasis in practice.

Perhaps a similar case can be made for the consideration of a private sector equivalent of corporate office and board roles in the case of the public service. That is, that in the same way as the consciousness of the general management functions in public management lay unrecognised for many decades and continues to evolve, it can be argued that there has been similarly little interest in the value that a dedicated CEO and corporate office could bring to the public service. Moreover, beyond the practice of appointing boards to oversee government business undertakings, there is also (still) limited collective consciousness and/or willingness to consider the added value that private sector–style boards might bring to the public service with their diversity of skills and experiences, and in particular the dedicated role of the statutory director to the health of the organisation. A way must be found in which the independence of such a board could be aligned with the interests of government to produce better outcomes for the Australian public.

An important question in considering the differences between public and private sectors and the implications for reform is whether there are particular institutional or other operating environmental differences that justify the legislated differences between them. Are there differences between public and private sectors that warrant these structural and role differences? How effective are the existing public service structures and relationships? How can public service performance be improved through changes to the structures and relationships? [20]

5.2.3.6 Differences between public and private sectors

As noted in the introductory chapter there is much academic literature on the subject of differences between public and private sectors and whether they matter and on the related discussion of the adoption and adaptation of private sector management tools and research for public sector use. Much of the associated debate, however, is more ideological

---

20 Many of Allison's recommendations for the development of an equivalent general management capability in public management can be observed today in the subsequent creation of schools of government to teach public sector management. I wonder, however, whether the premise on which such schools are built, which requires a different educational framework for public sector executives, is the right one?

than evidence-based, with arguments pointing to fundamental differences including: presumed different motivation, an absence of competition, and a lack of private sector–style accountability. Although these sorts of arguments point more to differences of degree than root causes, they are made because these difference are viewed through the erroneous paradigm of a monopolistic as opposed to competitive public service.

I have already addressed the issue of motivation and argued for the presumption that public servants are no less self-interest seeking than their counterparts in the private sector. In Chapter 7, I further argue that there is little in the way of the private sector management tools and concepts that could not reasonably be adapted to public sector use. Certainly there are some differences of degree, but they do not justify a fundamentally different approach to the structuring and management of the public service. All organisations (should) have objectives, clearly identified shareholders/stakeholders, and a group responsible for delivering one to the other necessitating the same sorts of organisational leadership, management and oversight, irrespective of what sector of the economy they operate within. There is, however, a line of argument for inherent difference that requires consideration.

While I am unable to find satisfactory arguments to justify the a priori absence of an effective regime of government governance and public service governance in relation to public administration, the absence of a systematic regime of governance and of private sector–style structures can be explained by the existence of the Cabinet as the real board equivalent of the private sector. It can reasonably be argued that Cabinet is the peak oversight and decision-making body for the business of government, that through the political party (parties) it represents, it is answerable to the electorate on a regular basis and that, through the established institutional (parliamentary) structures and electoral accountability, Cabinet provides adequate 'oversight' of the total business of government including the public service. The absence in the Public Service Act of key oversight responsibilities for the Secretaries Board, and the existence of a set of independent watchdog and integrity bodies (auditors-general, anti-corruption bodies and ombudsmen) to support the government, is evidence supporting this argument.

Both in principle and on pragmatic grounds the argument doesn't hold water. Taken as the primary justification for the different structures between the public and private sectors, the argument fails to recognise that the public service is a separate organisation established under its own Act of parliament and which, in the words of a former APS commissioner, 'endures'. The political parties that form government are, in contrast, private organisations with a mandate to govern for a maximum period and whose primary organisational responsibility is to pursue the charter(s) of their members. Therefore, whilst the role of governing clearly lies with the elected government as supported by the public service, it is inappropriate to view the public service as a merely subservient extension to, or appendage of, government, as there are distinct differences in the legislative foundations of the two. One might further observe that there are distinct differences between the business of government and the business of the public service, with the former focused on the political dimensions of government and the latter on the administrative. From a public policy standpoint, differences between the government and the public service could easily be considered as important as differences between the public and private sectors.

A second and equally fundamental point of principle goes to the detail of the legislated responsibilities for the public service in the Public Service Act. The APS was established to serve not just the government of the day but also parliament and the Australian public. Section 3 of the Act, which sets out its objects states this intention as, 'to establish an apolitical public service that is efficient and effective in serving the Government, Parliament, and the Australian public'. Nowhere in the Act does it indicate that serving any one of these is to be subservient to the others. Clearly the APS is an organisation deserving of the sorts of structures and resourcing to meet the goals of its multiple stakeholder groups.

My third point of principle goes to the associated argument that the establishment of the dedicated public sector watchdog and integrity bodies (such as they are) with a duty to oversight the operations of the APS is further evidence of an existing holistic view of government embracing the government and public service as 'one'. Even if this were the intention, it would be ill-advised to place so much weight on ex post governance and so little on the establishment of ex ante incentives that should come with the public service taking responsibility for its own governance. A further point of difference is that the public service and government are subject to quite different kinds and levels of scrutiny.

By assuming that pursuit of self-interest is the primary motivation for individuals in politics and the public service, what sort of collective behaviour can be observed? Whilst acknowledging that individual motivation may not be translated directly into organisational behaviour because of institutional and contextual modifiers, evidence indicates that, in the case of politics, the pursuit of office is the primary goal and pursuit of good policy and 'seeing all Australians' is only seen as an optional means to this end. The sort of political behaviour that the electorate observes does not (necessarily) align with community expectations of good policy.

What, in the case of the public service, is the reward system? If the public service is closely tied to the operations of government and the prize (of career development) is awarded on the basis of political notions of 'responsiveness' then, for all intents and purposes, the public service is merely a vehicle supporting the endeavours of the incumbents to stay in office. Viewed in this light, the public service will be entirely reactive and transactional: all Australians will not be 'seen', and the public service will neither 'endure' nor have regard to the national interest in any productive way.[21]

This is the wisdom in Simon Longstaff's observation of the realignment of the interests of the public service with the government of the day some 30 years ago and is substantially the position today. If the APS is to serve the Australian public and if good government is to prevail in the future, it is necessary for the public service to be provided with sufficient capability and degrees of freedom to be more than merely responsive to the needs of the government of the day. It is not enough, therefore, to argue that Cabinet is the real public service board: the public service must have its own effective board, even if this requirement is only seen within the boundaries of the existing public service Act.

5.2.3.7 Differences within the public sector

Yet another question that arises in this context of differences between private and public sectors concerns differences within the public sector. Given that the elected officials, not the public service, lie at the heart of

---

21   There is an important side issue here that explains, in part, the more visible self-interest-seeking behaviour of governments today. Mulgan (2009) points to the loss of trust and community activism together continuing to reduce the pool of authority to be shared between government and public service that is available. In this scenario the government only maintains its share by diminishing that of the public service. This hypothesis could explain in part the behaviour of governments in diminishing the capacity of the public service to 'play the game' and points to further pressure for such change.

Australia's government, and given that these elected officials belong to private organisations pursuing their members' goals, one could well ask why there is not an equivalent act of parliament prescribing roles, values, and conduct for the elected officials in the same way as the Public Service Act prescribes such matters for the public service. Certainly there exists a ministerial code of conduct but this is a document of the government of the day 'enforced' at the whim of the prime minister, with none of the authority that is prescribed for public servants through the Public Service Act. This legislative absence is particularly acute given that ministers and other elected officials have unlimited power in regard to the determination of policy.

The somewhat heavy-handed regulation of public servant employment and behaviour compares unfavourably with the light touch of regulation of the behaviour of elected officials when one considers where power is exercised in government, and that this power is exercised by private organisations. A clear manifestation of this difference can be observed in relation to the practice of ministerial responsibility and accountability. There are no dedicated, written, and enforceable guidelines and it is very much up to the prime mister of the day how such a concept is practised.

5.2.3.8 How effective are the existing public service structures?

Our next question considers how the public sector is performing given differences between public and private sectors in goal-setting, oversight structures and relationships. Is what is in place working despite some evident missing links? The evidence suggests not, with public service arrangements for oversight of their activities falling well short of their private sector counterparts. This evidence comes in the form of the academic and auditor-general reports considered to date; but perhaps some reinforcement is needed. The UK National Audit Office (NAO UK) report *The centre of government* examines the role of 'the centre' in UK Government, and draws together insights from previous NAO UK reports and comments, in particular from the 2014 findings of the Committee of Public Accounts (NAO UK 2014). (In the United Kingdom, the Cabinet Office and the Treasury comprise 'the centre'.)

The committee's examination of civil service reforms concluded that the Cabinet Office and Treasury were failing to act together as an effective corporate centre, that the centre did not provide the strong corporate leadership the government required, and it recommended defining a new operating model for the centre of government. This would include the centre taking more control of key corporate functions such as finance, human resources and information technology, and the centre using its strategic position more effectively to ensure that government joins up its thinking and learns lessons from its past mistakes. Additionally, the report noted that both the committee reports and previous reports of the comptroller and auditor-general called for more strategic leadership and coordination from the centre in areas such as assessment of the key risks to government achieving its objectives.

In reaching these conclusions, the report identified the central agencies as undertaking strategic, coordinating, and corporate improvement roles. The report pointed to the need for greater integration, placing increased emphasis on long-term planning, greater cross-government integration, and the extension of central government leadership beyond matters of national security and prime ministerial support. The report identified particular needs/opportunities to include collection of information across government policies and programs, the sharing of good practice, and the provision of strategic leadership; exploitation of the government's collective strength; incentivising the right behaviour including promoting collaboration, integration and innovation; identifying and implementing more efficient and effective ways of working and presentation of a coherent view of government; improving government capability and articulation of a clear operating model for government incorporating clearer accountability; taking a strategic (i.e. whole-of-government) view of activity, performance, and risk, and allocating resources accordingly; and placing more emphasis on long-term planning.

If the NAO UK 2014 report found systemic weaknesses in the execution and conception of responsibilities at the centre of public administration in government, then a 2010 report, also by the NAO UK, provided a very good example of this oversight failure. Some of the conclusions from *Reorganising central government*, noted earlier, pointed unambiguously to the deficiencies of a system without effective central leadership and management (NAO UK 2010). The report's recommendations were:

a. There should be a single team in government with oversight and advance warning of all government reorganisations.

b. For announcements of significant reorganisations, a statement should be presented to Parliament, quantifying expected costs, demonstrating how benefits justify these costs and showing how both will be measured and controlled.

c.   Intended benefits should be stated in specific measurable terms that enable their later achievement (or otherwise) to be demonstrated.

d.   The planned and actual costs of reorganisations should be separately identified within financial accounting systems so costs can be managed and subsequently reported.

e.   A breakdown of planned and actual costs and financial benefits of every significant central government reorganisation should be reported to Parliament in the organisation's annual report in the year the reorganisation is announced.

f.   Each body at the heart of a central government reorganisation should share with the Cabinet office an analysis of lessons learned within two years of the date of the reorganisation.

5.2.3.9 How can public service structures be improved?

It is clear that 'the centre' is a virtual and notional collective representation of the individuals and organisations expected to provide the strategic drive and oversight of the public service. In Australia it is a role variously played out by the central agencies (PM&C, Treasury, Finance, and the APSC), the Secretaries Board and the two key individuals who head PM&C and the APSC. Notwithstanding these features, the structures, roles and responsibilities associated with these bodies and key individuals clearly fall some way short of the collective private sector equivalent. I have noted shortfalls both in regard to board-level direction and in regard to management. A reasonable question is, then, what could an effective public service look like in this context – in strategy, in oversight, and in organisational, terms?

In considering the operations of the public service in the context of equivalent private sector structures and operations, it is clear that what is missing at a whole-of-public-service level is the fundamental capabilities and mechanisms by which the public service could be led, managed, and developed in a strategic manner, and account for its activities to government, the parliament, and the Australian public. In particular, as spelled out in the ASX Board Charter, the role of the private sector board includes a number of key leadership and management ingredients that are absent from the public service conception of the centre. These include production, review, and approval of corporate strategies; oversight and monitoring of organisational (i.e. whole-of-public-service) performance; protection of the (public service) brand and reputation; and reporting to and communicating with (all) stakeholders.

Arguably, none of these activities lies outside the collective charter of the Secretaries Board, the secretary of PM&C and the APS commissioner. And a number are practised at the departmental level. But, in the absence of a real rather than virtual corporate headquarters with dedicated leadership and supporting resources, these matters are unlikely to receive systemic and corporate attention, being relegated to the basket of projects and occasional reports at best. Notwithstanding this observation, I have been unable to find a government jurisdiction in which the institutional and reporting arrangements as outlined above match even approximately that of the private sector for its public service arm.

Whilst many national and state jurisdictions have a board and a notional, sometimes designated, head of the public service, I have been unable to discover any democratic jurisdiction that duplicates the private sector practice of having a designated CEO with overarching responsibility for the strategic direction and results of the business and a board with higher, corporate-level, oversight responsibilities. In Australia's case, the key players in public administration are the individual departmental secretaries. It is they who have full responsibility and accountability for the operations of their departments in reporting to their portfolio ministers. In New Zealand and Canada some measure of this public administration independence exists in regard to recruitment and employment matters, but this falls a long way short of strategic oversight.

There is, nonetheless, a case to be made for a board that is separate from the executive management group, and a CEO/MD who is dedicated to the corporate role; these are the key sources of organisational leadership associated with determining what a business does and how it does it – addressing the questions of where to play and how to win at the highest organisational level – and actively building the systems, capabilities, and supporting synergies across the business to deliver on the organisational purpose. The business I am referring to here is not the business of government but the business of the public service. Viewed from a government and public service perspective, this is the role that should lie at the heart of the concept of 'the centre' in public sector terms.

I have argued strenuously that the public service lacks properly tasked and resourced strategic management and have examined in a preliminary manner the concept of strategy as it might apply to the public service role, along with alternative accommodating organisational structures. Whether one follows the arguments of Mintzberg (1979), Williamson (1970),

Porter (1985), Grant (1995), Lafley and Martin (2013), or McGrath (2013), a dedicated team could add great value to the development of the public service and its contribution to good government.

In looking at equivalent corporate structures where there is active strategic leadership in large organisations, there is invariably a separate peak coordinator's office. Williamson saw the value of this role in terms of both detachment from day-to-day activities making time available, and the use of this time to devote to corporate (i.e. whole-of-organisation) activities.[22] It is to the benefits of this dedication of resources to leadership at the very top that he attributes much of the popularity of the multi-divisional organisational form in the private sector during the last century. Robert Grant, along with Allison, attributes to this the substantial productivity gains in the private sector of the US economy in the latter decades of the 20th century.

When seen in the context of the history of corporate strategy, this 'head office' role initially was viewed as one of portfolio management. The synergies sought from this activity were to be generated at the corporate level and delivered to the operating divisions, often through economies of scale: cheaper finance and raw materials, risk spreading, and shared use of marketing channels and supply chains. Subsequently, the focus shifted to the active creation of synergies between business units when the top-down synergies proved elusive. This head office role was to be played by 'the peak coordinator' with a supporting team of specialists to work with the divisions, all divorced from the day-to-day activities of the divisions, each led by a senior manager sharing an executive committee with the CEO. Sitting above the CEO and the executive committee is, of course, a board determining which businesses to be in to achieve the organisation's purpose. It is consequently tempting in this context to recommend a similar structure for the public service, where there is presently an executive committee with the title of Secretaries Board and no dedicated leadership and support team to lead the organisation.

---

22 In utilising the American literature on organisational form and behaviour, it is important to be mindful of Garratt's point that the vast majority of large American companies and boards are chaired by the CEO. As a consequence, American academics conflate the board and CEO/corporate office roles, treating them as one. Williamson (1970) is an example in his discussion of the peak coordinator's office. In this instance, it is important to bear in mind the distinction between board and CEO/corporate office roles.

One option on a direct translation basis would be to (1) establish a separate public service board reporting to the prime minister on a whole-of-public-service basis; (2) appoint a public service CEO with a dedicated team to assume the corporate CEO's role; (3) populate the public service board with external (to the public service) representation except for the public service CEO; and, (4) recognise that the present Secretaries Board is in practice an executive committee and call it such (the public service executive committee) to be chaired by the public service CEO. To give proper effect to this model the APSC would need to be abolished along with the roles of the APS and Merit commissioners, and their functions distributed to existing departments in line with the recommendations of the 2014 National Commission of Audit. Accordingly, the role of secretary for PM&C would revert to the role of a departmental secretary.

There would, however, remain some difficult organisational issues to deal with that should not be glossed over. These relate to the existing location of activities in a range of departments that embrace public service activities that would normally be part of the responsibilities of the corporate office. These include any whole-of-government coordination responsibilities assigned to PM&C, along with the primary policy role played by Treasury and the accounting function of Finance. In some cases it might make sense to draw such functions back to the corporate office, whilst in others it may make sense to leave them undisturbed. One way of dealing with the latter would be through service agreements between the corporate office and the responsible departments.

The case for such a general 'solution' lies heavily with the additional skills and time that a (largely external) board and corporate office would bring, while the key to such a structure working in the public interest would lie with the level of independence accorded to the public service board in the appointment of the departmental heads. This independence could come from two directions. The first would need to be a primary responsibility to make recommendations of these appointments to the prime minister with a substantial understanding that they should be accepted. The second direction would be the independence from political and bureaucratic influence of individuals appointed to the public service board. In other words, a board composed of individuals with sufficient standing in the community to discourage the prime minister from taking a 'hands-on' approach to the recommendations and decisions of the board.

I have looked through the literature on this subject as well as at the structures of the civil/public service in a number of countries but can find any such administrative model. Were it achievable it would be my first choice.[23] A compromise, and distinctly second-best position, would be to effectively roll the duties of a fully-fledged board and head office into one by maintaining the Secretaries Board (as a board of secretaries) as the peak structure, with a full-time chairperson (head of the public service) and support staff. Attracting the right sort of person would require a number of the other changes, including a revamped charter for the Secretaries Board, the right to publish an annual report, the downgrading or abolition of the APSC, and the confirmation of a career-driven public service. The skills and experience of such an appointee would be important with a primary recommended focus on mixed public and private sector experience at chairperson/head of public service level.

The third best option is one from the past. Until some 30 years ago, the lead department in the Australian system – PM&C at the national level and Premier and Cabinet at the state level – was an auditor, observer, and monitor of the activities of the other departments, oversighting the implementation of the government's agenda. It held no operational responsibilities and, along with an active public service board, had substantial capacity to provide much of the leadership so missing today. Since then, these departments have assumed major operational responsibilities thereby negating much of their inherent capacity to provide strategic leadership. My third option would be a reversion to this modus operandi with the assumption of whole-of-public-service leadership by the lead department, with its head being designated as head of the public service and with support staff being added to undertake 'head office' functions. In a de facto fashion, this seems to be the position today.

---

23 See Mulgan (1998–99) for a useful background paper on this subject.

5.3 Proposed changes to the Public Service Act

A brief summary of proposed changes to the Public Service Act is presented in Table 5.4. The first set of changes proposed to the Public Service Act involves clarification of what was intended in the original drafting. Top of this list is the rather large curiosity in the present drafting of the Act, which is the requirement for the public service to serve the government, parliament, and the Australian public (items 12 and 13). Some small hints of what was intended are provided in the Act but it remains largely unexplained how exactly the public service is able to serve all three given the inevitable conflicts that arise.

The focus of the second set of changes is on reinforcement where important clauses are not sufficiently detailed to be enforceable. The Public Service Act establishes one of the core public service values as the provision of frank and honest advice based on best available evidence, but provides no incentive or protection for a public service that honours this value in the face of government reticence to receive good advice. Changes to the Act to address this matter are highly desirable for it is clear that this is the primary role that the Australian public expects the public service to undertake on its behalf (items 7 and 9). In addition, public service responsibilities for performance measurement and government governance need to be spelled out to make them workable (items 10, and 15).

The third set of changes focuses on areas that the drafting of the present Act 'got wrong'. The major area in this regard lies with the underlying NPM philosophy and the focus on the department as the apex of public administration. A new philosophy of strategic management of the whole public service embracing cooperation, collaboration, and coordination across departmental and sectoral lines needs to replace this philosophy. Items 1 to 4, and 8, are designed to address this issue. The final changes proposed are the additional clauses required to adjust to the changing times. These are primarily items 5, 6, 11, 14, and 16.

Table 5.4 Proposed changes to the Public Service Act

Changes proposed	Mechanism
1. The reintegration of the public service and its holistic management strategically, structurally and operationally, underpinned by a switch from the prevailing NPM philosophy to one of joined-up and networked government.	The whole act needs rewriting with the new philosophy.
2. The establishment of a properly tasked board.	Change required to the Public Service Act (and also the PGPA Act as well).
3. The establishment of a public service CEO and properly resourced corporate head office.	Change is needed in the Public Service Act.
4. The development and maintenance of a corporate strategy for the public service by its board and management based on its competitive advantage.	Change is needed in the Public Service Act, but much could be achieved without legislative change.
5. The assumption of a responsibility for public service governance by the public service.	This could arguably be achieved without legislative change but would be enabled by it.
6. Publication of an annual whole-of-public-service report by the public service.	This would most likely require change to the two guiding Acts.
7. Confirmation and strengthening of the Australian Public Service as a career public service, built around performance not permanence.	The clause that outlines this objective needs to be strengthened both as an objective and by the establishment of associated mechanisms and responsibilities to promote this objective.
8. Clarification of the goals of the public service.	Requires a new sub-clause in the Objects of the Act.
9. Strengthening of the public service's ability to provide honest and frank advice on best available evidence. The obligation on the APS to provide frank and honest advice needs to be matched by a ministerial obligation to receive it.	Change is required to the Act. Ministerial ability to make and influence public service appointments needs to be circumscribed. More broadly, duties and obligations imposed on the APS need to be matched by a ministerial/government obligation to enable their performance.
10. Formal allocation of responsibility for the public administration component of government governance to the public service.	This could be achieved through the Public Service and PGPA Acts but much could be achieved without legislative change. (The Victorian Act formally assigns this responsibility to the state public service.)
11. Allocation of partial role in building trust in government.	Requires a change in the Public Service Act.

Changes proposed	Mechanism
12. Clarification of ministerial accountability to locate public service accountability to the Australian public within it.	This requires change to the Public Service Act.
13. Clarification within the Public Service Act of the content and manner in which service to (a) the government, (b) parliament and (c) the Australian public, is to be provided.	This requires careful drafting in the Public Service Act including acknowledgement of conflicts and their resolution.
14. A reconsideration of the respective roles of the public service and the watchdog and integrity bodies in government governance.	This has implications for the Public Service Act and the Acts under which bodies such as the auditor-general and the ombudsman operate.
15. Improving public service performance reporting by building it around good (internal) management information rather than (external) performance reporting.	This requires upskilling of public servants and cultural change for public servants to take responsibility for program-level reporting, without being constrained by Treasury/Finance. A change to the Public Service Act that goes beyond an 'effectiveness' responsibility to a customer/public value responsibility (as a journey) could reinforce this refocusing.
16. The formal assumption of responsibility for its brand management by the public service.	A change could easily be made to the Public Service Act to achieve this.

Four further comments are in order. Clearly, the public service contribution to good government could be improved in a range of areas, including performance measurement and management, governance, and strategic management. Some of this 'under performance' is directly due to the organisational prescriptions of the Public Service Act, whilst other parts are more behavioural in nature and can be associated with an absence of 'the right' incentives and protections in the Act. Moreover, some part, however measured, will be due directly to the public service itself. My interest is not the assignment of responsibility for under-performance as a precursor to 'fixing' it, rather to identify the nature of this underperformance and look to structural solutions primarily through changes to the Public Service Act. I expect that much could be achieved in the public interest through such changes.

With an eye to the future I have also pointed to some changes that could be made to the Act to accommodate a changed role for the public service in a changing world. One such change relates to the decline in the regard with which communities hold their governments today. Some measure of faith and trust in governments needs to be restored. Not only because the (present) alternative is costlier, but also because communities can become ungovernable if cynicism and lack of trust come to dominate attitudes towards politicians and the associated institutions. The public service has a role to play here in underpinning community faith in our institutions and our politicians by demonstrably upholding the values and code of conduct and actively implementing the employment principles set out in the Public Service Act. This could be reinforced by a strategically led and managed public service that is self-aware of its 'brand' as a major contributor to the quality of government in this country. The UK Civil Service Board has assigned such a responsibility to Her Majesty's Civil Service, although this is limited to promoting the civil service as an attractive place to work. I have a more commercial application of the concept in mind, one focused on its customers (the Australian public in this instance) employing notions of brand value and its component parts, and a plan to build brand equity over time.

One public service, and the concomitant philosophy embedded in the Act to enable and encourage this, is an imperative. A new Act is required with a new philosophy of government and set of objectives, the achievement of which is specifically enabled by the Act. Whilst an objective of establishing an apolitical public service that is efficient and effective (Clause 3(a)) is not out of place in a public service Act, a higher purpose would be supported by a statement along the following lines: 'The creation of a strategically managed and cohesive public service actively managing its own business and reporting to government, parliament, and the Australian public on a whole-of-public-service basis'. I would also like to see a set of defined terms included in the Act that establishes the public service responsibilities for governance beyond the simple notions of performance measurement engaged in the PGPA Act. This would better encourage the public service to develop a capacity to take a holistic view of its own activities, to execute strategies to better support the government of the day and future governments, and better acquit their responsibilities to parliament and the Australian public.

The discussion of changes to the Public Service Act have so far focused directly on changes to improve the operations of the public service primarily from the standpoint of enabling the APS to become a more effective organisation producing better outcomes for the community. In addition to the recommended philosophical changes to the Act, another set of changes should be made to improve its usefulness from a public policy standpoint.

As it stands, the Act is prescriptive about how things should be done, to a lesser extent about what should be done (but still mostly described in process terms), and provides little indication of how the performance of the APS should be judged. A related point is that, while there have been regular changes to the Act over the last century or so, it has only been rewritten twice. I propose a more prescriptive Act in relation to the performance of the public service, containing a sunset clause and a requirement for review every 10 years. Such an Act could be drafted within the existing framework, incorporating the recommended changes in Table 5.4 and, most importantly, including process, output and outcome-based public service performance targets highlighting the prime areas intended for improvement.

It could read like a high-level business plan but would make clear the changes and manifestations expected of the next decade of development of the APS. These might include improved focus on the triad of outcomes, leadership, and effectiveness, but should also establish important component parts and signposts. Underpinning this prescription should be the notion of the integrated management of the public service built around capabilities (continuing the present work in this latter regard). In this manner, the Act could be prescriptive about public service performance. The alternative to this level of prescription in the Act would be to prescribe this level of content for the plans of (new) board and CEO.

5.4 Conclusions

In this chapter I have sketched out major changes to the role and responsibilities of the public service that I believe to be in the public interest, and have pointed to some consequential changes to the Public Service Act. Such changes are warranted by the changing context and nature of problems that need to be addressed from within the public sector and the ill-conceived foundations on which the 1999 Act was based.

Whilst a more responsive public service may well have been a desirable aim for governments back in the mid-1980s, when serious discussions about changing the original 1922 Act first emerged, by the time that changes were embedded in the 1999 Act, these NPM foundations were under serious challenge and a number of governments had already started to explore new models of government. Ironically, whilst the 1999 Act was designed to bring the public service to heel, it is clear that, by that time, the public service needed to discover new ways of framing and addressing public policy problems and that fragmentation of the public service and decimation of its policymaking capabilities would significantly diminish this capability.

The unfortunate feature of these changes is that the notions of a responsive public service, and one with sufficient independence of thought to solve the thornier public policy and service delivery problems, are not necessarily in conflict. They need not have been seen so at the time of the NPM reforms, when wicked policy problems were emerging as an important challenge for public administration. They can be seen as even less so today for, over the last two or three decades, there have been substantial developments in the academic literature in relevant fields including organisational design (for example, how to balance stability with change), strategic management (how to manage strategy in a rapidly changing environment), and public sector innovation (how to manage innovation collaboratively and strategically for results).

In order to entertain broader possibilities, it is necessary to look outside government and the public service for inspiration. By stepping outside the confines of the Public Service Act and the current experience and considering, it is possible to do more than incrementalise on a present unsatisfactory situation. One way of framing an alternative role would be to look at the activities of the public service as a business, and ask the question: if the public service were an independent business within the confines of the industry called public administration, how might it conceive, structure itself and behave? This would involve looking at the public service as a competitive business, competing against a range of alternative suppliers.

An alternative frame of reference would be that of public policy, considering the role that might emerge from the public service acting in the public interest. The necessity of goal specification would remain, but it would clarify the question of whose goals are the focus. In the case of the former, I suggest the maximisation of its influence as an appropriate goal of an independent public service, and, in the latter, the goal of any public policy–driven changes should clearly be some measure of community welfare.

These alternative approaches might be expected to yield different profiles of public service activity – a competitive public service versus an acquiescent one – and point to some possible changes. In the end, of course, the goal must be the improvement of community welfare and the public policy criterion must prevail, but it may well be that pursuing the notion of a self-seeking and independent public service will throw up some ideas that would not otherwise be identified and that might pass the public-interest test.

6

Organisational design

6.1 The setting

Fiscal pressures and the impacts of complex policy problems have led to a variety of responses from governments around the globe. In Australia's case, government and public service responses have included a focus on joining up services across and within departmental boundaries, the creation of super-departments (to internalise the coordination problems), the use of a variety of task forces, and the placement of 'commissioners' and 'ombudsmen' in the bureaucracy to build greater cohesion and urgency into service delivery. The government response to fiscal pressures has been to target smaller and more efficient government through a reduction in public service numbers, de-layering the public service, the establishment of shared back-office facilities, and to search for greater efficiencies through contestability and outsourcing.

In previous chapters I have canvassed independent opinion (academic, parliamentary, audit global and local) to form a view about government performance and, in particular, the contribution of the public service. Reflecting the views canvassed, the challenge confronting the public service can be described as a substantial performance gap across the related areas of coordination – within and across departments as well as across sectoral boundaries – along with performance measurement and governance.

The quantity and quality of policy advice provided to governments can reasonably be added to this list, given the progressive degradation of this central – at least in historical terms – public service capability.[1]

In addition, the associated academic literature points to the source of problems not simply lying with implementation and capability shortfalls, but in more fundamental structural and strategic management problems with the organisation of the public service. One such example, identified in Chapter 5, is the contribution to organisational leadership arising from an undue reliance on individual skills at the expense of an organisational, structural, contribution. Organisational leadership derives from structure, process, and dedicated resources along with the leadership derived from individuals in their respective roles. The following chapters address the public service performance challenge as a top-down challenge, viewing it in terms of a combination of organisational strategy and structure, and necessarily drawing heavily on the private sector literature in these closely related fields.

Reviewing the academic literature on organisation is no easy task. There is an almost boundless body of literature that addresses matters such as the establishment of formal structures; the alternative organisational forms; the determination of 'the right' span of control; the number of organisational layers; the creation of a suitable organisational culture; and the creation of roles, position descriptions, and formal reporting relationships. There is also an associated extensive literature on organisational behaviour and conduct.

There are, nonetheless, features of the organisation of the business of government, both formal and informal, that narrow the field. My interest in 'organisation' lies in the choices made in the act of organising, the relationships established between different organisational functions, the behaviour that follows, and the impacts on performance. My starting

---

1   The powerful Australian Parliamentary Joint Committee of Public Accounts and Audit launched an inquiry (December 2017) into Australian Government spending on consultants, contractors, and labour hire following the earlier release of an information report by the Australian National Audit Office (ANAO) highlighting the growth in spending on contractors and the use of consultancy firms in circumstances where the public service was deemed not to have the skills to meet consultancy brief requirements (ANAO 2017a). On 11 April 2019, Senator JCPAA Chair Dean Smith issued a statement advising that the committee had decided not to issue a report.

point within this (still) broad field lies with organisational structures; the primary lens through which I examine the design of fit-for-purpose public sector organisational structures is one of strategy and performance.

Whilst the literature on private sector organisational design is extensive, there is much less on the subject of public sector organisadical design and strategy, and even less on the linkages between structure and strategy. In summarising the position on these important issues, Geoff Mulgan points to the radically different challenges facing public agencies (2009, p 22), the limitations of public sector organisation theory in making predictive statements (p 107), and the absence of a single formula for organising strategy in public organisations (p 3). He does, however, argue that governments must have strategies (p 3), and that strategy and structure need to be aligned (p 107), noting that, in the public sector, strategies often follow structures and that 'All too often fiddling with departments and agencies gets in the way of achieving results' (p 106).

When, however, it comes to the role of the public service in government, there is even less instructive literature. Whether it is Mulgan or Mark Moore, the focus of discussion of public sector activities is invariably on the whole of government, embracing both the political and administrative arms of government, either explicitly or implicitly (Mulgan 2009; Moore 2000). A discussion of strategy becomes one of the practice of government and description of the actors, with such terms as 'public officials' enabling the authors to embrace any or all of the elected officials and bureaucrats in their discussions.

The failure to make these distinctions devalues otherwise sharp analysis because of the different roles played by the two. It can also change the focus of analysis of the business of government because of the different playing fields. The notion of competitive advantage at the whole-of-government level is most likely to be one related to competition for territory and resources with other jurisdictions (even competition with taxpayers as to who spends their dollars), whilst for the public service it should be one of competition both for territory and influence with other entities within the single jurisdiction of government. Similarly, answers to the question of how best to organise may well differ depending on whether the focus is organising on a whole-of-government basis, for public corporations, or for the public service. Moreover, it is a legitimate academic pursuit to consider public service strategy and structure across many levels of activity within the economy, both within and across entity lines, while being clear about the boundaries of analysis.

The following discussion treats the whole of the public service as 'the organisation', being interested in the way in which the public service interacts with its customers and competitors. This involves the internal architecture of public service organisation and the rationale for the manner in which the boundaries are drawn between the various parts. My approach is to conceive of the Australian Public Service (APS) both as a single organisation, and as a set of separate operating units (departments), tied together by a common purpose, and administrative systems and procedures and variously overseen and/or driven by 'a centre'.

6.2 The role of organisational structure

The organisation of any business has many elements to it, one of which is the choice of the formal organisational structures.[2] Their importance lies in the fact that they make a number of statements about the goals of an organisation and how to achieve them. These include:

- First and foremost, structures provide the vehicle through which strategy is executed on the one hand, and the framework by which resources are deployed and managed and activities are accounted for, on the other.
- When viewed in hierarchical terms, organisational structures are an expression of the relative importance of their constituent functions and activities, and the resultant structures should be seen as the result of moderation of the various claims of these functions and activities for organisational leadership.

---

2   The English language is usually rich in alternative descriptions of similar circumstances but one situation where it is less so lies with the use of the word 'organisation'. Dictionaries typically list three standard uses, namely the act or instance of organising, an organised body, and systematic arrangement (Moore 1999). In this context, the primary use of the term lies with its structural meaning, as in organisational structures. The term is, however, also useful as a description of the process of building and managing a business, as in organising the business. Then there is the third meaning of any business, indeed the public service, as an organisation. I have tried to make the context of use clear so as not to diminish the clarity of interpretation of this useful word.

- They importantly condition both the internal behaviour of an organisation, and the manner in which it interacts with its external environment (its conduct).
- When viewed as an adjudication of the competing claims for resources, structures also determine the economies and dis-economies of size that the constituent functions can contribute to organisational efficiency.
- Viewed in efficiency terms, organisational structures can be considered as an optimal number of layers and span of control.
- When viewed in effectiveness terms, structures and their embedded administrative processes give effect to strategy and enable the management and oversight of organisational performance.
- Organisational structures also house the administrative systems designed to give effect to measurements of organisational performance and enable good governance.

Organisational structures play many roles. The particular value of setting the analysis of organisational structures within a strategic framework is that it encourages better understanding of organisational design options, for the organisational literature provides a plethora of models, including structural models, models of conduct and behaviour, some holistic many partial, some static, some dynamic, contributed by a wide range of disciplines. Many of these models emphasise the importance of context in framing an analysis of the organisational dimensions of the public service.

A strategic approach also helps to understand the causes and consequences of making choices. The causes can be viewed through the linkages between the structures and the strategy that they are expected to execute; the consequences can be seen through the impact on organisational performance. An absence of discernible strategy, an inability to capture (and manage) the major dimensions of performance, a mismatch between strategy and structures, or of the structures and the performance measures embedded in the administrative systems, will inevitably promote poor performance.

Focus – on the separate elements of strategy and structure and their interaction – receives very little attention in either of the academic literature or public discussion of government and public service performance. All too often the public service is viewed only as part of 'government', often lumped in with the rest of 'the public sector', rather than being viewed as an independent body established under its own Act of parliament with multiple constituencies to serve. Yet in the context of the history of corporate performance, organisational structure is seen to be a critical enabling, indeed determining, factor both in responding to and shaping the corporate operating environment. My focus on strategy in a public service context views its contribution as determining the business that the public service is engaged in, the way in which the totality of its activities is translated into a set of interlinked building blocks, and then arranged in a manner focused on meeting the organisation's goals.

That is not to say that I do regard the other parts of the business system – goals, operating environment, organisational capabilities, administrative systems, organisational conduct and behaviour – as unimportant. These are each important elements in determining organisational performance, but it is the organisational purpose embedded in its strategy that is the glue that holds these elements together and which provides the foundation for consistent organisational decision-making across all levels. Moreover, stepping back from the day-to-day activities of the public service enables consideration of alternative organisational structures against the required tasks, processes, responsibilities and accountabilities of the public sector.

It prompts the question of whether the public service should be conceived as: simply a set of highly routinised activities, hierarchically arranged and managed as a Weberian style bureaucracy; a set of functions or programs sharing an interest in delivering products and services to a common group of customers; or a set of independent businesses (departments), each with its own (complete) structure with limited central oversight. Stepping back also allows consideration of the factors that should determine the operating boundaries between the various businesses and whether the same factors that determine whole-of-public-service organisational design are equally suitable for departmental design. Depending on the conception of the business of the public service, different leadership and control models might be appropriate.

Of additional interest is the concept of organisational structure as a living entity, responding to an ever-changing environment in order to meet organisational goals. My interest in structures is not so much about the (static) layering of an organisation and the span of control, as to how the bits of an organisation fit together and function effectively, having regard to the required external interface determined by the organisation's strategy, and how the organisation adapts to changes in its operating environment. Structures play a critical role in this regard, making a statement about the respective functions' importance, and both in formally recognising the necessary capabilities to achieve this adaptation, and in establishing the information and decision flows that determine how an organisation learns and responds to its environment. Notions of exploration and exploitation, stability and agility, innovation, and the organisational forms to give effect to them, are relevant in this context.

There is a broad range of important features of the environment within which the public service operates including: the institutional setting; the impact of a changing fiscal environment; the performance of governments; the political environment; and the causes, effects and legacies of past successes and failures. It is necessary to recognise the role and importance of context in describing organisational options, while not unnecessarily using this recognition to constrain these options to those consistent with path dependency.[3]

6.3 Organisational change in the public service

During the 20th century, the multi-divisional organisational form became the structure of choice for large American and European companies, replacing holding company and functionally organised company structures as the dominant corporate structure. It was (and still is) especially well suited to companies with a diversity of products and markets for the cost-based and strategic management advantages it confers. The three major benefits that this organisational form brought to the private sector included the economies of scale arising from consolidating divisional requirements at a whole-of-organisation ('corporate') level, including materials purchasing, capital raising and management, and risk; the active creation of synergies across the operating divisions; and an expansion of the organisational capacity to 'lead', with the establishment of a corporate headquarters with a CEO unencumbered by daily operations and dedicated divisional support. Three further advances in the corporate management field enhanced these advantages, the first being a growing awareness of the proper functions of management enabled by the establishment of a corporate headquarters (a point made by Graham

---

3   It is difficult to view options for improved performance in other than path-dependent terms if the solution to operational problems is seen only in operational terms. It is necessary to view these problems in terms of organisational purpose, or strategy at least; i.e. change the definition of the problem if non–path dependent alternatives are to be identified.

Allison and noted earlier), the second being advances in cost accounting and overhead allocation, and the third, the development of the field of corporate governance.

Only limited organisational change has occurred in the APS over the last 30 or so years. While the multi-divisional corporate form was one of the pillars of the New Public Management (NPM) reforms, the major reforms were made around this structure – tweaking it rather than changing it to better align private sector interests with governments. Some organisational change was necessitated by the introduction of contestability and outsourcing programs, and use of the policy–provider split, but these impacts on organisational structures were relatively minor. Similarly, the introduction of output budgeting along with designation of departmental heads as CEOs was focused on vertical accountability rather than organisational change.

Even looking more broadly beyond the governing structures (markets, hierarchies and networks) to the content of the respective models of governance (traditional public administration, NPM, joined-up government, networked government, and anarchic governance), to the structures resulting from the overall manner in which the totality of public service tasks has been allocated over the last 30 or so years, reveals limited change. There has certainly been the introduction of executive agencies and super-departments, but undeniably one of the more enduring features of public sector management around the globe over the last century has been the relative rigidity in public sector structures in the face of many decades of change in the private sector. Academic commentators looking back at the evolution of models of governance in the public sector since the NPM revolution continue to note that endeavours to 'join-up' government, and deliver whole-of-government responses to today's public problems invariably take place alongside traditional bureaucratic structures. But perhaps the solution lies in another direction?

At first sight it is odd that there has been little high-level organisational change in the public service when private sector history suggests substantial change, and when both public and private sectors are subject to the same changing economic and social pressures. These pressures occur, for example, in the form of bottom-line pressures in businesses and the companion budgetary pressures in public administration during economic slowdowns, and the growing community pressures for involvement and transparency in the activities of businesses and governments that help shape their citizens' lives. Indeed, it may be that effective organisational change has been achieved by stealth in the public sector through an expanding toolkit of accompanying informal organisational arrangements and behaviours, as evidenced by increased use of task forces, 'commissioners', ombudsmen and tools such as matrix management allied with the networking of other players into formerly closed organisational processes. Looking beyond structural change, then, makes it possible to observe other important change in areas such as boundary management, with greater porosity required in a world of (more) open government and networking. The associated behavioural change involved with loosening organisational boundaries may well have an impact on operations as large as any structural change.

In order to reach a conclusion about the nature and impacts of organisational change, it is necessary to distinguish between changes to the whole organisation and changes to the individual operating units. The primary changes in private sector structures have occurred around the organising framework for the totality of business units, rather than within the individual operating units themselves. This has involved the addition of substantial dedicated capacity in the form of a corporate head office designed to create and capture benefits from the aggregation of a number of separate businesses. Below this level the various business units might themselves be organised in any number of complementary forms. One might describe this as a strategy of integration built around markets, and a logical step in the development of overarching corporate structures evolving from the functionally organised form, through the investment or holding company, through to the multi-divisionalised form. The latter moving first through the vertical phase (cascading benefits from corporate to divisional levels), to the horizontal phase (creation of synergies across business units).

Yet, if integration for the purposes of extracting benefits can be observed as the underlying rationale for corporate developments, the opposite has been the case for the public service. Where structural change built on integration has produced substantial productivity gains for the private sector as a whole, degradation of this integrating capacity and consequent fragmentation marks the comparative history of public service organisation, including degradation of the capacity of the centre (and partial distribution of its functions to the departments), and the devolution of responsibility to departments.

The other observable difference between the two is the move towards super-departments, a change that has no direct parallel in the private sector. The drivers for this change are twofold, the one being the elusive benefits driven by shared back-office facilities underpinned by the opportunity to rationalise the multitude of legacy systems within and across the former departments; the other being the failure of some decades of attempts to 'join-up' government and deliver solutions to the Australian public.

This change has been more noticeable at the state than federal level. In Victoria, for example, it has led to public administration being consolidated into seven departments. Moreover, in this process, a number of departments have not had their traditional boundaries changed – for example, Premier and Cabinet, Treasury and Finance, Education and Training – but several large aggregated departments have been created, namely Health and Human Services; and Economic Development, Jobs, Transport and Resources, this latter department supporting nine ministers and 14 portfolios with an ambit that in previous governments would most likely have been allocated across six separate departments.

Of course, aggregating departments with similar objectives but different tools and domains is no guarantee that expected benefits – in customer focus, communications, back-office systems rationalisation, and staff numbers – will be realised.

It might be observed that a parallel exists with growth by merger and acquisition in the private sector seeking synergies between the businesses. Evidence to support this hypothesis lies within these super-departments, represented by the processes put in train to secure such synergies. The golden age of mergers and acquisitions in the private sector, however, is some decades back and differences between the sectors can illuminate differences in timing.

Moreover, the accumulating evidence suggests that past models of governance changes have not delivered the improvements in public service cooperation and collaborative endeavours sought and that capturing the potential benefits of rationalisation and scale is no easy road to hoe. Of itself, aggregation does not solve the problems of converting services into solutions. Creating the conditions for more internal and external collegiate behaviour, and the necessary interactions to deliver and capture the benefits, remains an elusive challenge.

Several points from this brief discussion of the history of organisational change in the public service and its impacts on organisational performance are important from a public policy standpoint. The first is that there is an absence of strategy, even observable rationale, to the various organisational developments. If one might, ex post, attribute some linearity to the changes, it would be the growing reliance on the individual department to resolve its own problems, many of which are common to the public service. It remains an interesting research question whether public service coordination problems are more easily addressed with fewer (bigger) or more (smaller) departments to coordinate, and the conditions under which either might be preferred. From the top, fewer (bigger) might look easier, but I wonder what the results are like on the ground.

There are at least two issues here, the first is the absence of suitable management models to work with, and the second is the suitability of the underlying skill set of public servants. Evidence of the former is the continuing flow of academic literature exploring the need for new management approaches to address underlying management problems. In comparing models – such as 'competitive', 'authoritative', and 'collaborative' – academic agreement indicates that collaboration is the way of the future, however, this literature is at an early stage of development focusing on management paradigms and is not yet able to describe the decision-making model that gives effect to a continuous flow of successful collaborations across the public service, nor to the sources of new-found skills and collegiate intent that give rise to it.[4]

Argument for the latter – a deficiency in public service skills – is provided by Mulgan, who points out that the training of public servants in the disciplines that dominate the staffing of most public service departments misses out on the skills to understand how complex systems work. This concern is accompanied by his observation that the future is likely to bring more pressure to join-up government through a growing mix of horizontal and vertical structures (Mulgan 2009, Chapter 10 esp p 193 ff).

If this discussion suggests that there are unanswered questions – about the consequences of public service fragmentation (and the value of an integrative approach), and the development of new organisational and management models – then two further points follow the same line.

---

4   See, for example, the discussion of collaboration in Bommert who notes a number of shortcomings of this literature (Bommert 2010).

One area of common focus, and one in which there is little systematic evidence available on which to form a view, is the impact of size on organisational efficiency, a particularly pertinent issue in the presence of the fashion for super-departments, and the projected impacts of dis-economies of size.

Oliver Williamson has identified substantial a priori reasons for concern with this fashion. He attributes the capacity of the modern corporation to reinvent itself through organisational change as a means of escaping the inevitable inefficiencies arising from size. These inefficiencies stem from bureaucratic disabilities, in particular what Williamson characterised as control loss (the degrading of information as it moved through an increasing number of organisational layers), and sub-goal pursuit (the opportunity for individual managers to pursue their own goals in this context) (Williamson 1970).

What Williamson saw as distinctive about his theory was the corporation's capacity to avoid, but never completely escape, the growing size-based efficiency losses through changes in organisational form with the accompanying development of a strong and leading headquarters. As the bureaucratic disabilities Williamson noted are common to both public and private bureaucracies, and there is no evidence of similar organisational change in the public sector, the question is whether the public sector has somehow escaped these shackles through other means, or whether it is unknowingly suffering from severe indigestion associated with 'bureaucratic disabilities'. Williamson's theorising suggests that the prevailing public sector approach – of increasing operating unit size – could bring with it a substantial price in organisational efficiency terms even if there were some effectiveness gains secured. There is a discernible trend to establish super-departments and, in the absence of published data, scepticism about the motives and benefits associated with such amalgamations is justified.

The final point in this summary notes the impacts of organisational change as an important area where the limitations of our knowledge constrains the capacity of the public service to adjust to contextual change. I have noted some parliamentary interest in this issue in the United Kingdom and Victoria,[5] and I have also pointed to the Australian Public Service Commission (APSC) commentary in its *State of the service report 2013–14* indicating a high level of impact on the public service from the machinery of government changes associated with the election of Tony Abbott as prime minister in 2013.

The history of organisational change in the public service suggests no discernible efficiency-based rationale for the mixture of machinery-of-government changes and departmentally inspired restructurings. Relative to both its own history and the growing challenge to integrate activities – to join-up and network – the position of today's organisation of the public service is divided and lacking unity.

The question is whether there is a better way to organise. An examination of organisational design developments in the private sector provides a sense of the issues being addressed, along with the resultant structures.

6.4 Organisational design in the private sector

6.4.1 Themes in organisational design: Lam

6.4.1.1 One best way to organise

As described by Alice Lam, the classical theory of organisational design in the 20th century was preoccupied with the notion of 'one best way to organise'. The work of Max Weber on bureaucracy and Alfred Chandler on the multi-divisional form were most influential in their respective domains. During the 1960s and 1970s, however, the assumption of one best way was challenged by research into private sector organisation that related the organisational form to the context within which it operated. Key contextual factors were identified to include scale, scope, technology,

---

5   Following the publication of a Victorian Government Parliamentary Committee report in May 2016 into the costs and benefits of the substantial machinery-of-government changes that occurred following the November 2014 state election, the Department of Treasury and Finance published an operating guide (Nov 2016) for affected agencies. It is a process-driven document with a 100-day plan to establish a new entity, but no discussion of capturing the costs and benefits after the event, let alone building a business case before the event, despite the recommendations of the Parliamentary Committee (Parliament of Victoria 2016b).

and environment, and the evolving views of context and structure saw more adaptive and flexible structures developed. This is the first theme drawn from Lam's survey (Lam 2005).

6.4.1.2 Organisational integration

A second theme to emerge from this literature is that of organisational integration. The field of industrial organisation examines the relationship between industry structure and organisational performance. It sees individual organisational structure as both a cause and effect of managerial choice and as part of a whole-of-organisation strategy to compete effectively in its chosen environment. The organisational integration hypothesis directs our attention to the internal cohesiveness of the firm as a critical determinant of corporate strategy and innovative performance. This discussion of organisational integration offers useful insights into the public sector where building integrated networks and integration capabilities to confront complex problems is seen to be a critical element of the effective response to these problems.

6.4.1.3 Organisational networks

A third theme involves the growing literature on networks that shifts the primary focus of enquiry away from formal to informal structures, organisational processes, relationships, and organisational boundaries. Much of this contribution comes from the field of economics initiated by the work of Ronald Coase on the boundaries of the firm and the subsequent development of the field of transaction costs as an explanator of organisational boundaries (Coase 1937). The importance of these concepts – of organisational boundaries and transaction costs – is that they encourage an expansive view of 'the organisation' as one having access to an array of resources, not just those employed internally, and with more fluid boundaries. This array includes relationships with external organisations covering a broad range of activities – such as partnerships, professional associations, pre-competitive research arrangements, benchmarking, risk-sharing, industry development and collaborations. In some theories, these external resources are seen as sufficiently important to replace the concept of organisational capabilities with that of resources = capabilities + networks. Clearly, such organisations are more open to the external environment, which particularly suits industries facing continuous change, little in the way of fixed assets, and constituent firms competing on the basis of a transient competitive advantage.

6.4.1.4 Organisational cognition and learning

A fourth theme – based on a stream of research on organisational cognition and learning – focuses on internal processes, seeing the organisation as one that learns, acquires and creates knowledge. It is a multi-dimensional field of study regarding the acquisition, processing, creation, and application of knowledge within the organisation. Whilst much of this research focuses on the mental models – individual and collective – used to process information, an important part focuses on its acquisition and the porosity of the organisation's boundaries particularly in the context of learning, and the impact of structures on an organisation's capacity to 'learn'.

One stream of this literature focuses on the way in which organisations adapt to their environments. A recurring theme is the need to balance the forces of continuity and change. The architecture of the firm can be described as a combination of rules/routines/processes: skill sets and core competencies, hierarchies and structures, built around notions of competitive advantage and/or efficiency/effectiveness. The success of an organisation then derives from the standardisation and routinisation of basic organisational processes whilst simultaneously being able to capture and embed changes in the external environment into these routines/rules/processes. A number of similar and complementary solutions to this challenge are identified, including the need to balance exploitation with exploration (March 1991), the division of strategy into deliberate and emergent (Mintzberg & Waters 1985), organisational ambidexterity (Tushman & O'Reilly 1996; O'Rielly & Tushman 2013), a focus on the design of business (Martin 2009) and, more recently, transient advantage (as opposed to sustainable competitive advantage) (McGrath 2013).

Another stream of this same literature focuses on organisational inertia. One subset sees organisations that respond slowly to environmental change as being dominated by organisational inertia. The second strand builds on this and sees organisational transformation as discontinuous and occurring in a short period of time. The third perspective, which Lam describes as strategic adaptation, sees the interplay between organisation and environment as two-way, stressing the role of management and learning and the importance of continuous change and adaptation in coping with environmental turbulence and uncertainty. Achieving this balance is one of the prime duties of corporate headquarters outlined by Henry Mintzberg (what Rita McGrath describes as 'achieving the balance between agility and stability').

A particularly important component of the process of strategic adaptation is the acquisition and use of market intelligence. Over the last two decades there has been rapid private sector growth in the acquisition and application of 'business intelligence' fuelled by the development of electronic data-processing systems. This in turn has supported the notion of organisational knowledge management and an examination of the merits of different acquisition and processing systems – for example, the codified electronically stored system as opposed to the personalised, shared system relying more on social interaction for transmission. Another interesting recent development examines the strategy of global exploitation of local knowledge, which underpins the work on 'meta-nationals', a concept that is immediately relevant to the public service in terms of how to identify, capture, and multiply best practice across such a large organisation (Doz et al. 2001).

In keeping with the corporate strategy literature, a further distinction can be drawn between corporate (whole-of-organisation/whole-of-public-service) and business (divisional/departmental) intelligence. This distinction is relevant to an examination of the two-way relationship between the external environment and organisational structures. It is important to understand how an organisation translates strategy into structure and activity on the ground on the one hand, and filters market intelligence up the organisational tree to influence strategy. It also requires acknowledgement of the distinctive capabilities (core competences) required to develop and implement strategy (Hamel & Prahalad 1994).

Finally, a discussion of organisational learning and management needs to acknowledge the role of the board. In introducing the notion of the learning board to the discussion of corporate governance, Bob Garratt visualises the role of the board of directors as a point of convergence between two pyramids: the executive system of day-to-day management faces upwards towards the board, the other is an inverted pyramid that represents the outside world influences comprising trends, uncertainties, and disruptions, focused on the board. As described, the point of convergence is the board, responsible as it is for the immediate and long-term health of the business.

Garratt both coined the term and presents this notion of 'the learning board' in the context of the board role being to provide momentum, leadership, and movement, balanced with prudent control of the daily operations of the business (2010, p 33). As such, it is the board that is responsible for governance and strategy.[6] When viewed in this setting, it is not difficult to understand why Garratt emphasises the clear differences between board and management roles, the diversity of experiences and skill sets that successful boards require, and the difficulties of single individuals occupying both CEO and board chairman roles.

This broad stream of literature on organisational learning, which might be viewed holistically as an organisation negotiating with its environment, is also important because it acknowledges the need for an organisation to simultaneously exploit the competences that provide a competitive advantage in its chosen marketplace but remain open to the development of new competences (and the dismantling of old!) in relation to a changing external environment. One way of viewing the overall challenge is of the need to find ways in which order and chaos can profitably coexist and be converted into a set of integrated organisational responses on an ongoing basis. Developing structures and capabilities to cope with continuous organisational change, rather than seeing change as a discontinuous set of projects, is key to organisational success in such a fluid environment.

6.4.1.5 Inter- and intra-organisational collaboration

The fifth theme points to important differences between public and private sectors. Widely practised in the private sector to the point where it might reasonably be regarded as a core component of corporate strategy, inter-organisational collaboration comes in many shapes and sizes. These range from research consortia, joint ventures, strategic alliances and subcontracting, and span a wide range of functions and business processes. In turn, these collaborations range from networks deep in trust with close ties to those with weak ties that provide limited access. These various forms of inter-organisational cooperation are well developed in the private sector but less so in the public sector, which continues to discover the benefits of networking.

---

6   Interestingly, and again in the context of a discussion of the role of the board, Garratt draws a distinction between the board's role in policy formation and the development of strategy. He identifies policy as the highest level of organisational thought and action to achieve fundamental organisational purpose, describing it as concerning the political will of the organisation in relation to its ever-changing external environment. He describes strategy as the deployment of scarce resources to achieve organisational purpose and within the established policy framework. Without pursuing Garratt's distinction, I continue to raise the matter of board value-added in the public service context.

The observation of the many challenges of effective intra-public service cooperation, whether across multiple departmental lines in program delivery, or amongst central agencies in the provision of strategic direction, has been accompanied by a rapid expansion in theoretical research as to 'how to', but is yet to be followed by applied research assessing the merits of proposed solutions. Research into the governance of these organisational forms and networks may well in time offer insights into the prevailing problems of collaboration faced in the public sector. Such research should recognise the distinction between traditional (Weberian) coordination, and the collaboration that dominates today's academic discussions of public service teamwork. The literature on collaborative innovation, which seeks to develop models of public sector collaboration is the most developed form of the latter, an important part of which sees this form of innovation as the way ahead for a public sector struggling to maintain connection with its environment (Hartley 2005; Bommert 2010; Sørensen & Torfing 2011, 2012; Hartley, Sørensen & Torfing 2013; Lægreid et al. 2013). The risk is that a focus on collaboration rather than coordination risks reducing the 'solution' to a set of projects at the expense of focusing on the whole-of-public-service culture, with the benefits that might bring over time.

6.4.1.6 Organisational size and efficiency

The sixth and final theme from Lam's survey is the relationship between organisational size, age and efficiency. A set of issues outlined by Lam and developed by Mintzberg and Williamson can be considered in the context of the optimal size of the public sector as an aggregate entity and in terms of its component parts and boundaries. Mintzberg (1979) proposed that, as organisations aged, they became more rigid and hierarchical, whilst Williamson (1970) noted the diseconomies of scale associated with control loss and managerial discretion.

This theorising raises concerns about the organisational efficiency of public service activities given the scale and longevity of the structures employed. Given recent fiscal pressures on the public sector and the creation of super-departments to enable back-office economies to be more readily captured and the building of a customer-driven focus, more efficiency (inputs/costs) and more effectiveness (outputs/benefits) result. Unfortunately, as noted earlier, one area of public sector activity in which governance is especially weak is in structural change. There is little 'evidence' to base judgements upon, other than a regular list of concerns about the decision-making and implementation processes, and a lack of government interest in tracking the costs (or benefits).

In addition, a stream of audit reports at state, national, and international level casts doubt on the capacity of the public sector to capture targeted benefits from, for example, consolidated information technology–based activities. These conclusions are supported by recent research into three decades of reform and change in the UK central government, which concluded that information technology costs continued to rise over a long period, despite the advances of technology and the consolidation of operations (Hood & Dixon 2015). This broad subject is beyond the boundaries of this book but continues to lie in the background.

Table 6.1 Themes in private sector organisational design

Theme	Public sector relevance
1. One best way to organise	The dominant 20th-century structure for the public service has remained intact into the 21st century in the face of substantial private sector organisational change. Some change at the margin with super-departments and executive agencies.
2. Organisational integration	Achieving whole-of-public-service cohesion is important following the NPM fragmentation and emergence of wicked problems. Coordination, collaboration, strategy and structure all-important for one public service, along with culture.
3. Networks	The growth in networked policy advice and service provision encourages a focus on organisational boundaries and management of the external interface as well as on accountability mechanisms.
4. Organisational cognition, learning and adaptation	Fiscal pressures and social change make it important to build adaptive systems and capabilities and structures. Market intelligence, organisational memory, porosity of organisational boundaries, design thinking, and a career public service are all key features of this element.
5. Inter-and intra-organisational collaboration	So-called horizontal strategy or intra-organisational strategy is a core component of corporate strategy but seems poorly understood in the public sector. Strengthening strategic and operating linkages between government departments and external parties is important to the future of the public service.
6. Organisational size and efficiency	As size of government is largely a given in any jurisdiction, the real question is the impact on efficiency of the way in which the parts are conceived and assembled. There are important effectiveness, efficiency, and strategic management considerations that follow.

6.4.1.7 Drivers that emerge

Over the last two decades, the number one organisational problem addressed in the academic literature relating to public sector management is organisational design, and in the business strategy literature has been the management challenge of coping with change. In the public sector literature, the development of management models for collaborative innovation has been matched by a focus in the organisational literature on the simultaneous exploitation of existing competitive advantage alongside the exploration of new advantage. In the strategy literature, the focus has been on the emergence of design thinking and innovation as central to effective strategy, and development of the notion of transient advantage as a prospective replacement for sustainable advantage.

The core of the organisational response to this new perception of the operating environment – described by McGrath (2013, p xi) in terms of the need for executives to learn how to exploit short-lived opportunities with speed and decisiveness in volatile and uncertain environments – is the ambidextrous organisation. The modern origin of this concept lies with a seminal paper published by James March (1991) in which he made a number of observations, some counterintuitive, that are accepted today as conventional wisdom. March pointed to the central concern of studies as adaptive organisational processes, being the relation between the exploitation of certainties and the exploration of new possibilities. Adaptive systems that engage in one to the exclusion of the other are likely to find themselves with either too many undeveloped ideas or trapped in a sub-optimal stable equilibrium. The challenge is to maintain an appropriate balance.

In surveying the established literature, March pointed to the organisational tendency to build capability faster in exploitation than exploration and reward it accordingly, making adaptive processes potentially self-defeating. March then went on to model the conditions under which an appropriate balance might be achieved between the two, exploring the impact of factors such as the diversity of beliefs and knowledge between individuals, the gap between individual beliefs and the organisational code, the rate of organisational learning, along with the impacts of heterogeneity of learning rates amongst individuals, personnel turnover, and an organisation's competitive positioning. The conclusions drawn from his research point to the benefits of maintaining a diversity of views within an organisation – an organisation that is homogeneous in its thinking can very quickly run out of ideas and competitiveness –especially in a context of environmental turbulence.

While March did not address the organisational consequences of his findings, his research was followed by Michael Tushman and Charles O'Reilly (1996), who built on one of March's foundational insights: that different organisational structures are associated with different strategies and environmental conditions. Tushman and O'Reilly proposed that organisational ambidexterity – defined as the ability to simultaneously pursue both incremental and discontinuous innovation involving multiple contradictory structures, processes, and cultures within the same firm, was required for long-term survival. In doing so they challenged the academic wisdom of the time whereby organisations needed to shift structures to initiate and execute innovation (Tushman & O'Reilly 1996). Their proposal built on March's idea that organisations needed to simultaneously exploit their established competitive position and explore new options.

In a 2013 review of the then current state of research in the field following an explosion of interest over the previous 15 years, Tushman and O'Reilly noted broad-based confirmation of the concept along with further areas for research (O'Reilly & Tushman 2013). In doing so, they confirmed four points in line with their original conception of organisational ambidexterity: (1) that the focus of the original concept was the need for management to resolve organisational tensions, (2) that, above all, it was seen as a leadership challenge, (3) that the business challenge was one of leveraging existing assets to create new ones, and (4) that the resolution of the challenge should be viewed in terms of building new organisational capabilities.

They concluded that organisational ambidexterity had been positively linked with firm performance in terms of innovation, financial results and survival across a broad range of studies and methodologies. They also noted that the ambidexterity toolkit had been expanded to include structural options – simultaneous and sequential ambidexterity, and what is described as contextual ambidexterity, where the allocation of organisational resources to exploration is left up to individuals across the organisation.

In noting the different forms and definitions applied to the concept – but a strong body of empirical evidence supporting the broad concept – Tushmann and O'Reilly highlight the importance of context. This is an important issue because there are distinctive features of the markets within which the public service operates that need to be observed. In particular, Tushman and O'Reilly note that a simultaneous approach may be more useful in dynamic markets, or where there is a long history in a particular market, whilst stable environments organisations may be able to afford a sequential approach. What these authors, along with Bason, Martin and McGrath, argue, is that change needs to be built into an organisation's DNA. However described, it remains an activity that must be established, organised, guided, and driven from the top, even if the bulk of the activity takes place down the line at divisional level and much of it at the customer interface. The location of the bulk of activity should be considered as distinct from its oversight.

It should also be noted that this growing inter-disciplinary literature on organisational adaption is demanding of more rather than less central leadership, planning and supervision. It is clearly a headquarters function to determine the organisational activities. Moreover, despite McGrath's declaration that concepts such as core competences are no longer relevant, her argument is about the creation of a new organisational capability – of continuously releasing underperforming resources and seamlessly managing the associated change.

The final point of interest is that the research does not show how leaders manage the interface between exploration and exploitation and resolve the tensions created, a point noted earlier in the context of the public sector management literature on collaborative innovation. This may be a detail too far for the academic literature, but it is just this sort of detail, along with the detail of management information systems that enable corporate leaders to continuously form and disband project-based (innovation, policy service delivery) teams, on which successful public sector management depends.

6.5 Distinctive features of the public service

There are many factors that can influence the design of public service organisational structures. The different conceptions of governance may in turn result from ideas about how governments might best execute the role of the state. RAW Rhodes, for example, points to an array of different narratives of this relationship between the state and its associated form of government and governance (Rhodes 2017). Each such narrative carries with it a different concept of the state, its relationship with civil society, the role of government, the underlying mechanisms through which government is delivered and, consequently, the role and organisation of the business of public administration. Beyond that, it can be viewed as ranging from institutional settings down to the manner in which the government expects the public service to operate.

The breadth of associated organisational possibilities can be appreciated by (re)considering Table 2.3 and the outline of the differing governing structures associated with the five models of governance noted. At the level of the relationship between government and governance, the necessary choice is one of directly managing the mix of hierarchies, markets and networks variously associated with these models, and blending the associated organisational design options.

The underlying narrative is one that sees the hierarchical structure of management continuing to be in evidence, with the role of government being both to establish the policy agenda, and choose the balance of hierarchies, markets, and networks through which this agenda is delivered. This narrative underpins the discussion of performance measurement, which sees measurement of service outcomes as central to the delivery of 'good government', rather than measurement of network management or facilitation as the deliverable for government, though each option has a place within the diverse business of public administration.

A commitment to the Weberian model is common in departments such as defence and foreign affairs, however, the social and human services field employ a mix of all models (through to anarchic governance) overseen by a core of Weberian bureaucracy. And, even within individual departments, there is a mix, although the overarching structure is likely to be hierarchical. Whilst governments are evolving towards 'looser' forms of governance, much of what is in place is a legacy of the philosophy of hierarchies, markets, and networks, and can only be reasonably judged on that basis. If judged as poor, however, it would provide an argument to embrace a new narrative of the relationship between the state and civil society, such as those identified by Rhodes as networked governance, meta-governance, and decentred governance.[7] New organisational design implications would follow.

The technical design principles that relate to the mechanics of organisation design, including number of layers, span of control, and the stacking of functions, exhibit no obvious differences between the public and private sectors. Certainly, the public service is more prone to layering and narrow spans of control than the private sector. In looking at the environment within which the public service operates, however, significant differences are observable, which impact both on the primary design of public service organisation, and its ability to adapt to change.

The first thing to consider is the legislative setting. In many industries, the role of government is important – in setting the rules of the game, in regulation and in support – making policy settings a central factor in strategy and organisational design for individual businesses. In the case of the public service as a player in the business of government, it is clearly the most important factor. As such, the Public Service Act is critical to defining the role of the public service in Australia and the structures (and players) through which public services must be provided.

One direct (but not necessary) consequence is that there is currently no parallel to the private sector roles of board and 'head office', and there are important missing structures and elements of leadership, management, and accountability, including good governance and the practice of strategy. The public service is thus less able than it should be to place pressure on governments to pursue allocative efficiency and continue to make conscious and informed choices about the portfolio of policies pursued. Rarely, for example, do governments determine that they should withdraw from particular markets, a necessary part of maintaining a well-balanced portfolio of activities, at best fiddling at the margin with the classes of customer served by particular products and the level of service delivered. This lack of a culture of systematic portfolio review and change is likely to be mirrored in rigidities in public service organisation and

---

7   An interesting question in this regard is: where is the private sector headed? Certainly shareholder and community activisim are growing challenges for private companies but, interestingly, are pulling their boards in different directions, the former towards better financial performance (as perceived by the stock market) and the latter towards a stronger focus on non-shareholder stakeholder groups and 'non-financial' performance. If and until the stock market evolves towards a more holistic assessment of company performance this divergence seems likely to remain.

practice, where resources are 'owned' at the program and departmental levels, held hostage in McGrath's terms, further limiting prospects for whole-of-government allocative efficiency.

Another element concerns the rigidity of the structures (and underlying philosophy) imposed by the Public Service Act. Clearly, the Act prescribes the key public service structures and the importance of these structures is not that they prevent change – clearly some change has occurred over recent decades – but the undivided focus on the department as the primary entity within the public service and the individual secretaries as the key players is the source of important shortcomings. There is nothing necessarily ineffective about such a divisionalised structure, rather its major shortcomings are related to the missing additional management and leadership layers.

The present departmental structure, if complemented by board and corporate layers, could drive an effective public service. The placement of a collective management (as opposed to leadership) structure at the apex of public service organisation inhibits cohesion and, importantly, adaptation to change within its own ranks. 'Stability' is often claimed to be one of the more important contributions of the public service to government but stability of organisation should not be confused with stability of purpose, the latter able to accommodate (ongoing) change in the former.

Prescribed organisational form and stability in the public service is material. There are interesting ongoing developments in private sector literature and practice embracing such related notions as the ambidextrous organisation, exploration and exploitation, and design thinking.[8] Each of these concepts, along with that of collaborative innovation, offers a means of systematically addressing the challenge of a rapidly changing operating environment. And, whilst none of the alternative structures proposed in the private sector organisational literature may necessarily be blocked by the wording of the Public Service Act, and certainly not by any government intent on changing the Act, the underlying philosophy of the Act, its establishment of a master/servant relationship, and the practice of government permitted by the Act, militate against innovative public service activity. A departmental head seeking to build a more

---

8   Pioneers in this field of thought of flexible organisation design are Burns and Stalker (1961) and Lawrence and Lorsch (1967).

creative and productive climate for his team through experimentation with organisational form – for example, working out how to achieve the benefits of integrating the standard Weberian structure with the benefits of the free-form 'organic' structures – would certainly not feel enabled in the present climate.

Beyond the impact of the formal establishment of public service structures, the government's installation of a formal set of values, code of conduct, and employment principles has an impact both on what the public service does and how it plays its role. Consolidating this and considering the business that the public service is in through private sector eyes reveals a service industry business with a dominant customer, competition for this customer's business (the terms and conditions of which are set by the dominant customer), and no rights to compete for other business. A focus on structures and process is also observable, and an associated absence of clear goals and outcomes. This is not the ideal environment to enable a public service to deliver value to the Australian public.

It is the regulation of competition by government and the prescription of public service structures and conduct that makes difficult the achievement of both the most suitable organisational options for the time, and public service adaptation to a changing environment.[9] These legislative constraints are reinforced by governments showing no interest in good organisational design principles – despite their responsibility for the largest business in the country – and only occasionally does the government's interests and those of good public service organisational design collide; for example, with the rationalisation of back-office functions. Ironically, and if a growing collection of auditors-general reports at state and federal levels is to be believed, this is where public administration in Australia is at its weakest.

Secondly, and material to the structuring and operations of the public service, is the institutional environment within which the public service operates. One such element involves the existence of and roles played by

---

9   A specific example of government regulation of public sector competition is the establishment of the Australian Government Lobbyists Register and the restrictions placed on former politicians being involved in such activities. It is arguable that this has had the effect of legitimising rather than regulating this activity; perhaps a not unintended effect? Any attempts to open up government policy decisions to watchdog and integrity body decisions should start here. Judging by the number of registrants – over 500 – it must be big business. For a systematic assessment of codes of conduct in Australian and overseas parliaments, see McKeown (2012).

various watchdog and integrity bodies reporting directly to the parliament: bodies such as auditors-general, ombudsmen, and anti-corruption commissions. These bodies perform important audit functions in regard to public sector activity, but they also have an impact on the public service organisational form by playing an important role in public sector governance. The acquittal of the government governance function by the public service at the national level might be more effectively undertaken if this responsibility lay directly with the public service, and indeed were assigned to it by legislation.

A third and related institutional difference between the public and private sectors is the accountability frameworks. Whilst public and private sectors work to similar accounting standards from a record keeping perspective, the organisational focus on both achieving and demonstrating performance varies substantially from one to the other. Public and private sectors can account equally for their compliance with the laws of the land; however, the private sector's bottom-line focus on profitability and cash flow creates cohesion in the performance component of accountability that is notably missing from the activities of government. In addition, as corporate regulator, ASIC is active in enforcing appropriate standards of private sector governance, whereas the public sector equivalent – the Auditor-General for Australia – has no such enforcement powers.

A fourth feature that may produce different organisational responses is differences in the market environment within which they operate. Top of the list in the case of the public service is the difficulty of placing neat organisational boundaries around the delivery of solutions to public sector clients. The complex nature of many public policy problems (absence of data, problem and solution definition, integrated service delivery), along with the diversity of stakeholders (clients, citizens at large, community organisations), a number of which lie outside the transaction path for the assembly and delivery of service-based solutions, mark public administration activity out from much of the private sector equivalent.[10] This is a differentiating feature of the demand side of the market for government services. The consequence of this feature is that it requires a standard level of cooperation between the operating units

---

10   One example of the application of the concept of wicked problems to private sector activities involves the recognition that they exist in urban architecture, and that the architecture profession must 'redefine and release its potential for problem-solving and innovation within a new economic, societal, and ecological context' (Delft University of Technology 2015).

(the government departments) that appears to go above and beyond that required in the private sector (the divisions). This difference is amplified by a strategic approach to the identification of horizontal synergies in the private sector matched by corporate leadership in securing these synergies and overcoming boundary difficulties, by contrast with the public sector where horizontal coordination is supported neither by the culture nor a readily available toolkit.

The final element of difference is what might be described as the 'publicness' of the business of government that the public service executes on its behalf. This can best be understood in terms of the central players – the government and the public service – as well as the role of government, and the characteristics of public services. From an economics-based view of the role of government, its activities can be described largely as a combination of public goods (those which are non-rivalrous and non-excludable in consumption) and merit goods (excludable and rivalrous in consumption, which governments feel people will under-consume if privately supplied). Then there are the choices to be made about service delivery. As described by Williamson (1999), some of the important characteristics that determine whether particular government services should be delivered by the public or private sectors include asset specificity, privacy and probity. He argues further that when the problem of incomplete contracting arises – such as in the irregular nature of transactions being contracted – the case for public service delivery is stronger.

As a package, this set of differences between public and private sectors spans product and market characteristics, the legislative and institutional settings, and leadership and management. These differences constrain the role of the public service, limit the nature of competition in its markets, and restrict its ability to adjust to changing political, societal and market circumstances. Clearly, the public service could, at best, be considered a partner in its own fate with far fewer degrees of freedom of action than its private sector counterparts. In this sense, it has the freedom of operation that might be likened to that of a franchisee, where the products, markets, budgets, and earnings are largely determined by the franchisor, and it is on the quality of the execution of a limited and clearly defined range of tasks that 'success' depends. The question is whether this position really is in the public interest? Could the Australian public benefit if the APS had more such degrees of freedom?

In the face of a list of differences such as that above, it is important to recognise that most of them are matters of degree rather than principle, and that they do not necessarily demand the prescription of a different style of public service leadership and management. In the private sector case, whether a franchisee or franchisor, a small business or a big business, a service industry business, a miner or a manufacturer, all such businesses will have goals, shareholders, capital at risk, stakeholder management plans, and a number of degrees of freedom, some more than others, as determined by industry and market conditions and the regulatory environment. The public sector is no different in principle, whether a public corporation managing its financial capital, or a government department managing its reputation and influence, all such businesses and other organisations – public or private – should have a plan built around the elements noted above if they are to encourage effective whole-of-organisation pursuit of defined goals.

Certainly, the public service operates in a regulatory/institutional environment that is different to that faced in the private sector, with the obvious and central difference being that public sector organisations are subject to political direction and control that, as Naomi Chambers and Chris Cornforth (2010) point out, constrains the capacity of governing bodies to steer their organisations and leads to consequent differences in governance arrangements. The basic dictates of good strategic management are no less applicable because of it: know your customers, markets, and your competitors, and know yourself.

The public service operates in an environment with a number of important, distinctive features, but there are no reasons inherent in the public service that dictate that it should not be strategically managed and organised according to best private sector practice. The fact that governments choose not to see it in these terms leaves the APS and the Australian public all the poorer. An interesting exercise for APS leaders would be to seek out the unexploited degrees of freedom and see what might be done within the existing Act and institutional settings.

6.6 Organisational design in the public service

6.6.1 A whole-of-organisation approach

Lam's survey of the development of the alternative organisational forms in the private sector literature indicates a flourishing variety of options developed from the 'one best way' of the early years to several different forms addressing dominant environmental themes. These themes and the resulting organisational forms might be regarded as alternatives, but the various themes underlying these structures may be relevant for individual organisations, with the challenge being to blend and stack organisational forms according to the dictates of the local operating environment.

Mintzberg's framework for viewing alternative organisational forms was designed four decades ago to answer the question of how organisations structure themselves and it provides a simple way to view the design of all organisations, large and small. Mintzberg provides a whole-of-organisation approach within which the themes relevant to the public service can be considered. His primary interest was not the hierarchical nature of the structures, rather the way in which the various parts of an organisation fitted together and functioned (Mintzberg 1979).

Originally setting out to publish a survey of the organisational literature, Mintzberg saw the opportunity for a synthesis, establishing his framework around what he saw as the two fundamental opposing requirements arising from the organisation of human activity – the division of labour into various tasks, and the coordination of these tasks. In this light, the structure of an organisation can be simply defined as the total of ways in which it does this. In developing a set of organisational models around this simple notion, Mintzberg considered a range of factors including basic work and information flows, formal design parameters, and contingency factors (context), but settled on a suite of models described in terms of: (a) the way in which work was organised around its basic parts or functions, and (b) the coordinating mechanisms employed. He described all resulting organisational forms in five basic parts: the strategic apex, the middle-line managers, the operating core, the technocracy, and the support team.

The strategic apex comprises those people charged with overall responsibility for the organisation, including the chief executive manager and any others whose concerns are global. Mintzberg describes its three sets of duties as, firstly, direct supervision including the design of the structure, resource and people allocation, disturbance resolution, transmission of information to employees, and leading and rewarding staff. The second set of duties involves the management of what Mintzberg called the organisation's 'boundary conditions', its relationship with its environment – acting as spokespeople, liaising, and monitoring. The third set relates to the development of the organisation's strategy. He viewed strategy as a mediating force between the organisation and the environment, and strategy formulation as involving the interpretation of the environment, the development of consistent patterns in streams of organisational decisions, and the maintenance of a pace of change that was responsive to the environment but not disruptive to the organisation.

The operating core contains the workers who perform the basic tasks of the organisation whilst the middle-line managers form a chain joining the strategic apex to the operating core. The technostructure designs, plans, changes the work of others and may train the people who do it, but do not do it themselves. The support staff is composed of specialised units to aid the organisation outside the operating workflow. Essentially, the strategic apex, the middle line, and the operating core is the spine of the structure with the technostructure comprising the analysts who design the work flow, change it, and train people to do it. These are the five basic parts of any organisation, varying in relative size depending on the scale and content of the business.

In association with the five basic organisational parts, Mintzberg identified five coordinating mechanisms, considering them the glue that holds organisations together. The first of these, mutual adjustment (the foundation for the organisational model of adhocracy), works on the basis of the organisation's specialists adapting to each other along their unchartered route. It is a simple coordinating mechanism but works best in the most complicated and simplest of circumstances. The second is direct supervision (the foundation for simple structure) where one person takes responsibility for the work of others. Work can also be coordinated without mutual adjustment or direct supervision; i.e. it can be standardised. This may take any of three forms – standardisation of work processes (the foundation of machine bureaucracy), standardisation of outputs (the foundation of the divisionalised form) or the standardisation of skills (the foundation of the professionalised bureaucracy).

From this analysis, Mintzberg developed five models – simple structure, machine bureaucracy, professional bureaucracy, divisionalised form, and adhocracy – which remain a useful framework by which to consider any organisation. Table 6.2 presents the five organisational models, showing the correspondence between the coordinating mechanisms and the emergent models.

Table 6.2 Mintzberg's coordination mechanisms and organisational models

Coordinating mechanism	Simple structure	Machine bureaucracy	Professional bureaucracy	Divisionalised form	Adhocracy
Mutual adjustment					X
Direct supervision	X				
Standardised work processes		X			
Standardised outputs				X	
Standardised skills			X		

Source: Mintzberg (1979, Part IV, especially chapters 17–21).

The simple structure has little or no technostructure or support staff, a loose division of labour, and a small managerial hierarchy, with coordination undertaken by direct supervision and centralised power. This structure is common to the formative years of most organisations where the future cannot be predicted nor activities standardised.

The machine bureaucracy has highly specialised, routinised operating tasks, formalised procedures, a proliferation of rules and regulations, large operating units, relatively centralised power and an elaborate administrative structure. Such organisations are commonly found in stable environments, with the managers in the strategic apex concerned with fine-tuning their bureaucratic machines.

The professional bureaucracy relies for its coordination on a standardisation of skills, which often originate outside of its own standards (set by various professions), and considerable control over work is accorded to the operating core. The individual professions inside and outside of the organisation generally develop organisational strategies.

The divisionalised form is composed of semi-autonomous units. It is a mechanism to control and coordinate a large conglomerate with horizontally diversified products or services and a stable environment and may be regarded as a structural derivative of the machine bureaucracy. It is not an integrated organisation but rather a set of quasi-autonomous entities, each division having its own structure, coupled by a central administrative structure ('the headquarters'). In its top level, it is driven by market groupings.

The adhocracy comprises a highly organic structure with little formalisation of behaviour, job specialisation based on training, and reliance on mutual adjustment as the coordination mechanism. Managers abound but also perform as members of project teams and the distinction between line and staff disappears.

It is useful to note that elements of Mintzberg's framework remain pertinent today and relevant to a consideration of public sector structures.

These are:

- the inherent complexity but simple logic
- the whole-of-organisation nature of the models, whilst pointing to the likelihood that any organisation contains elements of each of these models at a point in time
- the balance achieved between the use of formal and informal structures
- the evolutionary nature of organisational form; the tendency for each of the organisation's five basic parts to pull the organisation in its own direction
- the role of context (what Mintzberg called 'contingency factors').

How can these five models be applied to the structure of the public service today?

When Mintzberg turned his mind to the relevance of these organisational forms to the public sector, he saw 'government' primarily as a combination of the divisionalised and machine-bureaucracy forms, observing at the time that government could be likened to a giant divisionalised organisational form with departments and other agencies exercising considerable autonomy but with 'the central administrators' residing in 'the headquarters' of this divisionalised organisation, concentrating on exercising budgetary control over its bureaucratic forms, performance monitoring, and the recruitment and training of its people. Mintzberg further noted that the divisionalised organisational form worked best where the divisions were organised along machine-bureaucracy lines with standardised 'outputs' lending themselves to ready monitoring and control by headquarters (see, for example, Mintzberg 1979, p 402).

The public service exhibits a number of features of the multi-divisionalised form – it is established as a set of quasi-autonomous entities (departments), with each department having its own structure coupled with a loose central administration, with its top-level structure driven by market (customer) groupings. There is also a set of central administrators – the group of central agencies – exercising budgetary control, monitoring performance and focused on the development of the workforce. And, within this overall structure, the divisions (departments) are commonly organised along machine-bureaucracy lines, certainly at their senior management levels although, below this level, other of Mintzberg's organisational forms may exist according to the context.

The machine-bureaucracy model continues to describe large swathes of public service activity because the operating environment has been relatively stable, and even changes of government and ministers, and the occasional discontinuity in the marketplace, have not necessitated organisational change, with changes in activity often taking place at the margin and the organisational structures at worst being 'fine-tuned'. In some cases, whole departments may be organised along these lines, while in others there may be a mixture of structures with the hierarchical, machine bureaucracy sitting atop it all.

Australian Government departments such as Treasury, Attorney-General's, Foreign Affairs and Trade, and the various elements of the Education and Training portfolio, most closely match the whole-of-department machine-bureaucracy model as individual organisational (divisional) units. Other parts of government more closely represent a professional bureaucracy in which aggregations of professionals perform specialised tasks, for example CSIRO, the Australian Competition and Consumer Commission, and the Productivity Commission. Similarly, an adhocracy and simple structures may well be present in small part across a range of government departments but, as with the professional bureaucracy, they are more likely to exist at lower organisational levels within larger structures organised around the machine-bureaucracy model. Indeed, I suspect it would be difficult to identify other than small pockets of public service activity organised in any other way.

Even where some departments find their names changed and programs regularly shuffled around, the machine-bureaucracy model continues to dominate. And, at the whole-of-public-service level, the multi-divisional form, where the departments comprise the divisions, continues to hold sway. Perhaps the one difference that exists today following the aggregation of (former) departmental activities into super-departments is that a number of these large departments are themselves multi-divisional forms. What remains a clear point of difference between the public and private sector versions of this organisational form, however, is the existence and role of the corporate headquarters.

Such a 'headquarters', if it exists in the APS, does so in virtual form, with 'the central administrators' comprising the Department of the Prime Minister and Cabinet (PM&C) (whole-of-government coordination), Treasury and Finance (economic policy, budgetary control and monitoring of financial and program level performance), and the APSC (focused on workforce matters), with the Secretaries Board playing a limited project-based supporting role. Regarding such structures from a corporate strategy rather than simply organisational design perspective reveals the absence of a variety of leadership and support functions – in Minztberg terms, components of the strategic apex – and both the centralised technostructure and support staff. What is largely missing today is a centralised strategic management and leadership role played by a dedicated headquarters group, and the direction setting and governance of a board.[11]

A question to explore is at what cost these organisational elements are 'missing'. Clearly they are missing by government design, and this is because successive governments have seen this to be to their advantage. An important focus for these missing leadership and management layers in the

---

11   Mintzberg's organisational design focus was primarily management; he did not concern himself with the role of the board role.

private sector is that of adaptation to a changing environment, a subject that could be argued to be the dominant theme in the organisational design literature of the last 20 years.

6.6.2 The role of corporate headquarters

6.6.2.1 Mintzberg

Mintzberg describes the top organisational layer as the 'strategic apex', comprising those people charged with overall responsibility for the organisation, namely the CEO, other top-level managers whose concerns are 'global', and support staff. The strategic apex has three sets of duties: direct supervision, management of the organisation's boundary conditions and its relationship with its environment, and the development of strategy.[12]

Mintzberg describes the role of strategy as mediating between the organisation and the environment in pursuit of the organisation's mission, with strategy formulation involving the interpretation of the environment and the development of consistent patterns in streams of organisational decisions ('strategies') to deal with it. Importantly, he sees this responsibility as including both the maintenance of a pace of change that is responsive to the environment and a need to review the organisational mission (its fundamental purpose) from time to time. He further notes that other parts of the organisation might play an active role in strategy formulation but that the strategic apex has the most important role.[13]

Whilst giving considerable attention to fleshing out his five organisational models, Minztberg devoted most attention to the divisionalised form, reflecting his observation that the vast majority of the Fortune 500 at the time – remember this is 1979 – were (and indeed still are) so organised. In this model, the divisions run their own businesses, determine the strategies for the markets that fall under their responsibility, and control operations. Headquarters shares in the setting of divisional objectives, undertakes whole-of-organisation planning, determines basic human

---

12   There is no universally agreed list: others might describe these functions today as leadership, planning, and supervision.

13   In later writings, Mintzberg made it clear that he saw the importance of the central role as one of organising, with the content of strategy being the prime responsibility of the divisions. See Mintzberg and Waters (1985). This issue – of responsibility for the content of divisional strategy – is much debated in the literature. See, for example, Martin's criticism of the practice of strategic planning in this regard (Martin 2013).

relations policies, finance and accounting systems, and determines budgets. In his discussion of the functions of headquarters, Mintzberg concentrates on six responsibilities:

- the formation of overall product-market strategy (including strategic planning)
- the allocation of financial resources (including the setting of divisional objectives)
- the design of the performance-monitoring system
- appointing divisional managers
- monitoring divisional behaviour on a personal level
- providing support services to all divisions.

At a general level, the corporate office role in organisational coordination and leadership described by Mintzberg might involve building a portfolio of businesses with a common dominant logic and the promotion of unity through the creation of a common set of values and beliefs to create a unifying corporate culture. In business unit strategy formation, Minztberg proposed a 'hands off' role, arguing that the primary responsibility for the formation of divisional strategies lay with the divisions, with corporate office probing, appraising, amending and ultimately approving, unless there was divisional relatedness of a strategic or operational nature, when the role for corporate office should be one of joint formulation (Mintzberg 1979, p 404).

6.6.2.2 Chandler and Williamson

Through the work of Chandler and Williamson, the divisionalised organisation became the private sector organisational form of choice for strategy execution during the expansionary decades of the 1960s and 1970s (Chandler 1962; Williamson 1970). Following Chandler's lead, Williamson developed and popularised the case for the divisionalised corporation, noting the limitations of the functionally arranged (U-form) organisation (a common public service departmental organisational form then and now), and the advantages of the multi-divisional (M-form) organisation.

As noted earlier, Williamson described the inefficiencies of unitary form organisations in terms of managerial discretion ('sub-goal pursuit') and what he saw as the inevitable control loss in large organisations. But his major contribution focused on removing the organisation's chief executive (whom he called the peak coordinator) from day-to-day involvement in the decisions of the various functional activities within the unitary form, enabling him/her to focus on strategic decisions and the overall organisational performance of the divisionalised form (Williamson 1970).

Williamson wrote of 'the general office' attached to 'the peak coordinator' and 'the elite staff', a 'team of top executive specialists' removed from operating matters, employed in this office dealing with strategic matters with the peak coordinator. By focusing the efforts of the divisions on competition and competitive positioning in their markets and allowing greater specialisation at the level of the customer/product/market, Williamson saw the opportunities for (managerial) sub-goal pursuit diminished, with the decentralisation of authority for these markets as diminishing the impact of control loss in organisations with a substantial product/market portfolio. He further argued that this raised the maximum effective organisation size – which he expressed simply in maximum span of control and number of organisational layers – by an order of magnitude but noted that he expected the same size-based inefficiencies to be encountered further down the road. And he expressed interest in the next generation of organisational innovations to address this limitation. Whilst Williamson's views were not so much competitive with those of Mintzberg as complementary, the same could not be said for those of Michael Porter and Robert Grant.

6.6.2.3 Porter and Grant

Writing shortly after Mintzberg, Porter observed that by the 1980s the pendulum in regard to the role of 'headquarters' in the multi-divisional organisational form had started to swing back towards active intervention in the business of the divisions. He saw this as following several failed decades of attempts to extract synergies at the corporate level to justify the conglomerate mergers of the time, on which foundations many of the multi-divisionalised corporations of the day were built. These mergers had been a particular feature of corporate America since the 1960s, built on the premise that the aggregation of diverse businesses offered corporate-level synergies based on scale in areas such as cheaper finance, currency management, risk management, and generally diminished overheads (Porter 1985). Porter, however, saw the benefits of a corporate headquarters, not so much in terms of benefits derived from economies of scale at the corporate level, rather in the active creation of synergies across divisional boundaries – what he called horizontal strategy – and the formation of external partnerships.

Grant (1995) provides a third and later view of the role and functions of 'headquarters'. He examined this role within the context of a divisionalised multi-business corporation and the separation achieved between strategic and operational management. He grouped the functions and responsibilities of 'corporate management' into four areas:

- managing the corporate portfolio of businesses and the resource allocation between them
- participating in strategy formulation at business unit level
- providing coordination between the different businesses
- controlling performance.

There are subtle differences between Mintzberg's, Porter's, and Grant's views of the headquarter's role, perhaps reflecting the evolving corporate context, with Porter and Grant clearly seeing a more active role in the divisional businesses than Mintzberg and, in particular, placing greater emphasis on the corporate office coordination role.

6.6.3 The strategic role of corporate headquarters

The academic study of organisation has highlighted the relationship between organisational structure and strategy in that some structures will be more effective than others in delivering an organisation's strategy. This linkage is important in a public sector context, as it is the corporate headquarter's role to develop and manage this strategy and follow through its organisational consequences. The evolution in private sector organisational form responded to market opportunities and changed strategic objectives can be traced back to the middle of the 20th century. It is clear, however, that while there is a developing literature addressing the structural and management challenges of balancing exploration and exploitation, experimentation in this regard is taking place within the context of the dominant divisional organisational form.

Table 6.3 draws this discussion together in a somewhat stylised form by linking the changing strategic objectives of business with the consequent organisational form employed and identifying the changing role of the corporate office. Whilst the timing of the phases is indicative at best – as with our discussion of timing with the models of governance – this table indicates the stability in the dominant private sector organisational form, and the ongoing changes within it, in the ambit of the head office role and the distribution of authority between the business units and head office.

Table 6.3 The evolution of the role of the corporate office and organisational structures

Strategic objective	Corporate office role	Approximate period	Organisational form & evolution
Address separation of ownership from control. Run profitable business for owners	Leadership and stewardship Manage organic growth Governance	19th/20th century up to today for non-diversified and smaller businesses	Functionally organised (U-form)
Expand business by creating a vehicle within which to hold purchased companies	Build a portfolio of companies Report on a consolidated basis	Up to 1950s/1960s	Holding company with autonomous subsidiaries
Build a diversified business to gain corporate economies	Extract corporate synergies; eg, finance, risk, and purchasing	1960s/1970s forward	Multi-division (M-form) with largely autonomous divisions
Capture horizontal (inter-divisional) synergies	Actively create synergies between divisions as justification for diversified business	1980s/1990s forward	Multi-division (M-form) with more active head office involvement in business
Build formal alliances at corporate and divisional levels	Build formal alliances with third parties at corporate level and assist divisions	1990s forward	Multi-division (M-form) with a wider divisional brief under corporate leadership
Open up the organisation to outside influences. Focus on organisational learning and continuous change	Encourage formation of formal and informal alliances across all organisational levels. Develop accompanying structures and management tools	2000s forward	Multi-division (M-form) with new accompanying adaptive structures and processes

6.6.4 Implications for the public service

Just as with the models of governance in the public sector, the underlying organisational model for large corporate activity has not changed for some four or five decades. Change in the private sector has been achieved through the redistribution of authority through an integrated two-way strategic approach between head office and the divisions. Head office is responsible for whole-of-entity direction and governance, the divisions having similar responsibility within their product/market domains, and with head office being primarily responsible for creation of the horizontal strategies that today are sought as the primary justification of such collective activities, along with the usual corporate synergies. What the public service and the private sector have in common in this regard is stability in overarching organisational structures. The central difference, however, lies with the effectiveness with which the two can respond to changing circumstances, with recent unsuccessful public service attempts to achieve whole-of-public-service responses to environmental change.

The NPM (re)organisation of the public sector around products and groups of services with performance measured by related output measures mirrored the first phase of private sector decentralisation of management, with departments placed at the apex of public service organisation and activities strongly focused on results (through output measures) in their own activity areas. The addition of whole-of-government strategic objectives shared amongst ministers was designed to balance the agency-level focus on their own activities with a shared responsibility for whole-of-government outcomes.

This attempt to share the government's strategic load through ministerial-level strategic objectives, in the absence of any detailed performance measures, resource allocation, and effective whole-of-government business plan, was always unlikely to deliver an effective whole-of-government strategic focus. Governments have moved on to develop a more networked style of public administration but, as a succession of national and international audit office reports have noted, this has also met with limited success, given that distributed government has not been underpinned by upgraded accountability and performance measurement mechanisms.

6.6.5 An Australian perspective

John Halligan (2011) noted evidence of five empirical models of the central steering role, ranging from a traditional integrated hierarchical model that is grounded in traditional public administration and emphasises transactional control over operational and delivery matters, through to a strategic governance model emphasising strategic planning and priority setting.[14]

---

14 Many criticisms are levelled at the concept of 'strategic planning', including its not uncommon description as an oxymoron; for example, by Garratt. In my experience, it is a term best avoided because it combines two inconsistent notions, namely strategy and planning. The objective of strategy formation should be to explore the viability of an organisation's fundamental purpose and its positioning to meet this purpose. Its objective is to explore the unknowns about businesses, markets, customers, products, and technologies, whereas the usual objective for any 'planning' exercise is to roll out what *is* known, commonly in financial terms. Planning for the execution of a confirmed strategy should follow its determination, but the strategy formation and implementation planning activities are separate and different processes. Where use of the term 'strategic planning' may be warranted is to denote part of the strategy formation process associated with the systematic exploration of the future, using such techniques as the Delphi method or scenario planning. But it is rarely used in this context and better avoided as a consequence.

In commenting on the Australian experience from a whole-of-government (including inter-governmental) perspective, Halligan noted that the general pathway of central steering has displayed features of all five models over a period of 25 years, but against a tradition of a strong centre in Australian Government. This is underpinned by the central role played by PM&C, and government that has become more complex and challenging and subject to higher aspirations over the period.

Halligan pointed to considerable reform following the introduction of NPM principles and practices and the development of 'a complex array of instruments across a broad range of key policy sectors and intergovernmental relationships', adding up to 'a formidable apparatus for steering and reviewing strategy and performance' which he equated with his high-end model of strategic governance. He noted at that time (2011) that the effectiveness of central steering under the strategic governance model could only be determined 'in the medium term'.

Indeed, in light of the questions already raised in this book on the operations of the national government and the APS, one could easily conclude: (a) that, if indeed a formidable apparatus had been assembled, it could hardly be judged a success today; (b) that this 'failure' is substantial enough to question whether indeed the apparatus was of a high-end model; and (c) given the observed failures in government governance, whether the range of governance models considered should have more obvious regard for the corporate equivalent. The real question is whether an historical view of the role of the centre in public sector life is an adequate yardstick by which to measure public sector governance. Indeed, I argue that the private sector would be a better public policy yardstick than own sector historical performance.

As noted, models of organisational design can be constructed around a mix of structural and contextual factors and, in addition to describing organisations in terms of layers, span of control and stacking of relationships between lines of business and/or functions, organisations can be described holistically in terms of their culture, their informal social networks and derived behaviours. Organisations can also be seen as a set of administrative systems and associated processes and an associated set of information technology systems that facilitate the information flows from these systems and processes; a family of functions and the associated skill sets at work; or, following Mintzberg, various collaborative mechanisms at work.

Halligan's chapter is a reminder to look to other (contextual) factors to explain organisational performance on a case-by-case basis. There may well be a formidable apparatus in place to steer whole-of-government strategy and performance, but if the organisational incentives and behaviours are not aligned with strategic and operational priorities – a common public sector problem – then 'the right' organisational structure will be of little value (See Halvorsen et al. 2005). As noted in Chapter 4, the designers of the Public Service Act may well have had good intentions in regard to independence of public service advice, but there is no protection for such public service action in the face of government indifference or hostility: on the contrary, unwelcome advice may readily be blocked and public servants shown the door (after due process of course). The UK National Audit Office report (NAO UK 2014) also invites consideration of incentives when collegiate behaviours are not being exhibited by the central agencies. Inadvertently enabling the wrong behaviours can readily undermine intentions to extract the right behaviours.

Ultimately, these factors – ranging from the social, administrative and technology systems, to formal structures – contribute to organisational performance. Understanding formal structures and functions and how they fit together are a threshold requirement for good organisational performance. The NAO UK 2014 report highlighted the need for placing increased emphasis on long-term planning, greater cross-government integration, and the extension of central government leadership beyond matters of national security and prime ministerial support. This points to a structural solution.

Structures are useful for strategic (focus) and operational (linkages and systems) reasons, but also in signalling organisational priorities and intent. An integrated and aligned organisation invites collegiate behaviour in a way that no amount of exhortation within a fragmented structure is likely to achieve. In addition, a peak coordinator (and his/her office), free from operational responsibilities, is more able to devote time to the strategic direction of the organisation, signalling this throughout the organisation, and building the sorts of collegiate behaviour that contribute to success. The supporting organisational structures – the stacking of the various functions and the right representation on a variety of executive and management committees – importantly shapes how individual employees see themselves fitting in and their consequent behaviour: who they communicate with, what they communicate and, importantly, what they (can) expect in return.

This discussion of the role of 'the centre' in the public sector asserts that, at the global level, the department remains the central operating unit within government and individual department autonomy with limited leadership and oversight by 'the centre' is a substantial handicap in delivering good government. The absence of operational cohesion and corporate leadership denies the development of a sense of self in the public service, and denies the public service the capability of taking a strategic view of its role and activities.

When viewed on a comparative private sector basis, the standard executive committees of senior public servants (such as the UK Civil Service Board and the Australian Government's Secretaries Board) established to provide strategic oversight of the implementation of government policies, do not have the skills (the relevant board experience), the time (having a full load of operational responsibilities with their departments), breadth of experience, nor the charter or the supporting resources, to devote to the sorts of high-level activities performed by the typical private sector board and corporate office. The quality of advice received by successive governments (and parliaments), the role and standing of the public service, and the quality of government received by the community, are all the poorer for it. A public service board and 'head office' is needed to develop the public service's strategic view of its place in government. This must centre around its role in the two pillars on which the existence of the public service role rests, namely policy formation and service delivery, informed by the triad of communities it must serve, a pre-eminent role in policy advice, a competitive position in service delivery, a role in legitimising government, underpinned by a systemic view of government that only it can provide. But this is not where it is at today.

The establishment of a strong centre comprising board and corporate office does not necessarily, however, effect a net transfer of power to the public service from the government. It might do so in the short term, and if the public service is to improve its contribution to good government, it must be given greater freedom to do so. It is not clear, however, that this additional freedom need be at the expense of the government of the day. Moreover, in the medium term, stronger government should result, through the impact of a more effective public service. Similarly, the establishment of a strong centre need not effect a net transfer of power from the departments to the centre as an effective 'centre' will enhance the strategic and operational capabilities of the individual departments.

The role of the centre is to see the business of the public service as a whole, to leverage the total business assets to deliver benefits through the departments, to leverage individual departmental assets to deliver advantages to the whole, to identify opportunities for and create inter-departmental synergies, and to appropriately frame the operating context ensuring that the departments are equipped with the tools and knowledge to respond effectively to their environments. The provision of global (versus local) market intelligence, the establishment of integrated performance measurement and resource-allocation processes, and the development of an integrated system of corporate and departmental memory are contributions from the centre that would strengthen individual departments and the whole public service. A well-resourced and dedicated centre will significantly strengthen departmental capacity to service ministers and improve their individual and collective performance.

6.6.6 A set of tasks for the centre

Whether 'the centre' of a business is described as its strategic apex, its headquarters, corporate office, peak coordinator's office, board plus corporate office or other; and whether its role is described in terms of direct supervision, setting the boundary conditions, and developing strategy; or leadership, planning and supervision, there are many such activities that could be undertaken by a corporate team free from operational responsibilities. The benefits of a dedicated head office team is the management of the organisation's portfolio of activities as a continuous process, and calibration of the whole-of-organisation capabilities, structures, and processes to pursue integrated decision-making across all levels consistent with stakeholder goals.

It is important to consider both the need for a strategic management capability and a core base of knowledge to underpin the associated strategic management decisions. The centre could undertake a number of supporting research tasks to build public service understanding of its business within an integrated, whole-of-public-service model (as described in Box 6.1). There is no more important capability in one's business than that of being able to think creatively about it. The curiosity to follow outliers in such research, rather than follow central tendencies, will almost certainly only come from those who know a business intimately rather than from those following a consulting brief.[15]

---

15 Roger Martin provides a useful explanation of how success in medical research (into autism spectrum disorder) was achieved through a careful examination of outliers (see Martin 2009, pp 33–39).

Box 6.1 A set of research tasks for 'the centre'

1. Develop an integrated map of the wicked problems confronting the public service, showing the linkages between the various components and the impacts that they have on each other. (This could be worked through to and up from sets of pairwise departmental comparisons of operating overlaps and with external parties.)

2. Develop and promulgate a model of government governance that acknowledges the existence of cross-departmental and cross-sectoral participation in the business of government.

3. Establish a central research capacity to develop performance measurement concepts and techniques that underpin good government (and public service) governance. Treat the measurement of public value as a suitable goal and this task as a journey.

4. Develop an integrated management information and program performance reporting system building through process and output to impacts, outcomes and public value. Establish a standard departmental data architecture map linking the various required data sources with their collection, aggregation and distillation of the required governance monitoring and performance reporting reports.

5. Develop empirical foundations for a public service strategy to enhance its standing and promote the legitimacy of government through publication of its annual report, active stakeholder management, public service brand development and promotion, and the creation of public value, all in the public interest. Examine both public and private sector foundations for such a (public interest) strategy.

6. Establish an ongoing capability to research the academic literature and published evidence on alternative organisational forms and associated management models for individual departments and for the collective of departments. Examine especially the models of organisational learning and adaptation to change.

7. Research the impact of the overall size of the public service on its efficiency, and the impact of the number and relative sizes of the public service departments (and functions) on whole-of-public-service organisational efficiency. Examine notions of the determination of the efficient boundaries of organisations and the determination of organisational efficiency.

8. Examine the limits to outsourcing both from efficiency (cost and organisational design) and effectiveness perspectives. Examine the application to the public service of the underpinning notion that an organisation does not outsource activities associated with its competitive advantage.

9. Develop a methodology to measure the cost of governing and to track the unit cost of public administration.

10. Examine the applicability of the concept of investment (in people and businesses) as opposed to consumption, to the breadth of non-capital investment programs, and the conflicts between strategies of containment and resolution (and the consequent costs), from both decision-making and accounting perspectives.

11. Develop a stakeholder management model for departmental use embracing the government and its customers, parliament and the Australian public, and establish integrated customer relationship management systems at appropriate levels across the public service.

12. Examine the establishment of an integrated centre and divisional (corporate) market intelligence capacity to shape and complement the market intelligence gathered and the memory 'stored' at the business unit (departmental) level. Develop an integrated model for departmental and 'centre' use.

13. Develop a central capability to identify, capture, and diffuse best local and international practice (and best possible practice where applicable) in policy development and formation.[1]

14. Develop a companion model of public service governance.

[1] Walter Kiechel's proposal of the notion of best possible practice is consistent with his idead that strategy is change, and a case to be cracked, rather than simply replication of someone else's status quo (See Kiechel 2010, Chapters 1 and 2).

Box 6.1 is not intended to be a full set of tasks for a public service head office but rather within the five elements of the role of the public service: advises policy formation, manages service delivery, provides leadership across the public service, delivers government governance, and contributes to the legitimacy of government. A number of related projects may already be under way within the APS; however, what is missing is the systemic view and strategic management of the public service to which this set of centrally driven and managed research tasks would contribute by forming a strong research base to underpin an effective leadership role from the centre. Were an 'independent' public service board to be created, such research would be a starting point in the development of an appropriate strategy for the APS.

6.7 Conclusions

The academic literature suggests that some ground has been recovered in the field of public sector management following the less fortunate impacts on public sector capability and performance ensuing from the introduction of the NPM reforms. Developments in the fields of strategic and collaborative innovation are continuing, as are private sector developments in organisational form and strategy. The international quantitative evidence available, however, along with parliamentary committee and auditor-general reports, suggests that important public sector management issues remain. Increasing pressure to deliver government services through horizontal mechanisms reinforce these difficulties, as do the associated increasing focus on networks and community involvement in the business of government, and the poor underlying base of performance measurement.

Academic research and national audit office reports continue to report on performance shortcomings. Other reports prepared by major international advisory organisations (see, for example, UNDP 2015) deliver similar messages. This chapter has focused on the contribution to these shortcomings of public sector organisational structures and the design of a fit-for-purpose organisational architecture for the public service that serves the needs of public service strategy and the accountability requirements of good government. I argue that,

- Reliance on an organisational structure that places the department at the apex of delivery of government services and sees the public service contribution as simply the sum of individual departmental contributions severely limits the potential for good government (at best, the public service can make the whole equal to the sum of the parts).
- The absence of a strong centre providing leadership and support to the constituent departments:
  - substantially constrains the conception and delivery of a coordinated and whole-of-government approach on the ground
  - restricts the systematic collection, distillation and sharing of experiences across the public service in addressing common operating problems and thereby the formation of institutional memory
  - hinders innovation and the capacity of the public service to provide the oversight of government operations in line with consistent decision-making and sound government governance
  - denies the public service and the public at large the opportunity to benefit from a public service contribution to the legitimacy of government and protection of the national interest
  - further diminishes public service capacity to create and capture the corporate and divisional benefits that any equivalent private sector organisation would target
  - ensures the existence of many public services rather than one.

Organisational structures are given life by the combination of the parts that are assembled and the linkages established between them. This is a package and the absence of any of the organisational pieces or associated linkages has downstream consequences for organisational performance and accountability.

In Australia's case, the absence of an integrated public service plan and associated reporting process, the absence of public service competitive strategy and competitive positioning, the presence of national audit office reports pointing to ongoing whole-of-government coordination difficulties, as well as published comments made by successive public service heads, support the view that there is an absence of an effective high-level and strategic public service leadership. This absence can be explored through the respective roles and structures of 'headquarters' in private sector organisational structures and its counterpart in the public sector, 'the centre'. I have also pointed to the prospective value-adding role of an independent board.

The public service lacks the strategic leadership evident in the structures and practices of equivalent large corporate entities, and this absence is attributable to a limited conception of the role of the public service, both by the government and public service itself. This 'limited conception' by successive governments is a deliberate strategy to constrain the substantive role of the public service to one of public administration, mechanistically administering the government's program. The organisational structure in place involving the fragmentation of the public service is well designed to give effect to this strategy. The strategy was most likely conceived of as a grab for political control of the processes of government some 30 years ago, and in its organisational form chose to ignore prevailing developments in private sector strategy (a focus on horizontal strategies) and organisational structure (the evolution of the divisionalised form), the linkages between the two, and in the services required by customers (the continuing emergence of complex problems and the requirement for solutions not services).

In focusing on securing political control of government while ignoring the changing marketplace, this grab for power by the politicians of the day was arguably always going to fail the broader communities that they were elected to serve. The 2007–08 global financial crisis exposed many of these shortcomings, with governments unable to throw money at their (public policy) problems, having to make choices, but lacking the information and decision-making apparatus with which to do this. The cupboard is bare, governments lack big policy ideas and the will to execute them and, because of this, voters around the world are impatient with their governments. It is not difficult to see the seeds of today's growing voter activism having been sown by the NPM reforms of the 1980s.[16]

Much of the discussion of solutions to this problem focuses on a different sharing of power between the government and the public service, whether prescribing a managerial role for ministers or reskilling the public service. An underpinning problem pointed out by Mulgan is that the pool of authority to be shared between the two is diminishing as trust in government declines and community activism rises. Attempts by politicians to retain their pool of authority leads to a reduction in the part managed by the public service. In this sense the political parties (governments) are continuing to become stronger at the expense of the public service, by default.

This also makes it difficult to find a solution to the present difficulties of government based on the transfer of some power to the public service, although inevitably the major shortcomings identified will inevitably involve more power for the public service. I believe that part of the answer should involve finding new ground, occupied by neither, on which to build a stronger public service. My proposal for an expanded role for the public service in promoting trust in, and the legitimacy of, government, is consistent with this view. Perhaps there is other ground than that which is already occupied – to be shared in the public interest?

In concluding this chapter on organisation, it is worth noting the reminder from Oliver Williamson that all organisational forms are flawed and that the choice is inevitably between flawed forms. Williamson also declares that, before declaring one organisational form to be inferior to another, the inevitably high costs of changing organisational form must be assessed. Some of these costs have been noted, however, more importantly, to develop public policy–based views of how the public service should be organised, it is important to understand the strategy the organisational structure is intended to execute.

---

16   There is a biblical form to this wisdom 'as you sow so shall you reap' (Galatians 6:7). Thus lies the irony in seeing Australia's national politicians attend the annual non-denominational religious service that precedes the opening of parliament each year. Perhaps if they want His support they should heed His words.

7

Arguments for better strategy

7.1 Introduction

Just as there are many different sorts of 'strategies' and 'plans' in life and business, there are almost as many definitions of strategy. Concepts of strategy, and to a lesser extent structure, are applicable to management at most levels in most organisations, with the scope for strategy and associated structuring diminishing down through successive organisational layers. The board and senior management do not have a monopoly on strategic thinking in an organisation, but they do have responsibility for the highest level of strategic thought focused on achievement of the purpose of the organisation (as determined by shareholders) and the broad deployment of resources to achieve this purpose.

What is strategy? A common theme in latter-day writings is that strategy is about 'winning'. Robert Grant's opening words to his book on contemporary strategy analysis are that strategy is about winning; he defines it as 'the unifying theme that gives coherence and direction to the decisions of an individual or organisation' (1995, p 3).[1] Grant outlines a number of features that contribute to success, including goals that are simple, consistent and long term; a profound understanding of the competitive environment; the objective appraisal of resources; and effective implementation. He places the concept of competitive advantage at the heart of the notion of strategy.

---

1 Grant helped popularise the resource-based view of the firm.

Different writers emphasise strategy's different dimensions. Roger Martin defines strategy as 'the making of an integrated set of choices that collectively position the firm in its industry so as to create sustainable advantage relative to competition and deliver superior financial returns' (Martin 2013). Martin elaborates on the necessary choices within the broader concept of strategy as follows, 'It is one integrated set of choices: what is our winning aspiration; where will we play; how will we win; what capabilities need to be in place; and what management systems must be instituted' (Martin 2014). And, with AG Lafley, he adds the notion of playing to win, not simply playing to play (Lafley & Martin 2013).[2] Martin goes on to break the practice of strategy down to the idea that 'Two choices determine success: the where-to-play decision (which specific customers to target); and the how-to-win decision (how to create a compelling value propositions for those customers)' (Martin 2014).

In turn, Michael Porter focuses on competitive advantage and positioning and the central role of the customer 'Competitive advantage grows fundamentally out of the value a firm is able to create for its buyers' (Porter 1985, p xxii). Rita McGrath (2013) emphasises the transient nature of competitive advantage, while Michael Lanning (2000) also places the role of the customer at the centre of strategy with his concept of the value delivery system. For his part, Henry Mintzberg sees strategy as the glue that holds an organisation together, enabling a consistency of decision-making throughout an organisation (Mintzberg 1979). What all of these writers recognise is that strategy creates organisational purpose and cohesion.

Lafley and Martin also ask, what is winning? This question provides content to Martin's notion of a winning aspiration and, in turn, they ask why it is important to make winning an explicit aspiration? They also point to the need to win with those who matter most, noting the risks of marketing myopia and the pitfalls of a product or technology focus at the expense of meeting the needs of customers. They observe that organisational winning might be expressed in any number of ways and briefly examine the mission statements of a small number of leading consumer marketing companies – Starbucks, Nike, and McDonald's – concluding that these companies don't just want to serve customers, they want to win with them (Lafley & Martin 2013, p 35). They argue that winning is hard, it takes hard choices, dedicated effort and substantial investment, and that, when

---

2   This concept is relevant to the public service as it could be argued to be 'playing to play'.

companies set out to participate rather than win, they will inevitably fail to make the requisite hard choices. Lafley and Martin ask the reader to imagine the likelihood of winning without explicitly setting out to do so. The following tests this literature by applying it to public service activity using the criterion of the public interest.

The history of the development of corporate strategy is of interest in a public sector context because of the changing focus of the corporate strategy literature and practice over the last 50 years, and the impact of economic conditions on this evolution. It is also of interest because of the parallels that can be drawn between public and private sector responses to the same, evolving environmental pressures. It is of particular interest because, despite the different paths taken, the content of strategic management in both sectors consolidates around the notion of people as the major competitive asset, and innovation as the means of staying on top of increasingly fast-paced change.

Strategy development and implementation is not easy, as illustrated by Bob Garratt's board-driven view of strategy, which indicates the scale of the challenge:

> I take from the Greek the key concept that strategy is the broad deployment of scarce resources to achieve a purpose. This is the role of the board of directors. This is a concept based on having a suitably varied group of independent thinkers around the board table capable of scanning the murky horizons of continuous change in the political, physical, economic, social, technological and trade environments, and then linking the data in broad deployment terms to deliver the organisation's fundamental purpose – the reason it exists. (Garratt 2010, p 8)

In business terms, in order for an organisation to achieve its fundamental purpose, it must locate an industry (or industries) where conditions are favourable to its goal and it must attain a position of advantage vis-à-vis its competitors that allows it to earn its target return on capital. Whilst the choice of industry is largely a given for the public service, it faces competition for influence and its services across the board, making notions of competition and competitive positioning entirely relevant.

The terminology employed in the following discussion of the public service as a competitive enterprise describes public sector activities as the industry of public administration. In standard industrial organisation terminology, individual businesses compete with each other in markets, where buyers and sellers are engaged in exchange. The sellers that compete for buyer attention for particular goods and services are collectively called the industry, where the boundaries of the industry are defined by the substitutability of their products in consumption. Gaps in the chain of substitutability in consumption lead to the definition of different markets and industries.

I describe the collection of activities of the public service as the industry of public administration, recognising that there are a number of interrelated markets in which the public service competes for influence and business, and differing degrees of competition faced by the public service in these separate but linked markets. In general, this framework can be used to analyse how individual suppliers might best position themselves to 'win' in their markets, and also how the organisation and competition amongst suppliers in any market affects the nation's welfare.[3] The focus of Chapters 7, 8, and 9 is primarily on the former, and Chapter 10 addresses the latter with a discussion of public policy.

Further, in describing public service competition in these markets, I focus primarily on the government as the customer but acknowledge that value propositions need to be delivered to other players in the value chain. The public service competes directly for the business of government – for example, the provision of policy advice and management and delivery of government services – but also competes more broadly for influence in the community, both to enhance its prospects of winning more government business, and to improve the profile of government administration.

7.2 The concept of strategy

7.2.1 The management century and the development of the tools of strategy

7.2.1.1 The management century

Walter Kiechel provides an insightful interpretation of the management context within which the development of the concepts and tools of strategy have taken place (Kiechel 2012). In a review constructed around the ongoing tensions between the two streams of thought in this field – the

---

3   For further discussion, see Caves (1967).

humanist and the numerist streams – Kiechel describes the 20th century as the management century, dividing it into three parts. He describes the period up to the Second World War as one of 'aspirations to scientific rectitude'; the second, from the late 1940s to a high point around 1980, as one of 'managerialism's good feeling and widespread public support'; whilst the third, from the 1980s up to the present day, as marked by 'a kind of retreat into specialisation, servitude to market forces and declining moral ambition'.

In describing the evolution of management thinking, Kiechel traces the emergence of systematic strategic thinking in the business world to the establishment of Boston Consulting Group by Bruce Henderson in 1963, the adoption of the term corporate strategy, and Henderson's development of the building blocks – the experience curve and the growth-share matrix – all underpinned by an analytical passion to take a sharp pencil and stopwatch to every aspect of a company's operations. A lengthy period without recession in the United States was disturbed by the oil shocks of the 1970s, and an accompanying economic malaise that Kiechel describes as ending the triumph of managerialism.[4] An intense period of change set in: high levels of inflation, the march of computer technology, and a lively market for corporate control as the stock market heated up. During this period, the era of humanist managerialism – one in which the corporation was regarded as a social institution in which the capacity and potential of manager and employee alike were to be respected – was confronted by a growing focus on the shareholders and the creation of shareholder wealth.

Kiechel observes that for the next 30 years – up to the present – the numbers-driven push for greater profitability and the cry for more respect for the humanity of production coexisted in uneasy tension. He cites the emergence of the re-engineering movement, which used the latest information technology 'in a turbo-charged push for efficiency and competitiveness', but which was later discarded as a management fad gone horribly wrong as an example of this tension. Kiechel paints a picture of growing disarray amongst the humanists who were unable to identify the practices that would bring out the best in employees, in contrast with

---

4   This observation – that managerialism's triumph ended in the 1970s – sits uncomfortably with its discovery by the public sector around the same time.

strategy and the numerical approach to management, which had a clear paradigm and set of frameworks developed in the first half of the 1980s through the work of Michael Porter.

Notwithstanding this disarray, Kiechel notes the emergence of two themes from the humanist side during this period, one of leadership and the other of innovation. He observes that the theme of leadership has fallen somewhat by the wayside as no consensus has emerged on exactly what constitutes a leader, but innovation is less controversial as both humanists and numbers people recognise its importance.[5] Whilst noting the ultimate difficulty of determining 'one best way' more generally when it comes to human endeavour ('no one yet appears to have been able to automate the invention of the new'), Kiechel ends on the optimistic note that management is, finally, focusing on how to make humans and their organisations more effective.

7.2.1.2 The emergence of corporate strategy

The emergence of corporate strategy in the 1950s and 1960s followed the long postwar period of unprecedented stability and economic growth, which was conducive to the expansion of large, global, and diversified enterprises. Companies confidently planned for growth, actively seeking economies of scale and scope through expansion into multiple markets. Growth through diversification followed, with a particular focus on conglomerate mergers enabled by the development of long-term planning tools and the emergence of techniques to make a 'scientific' choice of the products and markets.

The private sector enthusiasm for planning was paralleled in the public sector as governments and public authorities undertook long-term economic, social and investment planning. Tools were developed and applied in the public sector – such as cost–benefit analysis and linear programming – and were accompanied by the development of discounted cash-flow analysis and econometric modelling, providing a new array of tools to support 'scientific' planning for growth. This was the golden age of investment in public infrastructure.

---

5   Kiechel does not consider the part played by organisational structures in providing leadership, only the qualities of individuals. This is consistent with the American literature in this field, which conflates the role of the board with senior management and sees the CEO as the primary source of organisational leadership and inspiration.

By the mid-1970s, however, circumstances had changed for the private sector, with evidence accumulating that the expected synergies from diversified enterprise, the strategic foundation on which much corporate expansion was based, were not being realised. In addition, the first oil shock of 1974 and the associated growing macroeconomic instability made redundant the essentially 'linear' forecasting techniques on which companies (and governments) had relied. Slower, as well as more uncertain, economic growth also meant fiercer competition and smaller margins in the private sector, and pressures on revenues in the public sector. The incentive for business to concentrate on what it did best and withdraw from the rest was strong and the focus fell onto competitiveness within a prevailing paradigm of 'sticking to your knitting'. As public sector infrastructure needs were seen to be largely met, governments turned their focus to social problems and encountered the policy challenges documented by Horst Rittel and Melvin Webber (1973). So, whilst the bigger end of the private sector consolidated around what they did best, democratic governments refocused their efforts in areas requiring new structures, tools, and skills.

The consequence for the private sector was that top management began an evolutionary process of reconceiving its role in developing the strategy, moving away from planning for growth and expansion in the 1960s to portfolio planning in the 1970s, to sources of competitive advantage within the firm in the 1980s, and to internal sources of competitive advantage in the 1990s. Grant notes:

> Work on the 'resource-based view of the firm', and organizational competences and capabilities helped shift the focus of attention of strategic management toward dynamic aspects of competitive advantage, the importance of innovation, and the central role of internal processes within the firm. (Grant 1995, p 16)

In charting the progress of strategy's development as a means of understanding the foundations of business success, Kiechel describes its evolution in terms of focus, tools, and people (2010). This evolution – of focus and development of tools from the 1960s through to the present decade, could be condensed to the following:

- costs, competition and competitors (a focus on competitive positioning in markets)
- the value chain and value-delivery system (a focus on the customer and value-creating activities)

- shareholder wealth and financial management (a focus on finance and delivery of shareholder value)
- competencies, processes and capabilities (a focus on people and dynamics of organisational behaviour)
- time-based behaviour (the notion that speed of activity was critical)
- the resource-based view of strategy (based on internal and external 'resources')
- three versions of strategy as people (people as the critical resource for innovation and growth, networks, and private equity where 'the people' are the partners of private equity firms).

That progression has, however, been neither linear nor constant in impact, and nor have any of the 'tools' been completely replaced by another. Indeed, all of these tools would find a use today on their own or in tandem. In addition, there have been other contributors to the strategy evolution, such as the quality movement and business process re-engineering that have similar claims for inclusion on this list. The list's value is as an indication of the steady evolution of focus for businesses advised by large consultancy firms, from competitive positioning in markets, to capturing customers through the creation of value, to the internal focus on people.

What this represents is a continuous search by the consulting community to find measurable models and sources of sustainable competitive advantage that could form the basis of lucrative consulting assignments and relationships. The preference for measurables – for example, costs and time are clear measurables – superseded the focus on competences, capabilities, and resources. In this light, it is important to maintain a healthy scepticism about the tools and their promoters who emerge from time to time, noting that ongoing academic research about what works, in particular in regard to sustainability, has driven much of the development of consulting tools. The other relevant discipline is that of 'matching' the tools to the prevailing economic and social conditions to see if they fit the times.

This chronology gives limited credit to the notion of new product, market, or technology development, as a preferred source of competitive advantage. This is despite the obvious advantages of success in this field. Kiechel notes this anomaly without explaining it, but it may be associated with the absence of suitable consulting tools by which to 'sell' it. In keeping with the emergence of the focus on people in the strategy literature, and the associated development of the design-thinking literature, the tools may be at hand for more organisations to take the challenge of innovation upon themselves and elevate this to the primary focus of their ongoing business success. There are companion developments in the public sector management literature that give substance to this view.

Kiechel attributes to Porter two of the landmark advances in corporate strategy history, the first being the concept of positioning and the second the value chain. In his development of the concept of the value chain, Porter fundamentally changed the unit of analysis of strategy development. Until the publication of his *Competitive advantage* in 1985, the level at which strategy development was typically undertaken was high-level functional – for example, manufacturing cost, marketing cost, or research and development cost – occasionally resource or capability-based where costs could be determined. Porter conceived of a business as the sum of a set of discrete activities, with the value chain being the organising principle, and with its particular merit being that the concept arrays these activities in roughly the same order as they are done. Activities were conceived of as the basic unit of competitive advantage, being narrower than traditional functions, cutting across organisational units and being what generate cost and create value for buyers. In private sector terms, this involves discrete activities, such as processing orders, calling on customers, assembling products, and training employees (Porter 1985, p xv). The value of this concept was that it provided a framework for understanding how these detailed, discrete activities had to change in order to give effect to the higher order strategy chosen with respect to markets. It provided a clearly linked means to implement the higher order positioning strategy.

7.2.1.3 The position today

Kiechel's framework through which to view the last hundred or so years of the development of management as a formal discipline evolving from supervision to leadership, and the management tension between people and numbers, can also be used to locate the tools and concepts of strategy today. There are a number of elements to this state of play that revolve around management tension and can perhaps best be seen through the position of innovation.

As Grant and Kiechel have noted, innovation emerged in recent decades as a primary focus for organisations pursuing growth. In the 1960s and 1970s, achieving success in the private sector was seen as a matter of choosing products and markets, planning for growth, and taking a ride. In a period of strong overall economic growth where market growth was more important than market share for profitability, this was a sufficient foundation for the success of many businesses. But in periods of slower economic growth, such as was experienced in the 1980s and has been experienced globally over the last decade, competition through innovation offers a more sustainable path to profitability than competition for market share. Moreover, pursuit of innovation is a robust strategy as it can also deliver 'success' in rising markets as well. The issue noted in an organisational structural context in Chapter 6 – how to simultaneously and seamlessly pursue success in established businesses whilst developing the next generation of businesses – thereby comes to the fore in a strategic context.

Clayton Christensen (1997) and Christensen with Raynor (2003) position the challenge of growth through innovation in the mainstream of business literature. This has been followed by an ongoing debate about where strategy and planning sit in relation to innovation and change. The foundations of this debate can be traced back at least as far as an empirical study by Mintzberg and colleagues at McGill University in the mid-1980s of the long-term development of strategy in a number of organisations, leading to criticism of the 'rationalist', 'scientific', view of the strategy-making process.

Mintzberg and colleagues argued that the picture of strategy making that emerged during the 1960s and 1970s, of a top management–determined strategy handed down for implementation by lower-level managers, was a fiction. This led Mintzberg (with James Waters) to distinguish between deliberate, and emergent strategy, where in the latter the process is less structured, more diffused, and the hard line between formulation and implementation is less apparent (Mintzberg & Waters 1985). Mintzberg later argued that not only is 'rationalism' an inaccurate representation of how strategies are formulated, but it is also a poor way of making strategy as it precludes learning. He describes a preferred view of the process of strategy making as crafting (Mintzberg 1994a, 1994b).

Porter countered much of Mintzberg and Waters' argument by pointing out that both corporate and business unit levels contributed to the successful strategic management of an organisation. He described the former as concentrating on whole-of-organisation strategies and playing the critical role of building synergies across business units, and the latter strategising at a market-level. Presented in this way, strategic management in large organisations becomes not so much a question of who does it but, rather, a matter of all parts of the organisation contributing under central direction within their clearly defined domains and varying time frames (Porter 1985). This did not, however, stifle the intense debate that ensued around the capability of the leaders of multi-divisional businesses to plan for their whole organisations, and the related merits of strategic planning.

Grant sought to balance the ongoing debate by arguing that strategy development was a multidimensional activity involving rational analysis, intuition, experience, and emotion, but that to downplay the role of systematic analysis in favour of intuition and vision was to ignore the opportunity to organise and assess the vast amount of information available on a firm and its environment, and deny the opportunity to systematically analyse the reasons for business success and failure and apply the lessons to the formulation of strategy.

This debate, or a latter-day version of it, continues and, in retrospect, much of it is more about semantics than substance (who should do it rather than where the balance should lie and what the content should be called). Indeed, the notion of strategic planning is a convenient whipping boy when the concept as commonly described and practised has no real place in a discussion of strategy. Martin, writing in 2014, points to Mintzberg's position as eminently sensible, in particular his advice that managers overestimate their ability to predict the future and plan for it in a precise and technocratic way, thereby wanting to encourage them to watch carefully for changes in their environment and make adjustments to their strategy as events unfolded (Martin 2014). But he adds his own advice in arguing that this is typically not what managers do, as they use the argument that because the future is unpredictable and volatile, it does not make sense to make strategic choices until the future becomes sufficiently clear. Martin argues this is a dangerous corporate approach leading to 'fast follower'–based choices that will never lead to the creation of unique advantages. He argues for a solid dose of empiricism to be added to the discussion.

In recent years, however, literature has moved on from addressing the issues of how to plan and who takes responsibility for it in a corporate context, to focusing on the organisational and management issues of successfully executing and integrating the exploitation of its present advantages whilst continuing to create new ones. In response, the strategy literature has turned to the relationship between strategy and innovation and a questioning of the continuing value of the concept of sustainable competitive advantage in an age of turbulence and rapid change in corporate markets. These are important issues when considering the application of the strategy and innovation literature to the public sector, along with the reminder from Kiechel (and others) that there is unlikely to be 'one best way'.

McGrath's recent and important contribution to the literature on competitive strategy argues that the separate fields of competitive strategy, innovation, and organisational change were coming together, but the notion on which the field of competitive strategy was based – that of sustainable competitive advantage – was outdated and even dangerous in the face of a rapidly changing environment. She argues that to win in this environment, business executives need to balance agility with stability and that 'to win in a volatile environment executives needed to learn how to exploit short-lived opportunities with speed and decisiveness' providing a perspective based on the idea of transient advantage (McGrath 2013, p xi).

The underlying concept – that advantage is transient – is not new, as much of the evolution of the corporate strategy literature can be seen as a search for sustainable competitive advantage – occasionally giving up and focusing more directly on the end game of making money for shareholders. Nor is the 'solution' new – of the need to balance agility with stability – first being introduced by March in 1991. Michael Tushman and Charles O'Reilly gave an organisational dimension to the concept in 1996, as did Christensen in 1997, and with Raynor in 2003. This latter dimension was complemented by the integrative comments of Martin in regard to innovation and strategy in his 2009 book *The design of business.*

What McGrath did in her 2013 formulation, however, was to lay out how to do it, with the development of her 'strategy playbook' taking a further step down the path of integrating the notions of competitive strategy, innovation, and organisational change, whilst focusing on a dynamic notion of success rather than the static equilibrium concept of the past.

The publication of McGrath's playbook and her criticism of the Porter-based theory of competitive advantage and positioning has opened up a lively debate about the nature of competitive advantage, although much of it ultimately, again, is about semantics. In a 2017 debate in the *Harvard Business Review*, Lafley and Martin claim that 'The death of sustainable competitive advantage has been greatly exaggerated' (Lafley

& Martin 2017). While, in response, McGrath demands flexibility in management, observing that many of the 'jobs to be done' have not changed over the centuries:

> but how that job gets done has changed dramatically. If incumbent companies stay focused on the job itself – rather than on the specifics of how it gets done at this moment in time – they may be able to invent a better way before the competition does. (McGrath 2017)

The study of public sector management addresses a number of points and questions that arise from this discussion of the concept of strategy. Three points of importance can be taken from McGrath's work. The first and obvious one is to recognise the importance of context. Not all industries face the pace of change and short time frames that McGrath describes of transient advantage and on which she builds her approach. In the *Harvard Business Review* exchange, McGrath draws a distinction between a classical strategic setting – one with clearly delineated boundaries, a stable competitive base, no major disruptions, and a strong competitive base that, once established, can be maintained – and one where industry boundaries are blurry, traditional barriers to entry are eroding, emerging technologies are eroding competitive constraints, and environments are unstable.

Certainly, in the period from Federation until the introduction of the New Public Management (NPM) reforms in the 1980s in Australia, the industry of public administration closely approximated the former. The reforms introduced to public sector management in the 1980s, however, fundamentally changed its competitive position after nearly a century (in Australia's case) of negligible competition; and the level of competition has continued to rise. Moreover, changes in the political environment, with the emerging decline and splintering of political parties, and its aftermath, are likely to represent a further major challenge to the influence of the public service. Any such changes are likely to challenge both the policy advisory processes and the content of public policy that the public service has traditionally relied on. The public service has a central role to play in the public interest in avoiding the worst outcomes of the sorts of policy compromises that occur with coalition governments, namely policies that no one supports. This environmental change, should it continue along its present path, is one in terms of its impact on the public service that may well be seen to be, similar in terms to the NPM reforms, some 20 or 30 years down the track.[6]

The second point involves the role of the centre. The need to balance exploration and exploitation (stability and agility in McGrath's terms) brings to the fore the resource-allocation process, both for the way in which resources are first allocated and the speed with which resources are reallocated. Indeed, in McGrath's world, the various operating units in a business become custodians rather than 'owners' of resources with resource allocation an almost continuous process – gone, in McGrath's world, are the dominant formal reallocations of resources associated with annual budget and planning processes, to be replaced by quarterly, even continuous allocations between existing businesses.

This places heavy demands on the centre for a carefully designed, tightly led and managed resource-allocation process. McGrath writes about healthy disengagement: escaping the tyranny of NPV (net present value); freeing up hostage resources; access to resources, not ownership; and proactively retiring assets. Geoff Mulgan agrees with this sentiment, noting that, in the public sector, effective strategy requires money to be liberated from the past for the needs of the future, and writes of the appetite for change and the change margin, but notes that in most governments, this margin is as small as 1 or 2 per cent of spending within a budgetary year, with past commitments and pay increments taking up most available annual resources (Mulgan 2009, p 105; McGrath 2013, p 77).

Whilst the proximate source of competitive advantage can be found in business units with deep customer relationships, as described by McGrath, the ultimate competitive advantage lies with resource allocation and management capability as it drives the balance between the present and the future, with the pace of changing resource allocation being the grounds of competitive advantage. It is not fashionable to argue that sustainable competitive advantage can be built on organisational capabilities or competences, and McGrath's argument aligns very closely with that of Gary Hamel and CK Prahalad who focus on a business's core competences as the best way of competing for the future (Hamel &

---

6   I return to the question of the role of the public service in a world of coalition governments – in its own interests and in the public interest – in the final chapter.

Prahalad 1994). By identifying the crucial role that the resource-allocation process plays in business success, McGrath links the standard resource-based and customer-driven approaches to competitive strategy.

The third point involves the data requirements of this system. McGrath's resource allocation and management system demands the generation of data to continuously fine-tune the allocation of resources. High-quality data systems and absolute transparency across business unit and corporate levels facilitate the processes. McGrath argues that, in a world of transient advantage, this data can give meaning to the difference between the competitive life of an asset and its accounting life, and the associated incentive to leverage relationships and assets of others rather than invest heavily in own-organisation long-life assets that have a relatively short competitive life. More broadly, this discussion of the concept of strategy points to the need to carefully align it with its context.

Nonetheless, some elements of strategy have not changed. The commonly accepted doctrine that the purpose of strategy is to identify and actively manage the foundations on which a business can be successful remains influential. Clear goals and an understanding of winning continue to underlie this focus, and 'to win' in business, an organisation must be better than its competitors. A business should choose its battleground and actively compete, and the arbiter of victory or loss is the customer, thus, no competitive strategy can afford to be cast in stone. Whilst the notion of competitive advantage should underlie an organisation's strategy, competitive advantage should be conceived of in terms of customers and the people, capabilities and processes that give it life. Beyond that, the discussion of strategy comes down to the alignment of markets and businesses with an organisation's fundamental purpose, the balance that the business should seek between maximising returns from the present and the future, and how it should do this.

I argue that the tools of strategy can be applied to any organisation, and that the challenge of making them relevant comes with the careful delineation of the context, not the choice of tools themselves. The tools can add value in any context, but has the environment been defined in a way that enables them to do so? Perhaps the key to doing this can be unlocked by design thinking, which avoids the path dependency of prevailing discussions in identifying mysteries and seeking to unravel them? The challenge, of course, is to identify these mysteries in a way that disassociates the thinker from the existing boundaries of thought once one defines such areas of interest as 'mysteries'. For example, examining data associations in pursuit of a causal relationship might involve focusing on outliers rather than the bulk of data that constitutes the central tendency.[7]

Consideration of the application of the concept of strategy to public administration is challenged by the legislated constraints on the business the public service is in. The public service is seen to have little control, and not much more influence, over the choice of its activities and the allocation of resources to these activities. Moreover, notwithstanding the occasional external jolt to the practice of public administration – from governmental or environmental change – the core tasks of public administration have been largely stable for decades, one might say centuries. Why could it possibly need a strategy?

I argue that public administration is competing for business, whether it chooses to recognise this or not; that it is losing the competitive battle; and that it is in the public interest that it recognises and responds systemically to this challenge. The public service is not well equipped to support a strategic approach to its business, knowing little in a systematic manner about its competitive position – about its costs, customers, and competitors – leaving it poorly placed to take a strategic approach to its business.

7.2.2 A simple strategy framework

Whilst most leading business strategy authors choose to emphasise different points in their own 'takes' on strategy, they all seem agreed that the foundation of good strategy is choices (see, for example, Porter 1985; Grant 1995; Christensen & Raynor 2003; Martin 2009; Lafley & Martin 2013). And from their various discussions of content and process a generic framework can be proposed. This is presented in Fig. 7.1

---

7   In his book on design thinking, Martin (2009) presents a fascinating discussion of what he calls 'the reliability bias', which encourages the identification of patterns in chaos, rather than discarding those data points that do not fit the pattern. He distinguishes between reliability and validity in understanding data associations. In a similar vein, McGrath (2013) encourages seeking something new in pursuit of competitive advantage: it need not be a new product or technology but it could be a new market or a new set of customers that develops from the reconception of the existing business.

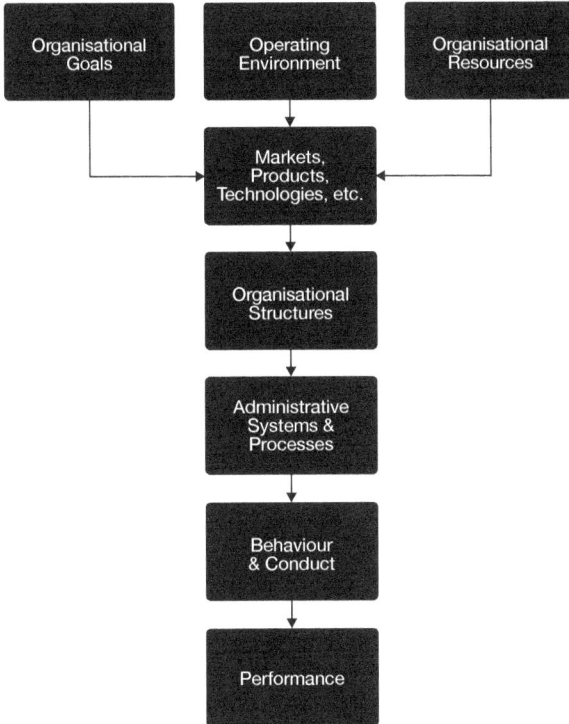

Figure 7.1 The basic strategy development framework

Given an organisation's fundamental purpose, a standard way of developing a firm's strategy is to first consider its goals (what winning looks like), search the operating environment for businesses that could best align with these goals, filter them through the resources available (internal capabilities plus suppliers, alliances, and partnerships) to determine the activity mix that the organisation should (and should not) undertake. This is followed by making choices about organisational structures, management and administrative systems and processes, associated with desired organisational behaviour and conduct, all of which contribute to results. Fig. 7.1 presents this analytical structure.

Conceptually, this process can be divided into two stages.[8] The first involves determination of the product, customer, market and technology mix, with regard to organisational goals and underpinning capabilities. Questions to ask include, what does a win look like (goals/targets); where

8   It can be argued that strategy development is one integrated and iterative act involving its formation and implementation. For expositional purposes I have treated it as separate stages.

to play (choice of customers/activities); and how to win (development of compelling customer value propositions)? The second part of the process, and integrated with the development of the first, involves choosing an organisational structure and supporting management and administrative systems that accommodate and enhance the chosen customer and market focus. These structures, systems, and processes need to harmonise with organisational behaviour and conduct.[9]

Important issues involve the determination of the intra- and extra-organisational relationships, achieving the desired values and behaviours, and the enabling management and administrative systems. This critically includes servicing the organisation's governance needs – the collection, integration, and aggregation of information across organisational levels to accommodate reporting against internal performance targets at multiple levels, but which at a corporate level must also accommodate a compliance component to fully address whole-of-organisation governance requirements. The final piece of the strategy framework is performance, viewed primarily in terms of the meeting of the organisation's goals.

There are many variations to this core business strategy framework, depending on what needs to be emphasised and to what level of detail. Any single element could be expanded into a self-contained diagram; pairs of (or multiple) elements could be presented with feedback loops; and the map could provide for multiple business divisions and information flows between head office and the divisions or functions (or both), depending on the organisational form and the respective roles of head office and the divisions in the planning process – the latter could also give effect to the organisation's choice of balance between deliberate and emergent strategy.

The entity could also be considered as a social/human organisation, rather than as a set of product- and market-based interactions, embracing communications (hard/soft) flows between head office and the divisions, between functions, and with third parties, giving effect to the concept of internal and external boundary conditions. Moreover, these flows might be presented, for example, in terms of the relative quantities and

---

9   There is a useful distinction between the (internal) behaviour of people within the organisation, and the (external) conduct of the same people in their external relationships. I have used the term 'culture' minimally because it is difficult to define and quantify and is often used as an ill-defined catch-all for human behaviour. From an analytical perspective it is more useful to concentrate on organisational leadership, which drives the alignment of people with organisational goals and strategies.

the balance between hard and soft communications. Other refinements might be possible in terms of the content of the communication and the respective roles of the parties – some communications might be regulatory based with government agencies, some might be marketing based with customers/suppliers, yet others might be professionally based exchanges between internal and external parties (e.g. between lawyers interpreting the trade practices legislation), and many would be between 'head office' and the divisions.

7.2.3 Application of the framework to the public service

The application of the simple framework to the public service raises three sets of issues. The first is the key contextual issues that distinguish the public from the private sector – these might be viewed in terms of the institutional and legislative differences. The second is the internal differences between the public and private sectors. And the third lies in their interface and should be considered primarily in terms of behaviours.

The institutional and legislative features of the public service are a major point of difference. The role of government as a determining presence, the legislated role of the public service in regard to the public and the parliament, the embodiment of these relationships in a dedicated act of parliament, the role of watchdog bodies in regard to the public service, and the central agency role and public nature of the business of public administration are also important differences. Then there is the nature of the public service itself, with its mixture of public, merit, and private goods and services; funding and staffing differences; and resourcing levels, allocations and senior management appointments determined by governments.

Moreover, differences in funding and staffing are matched by minimal choice over the business of the public service and a lack of a market price for services (Ludwig von Mises' economic calculation is not there to determine value). And, importantly, the continuity of the public service is legislated for – as a business it cannot fail. Moreover, governments largely determine the organisation of the public service in an overall sense and its division. Finally, it can be argued that the public service has limited control over organisational behaviour beyond its formal rule-driven component because of the nature of its relationship with government and the impact that both formal government policies and behaviours, especially of ministers and staffers, can have on departmental and public service culture.

Yet there are many similarities, especially with big business. The tasks of management are similar in a generic sense: there are customers (clients) and stakeholders, goods and services to be procured and delivered to clients, budgets to be managed, capital projects to be overseen, around 160,000 staff to be managed and developed, and there is a brand to be managed. When viewed as a competitive business, the public service has some serious competitive advantages, namely a legislated role (through the role of secretaries) as principal official policy adviser and manager of service delivery, guaranteed funding, and a seat next to (the ear of?) government – advantages that many businesses would pay dearly for. Discussions of the role of the public service typically tend to emphasise the constraints of government but, surely, this is a very powerful base to work from?

Moreover, the problems of government today – its short-termism and failure to invest; its piecemeal, fragmented, and low-level approach to policy; and the absence of a moral compass, even common sense (as measured by the pub test), amongst many parliamentarians – must be considered in light of how the relationships between the government and the public service, in its legislated and practised forms, is a key variable in any mix to improve the quality of government. The existing institutional and legislative arrangements should not be taken for granted and a better way must be sought within the broad ambit of a representative government served by the public service. The limitations of path dependency must be eschewed and, in public policy terms, public administration should be treated like any other activity in the economy, seeking to secure its best contribution. The legislature must not be used to serve private interests – in this case the private interests of the political parties and their supporters.

There are a number of possible sources of additional public value to be generated from a strategically led and managed public service. The first is that, when used to its best advantage in the private sector, strategic management focuses on choices between what to do and what not to do. This focus is in short supply in contemporary politics – there are too many problems to solve, too few resources to solve them, and little appetite to disengage with any group already being serviced from the public purse. If only for fiscal reasons, governments need a more strategic approach. The public service must find a way (or be empowered) to assist governments to make better choices and invest.

Much of the necessary analytical infrastructure and data collection is missing from public administration, including to better inform government of the consequences of its choices, to better manage its own activities, and to apprise the Australian public of the outcomes of government activities. A top-down focus on strategy, through a board and dedicated executive team, would ensure the establishment of this analytical structure consistent with statutory governance obligations. Accompanied by a capacity to practise the values and code of conduct set out in the *Public Service Act 1999*, the established role could contribute to more government decisions based on public value rather than political advantage.

The public service must reconceive itself as a competitive enterprise, develop a strategy, and actively compete for the strategic high ground it has given up over the last 30 or 40 years. Political parties are private organisations established to serve their stakeholders – they are no different in principle to the many other private organisations that seek advantage from government, whether through accommodating policy settings or from supply contracts. While our government is run by private enterprise, the Australian Public Service is established under an Act of parliament to serve – the government of the day, the parliament, and the Australian public. Only the public service has the legislated requirement and incentive to take an integrated and high-level view of the role and performance of government.

Central to the notion of strategy in the private sector is the concept of winning through effective competition. The private sector strategy literature is sometimes dismissed as inapplicable to the public sector because of the presumed absence of competition, but that assumption is misplaced. Certainly there is competition between political parties and individuals for office, but competition abounds in the business of public administration: there is competition amongst promoters of different political belief systems, policy frameworks, policies, and service delivery options, and this competition continues through the life of every government.

More importantly, amongst the elements of the governing parties (factions, parliamentary and organisational wings), there is competition for influence over, and ownership of, policy, including from the various think tanks and universities, and the community-based and private enterprises that wish to be the beneficiaries. There is a plethora of individuals and organisations that attempt to influence government decisions to their immediate benefit and of their clients. Right across this spectrum, the public service faces competition for influence, within its legislated policy advisory and service delivery management roles. Thus, there is a strong case to reconceive the public service as a competitive enterprise, to apply the concept of strategy to its activities, and consider how to enhance its capacity to meet its charter to serve the Australian public.

7.3 The concept of strategy in the public sector

7.3.1 The public sector strategic management literature

This examination of the concept of strategy and its linkages to structure leads to a consideration of the views expressed in the public sector management literature about the application of this category of private sector literature to the public sector. Public sector literature on strategic management is beginning to address some of the core questions with regard to strategy in the public sector. Articles by Theodore Poister and colleagues, and Jesper Hansen and Ewan Ferlie in the United States have examined the applicability of core strategic management theories – such as the resource-based theory and Porter's theory of competitive positioning – to the public sector, focusing, for example, on the determination of factors such as degree of fiscal autonomy, standardisation of services, and the presence of competition, as key determinants of suitability (Poister & Streib 1999; Poister, Pitts & Hamilton 2010; Hansen 2007; Hansen & Ferlie 2014).

The various theories of public sector strategic management range from viewing the organisation as a bundle of capabilities (the resource-based theories), to one of viewing the degree of competition amongst buyers, suppliers, and competitors as the prime determinant of organisational strategy. Both have a potentially useful perspective for the public sector. Most observers, however, are equally sceptical of their applicability to the broad range of public sector activity. For example, John Alford and Brian Head point out that, when considering the adaptation of the tools of corporate strategy to the public sector, '"government agencies" generally do not have the full set of freedoms borne by businesses namely goal setting, financial, recruitment, choice of business lines' (Head & Alford 2015). And, in turn, Hansen has made the point that only certain types of public sector organisation are suitable for the application of the Porter and resource-based strategic management theories (essentially those that have predominantly private sector characteristics) (Hansen 2007). I make five points in response to this hesitation.

First, whilst a useful starting point, market structure tests of suitability are largely built around a benchmark of autonomous firms and competitive market structures, which underestimates the prevailing level of competition for the business of government. This underestimation occurs because the competition is not necessarily competition of a conventional product features and benefits and price-driven kind and is rather a battle of ideas and for influence and, therefore, is harder to characterise and analyse. As argued in Chapter 8, the models are no less applicable in prospect to public sector/public service activity.

Secondly, much public sector management literature concludes that the private sector strategy literature has limited application in the public sector domain. This is rooted in a particular view of the NPM experience, which resulted in many critics arguing that differences between the public and private sectors were so great that business practices should not be transferred to the public sector. It is arguable that some of the tools were poorly chosen and others imperfectly implemented, and that a careful assessment of the NPM experience does not invalidate the general concept of application of private sector tools to public sector management.

My third point follows academic research into the applicability of private sector management tools to the public sector. In a 2002 meta-study, Boyne concluded that there should be no general presumption against the application of private sector management techniques to the public sector. He examined both the theoretical arguments and evidence from 34 studies and determined that the balance of evidence did not support this presumption, despite the dominant view in the public policy and administration literature that public and private organisations were so different that NPM-style prescriptions were inappropriate. He concluded 'Therefore the injunction that public managers can learn useful lessons from private managers is worthy of serious, but cautious, consideration' (Boyne 2002). Furthermore, whilst not settling the score on this count,

Boyne's article left researchers open to find that any shortcomings arising from implementation of the private sector–driven NPM were a consequence of inadequate implementation rather than unsuitable tools.

Qualified support for this view is also provided by Mark Moore, who examined the development of a corporate strategy for three different sorts of organisations – private for-profit, non-profit, and governmental – and considered the managerial tasks undertaken in each in the development of a corporate strategy. He argued that the essential difference between private for-profit organisations and governmental organisations is that financial performance dominates the strategic thinking of the first, whilst the creation of public value and mission attainment is central for the last. According to Moore, the form of such strategies, and the analytic tasks used in developing them, is the important distinguishing difference but that organisations in all three sectors need strategies to remain purposeful and effective (Moore 2000).

Moore went on to develop a strategy formation model for government organisations that incorporates the three elements of value, legitimacy and support, and operational capacity. He supported the notion that governmental organisations should plan and develop strategies, although he argued that the content and processes of strategy development for these organisations should differ from those of the for-profit sector. Unfortunately he did not make the critical distinction – which is central to the concept of legitimacy – between different forms of governmental organisation, variously describing government bureaucracies, and the efforts of elected representatives and officials, as one.

For governments (the elected representatives), the concept of legitimacy has elements of voter mandate and the standing of government in the community. This 'legitimacy' provides an umbrella, the authorising environment, under which the public service operates. The concept of government legitimacy is no less important for the public service for it helps to define the boundaries and limits of government activity and the role of the public service in its development. As argued in Chapter 5, when viewed in Moore's terms, there is a role for the public service to play in legitimising government.

Whilst there are some distinctive differences between private and public sector management, they do not invalidate the application of the notions of industrial organisation and strategic management to the public sector.

7.3.2 Application of the concept of strategy

The concepts, language and, most particularly, the environment may well be different when applying strategic management to the public sector. Table 7.1 aligns these key issues in the development of a public service strategy with the core elements of our strategy framework.

Table 7.1 A public service strategic management framework

Framework	Associated concepts and issues
Complexity of the environment	Degrees of wickedness, community involvement, services and solutions, solution and resolution, manifestations and root causes, containment and elimination, trust in government, a diminishing pool of authority, government by private enterprise, government short-termism, the 24-hour news cycle.
Organisational goals and belief systems	An integrated organisation; goals and their boundaries: alignment; the requirements of the Public Service Act – serving a triad of communities; values, conduct and behaviours; the concept of public value.
Organisational capabilities	Leadership and the role of 'head office'; competences and capabilities; strategic management; cross departmental and cross sectoral collaboration, coordination, and cooperation; organisational learning; a career public service; activity and performance measurement; hostage resources; resource-allocation processes and supporting management information; systemic policy capability, 'seeing' all Australians, looking over the horizon, and actively managing itself.
The activities	Competition for influence, competition for business, active management of self and government stakeholders, build confidence in government, build and capture public value and promote its own achievements in the national interest, sustainable rather than transient advantage. Who is the customer?
The organisation of resources and administrative systems/ processes	Organisational structure; strategy and structure; a learning organisation; inertia, change, and adaptation; organisational boundaries; innovation; vertical and horizontal collaboration; networks; outsourcing; information flows; data architecture; integrated organisations; organisational form, size, efficiency and effectiveness; performance measurement, government governance and accountability; public service governance.
Behaviour and conduct	Values, behaviours, code of conduct; organisational structure and behaviours; aligning behaviours with organisational goals; organisational boundaries and conduct; leadership; structures.
Performance	Due process; inputs, outputs, impacts, outcomes and public value; services and solutions; cooperation, coordination and collaboration; government governance and public service governance.

The framework of Fig. 7.1 can be applied to the public service with reference to the end game for government being the delivery of a set of valued services to citizens so as to achieve re-election. For the public service, with its duty to serve the Australian public and parliament as well as the government, the challenge is to balance the requirements of the government of the day with the needs of governments of the future, and with the competing demands of all three constituencies. The hallmark of its success is the influence it exerts over the policy choices of government in the longer-term and the quality of its ongoing financial and program administration. If it is to be successful in these terms, it must create room for activity choices rather than have all of these choices made for it by government(s), and it must see itself as an entity separate from government. From a public policy standpoint, there must be more to public service life than administering today's government's policies; it must have its own strategy.

7.3.3 Public sector innovation

Innovation has emerged as a management tool to respond to the challenges of an unfriendly operating environment incorporating slow overall market growth and fierce competition for market share in established industries. Kiechel's observation that innovation as a management concept sits comfortably with both the humanist and numerical streams of the management literature, which gives it credibility that other management concepts may not have.

The writings of March, Martin, McGrath, and Tushman and O'Reilly on associated developments in organisational structures and processes are designed to spell out how to do it. The most useful framework within which to view this literature is March's distinction between exploitation and exploration (March 1991). A lesson from this article is the natural tendency for exploitation to progressively dominate exploration through application of standard corporate resource-allocation processes in the absence of a concerted effort to the contrary. This substantiates the desire to seek a structural resolution to the problem of resource allocation – for example, ambidextrous organisations – but does not solve it. Other solutions are proposed in terms of formal and informal allocations of an individual's time to the two tasks. This literature is developing.

In the case of the public sector, innovation as a tool of general management has yet to achieve the status that it has in the private sector. Whilst innovation does occur in the public sector – it may be viewed as 'ministerially driven', or 'bottom-up', and may be 'top down' – what it invariably is not is systematic, systemic or strategic.[10] Moreover, current research into innovation in the public sector is still in its infancy, albeit growing rapidly and in a number of disparate directions. There is a basic human capacity to observe and learn through repetition and curiosity, and address 'mysteries', which underpins a level of innovation through all human activities across public and private sectors. Yet beyond this 'operational' or 'business improvement' innovation (Bason calls it random incrementalisation), the drivers of public sector innovation remain obscure. And, because it is uncertain why innovation occurs, there is less validation of subsidiary dimensions of innovation – including whether it is a learning process, problem- or capability-driven, and whether its core is incremental or radical, systematic or episodic, self-directed or management-led in nature. Consequently, the process is less able to be automated.

It can be argued that this absence – of a systematic, systemic and strategic approach to innovation across the public sector – is due to the absence of competitive pressures. Certainly, there are competitive pressures within the public sector for budget. The usual commentary, however, is focused on the absence of external competition for the business of the public service. This observation may well be true in some parts of public administration that do not readily allow competition, as in Oliver Williamson's example of foreign affairs (1999), but, as a broad-based perception, it is wrong. The public service around the globe is in a battle for influence over government policy and expenditure decisions, and is steadily losing market share, as governments increasingly look to third-party service providers and influencers to meet their needs.

---

10   There is value in distinguishing between the three terms systematic, systemic, and strategic. I use the word systematic to mean methodical, carried out using step-by-step procedures, and/or constituting a system, where 'the system' is the innovation system. Systemic, on the other hand, describes something that happens or exists throughout a whole system, it is whole-of-body, where 'the system' is the public service/sector. Strategic innovation, as defined by Bason (2010), is associated with setting organisational direction ('the what') and the need to find innovative solutions to create the desired value around this direction. I contrast this with operational innovation, which is associated with the day-to-day tasks of the organisation and which might ordinarily be associated with business improvement activities.

Another argument commonly advanced to 'explain' low levels of innovation is that of the public service's risk-aversion, which, in its more enlightened forms, recognises career, financial, and political risk(s). Whilst the presence of these risk forms is acknowledged, with the latter a unique feature of public service activity, I argue in Chapter 9 that, to the extent that risk-aversion exists, it does so substantially because there is no organisational framework within which entrepreneurial individuals, even those pursuing relatively low-level operational innovation, can lay off this risk. In the absence of a suitable organisational framework for the management of associated risk, it becomes career threatening. Career risk, then, is an important factor. State and federal government reports continue to identify the absence of suitable organisational risk management frameworks, regularly recommending that suitable governance and accountability frameworks be established in such cases.[11] [12]

Notwithstanding these valid reasons why levels of public sector innovation may be sub-optimal, there is an emerging public sector literature exploring the foundations on which a more innovative public sector might be built. There are two streams to this literature. The first is that of collaborative innovation, which reflects the growing focus on the need for tools to deliver effective vertical and horizontal coordination in a model of increasingly distributed government; this has been the major development in the public sector management literature over the last decade and a half. The question being posed is how public sector managers can deliver more effective public policy responses to problems that cross departmental and

---

11   The management of individual and organisational risk from public service activities is a weak point in many departments, not just in regard to innovation. One such example is the risk associated with undertaking controlled burnoffs in Victoria, where the responsible staff have been reluctant to do this because of the risk of breakouts and widespread damage, and the consequent impact on their careers. This followed a breakout from a controlled burn in country Victoria at Lancefield on 30 September 2015. The consequence is a system in which accountability is shared, with no one and everyone responsible in the event of a disaster, much like the Australian Government home insulation case noted earlier.

12   Risk management practices in the public sector are more developed in regard to third-party arrangements than internal operations, especially in regard to the variety of risk-sharing partnership arrangements with the private sector, however, further development is required here. No matter how government contracts with the private sector to lay off commercial risk, and whatever it might pay to do this, the prospect of failure by a commercial partner always leaves the government wearing the commercial risk as a consequence of the associated political risk. Governments are ultimately unable to avoid the commercial risk of jointly sponsored projects hitting hurdles and, as the Australian Government's Productivity Commission points out, governments must avoid both implicit guarantees that create perverse incentives that weaken risk management ('too important to fail'), and the pursuit of a risk-minimisation strategy that runs the risk of inflating overall project costs (trying to lay off all of the commercial risk) (Productivity Commission 2014a).

sectoral lines with the recognition (a) that fashioning these responses must become a priority for organisational leaders, and (b) that being innovative is necessary, given the uniqueness of individual problems. An important part of this research has focused on understanding how, in a world of overlapping problems and root causes, managers can be confident that actions will have satisfactory system-wide effects, whilst another has started to examine the organisational management issues, and a further part is exploring the influence of context on the performance of different management models.

The second and more recent steam of literature sees innovation as a whole-of-organisation challenge proposing the development of a systematic approach, and a supporting organisational culture. In *Leading public sector innovation*, Bason observed that most public service–led innovation is of a low level, not managerially driven, emerging in an incidental or random manner from the bowels of public administration, and ill-suited to delivering the kind of radical solutions needed (Bason 2010, p 15). Bason sees the challenge as creating an innovation strategy and its integration with robust organisation-wide processes to ensure continuous learning and improvement (Bason 2010, Chapter 6, esp p 120 ff). Eva Sørensen and Jacob Torfing highlight the accidental and episodic character of public sector innovation and its lack of enhancement of organisational-innovation capacity (Sørensen & Torfing 2012, pp 4, 8). Mulgan highlights the small budgets and lack of public sector commitment to innovation (Mulgan 2009).

What this set of public and private sector literature has in common is the articulation of a common problem for established organisations – how to balance the present and future in an increasingly volatile and unfriendly environment. This label applies whether the discussion involves the merits of transient advantage over sustainable competitive advantage, of ambidextrous organisations over processes embedded in existing organisational structures, or how to effectively integrate the tools of design thinking into established organisational processes. As Bason observes, one of the key challenges in building a culture of innovation in the public sector is to recognise the equal validity of innovation and operational activity: 'Innovation can be perceived as a barrier to "real work". Conversely "real work" can be a barrier to innovation' (Bason 2010, p 120). This is the challenge that March wrote about in 1991.

The public service must become innovative to meet the needs of effective coordination. This requires leadership, not management, which treats it at present as an incidental outcome from the prevailing day-to-day activities.

The necessity to promulgate associated organisational (management) rules, and administrative systems and procedures as well as develop new capabilities practically demands that innovation be treated as a strategy not just at the level of the individual department but on a whole-of-public-service basis. It should be one of the key elements in a centre-driven public service that takes as its challenge not just how to do things but what to do.

7.4 Conclusions

The field of corporate strategy has recently recognised the management tools needed to integrate the exploitation of existing market advantages, along with the exploration of new such advantages. Developments in this literature – the application of design thinking, the development of the notion of transient advantage, and a focus on the development of organisational capabilities to manage the integration of exploration with exploitation – have seen a blurring of the distinctions between innovation and strategy. For some, innovation is the new strategy, for others it is an important platform in corporate strategy. Where it sits in an organisation's hierarchy is a function of its history and the pace of change in its markets; how successful it is likely to be is a function of its capacity to observe and assess change and form an effective response. The private sector management literature is converging on the view that innovation should be central to the way organisations think strategically and operationally with a developing view in the public sector management literature that innovation may also be necessary for survival.

The prevailing debate about the concept of transient advantage can be seen as a metaphor for the broader debate about the direction of corporate strategy. McGrath argues that the utility of the concept of sustainable competitive advantage, which underpins Porter's work and remains at the heart of much contemporary strategy analysis, has passed in an age of turbulence and rapid change in corporate markets, and that the concept of transient (as opposed to sustainable) advantage has greater utility today (McGrath 2013). There is much dispute around this subject but it can be argued that the concept of competitive advantage continues to be useful despite shortening product life cycles, and that what is needed is an additional capacity to generate and integrate innovations if they are to survive. The equivalent point of agreement in the public sector literature is that the public sector must elevate innovation from its present status of random incrementalisation to one of strategy that drives the public sector.

Similarly, where Head and Alford see the potential value of the adoption of the tools of corporate strategy in the public sector, noting that it widens the horizon of choice from simply how to do things to what to do, context is also a necessary consideration (Head & Alford 2008). In the context of a multiplicity of players involved in fashioning and delivering solutions to complex public sector problems, Head and Alford see making choices about what to do, through the use of tools such as strategic positioning and determination of core competences, as potentially beneficial when applied with flexibility in goal-setting and strategy development.

These tools are rarely focused on the external interface in a public sector context. At the heart of the determination of corporate strategy lies the concept of competitive positioning. Within the public service there has been too little attention paid to goal-setting (winning) and what to do (as opposed to how to do it) and the organisational and skill requirements for both the general and specific solutions to today's problems; and too much attention paid to collaboration at the expense of competition.

This public sector focus on the internal to the exclusion of the external, on capabilities and competencies rather than customers and value chains, one that has been described in a corporate context as 'the four walls approach to strategy' – might well also explain a public sector lack of interest in obtaining and retaining systematic market knowledge. Laura Tingle (2015) noted destruction of corporate memory in the Australian public sector, but it is more importantly an absence of the proactive acquisition of market intelligence of the sort that would be used by any large corporation to inform its allocation of resources.

Every organisation has actual and/or potential competitors for its business now or in the future and one of the key elements that a successful strategic approach to an organisation's business must deliver is information on competitors, on customers, on underlying demand and supply trends, on the impact of technology, on market and organisational risks, all married to information on its own business. At the whole-of-organisation level, this information must support regular reviews of the businesses it is in, and at the operating or business unit level (in public service terms, the individual department) must focus on its competitive positioning, together addressing the questions of where to play and how to win on an ongoing basis.

The systematic accumulation and interpretation of market intelligence should be a dedicated function in any large organisation, and play a critical role in shaping its strategic outlook. Market intelligence in a public sector context should comprise the information that is collected at individual department level and at whole-of-public-service level. This may range from 'global' developments in consumer, political, industry, social, and environmental behaviour (the core of corporate market intelligence), through to such behaviour in local markets allied with competitor analysis (the core of business unit market intelligence). A central capability is required to support this critical function.

The public service must use all of the tools available to competitively position itself amongst the players in the system and actively compete for influence amongst them. In the words of the early strategists (who were military men), the public sector should choose its battleground, build its capabilities, and engage in war. Anything less will see its legitimacy and competitiveness further eroded at long-term cost to the community at large. To achieve change, the public service must reconsider its role in delivering good government, acknowledge both the commonality and divergence of interests with the elected representatives, and build new capabilities and processes to deliver beneficial outcomes. Fundamentally it will need to determine its competitive advantage in the political game and actively compete.

Unless the public service reconceives itself holistically, acknowledging that it faces a Porter-type challenge to actively compete for its share of the business of government, it will continue to lose relevance as a player in the game, continuing to 'play to play' rather than playing to win. A 'decision' by the public service to actively compete rather than retreat in the public policy space would require its re-conception as a competitive organisation with its departments equipped to compete.

Context is essential for the prescription for any single organisation. Whilst there may be some common high-level imperatives for all organisations in the face of widespread economic and social change during particular periods of history, there will always be differences as to how individual organisations might best respond. The pace of change in individual input and output markets will vary and different organisational structures, different balances between exploration and exploitation, perhaps even different capability development and accompanying resource allocation processes, will be required. The importance of these contextual elements may vary as much across individual business units within a large organisation as between organisations. It is important that the public service understands and responds.

8

The competitive advantage of the public sector

8.1 Introduction

The starting point for any discussion about the competitive positioning of the public service should be a clear understanding of the role of government. I do not mean the underlying political, indeed economic, arguments for the range of interventions that any government might undertake, rather I mean the chosen role. And, within this context, I distinguish the role of the public service from the role of the elected officials within 'government'.

I acknowledge that the decisions about choice of government activities clearly lie in the hands of the elected officials, as does the role that the government chooses to play in the design and delivery of any particular activity, and the consequent chosen role(s) for the public service. I nonetheless argue that the role that the public service could play in meeting its responsibilities to its legislated triad of communities ranges more broadly across this spectrum than it presently plays. I also argue that, by virtue of the content of the *Public Service Act 1999*, the Australian Public Service (APS) is entitled to, and should, view its existence as separate from the elected arm of government.

With this as a starting point, the public service can be considered like any other independent organisation with goals and stakeholders, requiring effective management to connect the two. At the heart of the effective organisational management lies an ongoing plan to convert goals into activities. This plan is supported by choices made with regard to activities, and demonstrating how these activities can be converted into the targeted outcomes. It is to the strategic choice and mix of public service activities – the public service activity portfolio if you like – that I now turn.

It is not immediately obvious how best to apply the concept of strategy, as developed in Chapter 7, to public service activity. Neither the corporate strategy literature nor the public sector management literature is of much assistance here, as there is little published research that brings the two together, certainly not with a primary focus on the role of the public service. There is a substantial literature on the application of selective private sector business practices to public administration; for example, public sector procurement outsourcing and contestability. This literature focuses on the management of these activities rather than on the strategic context within which decisions are made and the processes of competition between the public and private sectors. Similarly, the major stream of literature on public sector management that treats the public service as a competitive endeavour, is focused on motivation and internal competition for resources and status, for example through budget maximisation and turf acquisition, rather than on competition for influence in broader markets. This chapter focuses squarely on determining competitive advantage for the public service in the broader context.

Michael Porter's analytical framework in *Competitive advantage* (1985), in which he explores competition at the level of the individual firm, is applicable to this discussion (Porter 1985). In conjunction with the preceding volume, *Competitive strategy* (1980), Porter's activity-based framework, which focuses on competitive advantage and its sustainability, has been the basic language of business strategy for over 30 years. The major benefit of using this framework is that it provides the foundations for thinking about strategy across multiple businesses (departments), which is essential when treating public service endeavour in a systemic manner. It also provides an integrated framework within which to consider the role of 'the customer', the emerging concept of public value, and the coordination problems confronted by the public service. The latter can be considered through the process of strategy implementation, with Porter paying special attention to the establishment of beneficial horizontal relationships between businesses within a large organisation.

The analytical starting point here is the public service status quo, with a large number of embedded decisions about roles, responsibilities, and a broad range of make-or-buy policies and decisions. Many of these decisions were 'imperfect', embodying primarily political motives and/or limited analytical frameworks and inadequate information, but they are a starting point. The aim is to construct a competitive strategy for the public service in this environment noting that, while the public service is a captive of the public sector and clearly dependent on government, it is nonetheless exposed to competition across a broad spectrum of government activities.

This chapter outlines Porter's framework and applies it to public service activity. While there is much detail in the Porter model that is worthy of notice – for example, his five-forces model to determine industry profitability and the nine generic pursuits that comprise the value chain – its application in any depth here would detract from the proposed in-principle examination of the applicability of a strategic framework to the public service.

A lucid set of observations about the application of standard strategy models to public organisations is delivered by Geoff Mulgan, who notes the existence of a vast literature on strategy (from Sun Tzu to Michael Porter). He outlines the common principles and factors to be borne in mind in every field, but points to a radical difference in the challenges that public agencies often face. One of the most important differences he points to is the role of time and the need for public organisations to take account of intergenerational considerations, which is certainly not an imperative in the private sector calculus.

In answer to the question of whether strategic methods are applicable across sectors, Mulgan suggests that, although some questions are universal, the answers are not; smart strategies are specific to their contexts (Mulgan 2009, pp 22–23). Interestingly, it is one of these differences – what John Alford and Janine O'Flynn describe as complexity, referring specifically to the interdependence between policymaking and service delivery – that enables the public service to 'see' government activity as a whole and, in the process, becomes the foundation of its competitive advantage (Alford & O'Flynn 2012).

8.2 The concept of competitive advantage

The organisational objective around which Porter built his competitive advantage framework was the aim to establish a beneficial and sustainable position against the forces that determine industry competition. This competitive advantage is created through the choice of a competitive strategy built on two elements – industry attractiveness, and the determination of an organisation's relative competitive position in its chosen industry. Determining the relative contributions of the two on a case-by-case basis is important, with Porter first noting that not all industries offer the same potential for long-term profitability, then noting that some firms are more profitable than others, regardless of what the average profitability of the industry may be.

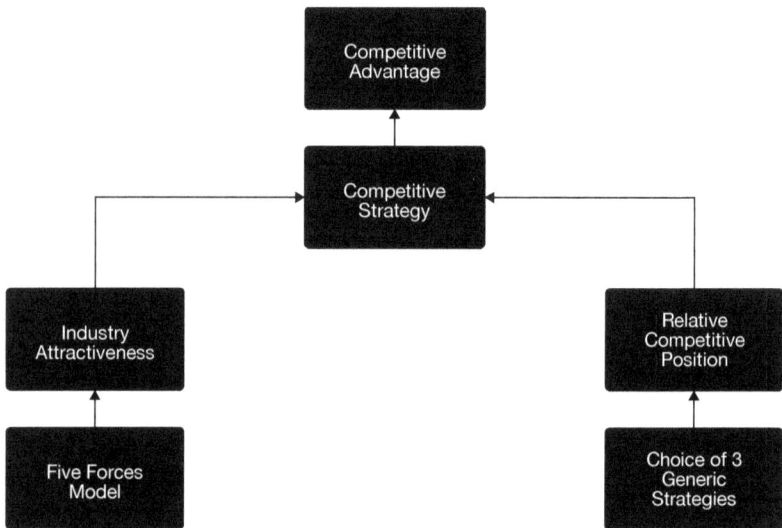

Figure 8.1 Organisational-level competitive advantage
Source: After Porter (1985, Chapter 1).

Porter's five-forces model is distilled from the industrial organisation literature of the 1950s and 1960s and incorporates the five elements of suppliers, buyers, industry competitors, potential entrants and substitute products. Porter uses the model to determine industry attractiveness, and the choice amongst three generic strategies – cost leadership, differentiation and focus (either cost focus or differentiation focus) – to determine a firm's relative competitive position. Fig. 8.1 presents these relationships in simple diagrammatic form.

Porter argues that the concept of competitive advantage cannot be understood by looking at the organisation as a whole, because it stems from the many discrete activities that a firm undertakes. He declares that it is best understood at the individual product or business line ('industry') level and he introduces the value chain as the tool for this purpose. The value chain disaggregates a firm into nine strategically relevant activities that, at the product, business line, or strategic business unit level, may be the source of competitive advantage. These comprise the five primary activities – inbound logistics, operations, outbound logistics, marketing and sales and service; and the four support activities – firm infrastructure, human resource management, technology development, and procurement. Porter describes the value chain as a systematic representation of activities that are performed to design, produce, market, deliver and support an organisation's products, and goes on to detail the nine generic pursuits that comprise all value chains (Porter 1985, Chapter 2). The value chain is primarily a discrete function-level description of a business in which, for example, human resource management might be regarded as the function and employee recruitment, remuneration, and training as activities.

To apply this concept to the pursuits of the public service, the public service needs to be similarly described in a disaggregated form – its functions and the distinctive features of its activities, the separate markets within which it competes, and the value that it delivers. Previous discussion of a number of ways by which the endeavours of the public service might be disaggregated – for both organisational design and strategy purposes – supports this endeavour. One such perspective is that of a set of departments that correspond loosely with the private sector notion of a product, business line or industry; for example, departments of health, defence, agriculture, and the environment. Closely aligned to these definitions are notions of programs and services, although not necessarily contained within the boundaries of one department.

The public sector can also be described in terms of functions, such as the Department of Finance's family of functions that were employed as the foundation for its Efficiency through Contestability Programme (based on the APS Job Family Model), or by the overlay of the strategy framework outlined in Chapter 7 of this book. To be of value, any such framework must allow for differences on a case-by-case basis.

In the case of the public service, it is important to keep an open mind about where within the ambit of the public sector domain that public service competitive advantage can be found, especially as such advantage may already exist in various parts of the public sector system but remain to be developed/exploited. This approach supports Porter's view that the primary argument for the existence of diversified businesses lies in the synergies that can be secured across the individual businesses, and that the competitive advantages enjoyed by business units in any line of business activity within a diversified organisation is necessarily a combination of (a) cascading organisational elements down to that business unit, (b) horizontal advantages across from that business unit to other business units within the total organisation, and (c) the advantages it creates directly in its chosen markets.

Some of the contributing elements to competitive advantage in individual markets may, then, derive from the corporate (whole-of-organisation) level (e.g. a capacity to absorb important risks, raise capital more cheaply, or form third-party alliances). Some others may derive from cross-divisional alliances (e.g. customer loyalty programs or shared facility use); the divisional (department) level (e.g. the existence of proprietary manufacturing technologies or a well-established set of marketing channels); and others may derive from the value chain of individual business lines and products (i.e. programs and services) themselves (e.g. strong brands).

The public service is underpinned by a bottom-up philosophy of fixing problems from a disaggregated structure. In contrast, the corporate strategic approach is a top-down focus on the creation and capture of synergies to justify the structure. The difference in practice is that the corporate approach regards as its mission the creation of a whole that is greater than the sum of the parts, whereas the public service approach focuses on the problem that, in operation, the whole is somewhat less than the sum of the parts, and there is an ongoing (but never satisfied) need 'to catch up'.

Beyond the philosophical foundations of various business forms and the structures and processes for capturing and distributing a variety of synergies, there are important contextual differences that can drive competitive advantage. Key differences include the presence of political as well as commercial risk, the diversity of services, the high degree of interdependence amongst public service activities, the 'enduring' nature of the public service (indeed, it cannot fail), the matters of time and intergenerational equity, and its role in the maintenance of trust in government. Other differences, noted by Mulgan, include constraints such as the existence of political factions and the limitations of tax-raising powers; whilst Alford and O'Flynn include the use of public power, the political benefits of externalisation, and the role of the public sector as custodian of values orientated to the public interest (e.g. probity and fairness) as complicating contextual factors (Mulgan 2009, p 22; Alford & O'Flynn 2012, pp 44–49).

Some differences between public and private sectors are merely matters of degree; for example, the ultimate limits placed on departmental expenditure by the government's exercise of its tax-raising powers, product diversity and complexity. In contrast, the existence of political benefits of externalisation, the role of custodian of public values, a concern for external effects, the need to 'see' all Australians, the impact on trust in government of public administration failures, and the matter of intergenerational equity, are not matters of private sector concern and are genuine points of difference between the two sectors.[1]

In turn, a number of these 'differences' are the foundations on which an activity is considered appropriate for public sector intervention and management. And, in some cases, the argument for government intervention extends through to public sector delivery of the good or service whilst, in others, the argument for a direct role for government stops with the intervention, and outsourcing becomes feasible. In that instance, factors such as the availability of suitable external options for outsourcing and the impacts on internal operations of such activity, enter the calculus.

When considered within the ambit of activities that a government chooses to undertake, some of these factors are likely to be more important than others in determining the competitive position of the public service in policy formation and service delivery. The strength of potential competitive advantage for the public service is not necessarily tied to these differences – a mandate is different from a potential competitive advantage. At the level of individual services, the distinction between the provision of

---

1   There are, arguably, parallels between public sector political risk and private sector reputational risk.

standardised and tailored services is important, especially when viewed from the perspective of management of a portfolio of diverse and complex services, which enables the development of organisational competences.

For instance, in the case of service diversity, Ian Miles has noted the different patterns of interaction between suppliers and clients, distinguishing between the provision of relatively standardised services, and services negotiated between supplier and client. Miles points out that specialised services require greater exchange of knowledge between service provider and client, and that the learning process is a fertile basis for innovation; this provides opportunities for the creation of competitive advantage in the latter that are not available in the former (Miles 2005, p 441). Similarly, in the case of complexity, Alford and O'Flynn point to the interdependencies, both service and organisational, that can form the basis of public service competitive advantage (Alford & O'Flynn 2012, p 45).

Moreover, based on Williamson's notion that it is harder to write a suitable contract in circumstances where 'the product' is not standardised – both in terms of the services to be delivered and in terms of the costing of the services – than under the alternative situation of routinised services, contract writing and management in circumstances of diverse and complex products can be another basis for the development of competitive advantage. There are strong arguments for recognising these as sources of competitive advantage for the public service in competition between public and private sectors for policy advisory and service delivery activity. These possibilities at the program and service level, once elevated to the department and whole-of-public-service level, offer a basis for the creation of public service competitive advantage.

In so arguing I propose that it is not the absolute advantages of the public service that enable it to compete more effectively with the private sector for the business of public administration, rather it is the competitive advantages. This view – that the public service has opportunities to create competitive advantage through the taking of a systemic view of their activities – is reinforced by Porter's notion of economies of scope: where systematic and systemic knowledge of the breadth and diversity of the services to be delivered is required to best tailor services to individuals. This notion equally applies where there is a breadth of services to be delivered to individuals, as in the human services case; where the manner in which the impacts of these services overlap is uncertain; where rules cannot readily be written for the management of these overlaps (and for delivery contracts); and, whether they are positive (reinforcing) or negative (destructive) in nature, where the cost, management, and outcome arguments for one service provider is strong.

8.3 Industry attractiveness

8.3.1 The concept and its relevance to the public service

Fig. 8.1 identifies the two components of competitive advantage described by Porter, the first of these being industry attractiveness, and the second relative competitive position. The relevance of industry attractiveness in a private sector context goes to the choice of industries in which to compete, and there is a broad range of factors that can influence the attractiveness of industries to corporations – these are commonly considered in terms of market structure and market conduct. Key elements of market structure include buyer and seller concentration, product differentiation, the rate of technological change, the barriers to entry of new firms, the level and nature of government regulation, industry growth rate, the ratio of fixed to variable costs in the short run, and the price elasticity of demand. In turn, market structure helps determine market conduct and, together, they determine individual firm and market performance.[2]

When considered in terms of the overall business of government, the public service as captive to the public sector has no such apparent choice of industry. It is a creature of the government created under an Act of parliament specifically to do the bidding of governments and, fundamentally must do what it is told to do, where it is told to, by the government of the day. Indeed, the public service is in the unenviable position of being tied to its 'industry', arguably having a monopoly customer, facing competition across the range of activities that it is required to undertake, and with limited apparent capacity to compete.

---

2   Interestingly, national trade practices legislation does not commonly bind government entities by similar competitive constraints, which is a relevant point in relation to public sector competitive positioning.

The role of the APS as principal official policy adviser to ministers is executed through departmental secretaries. The use of the word 'principal' admits the presence of other 'official' policy advisers, and places no limit on 'unofficial' policy advisers. In practice, governments and ministers take advice from many quarters and often in competition with, or as a substitute for, advice from the public service. Similarly, in its role as manager ensuring delivery of government programs (again through departmental secretaries), the APS may have an overarching role in management, but faces systematic 'competition' in service delivery, which is internally driven through the Australian Government's Efficiency through Contestability Programme. These important considerations for competitive positioning raise the question of whether the public service has the capacity to improve its 'industry attractiveness', tied tightly as this element of competitive advantage is to the fortunes of successive governments.

The public service has a strong incentive to improve its competitive advantage, given that the 'industry attractiveness' of government, at least from a community standpoint, is diminishing. Furthermore, from a public service perspective, the business of government can be described as having declining attractiveness. It is becoming more difficult to execute as time goes by; the electorate is becoming better organised, better focused and seems to understand the benefits of building issue-based coalitions better than the government; the major parties are increasingly struggling to govern in their own right and fragmenting, while the number of small parties is growing in number and numbers; social media is proving a powerful weapon for local and vested interest groups to broaden interest in their issues and thereby raise the political stakes; the increasing turnover of governments and party leaders within government is making the task of senior public servants ever more difficult; global and local fiscal pressures, along with changing ideological views, have led to targeted reductions in public service numbers; and effective external stakeholder management is both a growing issue and something of a slippery slope for public servants.

Add to this list the loss of career opportunities in the public service, the rise of wicked problems, and the low and declining community regard for politicians, then a picture emerges of a public service operating environment that (a) has substantially deteriorated in the last 30 years, and (b) is likely to continue to deteriorate in the absence of any game changer. Moreover, most of these factors have a cost to the community in terms of diminished government and public service productivity and effectiveness and point to a rising cost of governing. If it were possible to measure the cost of governing on a standardised outcome/value basis, it would likely reveal that the (unit) cost of government had risen several fold in real terms over the last 30 years. If the public service were a private sector business, it would surely be looking to address the attractiveness of its industry as long as it remained there, and equally surely would be looking to find more attractive industries for its shareholders' capital.

At the same time, casual observation suggests that the general community continues to hold the public service in relatively high esteem – certainly their frontline public servants – and politicians in relatively low esteem, and that it looks to the public service to make an important contribution to the quality of government that it receives. The public service can, thereby, raise the general perception of government performance and its perceived legitimacy by improving its own performance in this regard, and/or attempting to improve the performance of the government (as perceived by the community at large).

The statement of APS values and associated characteristics contained within the Public Service Act provides a ready framework within which to develop a systemic and systematic approach to this challenge. The public service could usefully develop a plan that demonstrates and markets their active pursuit of these values through their associated behaviours. The Act provides a broad canvas on which this might be done, setting out five values – committed to serve, ethical, respectful, accountable, and impartial – and a raft of associated lower-level characteristics, including professional; objective; innovative; efficient; demonstrates leadership; is trustworthy; acts with integrity; open and accountable to the Australian community; apolitical and provides government with advice that is frank, honest, timely, and based on the best available evidence. The Australian public expects the public service to demonstrate these characteristics behind closed doors, and it should welcome and value their public demonstration.

A simple approach to this challenge would be for the public service to measure annually its performance against behaviours consistent with these values, and in a way that spanned key stakeholder groups. One measure would involve comparing internal and external perceptions. A more sophisticated approach would attempt to construct an integrated performance index assigning weights to the measured values/behaviours as a starting point. A further level of sophistication could involve a comparison of performance with aspirations. Importantly in any such exercise, the public service must acknowledge the three communities – the government, the parliament and the Australian public – along with major contractors, suppliers, for-profit and not-for-profit groups, and services recipients. The results will likely vary considerably in terms of the different stakeholder groups and the values they place on different behaviours.

For example, the Australian public will be most inclined to assign top weights to those characteristics associated with demonstrated professionalism involving impartiality and the provision of frank advice, along with the quality of the interface in the public's role as service recipients. While the government assigns top weights to qualities such as commitment to service, respect, and trustworthiness, the business community rates most highly public service access, along with demonstrated efficiency and productivity. The public service may give more weight to leadership (including by agency heads and the Secretaries Board), coordination, innovation, integrity and trust than other parties and see those as integral to its effective, ongoing operation. On a paired basis, the public service would undoubtedly value measures differently in light of the communities they serve, and in turn find significant variation between each pairing.

Such an annual market-research exercise would be a useful way to open up a continuing internal discussion about how the public service might best serve its legislated triad of communities, with this discussion being facilitated by a diagnostic element in the market research. Active marketing of the results of these surveys through an expanded stakeholder management program would have dual benefits. This market research could usefully build on the present annual public service surveys and capability reviews undertaken by the APS Commissioner.

The public service could also build itself as an integrated entity, not just rebuild it in the image of the postwar public service, but in the manner of an integrated corporation. This would contribute substantially to the effectiveness of the APS by removing confusion in the minds of many public servants, who almost certainly believe that there are many versions of the APS built around departments. It might also encourage more cooperation and less competition for resources within the public service. As Ian Watt, then secretary to the Department of Prime Minister and

Cabinet suggested in a speech to the APS, the public service could start the journey forward 'by seeing ourselves as one APS and behaving as one' (Watt 2013). The establishment of 'one APS' in the minds of the private, not-for-profit, and community sectors, would also contribute to public service productivity by diminishing attempts by outside parties to wedge departments to gain leverage in securing favourable ministerial and cabinet decisions.

Thirdly, the public service could endeavour to directly raise the standing of the government in the community. Externally identified shortfalls in whole-of-government coordination, governance at the policy/program/project levels, and the reporting of outcomes from government expenditures are areas where the public service has primacy of action. Demonstrated success in these three areas would garner increasing support, certainly across parliament and the Australian public.

To achieve improved community standing the public service must get on the front foot, rather than finding itself continuously on the back foot with negative reports from the various watchdog and integrity bodies, which are picked up by the media. The public service needs to take control of its image (its 'brand') and actively demonstrate qualities that its stakeholders want to see, within the bounds of 'enduring' and 'looking over the horizon'. It needs to conceive of itself in terms of the various elements of a brand and market itself accordingly. The starting point for such a journey should be external perceptions, expectations and aspirations for the public service.

8.3.2 Trust in and the legitimacy of government

Arguments suggesting that the cost of governing is steadily rising have primarily focused on the administrative – that is, public service – level of government. Additionally, however, cost measured in terms of overheads as well, including the costs associated with elected officials and the operations of parliament, along with the various watchdog and integrity bodies, should also be included. I have questioned the efficiency of existing organisational structures within government, along with the effectiveness costs (benefits foregone) of the chosen structures. I argue, following Oliver Williamson, that large and growing structures create inefficiencies, and that given the starting size and growing propensity to create super-departments within government, there is good reason for the public sector to look for new organisational structures to properly match the tasks of government. The unit cost of government – considered in terms of the cost of delivering a unit of public value – is rising steadily.

A central concept in this notion of cost is associated with trust in and the legitimacy of government. In an ABC News Vote Compass opinion poll (149,000 respondents) ahead of the 2016 Australian federal election, ABC News reported that 'Malcolm Turnbull leads Bill Shorten on the question of who voters trust'. On a 10-point scale, this lead was one point averaged across two questions about the trustworthiness and competence of the three major party leaders. The fact that the incumbent prime minister's rating averaged five points on a 10-point scale (5.3 for 'competent' and 4.7 for 'trust') drew no comment from the media, although in the private sector and, no doubt, in the media itself, such low performance ratings would see incumbents very quickly pointed towards alternative career opportunities by their employers.

The community has unfortunately become inured to poor performance from governments. Yet this poor performance challenges the legitimacy of government itself, and directly impacts on the ability of the public service to serve the government of the day. It is for this reason, and the costs that this imposes on our community, that I am interested in the concept of the legitimacy of (the Australian) government. My focus is not the underlying authority that established legitimacy but, rather, the impact of the practice of government on this notion.

Simon Longstaff (2015) points to a community-wide phenomenon where individuals and institutions look one way and go the other, say one thing and do something else. According to Longstaff, this can be observed in a range of institutions, such as corporations (e.g. financial institutions), religious organisations, or public institutions like parliaments, political parties, and politicians. This practice has reached the point where there is deep and public questioning of these institutions and the individuals who (allegedly) serve them. He suggests that many institutions that were established with great moments of insight have been allowed to develop 'all sorts of magnificent elements in their exterior' whilst the insights that gave rise to them have been forgotten. He further describes the hypocrisy practised within our great institutions by people who look one way and go another as producing cynicism that eats away at the bonds of association within a community or weakens an institution.

Longstaff continues that political systems should be defined by where the ultimate source of authority happens to lie. In the case of a democracy, the source of authority is ultimately located in the persons governed and absolutely essential to this is their giving consent to be governed. He further argues that the gold standard is informed consent, and the only way that this can be achieved in a democracy is if those who are seeking to exercise public power through the result of an election give a truthful account of what it is they propose to do. Longstaff argues that politicians with their partial gaze, with their custom of looking one way and going another, and with their temptation to claim that they have a mandate, even though what they do might be at odds with democracy itself, are having a profound effect on (community) trust not just in politics and political parties, but in our political institutions.

The concept of trust is vital to the effective operation of our political institutions. Longstaff notes that high-trust systems operate with little cost, whilst low-trust systems are expensive to operate. He points to the Independent Commission Against Corruption (ICAC) and a parliamentary ethics commission in New South Wales as examples of cost generated when trust breaks down. There are many such examples across the national and state parliaments involving the establishment of anti-corruption commissions (but not yet at the national level!), ombudsmen, lobbying registers, 'commissioners', and others to deal in an ex post and costly manner with the administrative failings of our system of government (pointing to an important absence of adequate ex ante incentives embedded in our political systems and processes).

Perhaps the high-water mark of this failure is the appointment of a freedom of information (FOI) commissioner in Victoria in 2012 to deal with the tardy compliance of public sector entities with the *Freedom of Information Act 1982* (FOI Act). The legislated role of this commissioner is to educate and monitor compliance with the Act (but not resolve complaints), functions that already lay within the ambit of the auditor-general's brief and on which compliance the auditor-general had been highly critical in the past. In its last systematic audit of agency FOI performance in 2012, the Victorian Auditor-General's Office (VAGO) noted that the public's right to timely, comprehensive, and accurate information was being frustrated by a systemic failure by the Victorian public sector to support this right in line with parliament's intent, and that the prevailing culture and lack of transparent processes was allowing the responsible officers – secretaries and chief executive officers of agencies – to avoid fulfilling their responsibilities (VAGO 2012). In a subsequent report, *Access to public sector information*, to the Victorian parliament, the VAGO was highly critical of both the agencies with whole-of-government leadership and oversight, and those with primary information management responsibilities (VAGO 2015).

A further example of declining trust in our political system involves the sale of public assets. Rod Sims, chairman of the Australian Competition and Consumer Commission (ACCC), stated in 2016 that he had been a strong advocate of privatisation for 30 years but, in the face of government structuring of asset sales to maximise profits at the expense of consumers and businesses, he had almost reached the point of opposing it. This was damaging Australia's cost structure and increasingly being opposed by 'people in the street' because of rising prices (ACCC 2016).[3]

These sales are reflective of politicians with short decision-making time horizons and implicit discount rates way above community and standard public sector (even private sector) rates. The downside of the sales bonanzas claimed by politicians when proceeds exceed expected rates is, unfortunately, much higher future fees and charges. Where sales prices should reflect an appropriate social (i.e. public sector) discount rate (where social rates clearly lie somewhat below private sector rates) it is arguable that any such sale based on private sector discount rates will result in consumers being short-changed.

The point of this discussion is that the Australian public already bears a high cost for a lack of trust in our political system. As Longstaff points out, it is costly to make allowances for political commitments that possibly (probably?) will not be honoured. The 'expense' is not just monetary but includes the depreciation of the robust character of our democratic processes. In noting this decline, Longstaff observes three features underlying the change: parliaments do not belong to political parties, rather, they belong to the citizens; political parties are, after all, private associations with every right to pursue the objectives for which they were formed; and politics is more focused on the gaining of power than a shared understanding of the purpose for which power was being sought.

---

3   See also Potter (2016).

Longstaff concludes that this decline in trust, the absence of informed consent, the determination to express all discussions in some kind of demonstration of economic utility, the absence of an ethical dimension to the discussion of politics, and the political parties contending for power in ways that destroy trust in our institutions, are leading towards a loss of legitimacy. Worryingly, he argues, while we can survive a loss of trust at some financial cost, we cannot survive a loss of legitimacy. Legitimacy, he argues, comes partly from tradition, partly from the integrity of what is done, and partly from competence but, ultimately, the legitimacy of democracy derives from consent and the quality of consent.

In closing, he points to methods of possible repair. The first is to develop a common ethical foundation for the way in which politics is practised in Australia. The second, which is relevant here, points to the need for another discussion about the role of the APS, which in the presence of the partial political gaze of these times – for example, on marginal electorates and 'high-yielding' classes of citizens – Longstaff argues is the one bit of government that must see every single citizen, irrespective of where they live and what electorate they are in. He suggests that the realignment of the APS with the interests of the government of the day, which took place during the 1980s, deserves a solid rethink given the ongoing consequences.

This view aligns with the historical review of the impact of the New Public Management reforms, the comments from APS commissioner Stephen Sedgwick in the 2013–14 state of the service review, and with the observations of Laura Tingle in her 2015 *Quarterly Essay*. It also finds a place in Chapter 2's discussion of the role of the customer, which referred to the role of the customer in considering the task of government and briefly examined the development of the concept of public value. The three components of public value offered a new paradigm and a different narrative for public sector reform on the basis of the services (seen as the vehicle for delivering private value); the program aims and outcomes (which include higher-level aspirations of other citizens); and the impact on, trust, legitimacy and confidence in government.

The legitimacy of our parliamentary institutions and the associated level of 'trust' in our politicians is an important structural feature of 'the industry' in which the public service competes. As such, the public service has an interest both in capturing it as part of its role in performance measurement and good governance, but also as an incentive to improve it as one of the key structural features of its industry impacting on its activities. Whether trust in the public service should be conceived as a separate measurable from trust in the government is a moot point, but clearly the public service has a strong incentive, closely aligned with public interest, to change existing perceptions of government and improve the attractiveness of its industry.

8.4 Competitive positioning

8.4.1 The core competitive strategies

The second part of the public service strategic challenge is to determine how best it might compete within the given landscape of its government-legislated domain. To do this it must establish what its markets are, who its competitors are in these markets, what the modes of competition are, and determine where and how to outcompete its rivals. Whilst the public service may sometimes have little choice about the competition it confronts, it does have control over how and where it competes.

Porter identifies three generic organisational positioning strategies – cost leadership, product differentiation, and focus – and he uses the value chain to disaggregate and reassemble the activities of the firm around customers as the foundation of competitive positioning and competitive advantage. In the private sector, a strategy of cost leadership, for example, might be successful where there is a sustainable cost advantage. This cost advantage might derive from scale; for example, with economies available in one or other important inputs; or it might result from access to a specialised input not readily available to competitors. An example of the former might be a raw material and of the latter specialised workforce skills. In the case of the public service, an example of the former could be military intelligence and the latter could be diplomatic skills.

A competitive advantage from product differentiation occurs when a set of product features deliver greater benefits to customers than competitors' products. The source of this advantage can lie with exclusive access to a specialised input, such as intellectual property, a proprietary delivery system, unique product design features, or even the materials used in a product. Examples of this advantage associated with the role of the public service could be product consistency associated with scale, for example, in the provision of schools and hospitals. It might also exist where national standards are seen to be an important part of the creation of public value and where there is seen to be a provider of last-resort responsibility residing with the state and, especially, associated with the tailoring of packages of services to individual needs.

Deriving a competitive advantage from focus is harder to define. Porter defines this advantage in terms of the disadvantages of its alternative, namely the existence of costs of coordination, compromise, or inflexibility in serving multiple market segments. By optimising its value chain for only one or a few segments, the focuser achieves cost leadership or differentiation in its segment or segments compared with more broadly targeted firms that must compromise. As Porter explains, a focus strategy involves the entire value chain, not just one functional activity. The competitive advantages of this strategy may, however, derive primarily from one activity in the chain (Porter 1985, pp 15–17, 264–71).

Overlapping with each of these strategies lies the strategy of scope, which can be defined in either supply (or cost) or demand (revenue) terms. When considered in supply terms, an organisation may be able to purchase inputs more cheaply on a unit basis by servicing more than one market with its products (as long as there are no compromises necessary when focus is diluted). When considered in demand or revenue terms, benefits of scope are derived from the customer value generated by supplying more than one product to a customer. An example of the latter occurs with complementary products through brand extension. Scope lies on the opposite end of the same spectrum as focus and, in reality, it is not so much a third generic strategy but one derived from another generic strategy (Porter 1980, pp 53–59).

As discussed in Chapter 4, the role of government is built on the notion of interventions in an otherwise effectively functioning economy and society. These 'interventions' occur for a variety of reasons based on the public good, inherent market under- or over-supply, and a mismatch between market prices and social costs and benefits. Other reasons for desirable public interventions in the economy are based on the absence of markets in social goods and services. Many of these interventions have an associated layer of public or merit goods and public value in addition to the private value. The reason why governments provide particular goods and services can incorporate a mixture of these factors of market structure (e.g. natural monopolies); cost, customer, or community bases; and the existence of externalities. Some interventions are based on comparative advantages (relative advantages based on matters of degree), whilst others are based on absolute advantages.

The complex nature of supply-driven government activities does not readily lend itself to the simple framework of consumers and markets driven by private costs and benefits that Porter creates for strategy development purposes. This is unsurprising given the focus of corporate strategy on the customer as the driving force for existence, and the focus of government interventions on perceived gaps in supply. There is a difference between a raison d'être of creating supply and one of creating demand. It is the fact of competition for the business of government that makes Porter's framework applicable to the activities of the public service, and the interdependencies between the policy advisory and service delivery activities pointed to by Alford and O'Flynn that defines the nature of public service competitive advantage.

There is also a difference between the inherent advantages that government may have for the initiation of supply, and the choice between public service and private sectors for its delivery. The discussion that follows is based on the assumption that the government decision to supply is taken in principle, but the detail of program and service choices, the choice between public and private sector supply, and activity governance is yet to be determined.

There is no data for the second core strategy – cost differentiation – when considered in terms of the central markets for policy advice and service delivery. Broad-based observations, however, point to the need for further examination of this matter, starting with the policy advisory role. The complex policy advisory market is played out behind closed doors, with many and often changing groups of both internal (to government) and external players, some offering 'free' advice (e.g. lobbyists, think tanks, internal advisers), and others (a variety of specialist and generalist consultants) offering advice for a fee.

Our nation is shaped in this shadowy market of political donations and deals, where government ministers exercise largely unfettered and unaccountable power. In this market – where the APS is competing both for influence and the national interest – the public service usually maintains a competitive quality advantage when it comes to knowledge of the public administration and customer-based components of government. This advantage is balanced, however, by lobbyists and consultants who have more detailed knowledge and ready access to the local industry dimensions (the supply side of the market) and the international dimensions of the policy challenge. In addition, the advice of lobbyists – but not consultants – is invariably free and often backed by a tailored piece of research.

The public service has a distinct cost advantage when it comes to front-end policy formation where open processes are to be pursued, and where all reasonable options are systematically identified and assessed on the available evidence. Consulting firms charge a daily rate of up to five or 10 times public service direct costs. In addition to the direct and short-term costs considered here, there are also the longer-term opportunity costs, which are associated with loss of corporate memory and capability with outsourcing the important policy advisory role. 'Cost' (short or long term), however, is not the prime criterion on which advice sought by politicians is valued. Rather, it is a combination of the perceived independence (or, more accurately, the plausible deniability of its absence), the reputation of the provider, risk aversion (which manifests itself by a desire for third-party service provision), and the likelihood that the result will be 'acceptable'.

When it comes to service delivery and the consideration of cost differentiation as a strategy, there is a more formal market established under the government's Efficiency through Contestability Programme. In the face of the underlying ideological bias, the overt political desire to use this as a downsizing tool, the loss of institutional memory and strategic capabilities, and the cost biases built into the processes, this is a problem for the public service that is unlikely to be overcome through improved efficiency. The public service has been deliberately placed at a competitive disadvantage by the government. Cost is seen as central in service delivery (which it should be but not in its present form) and largely irrelevant for policy advice (although it should not be).

Were 'cost' to include both the short-term direct (out-of-pocket) costs, along with longer-term and opportunity costs, the public service would have a much stronger demonstrated competitive position in its policy advisory and service delivery roles than is accorded it by any contestability program. This overall cost-based position would be further strengthened if the policy formation and advisory function of government were subject to the same government watchdog and integrity body scrutiny as their expenditure and service delivery activities. Process and value-for-money scrutiny would add transparency and integrity to the processes, and lead to the highlighting of cost differences that would materially aid the establishment of a level playing field for the public service in competing for the business of government.

The application of the notion of product differentiation to the activities of the public service is best encompassed within the interdependencies pointed to by Alford and O'Flynn (2012) that describe public service advantages over the private sector (and non-profit competitors). These interdependencies may exist in the conception and design of services to complement existing services; they may exist in the identification for the delivery of services jointly; and they may be found within existing policy groupings, and within and across departmental boundaries. In a world in which public value became the standard-bearer for public sector effectiveness, the position of the public service in supporting government would be further strengthened by its understanding of the business of government and its capacity to develop appropriate measures of the second and third elements of this criterion, namely the community (non-consumer) valuation of individual services and its contribution to the legitimacy of government.

The public service is uniquely placed to occupy this ground because only it has a clear line of sight from the ideological foundations of policy, the conception of particular policies, through service delivery to valuation and back again. It is the interdependencies of these parts, whether viewed in terms of the aggregate of departmental activities, individual departments, individual policy frameworks, programs or services and governance that is the competitive advantage of the public service. However this advantage is described, in cost (i.e. the cost of public administration) or product differentiation (i.e. the service provided to the government) the advantage is based, in terms of the Porter schema, on scope. The competitive positioning and advantage of the public service lies in its systemic view of the role of government, and unique understanding of the interrelationships of the parts, and their prospective contribution to the whole.

When seen in terms of whole-of-government policy formation and service delivery, these 'parts' become a supply chain commencing with the ideological foundations, political belief systems, and derived societal goals; and moving to the policy frameworks, policies, programs, services (and solutions) that are delivered; the organisational and administrative systems options; and the service delivery, accountability and governance choices to be made. The chain should also extend beyond the traditional public service focus on public administration to active engagement with the national interest and the legitimacy of government, which is a clear point of product difference with most third-party advisory and service providers.[4] The advantages of access and physical and legislative proximity to government should also be considered for identification and exploitation by the public service.

Just as grasping and implementing this concept of scope is important to the overall competitive positioning and construction of sustainable competitive advantage for the public service, so it is important to build this advantage on a strong competitive position in the policy field. Policy is ultimately the best vantage point from which to see the whole supply chain. It is the policy choices and their ideological foundations that determine the deliverables of governments and (should) shape the governmental structures and administrative systems that establish how they will be delivered and measured. Good policy practice sees as a whole all of the activities involved in the process of meeting government objectives, from the choice of policy frameworks and instruments through service delivery to accounting for the meeting of these objectives. Only the public service has an interest in the whole system, from the initial stages of policy formation through to its implementation and evaluation. A strong competitive position in the policy formation market is critical to a successful public service–wide strategy of scope.

This recommendation – of building a competitive advantage around scope, based on strength in the policy advisory position – is consistent with Porter's notion of the value chain, where a competitive advantage across a range of activities is often built around one element. The public service cannot afford not to be (more) competitive in this field. This policy-driven competitive advantage must be based on systematic research across jurisdictions; the construction of an evidence-based knowledge bank on policy frameworks, programs and services; the delivery of services, and the supporting governance structures and administrative systems used to monitor performance. It must capture, evaluate and disseminate its

---

4   It is arguable that the ultimate and critical (from a public policy standpoint) competitive advantage is organisational motivation, which is the primary difference between the public service and its competitors. For private sector competitors, this motivation focuses on the goals of its shareholders, whilst the focus of the public service is on the national interest. The resulting differences can be substantial in the case of policy advice but are narrower in the case of service delivery activities. As noted, however, it is with the former that real damage can be done to the national interest.

corporate experience and promote the benefits of this system-wide view. It must also include data on competitors and accommodate the needs of institutional memory that is so lacking today. It must be complemented by access to systemic public sector frontier thinking on organisational structures and operations, and it should stay abreast of developments in the field of corporate management and strategy.

While there is evidence that the public service has belatedly adopted some of the management tools developed for private sector use over the last 40 or 50 years – whether it is the devolution of authority in the 1980s, the recent discovery of innovation, or the information technology–driven projects of today, even the introduction of executive bonuses in the 1980s and the (recent) establishment of super-departments – the public sector has variously been tardy, failed to learn the lessons of private sector experience, and has often poorly implemented these tools.

8.4.2 Interrelationships amongst business units

In addition to the competitive strategies that an organisation might employ at the product and market (business unit) levels to build competitive advantage, there are other, corporate, strategies that enhance the competitive position of organisations in these separate markets. In promoting the benefits of these horizontal strategies, Porter provided some history that resonates today when taken in conjunction with Alice Lam's history of organisational innovation (2005) and Walter Kiechel's review of management in the 20th century (2012). The strategic role played by the head office in the building of synergies between the various divisional units, so-called horizontal strategy, is of key interest here.

Porter noted that the concept of synergies was used as justification for many corporate mergers and acquisitions in the United States during the 1960s and early 1970s. The foundation of this concept was the corporate-level synergies to be created through the sharing of risks and economies of scale, which were to be cascaded down to the business units. Enthusiasm for the concept waned in the absence of their materialisation and was followed by decentralisation with authority for results devolved to business unit managers. Porter argued that there were forces at work by the mid-1980s compelling firms to re-examine their attitude to synergy. Since then, the ambit of corporate strategy has built on the notion of value to be created between businesses internal to an organisation, then extended to include a focus on formal alliances with external organisations (e.g. pre-competitive alliances in technology development), and subsequently extended to a broad range of formal and informal networks and arrangements spanning most business functions (Porter 1985, pp 317–23).

The public service has followed the private sector in the establishment of formal alliances with external parties, most notably through the use of public–private partnerships and, as noted in the discussion of models of governance, is now using networks to engage with a widening range of third-party collaborators. The weak part of the cooperative toolkit lies with the core business of delivering a whole-of-government approach to services and solutions, being somewhere still stuck in the decentralisation phase of the 1980s, and having ignored the focus on the systematic construction of synergies across the whole organisation. Even though Porter was writing in 1985, and about the private sector, his words are startlingly relevant to the contemporary public sector, given that present-day academic literature and auditor-general reports around the globe note the shortcomings in public sector coordination and the pressures for more effective coordination at the whole-of-government level.

Porter points to three broad types of interrelationships amongst business units: tangible, intangible, and competitor relationships. Tangible interrelationships arise from opportunities to share activities in the value chain among related business units due to the presence of commonalities of various types among buyers, channels, technologies and other factors (Porter 1985, pp 322–26). They lead to competitive advantage where cost or product differentiation benefits are gained. The former might derive from economies of scale, whilst the latter might derive from added customer value. Porter usefully notes that there are costs to sharing, including costs of coordination, compromise and inflexibility, and Williamson reinforces this point from a transaction-cost perspective. The other useful reminder from Porter is that some such relationships are more beneficial than others, not so much because of their intrinsic value but because they are more difficult for competitors to match.

Intangible interrelationships lead to competitive advantage through the transfer of skills (and experience) amongst the separate value chains. These relationships are important to competitive advantage where costs are lowered or differentiation is enhanced. Porter points to these relationships arising from a variety of similarities amongst business units, including similar classes of customer, similar generic strategies, and similar configuration of the value chain. He points to the necessary importance of identified similarities for competition if they are to have any commercial value.

Porter's third category of interrelationship is also of interest and relates to competitor interrelationships. Such relationships are present when a competitor competes with a diversified firm in more than one (common) business unit. These are so-called multi-point competitors. Single-point competitors with different patterns of interrelationships are also important because they bring different sources of competitive advantage to an industry. Porter argues the general case for explicit horizontal strategy and makes a number of important points in the context of the weaknesses of horizontal coordination in the public sector.

The first is that large, diversified organisations impose costs on their respective business units – through overheads and constraints imposed by corporate policies. Aggregation is a liability in a corporate context when the organisation does not make an offsetting contribution to the competitive advantage of the business units. The aim of horizontal strategy is to coordinate the goals and strategies of the business units to create opportunities for offsetting contributions and competitive advantage in individual business unit markets.

According to Porter, horizontal strategy cannot be left implicit or allowed to emerge from business units on a bottom-up basis. In the absence of a corporate-led horizontal strategy, the pressure is to optimise individual business unit performance at the expense of corporate performance.[5] In the same vein, without such a horizontal strategy, business units may value interrelationships differently (they may deliver differential benefits) making it difficult to achieve agreement; business unit strategies may well weaken the competitive position of other business units by not taking the broader view; coordinated pricing and volume strategies across business units may deliver corporate benefits through, for example, increased purchasing power; business units tend to form alliances outside rather than inside the organisation; and, transfer of know-how amongst similar business units will not occur (pp 365–68). Overall, Porter argues that 'Without an explicit horizontal strategy there will be no systematic mechanism to identify, reinforce, and extend relationships' (p 368).

---

5   Arguably, the same pressure exists within super-departments at business unit and function level.

Porter develops a seven-part process of strategy formulation for horizontal interrelationships embracing identification of tangible interrelationships, tracing them outside the boundaries of the firm, identifying possible intangible interrelationships, identifying competitor interrelationships, assessing the importance of interrelationship to competitive advantage, developing a horizontal strategy to enhance the most important interrelationships, and creating horizontal organisational mechanisms to assure implementation (Porter 1985, pp 368–75). Importantly, Porter also discusses the impediments to achieving these relationships. He outlines many challenges, including asymmetric benefits, loss of autonomy and control (especially important where there is a long history of decentralisation), different cultures, different procedures and supporting technology, perceived dilution of buyer relationships, turf protection, and biased incentive/reward structures. And he goes on to discuss a number of mechanisms that can aid in the achievement of successful interrelationships in the face of these difficulties.

Importantly, Porter points to the difficulty confronted by firms in achieving interrelationships in practice. He believes there are many 'natural' barriers to the successful implementation of such a strategy and that, unless a detailed and integrated process is carefully laid out and the whole process is carefully documented at every step along the way, and unless both the corporate head leads and divisional heads 'sign on', failure is almost inevitable (Porter 1985, pp 368–75).

In closing his discussion of horizontal interrelationships, Porter discusses the shortcomings of the multi-divisional organisational form popularised by Williamson in the academic literature (Williamson 1970, pp 113–17). Porter points to the need for further evolution of the M-form to produce a new organisational form that rebalances the prevalent concept of decentralisation in diversified firms with an overlay of mechanisms to achieve the important horizontal interrelationships. Porter suggested that divisionalisation in its traditional sense was no longer appropriate in many firms, noting that the new requirements of the diversified firm were for less simplicity, greater ambiguity, more subjectivity, and potentially more conflict (Porter 1985, pp 414–15). He noted that the new organisational form required a modification of rigid or narrow views on autonomy between the centre and business unit executives.

It is ironic that the public service around the globe adopted the divisional, decentralised organisational model at the very time that the private sector was experiencing misgivings about its utility. The public service implemented a restricted version of the M-form model, removing the top two layers and thereby compounding the difficulties of horizontal coordination. This mistake is yet to be rectified and, based on the view that at the operational level the distinguishing feature of the public sector is the extent of the existing horizontal relationships, this failure has almost certainly come at a cost and continues to undermine the effectiveness of public administration. Further, the creation of horizontal relationships through the diversity of public service activity, noting Porter's observation that diversity does not imply the absence of interrelationship (Porter 1985, p 415), should be encouraged. From a strategic management standpoint, the management of the horizontal relationships between departments, programs, and services remains virgin territory.

Finally, while the field of corporate strategy has moved on since Porter's observations in ways that recognise the need for greater urgency in responding to environmental change, in the face of greater environmental ambiguity, none of the associated developments has diminished the prospective benefits from improved horizontal cooperation in the public sector. Indeed developments in networked government have increased the demand for and benefits from both internal and external cooperation.

8.5 The markets and players

8.5.1 How many 'markets'?

There are many external players involved in the business of government today. This should be no surprise given that the Australian Government is far and away the biggest business in the country with projected expenditure to exceed $450 billion dollars in 2016–17 and accounting for over 24 per cent of gross domestic product. Taking a medium-term view of this expenditure could cast it as discretionary and, when allowance is made for the leveraging of significant parts of this total on shared projects with the states and territories as well as the private sector, the average annual amount of 'government' business to be 'won' by both government and non-government players is very large.

The business of government presents direct opportunities for many, including public servants, private sector suppliers of goods and services, politicians and their staff, professional lobbyists, and community-based and philanthropic organisations. It presents many businesses with sizeable commercial and rent-seeking opportunities, as well as individuals with a variety of employment opportunities inside and outside of the public sector. At the more senior levels of employment, career opportunities seamlessly cycle around in this milieu, moving from one sector to another with the individuals involved changing less regularly than the chairs they occupy. This happens nowhere more often than on the merry-go-round of public service media professionals.

A similarly concerning rotation takes place through ministerial and key business and community lobbying roles, despite legislation attempting to limit the impact of such activity. And 'career' public servants are not immune to this circus as they are attracted to senior government relations, consulting and public relations roles in the private sector. One measure of this interchange is provided by the Australian Government Lobbyist Register, which shows approximately 30 per cent of those on the register as former 'government representatives'.

As Tingle points out, the turnover in public servants can be sheeted home in part to the outsourcing of important parts of public service activity, particularly high-level policy advice. This denies senior public servants opportunities to practise and develop their skills in this field, which is arguably the primary attraction of a public service career. This loss contributes to a loss of institutional memory and leads to short-termism in the business of government represented by a focus on issues management, and the making of and repetition of mistakes, rather than on good policy development and implementation. This situation is less than satisfactory and falls a long way short of the Public Service Act's objective of establishing a career-based public service.

A discussion of public service competitive positioning requires consideration of the markets in which the public service competes, and the players within those markets. The taxonomy devised by Paul Windrum (2008; as discussed in Chapter 1, Fig. 1.3) is used to break public sector activity up into the manageable blocks of conceptual/ideological, policy frameworks, organisation/administration, services, service delivery, and systemic. This typology assists in taking a broad view of public service activity but needs refinement to better reflect the markets in which the public service competes. In Table 8.1 I identify five markets.

The first market is the market for political beliefs, Windrum's first category of public sector activity of conceptual/idelological. The second market can be described as the policy market, incorporating Windrum's second category – of policy frameworks – but including the design of programs and services. The third market is the market for service delivery (as per Windrum). The fourth and fifth markets deserve more discussion.

The fourth market derives from Windrum's third category – organisation and administration. The (quantitively) more important parts of the overall administrative task in which the public service faces direct competition lie with information technology and back-office functions. There is competition between commercial service providers and the public service. Being a strategic capability in regard to the delivery of effectively targeted services, and thereby the creation of customer value, this contributes to public service performance and is a field within which the public service must remain active.

The fifth and final 'market' is associated with the governance function, including performance reporting and compliance, and is the market for government governance. It is arguably part of the administrative function but deserves its own category The APS has a, but not sole, responsibility for government governance. The government has established other public bodies to play in this space – the auditor-general, a number of ombudsmen, and a variety of 'commissioners' who, in part, play a similar ex post governance role. They exist largely to report on the activities of the public service and 'compete' for this market with the public service.

Windrum's final category – systemic – is omitted here. Described by Windrum in terms of third-party engagement, it is indeed an important enabling factor and with regard to innovation, it is an area requiring consideration. There is, however, no 'market' for this activity (other than perhaps an internal one of competition for attention and resources), but this category primarily focuses on how the other activities play out and does not in any way constitute 'a market' in which outside parties actively participate. In Porter terms, the relevant markets of conceptual/ideological, policy, service delivery, administration, and governance can be regarded as the markets within which the external (to the public service) players and the public service compete for market share, influence and funds.

The systematic identification of the external players in the business of government across the identified markets is more difficult with elected officials who are subject to influence from many directions in the determination and administration of government services. Ideally the players can be matched with these respective markets and their nature identified as multipoint or single-industry competitors. Without that information available, an indicative approach as taken in Table 8.1 is the optimal way to list the players against the markets.

Table 8.1 Public service markets and players

External players	Political beliefs	Policy	Service delivery	Organisation & administration	Government governance
Public service	—	XX	XX	XX	XX
Universities	XX	XX	X	—	X
Think tanks	XX	XX	X	X	X
Political party machines	XX	XX	X	—	—
Professional lobbyists	X	XX	X	—	—
Industry associations	X	XX	X	—	—
CBO/philanthropic/ not-for-profits	X	XX	XX	X	X
Major commercial beneficiaries	X	XX	XX	XX	X
Ministerial staffers	—	X	X	—	X
Citizens' action groups	X	XX	XX	—	—
Watchdog/integrity bodies	—	—	XX	XX	XX

Key

— no (known) involvement

X some involvement

XX strong involvement

8.5.2 The market for political beliefs

While embryonic in its content the following comments can be made on the basis of Table 8.1 above. Consideration of the various influences and influencers involved with the formation of political beliefs, the development of new ideologies and their consequent impact on public service activities indicates that the public service is not a player in this market. Interplay between party machines, universities, research institutes, and think tanks (some of which are established for this purpose) provide the interaction that determines what beliefs and policy frameworks elected parties bring to government. This is not, however, just an unbounded market for ideas. It is clear from the past 30 or more years of changing models of governance that what drives mainstream ideas of both the demand and supply sides of this market are global, social and economic trends, and these factors drive belief systems, organisational forms, and governance models across the whole economy, not just the public sector.

In this market, consistent with an observer status, the role of the public service is twofold. It must keep a watching brief on both the local and global debates and be ready to effectively implement the agenda of any government elected with 'new' political beliefs, world views and operating models. Equally, it must determinedly bring to its role institutional memory of the upsides and the downsides – what one commentator has referred to as the welcome transformations, unfulfilled promises and unintended negative effects of the New Public Management regime (Sørensen & Torfing 2012, p 6), which Tingle (2015) asserts is missing in the public service today.

8.5.3 The policy formation and advisory market

There are six overlapping groups of players in the policy formation and advisory market, which makes it the most competitive of the markets in which the public service competes.

1. The public service has legislated responsibility to advise governments on policy matters.
2. Party machines (and their assorted associates), universities, and think tanks, are likely to take an academic and/or holistic view of policy consistent with their production of political ideas.

3. Commercial purveyors of policy ideas, solutions and experience drawn from their experience in other jurisdictions, include generalist consulting firms and industry specialists.

4. Vested interest groups want a particular slant on policy for their members – these are primarily 'industry' associations with commercial, social, and environmental roots.

5. For-profit and not-for-profit groups are potential direct beneficiaries of government policy decisions. They include the major commercial entities (including miners, manufacturers, aged-care service providers, and banks), community-based organisations, and philanthropic organisations.

6. Uncommitted players who 'facilitate' meetings and representations amongst the other parties are usually with good access to the decision-makers – namely the lobbyists and ministerial staffers.

The basis of competition in this congested market should include local contextual knowledge and associated history, knowledge of the global market, cost, and the capacity to provide good advice about policy frameworks, policies, programs and services that meet government policy objectives. Once upon a time the public service had a monopoly on policy/service advice, but this has been eroded over a number of decades to the point where its capacity to provide solutions to policy problems that move beyond a local domain is in question.

World-class pockets of public service expertise exist that could undertake the highest level strategic/systemic policy advisory consulting projects. Moreover, most business people (and also a number of politicians) do not understand the concept of 'policy' beyond their immediate interests, so that those with a broad-based understanding of public policy, namely the public service, should be able to build a competitive advantage. This should be the ground on which the public service establishes its primacy across the business of government. Government suspicions of public service motives and expertise, however, and the determination of successive governments to take out some insurance on these high-level projects by hiring a 'name', continues to contribute to an ongoing decline in this critical public service capability.

This fiercely contested market has downstream impacts of significance for public policy. The large number of registered players, along with the many others who play the game outside of the Australian Government Register of Lobbyists, suggests that, at the lobbying level, this is a profitable business (and deserving of its own governance regime).[6]

8.5.4 The service delivery market

There are two components to the service delivery market: the management of service delivery, and the delivery of services themselves. The Public Service Act legislates for the public service to have a monopoly control over the former, ensuring delivery of government programs, but it faces extensive competition for the latter. In common with the market for policy formation, there are many players in the market for service delivery who seek to influence policy in the direction of the solutions, goods and services where they (or their clients) can play a part in supply. As with policy formation, the bigger the stakes the bigger the political, commercial and community pressure placed on the government and involved officials. The rewards available to those inside government to produce a particular outcome can be just as irresistible as in the private sector, making the probity of processes critical for such contests.

The service delivery market differs markedly from the policy formation market in terms of the structure and intensity of competition. The service delivery market is highly diverse, reflecting the range of industries – including health, transport, agriculture, law and order, defence, international relations, and foreign trade – and the multiplicity of government activities that may be undertaken within each of these industries. The policy formation market, in contrast, comprises a range of large/international competitors that span the field of public policy – for example, the universities and think tanks often from an ideological perspective, and the major consulting houses from a business perspective – accompanied by a large range of smaller special interest players.

What these markets have in common is the broad range of national and international companies involved in them, with service delivery having the added layer of complexity of equipment and systems purchasing as part of a service delivery program (for example in the fields of transport and defence). Governments have the opportunity to meet local and/or

---

6   This register can be viewed at lobbyists.ag.gov.au/register.

international political objectives in policy and outsourcing decisions, and policy decisions regarding foreign government activity on Australian shores has important implications for supply of goods and services under government contracts.

8.5.5 The market for organisation and administration

An active component of the Efficiency through Contestability Programme is the rationalisation of the various information technology legacy systems in the APS and the creation of shared back-office facilities. This is a challenging task, with a large number of private sector service providers already involved in providing government agencies with a range of corporate services. The APS Shared Services Centre, established in 2014, was reported in 2015 to be providing services to 13 government departments and agencies. A critical Australian National Audit Office (ANAO) report followed in 2016 and, early in 2017, the centre was quietly closed and over 600 public servants were disbursed. Press reports indicated that some $210 million of taxpayers' funds had been lost. This followed similar failed attempts to establish such centres by state governments in Western Australia and Queensland.

What will be the future of the market for administration is unclear, as good reasons remain to seek efficiency gains from such facilities. A Department of Finance discussion paper (2015) highlighted the challenges and opportunities involved and identified over 200 unique Enterprise Resource Planning (ERP) systems across the APS, with no common data definitions, process and contractual arrangements, and approximately 85 internal service providers across 96 non-corporate agencies with 239 individual relationships with private sector organisations.[7] Despite the obvious challenges, this was seen as an opportunity for substantial efficiency gains through the reduction in public service numbers involved, in an estimated annual spend of some $3.5 billion to $4 billion annually. The program goal was seamless provision of services across tiers of government, without duplication or overlap.

---

7   Enterprise Resource Planning (ERP) systems refers to the collection of systems and software packages used by organisations to manage day-to-day business activities, such as accounting, procurement, human resource management, and project management. ERP systems are designed around a common data structure and usually a common database that enables all users, from CEO to accounts payable clerk, to create, store, use and leverage the same data derived from common processes.

Despite this public sector information technology failure, many private sector service providers remain involved with government departments in Canberra. And, whilst enthusiasm has diminished for large-scale rationalisations, this remains an active market in which the driving competitive force is the capture of efficiencies through rationalisation and consolidation of both software and hardware, whether the services themselves are ultimately delivered by internal or external providers. Particular benefits are expected in terms of efficiency, effectiveness, agility, and scalability from the consolidated provision of back-office services, but it is equally important that APS capability benefits are sought and acquired. This is important both at the strategic, whole-of-public-service level, at which public service operations are 'managed', but equally important on the ground where an active understanding of the systems and their capabilities can be married with services to customers, which must remain the primary focus of overall public service activity.

It is important that clear and integrated notions of strategic capabilities underpin customer-driven transformations. An effectively managed back-office rationalisation program would recognise the contribution that strategically managed capability would make to the overall public service–positioning strategy, and would not allow the more obvious head-count driven efficiency gains to overwhelm the case for primacy of focus on the customer in a customer-driven business.

8.5.6 The market for government governance

The fifth public service 'market' is that of government governance. Until the 1980s, the role of auditors-general around the globe was primarily restricted to financial auditing. With the arrival of output budgeting, public sector auditors refocused their attention on performance reporting, certainly as it related to the public service. The public service has responsibility for important parts of government governance under the *Public Governance, Performance and Accountability Act 2013* and the Public Service Act. Whilst the word 'governance' is not used to describe these responsibilities the Acts are clear that departmental secretaries cannot acquit their specified ministerial and whole-of-government responsibilities without fulfilling their governance duties. Therefore, while the public service bears the major public sector responsibility for government governance (but clearly not for the conduct of parliamentarians and ministers), and the watchdog and integrity bodies have parallel audit responsibilities, these latter – the Auditor-General for Australia and the Commonwealth Ombudsman in particular – 'compete' in this market through the requirement to publicly report on their respective responsibilities. In the absence of similar public service reporting, these bodies shape public opinion of the quality of public service performance.

The Australian public has no way of knowing, for example, whether or not the issues identified in the published reports are typical or isolated instances. If what the general public is exposed to is only the bad news about the activity, then it might be forgiven for assuming that public service performance is perennially poor. In this manner, watchdog and integrity body reports can have a negative impact on public perceptions of 'the quality of government' that reaches beyond the reality. And, insofar as perception is reality, then in a real sense, the Auditor-General for Australia is a competitor in this market where the real competition is not for the responsibility to account for government activities, although it is in part, but for the perceived quality of public administration in Australia. In a sense, this is both an accounting and reputational market.

In this 'market' for governance with 'buyers' and 'sellers', the government is a purchaser of the public service's establishment of a governance framework and the regular delivery of reports on the related activities. The demand for governance is a derived demand (from accountability to parliament and the Australian public) that the government 'buys' (pays for) through a multitude of program-level grants and corporate services administrative activities across all departments, just as surely as if there were a single departmental and whole-of-public-service output called 'government governance'. The ultimate customers for this product are parliament and the Australian public, with the quality of the delivered product an important determinant of the public trust in and legitimacy of government.

It is arguable, then, that a public service on top of its game should neither want nor need an auditor-general conducting costly annual performance audits (costly in audit and public service time). I argue that the delivery of good governance outputs should be regarded as important to the public service as effective competition for policy formation and service delivery. The public service should take full responsibility for its performance reporting and aim to make the auditor-general redundant in this process. It must compete for its reputation.

8.5.7 A markets summary: Public service competitive advantage

In the competition for political and public influence the public service has strong corporate-level advantages, including the legislative foundations for its role, including in policy formation and service delivery; its central role in the delivery of good governance; and its physical proximity to government.

The breadth of the role, when viewed across the spectrum of government activities, can be regarded as a strength or a weakness, depending on how these corporate-level advantages are exploited and on the competitive positioning the public service has achieved in the individual markets. When viewed in terms of the individual markets in which it is involved, the public service faces strong competition in the policy formation market and ongoing competition in service delivery through its competitors and the Efficiency through Contestability Programme. It is only in the field of delivering good governance that it has an unassailable position with limited competition. The downside with the latter is the existing competition's reputational impact on the public service.

The public service has an interest in each of the five identified areas of government activity – the political belief systems (as an interested observer), the policy advisory role (its core business), the delivery of services (as an active participant), organisation and administration (as a strategic participant and observer), and good governance (as a near-monopolist), . It is ultimately the competitive advantages of scope, built around strength in the policy advisory role, on which it should build its strategy. This advantage needs to be exploited at a whole-of-public-service level, but it is only of value to the business of the public service if it can be leveraged on a daily basis at the business unit (department) level. It should exploit the advantages of scope that are based on linkages between the parts of the public sector market system on a pairwise and aggregate basis.

An understanding of the underlying belief system, how it plays out into policy, and how such policies have performed in other jurisdictions enables the public service to anticipate government actions and expectations as well as provide sound advice about tailoring its actions to the local market. This pairwise advantage also enables the public service to be creative and propose policy changes that may not be part of an incoming government's policy platform. Similar advantages flow from the relationships between policy formation and service delivery, and service delivery and the supporting information technology (and associated administrative) systems, along with the delivery of good governance.

The major advantages of scope go to the heart of the difficulties, both large and growing, in delivering the three stages of coordination necessary to effective government – that is, vertical coordination within government, horizontal coordination across government, and the growing challenge of delivering horizontal coordination across sectoral boundaries whilst maintaining accountability. This is the fundamental challenge outlined by the Auditor-General for Australia in successive reports, and the same strategic challenge identified by Porter in his discussion of interrelationships between business units in a multi-business corporation.

Notwithstanding the existing strong foundation of public service competitive advantage, much of this potential remains unexploited. For the public service to secure maximum return from the advantages of scope, the government must understand and support it in its endeavours to secure this advantage. To be of any benefit, this corporate advantage must be exploited at the operating level; that is, the individual departmental level. The advantage only becomes useful at the level where it can be converted into customer value through cost and/or product differentiation. These corporate advantages are accompanied by business unit (departmental) level advantages derived from the departmental structure's ability to focus on target client groups at the policy and program levels.

A government that fragments the public service structurally and/or operationally significantly blunts the efforts of individual departments. A narrow focus on efficiency serves to reinforce these impacts by breaking up integrated public sector systems into a series of loosely connected activities and markets. The prospective dismantling of strategic capabilities through a function-based department-level outsourcing program is likely to have a similar destructive impact on public service competitiveness because it takes neither a whole-of-department nor whole-of-public-service view of these capabilities.

Table 8.2 Public service markets and competition

Market element	Political belief systems/ world views	Policy, program, and services advice	Service delivery	Government governance	Administrative
Structure of the market	A number of major players across the public and private sectors Government is conduit	A two-part market on the supply side, with a number of large players with broad market coverage and a raft of narrowly focused special interest groups	A fragmented 'market' comprising a large number of differently focused supply opportunities with the public service as the monopoly manager and default provider	A small number of government players in addition to the dominant public service, each with its own but overlapping charters	Presently a fragmented market with a large number of individual public service providers integrated with a large number of private sector service providers
Major players/ competitors	Think tanks, universities and party machines Public service an observer not a competitor	Public service is endorsed principal official supplier. Major consulting houses as well as special interest groups compete	Public service is the major player, but large local and international companies involved in some market segments, especially where equipment is involved	Public service faces competition from the auditor-general for performance reporting and limited competition from other watchdog and integrity bodies in areas of probity, integrity, maladministration	Public service presently a major player as integrated service provider on an agency-by-agency basis but with large numbers of private sector players across the service spectrum
Key elements of competition	Assessed merit of ideologies and ideas	Experience, often of an international nature Local market knowledge Political risk Insurance = a 'name'	Short-term costs/out-of-pocket expenses for most services. Whole-of-life costs for	Focus on adequacy of performance reporting as well as probity and integrity on an exception basis	Driving force for change is rationalisation of systems and providers to achieve savings and agility

Market element	Political belief systems/world views	Policy, program, and services advice	Service delivery	Government governance	Administrative
Public service competitive advantage	Understanding whole-of-systems implications of changing political ideologies and belief systems	Public service has proximity and Act endorsement. Knowledge of what is and what works based on best available evidence. Understanding whole-of-systems implications	Public service has monopoly on management of service delivery. Depth of local knowledge of what works but has the Efficiency through Contestability Programme to contend with. Can provide integrated upstream and downstream advice	Has primary responsibility under the Public Service Act and should value and exploit it	Incumbency and maintaining an integrated horizontal and vertical view of systems and from policy formation to customer
Public service competitive positioning strategy	Observer – ready to advise about downstream implementation implications – policy, service delivery, organisation, administrative systems, and outcomes	Active participant ready to advise about downstream implementation implications. Should be the public service's core business and competitive platform. Aim for a monopoly in this field. Develop whole-of-public-service centre and compete on scope	Needs to identify and maintain strategic capabilities at both department and whole-of-public-service levels whilst competing selectively to build supply-chain knowledge base	Needs to do better and make auditor-general irrelevant. Build results-measurement capability. Develop policy governance capability. Integrate with brand management. Work actively to build trust in government and legitimacy	Needs to identify and maintain strategic capabilities at both department and whole-of-public-service levels whilst competing selectively to build knowledge base in systems management and integration

The absence of a strong centre means the almost certain lack of whole-of-public-service strategic leadership and cohesion, which denies opportunities to generate corporate advantages and transmit them to the operating units; for example, through economies of scale and risk sharing activities. This absence similarly compromises advantages of interrelationships generated at the business unit level. This goes beyond the development of a capability to deal with boundary issues such as coordination problems, to a variety of projects that actively create value between business units on a bottom-up basis, rather than simply dealing with issues that emerge at the operational level between business units.

It is likely that the public service competitive position is continuing to degrade overall due to pressure to reduce the size of the public service combined with the government's outsourcing program. The public service's ability to 'compete' and fulfil its responsibilities under the Public Service Act are increasingly compromised by these actions of government and by its own lack of strategic management. A serious effort is required to arrest this decline in public service influence on government in Australia.

Above all, the public service needs to consider the point made by a number of public service heads, and well expressed by Simon Longstaff – that the alignment of the interests of the public service with the government, following the realignment by the government under Bob Hawke in the 1980s, needs reconsidering. The public service needs to work out where these interests align, where they compete, and where it can usefully occupy unoccupied ground.

8.6 Conclusions and summary

The public service must recognise that it is competing for its survival, which depends on it becoming better focused and organised in its activities, allocating resources across its different markets to build competitive advantage in a carefully chosen and balanced portfolio of activities. It cannot continue to retain all of its existing business on a department-by-department basis. It must change its business mix to secure its major competitive advantages, and position itself at the forefront of change in each market so as to capture the role of delivering change. This changed mix must involve:

- strengthening its understanding of the ideological foundations of political parties and policies. This would prepare it for a possible volatile future of coalition and minority governments with compromised policies with an honest-broker role or for reversion to major party rule
- regaining lost ground in the public policy space to reinforce its pre-eminent role in policy formation and implementation and its underpinning role in creating competitive advantage based on scope. The public service should identify the emerging fields of policy advice and accompanying tools and leverage this knowledge to ensure that it maintains its policy competitiveness
- maintaining selective involvement across the service delivery market whilst placing itself at the forefront of the development of tools to manage outsourced service delivery, especially in regard to networks
- maintaining active participation in the management of information technology systems across the whole public service, with its strength lying with an overarching perception of the customer. With organisation, the public service should develop a foundation understanding of the effectiveness of different structures and the functioning of the parts
- lifting its game with respect to government governance to the point of making the auditors-general performance-reporting role irrelevant. It must also take responsibility for its own governance and, if the opportunity arises, take responsibility for policy formation administration/governance.

The prospective foundations of success for the APS in strategy formation and implementation lie with its incumbency and the scope of its activities. Its incumbency – through the Public Service Act and its established position – provides a strong base on which the public service can actively build competitive advantage. It must build on its unassailable opportunity to take an integrated, whole-of-system, and whole-of-government view of the business of government, ranging from the ideological beliefs and world views that incoming governments may bring, through to the derived policy frameworks and programs, and into the management of service delivery (whether delivered in-house or outsourced). In Porter's terms, this position is scope-based, which enables product differentiation.

There is also the possibility of creating cost-based advantages in the area of formal policy advice. Engaging the major international and local consulting houses is always costly. A public service alternative of equivalent quality must be a less expensive option. While this caveat – on quality – is a challenge for the public service, there is no reason why it should not aim for a monopoly on the higher levels of policy advice. There will always be proprietary models and expert external advice that the government, even public service, will utilise, but there remains undoubted value in going down the path of establishing a public service vehicle for formal policy advice. The public service also needs to review its cost-based advantages in regard to service delivery.

There is much that the public service can do to improve the attractiveness of the industry in which it operates, including actively demonstrating that it performs according to the requirements of the Public Service Act and that, as such, it lives up to community expectations that it provide frank and fearless advice based on the best available evidence. Being part of 'government' increases community trust levels and the standing ('legitimacy') of government with the electorate. The public service should develop and promote its own brand as part of this exercise. The difficulty noted with declining trust levels in government is the rising cost of governing associated with community demands for more direct involvement in the processes of government. The associated problem for the public service is that, as a consequence, there is a diminishing pool of authority to be exercised jointly by the government and public service, leading to further constraints on public service activity. The consequent costs must be rising rapidly, diminishing the proportion of resources going to the citizenry as services.

A further point concerns where competitive advantage is conceived, occurs, and is realised. Porter (1985) makes the point that we can talk of 'competitive advantage' and 'competitive positioning' at the whole-of-organisation level but, to be of value, it must be realisable at the business unit/business line/product, and ultimately, customer level. It must create customer value by providing a better product at the same cost or the same product at a lesser cost. To be of any use, competitive advantage and competitive positioning at the whole-of-public service level must deliver identifiable value to customers through individual departments and programs. The value chain differs from one department to the next, and this is part of the challenge for an expanded public service centre: how can the public service use its competitive advantage of scope to deliver a benefit to individual departments?

The characteristics of public services include the respective merits of public and private bureaucracies. On a department-by-department basis, the foundations on which the role of government is built vary, as will the preferred role for the public service within these boundaries. These foundations, the nature of competition, and the preferred role for the public service also vary between departments and thus they are matters for individual business unit strategy. These differences are also reflected in horizontal relationships between pairs of departments, depending on operational overlaps and the contribution of corporate synergies.

Discussions of whole-of-government activities in the public service commonly focus on the coordination problems that arise from services delivered from individual departments that overlap with other departments. This is essentially a defensive role. Where the role of strategy is one of benefits created at the top of the organisation and cascaded down to the operating units, there is opportunity to create synergies at the business unit level that can be shared amongst the participating business units. Porter discusses this in terms of horizontal strategies and the interrelationships of business units, describing a number of categories in which such benefits might be created.

A beneficial strategy for public service pursuit of its legislative objective of serving the Australian public, however, needs to move beyond the notion of merely performing within the bounds of a business-as-usual approach. Re-establishing a competitive position on well-worn ground, however, has limitations and, whilst it must be done, it should be actively complemented by actions to change some of the rules of competition.[8] The public service should seek out disruptive strategies through an examination of private sector experience and its adaptation to the public sector.

Box 8.1 concludes this chapter by viewing the proposed changes to the style and operations of the public service from the point of view of the public service and articulates the strategy as the public service itself might view it.

---

8   Christensen and Raynor argue that, in competitive battles fought around incremental changes in products and services, *the incumbents* are likely to prevail, and only when the basis of competition is changed – through the attraction of new classes of customers, substantially changed products, or perhaps the use of new technologies to add product features – are established players likely to change the industry pecking order, or indeed are new entrants likely to win (Christensen & Raynor (2003) refer to the former as *sustaining strategies* and the latter as *disruptive strategies*).

Box 8.1 A public service role and strategy statement

1. We will adopt a simple mission statement – we create value for our customers – and around this mission will develop and manage a customer-focused, career-driven public service that is apolitical and pursues excellence in serving the government, parliament, and the Australian public.

2. We will develop our core competitive advantage around the scope of activities across the business of government – the underlying political beliefs, the choice and development of policy frameworks, instruments, programs and services, the management and delivery of services, and the measurement of performance. The foundation of this competitive advantage will be our policy knowledge and we will leverage this across our full range of activities.

3. We will build our competitive position in each of our markets around this overall advantage. We will keep a watching brief on political concepts and systems, we will build a pre-eminent position in policy advice, we will secure our (monopoly) role as manager of service delivery and selectively compete to deliver services, we will develop our role in governance and actively compete for influence, and we will strategically manage our role in the development and delivery of supporting administrative systems. We will strategise and manage together and separately on a whole of government, parliament, and Australian public basis.

4. We will underpin our competitive advantage through (a) the development of a globally focused policy capability to complement departmental capabilities, (b) the development of a centrally driven market intelligence system to integrate local and international knowledge of markets and competitors, (c) establishment of an integrated centre and department model of corporate memory, (d) the establishment of a central metrics capability to develop management information and performance reporting systems to complement government governance activities and the governance of the public service.

5. We will actively promote the institution of government by promoting the quality of public administration thereby aiming to raise trust in government by publishing an annual report on public service activities evidencing active service to the government of the day, parliament and the Australian public; by demonstrating the practice of the values, code of conduct and employment principles set out in the Public Service Act; and through stakeholder engagement.

6. We will aim to establish metrics for our overarching goals of influence and impact on good government, and will develop an integrated set of public service performance targets focused on (a) quantity and quality of service to our three legislated customer groups, (b) the development of our core capabilities, (c) the development of our brand, (d) the legitimisation of government, (e) our stakeholder management, and (f) our competitive performance. We aim to integrate the creation and measurement of public value into our day-to-day activities.

7. We will strengthen public service–wide capabilities in corporate strategy, market intelligence, strategic management, performance measurement, innovation (including in organisational innovation and change), with an underlying focus on our capacity to adapt to a continuously changing political, social, and economic environment.

8. We will establish integrated management information architecture and systems to link the (new) corporate-level activities with departmental operations to enable effective whole-of-public-service governance and better government governance.

9. We will win.

9

Adjusting to change: The role of innovation

9.1 Introduction

A central theme of this discussion is the need for organisations to constantly adjust to change. Whether expressed in the management literature in terms of balancing exploration and exploitation, or in terms of the application of the tools of design thinking; in the organisational literature in the concepts of the learning organisation and the notion of ambidextrous organisations; or in the strategy literature in a discussion of transient advantage and the divergence between deliberate and emergent strategy, the focus is on change and the central question of how organisations systematically change. Whether this challenge is explored in terms of capability development, organisational design, or the identification (and resolution) of mysteries, the various proposals necessarily involve a systemic view of and response to the challenge.

Organisations are living entities in which substantial change in one part will impact on other parts. More importantly, the major reason for a systemic approach is that successful change must be led, encouraged and allowed, across all levels, functions and businesses of an organisation. It cannot be contained to the top, but if it is not led from the top, systematic change will not occur. It must be encouraged in every part of the organisation. In a corporate world in which the pace of market change is seen to be accelerating, organisational and bottom-line growth is increasingly regarded as coming from disruptive change arising from market growth no longer delivering bottom-line growth. As a consequence, innovation has emerged as a management-adjustment mechanism to manage this change. If competitive advantage determines the primary location of an organisation's businesses, then innovation is the mechanism that enables this positioning to be continuously adjusted at many levels across the organisation. In this way, properly monitored and managed, organisations can integrate change with positioning and successfully balance deliberate with emergent strategy.

Empirical and theoretical research into the role played by innovation in the management of the public service is in its early stages of development. It is apparent from a recent stocktake of the empirical research, asking what it was we knew about public sector innovation, that there is no integrated body of theory and practice to draw on (Arundel et al. 2016).

Whereas the empirical research focuses on innovation activities as relatively lower-level matters of process, the emerging focus in the public sector management literature has been to elevate innovation to the level of strategy. This divergence – between the framing of existing empirical research into public sector innovation based on innovation process dimensions, and the strategic management of innovation – is important, as an understanding of how organisations engage with innovation (i.e. manage it) provides the foundations for government interventions to impact on innovation levels. In addition, both streams of research are concerned with 'public sector' innovation in the broad, often conflating the activities of government and public service and failing to distinguish the separable roles of politicians and public servants. It is equally not possible to automatically apply private sector experience of innovation to the public sector because of the imperative of contextual differences.

Sound public policy foundations can only be developed out of an understanding of what public sector innovation is, what part the public service plays in it, and how, through sound public policy, more innovation can be encouraged. One point that can be drawn from the developing literature on public sector management is the importance of the surrounding institutional, organisational, and management settings that frame research into public sector innovation activities. For example, for public policy purposes, lower/middle-level departmental innovation that occurred in an incidental manner – what is described in the public sector management literature as incremental or random innovation – can be viewed differently from similar occurrences taking place within a senior management–led whole-of-organisation strategic approach to innovation (e.g. in the presence of a whole-of-organisation innovation strategy).

The emerging literature on innovation as strategy follows a period in which the primary focus in the public sector literature was on process-driven collaborative innovation. Whilst collaboration is likely to be an important ingredient of a more innovative public sector, a number of the organisational and institutional elements – the culture, the organisational structures, the capabilities, the resource allocation processes, the governance and supporting management systems (including performance management and measurement), and the authority to innovate – are key determinants of an innovative public service and should be the primary focus of public sector innovation analysis. These are all properly matters for the strategic management of any organisation, providing a framework through which managerial behaviour may be influenced in the interests of public policy. If public service innovation is to play the central role of the umbrella environmental-adjustment mechanism for the public service, and be manageable in public policy terms, then it must be strategically conceived and actively managed, neither of which applies today.

A further challenge to the exploration of the notion of public sector innovation is that there are many alternative definitions, and numerous taxonomies and typologies of innovation that can be employed but none, it seems, readily able to meet strategic management and public policy requirements. By reconsidering these definitional and classificatory elements, however, it is possible to arrive at a definition through an examination of the separate contributions of the political and administrative arms of government, emphasising the organisational and management dimensions of the latter. Related questions – such as the 'manageability' of innovation from the point of view of the public service, and public service 'innovation readiness' – are also relevant.

9.2 Methodological issues

9.2.1 What is public sector innovation?

There are a number of definitional challenges to public sector innovation that revolve around the domain, the actors, and the context for innovation. The 'public sector' is a broad canvas on which to paint a picture of innovation, housing as it does many different sorts of entities (e.g. government departments, government business enterprises, statutory authorities, executive agencies, watchdog and integrity bodies, the institution of parliament), with a variety of different goals (e.g. service delivery, regulatory, profit-making, advisory), involving a broad range of fields (e.g. defence, health, transport, economic policy, public administration integrity), and reporting to a range of different bodies (ministers, department heads, government boards, and parliament).

9.2.1.1 The activities

Most writers define innovation using the novelty criterion – the assumption that change introduced to a new environment for the first time is innovation – and then progress to discuss a number of other dimensions of innovation, including impact, type, scale, process, and context (Fagerberg 2005; Hartley 2005).

A notable and important difference between the public and private sector literature is that, in the private sector literature, 'success' tends to be assumed in the definition of innovation, whilst in the public sector case, endeavour alone is the common starting point. This is ultimately inadequate for our own purposes because the public policy dimensions of public sector innovation must envisage effective use of public resources, therefore a definition of innovation must incorporate not just endeavour but also 'success'. If public sector innovation is to prove its worth, it must earn its keep.

Geoff Mulgan and Bason provide comparable workable definitions based on the two concepts of novelty and success. Mulgan defines public sector innovation as 'new ideas that work at creating public value', while Bason defines it as 'the process of creating new ideas and turning them into value for society' (Mulgan 2009, p 150; Bason 2010, pp 34, 45). 'Value for society', most commonly expressed in the public sector management literature as 'public value', notionally at least offers such a measure of 'success' aggregating as it does the individual consumer's valuation-in-consumption, and the wider community's recognition of its contribution to 'good government'. Indeed both Bason and Mulgan take an expansive view of public value. Mulgan identifies three main categories of value – value provided by services, outcomes, and trust in government; whilst Bason similarly describes service experience, results, and democracy – adding productivity gains to the value mix (Bason 2010, pp 44–47; Mulgan 2009, Chapter 10, esp pp 232–33).

Both acknowledge the difficulties in measuring and aggregating the components of value, with Bason pointing to the need for the achievement of positive value on all four elements ('a balanced scorecard'). Mulgan considers the limitations of available measurement techniques, observing the problems with monetising the elements and their non-aggregatability, and provides an interesting application of the concept of opportunity cost in public sector resource use – based on sacrifice by the community – as it might be viewed by citizens.[1] Other issues that arise with the measurement of 'success' include the measurement of a net benefit, the essentially destructive nature of innovation, and the distribution of benefits. The last of these three is another challenging measurement issue. The parties that may be affected by innovations – for example, politicians, public managers, street-level bureaucrats, and users – will evaluate innovation impacts differently because of differential impacts (single innovations can serve different purposes), which points to the need for trade-offs as part of any public policy evaluation.

9.2.1.2 The context

The variety of circumstances within which public sector innovation can take place permits a number of factors to be regarded as context and, therefore, a broad range of contexts to be described.[2] Particularly important in setting the scene for a public policy analysis of public service innovation are the institutional factors embedded in the notion of the alignment of government and public service. Context is the set of circumstances that define a particular event (public sector innovation), and it distinguishes external factors from those that are internal to the public service and which are the primary focus of change.

In twin Australian studies of public and private sector innovation activity, Kay and Goldspink undertook a set of interviews with departmental secretaries/deputy secretaries, and CEOs (Kay & Goldspink 2012a, 2012b). Kay and Goldspink's comparative research into the Australian public and private sectors was derived from a set of interviews with departmental secretaries and deputy secretaries. These studies evidenced distinct differences between public and private sector innovation on the one hand, and within each sector on the other. The research provides clear pointers to ways in which the level of public service innovation

---

1   Mulgan's notion of opportunity cost is squarely focused on citizens and what they are willing to give up in return for proposed benefits. He identifies the various 'sacrifices' as monetary, disclosing private information, the granting of coercive powers to the state, giving time or 'other personal resources' (Mulgan 2009, p 231).
2   Mulgan's method for dealing with this maze is to describe it in terms of 'the field of battle' and how knowable it is, describing four types of fields – direct causation, multiple causation, complex fields, chaos. The field type affects the kind of strategy and how tightly the strategy can be controlled (Mulgan 2009, p 79).

can be increased. The authors' examination of 84 'innovation stories' across the public and private sectors divides the playing field according to the twin dimensions of uncertainty and pro-activity. They identified three distinct approaches in the private sector according to the level of uncertainty – covering 'incremental', 'evolutionary', and 'revolutionary' forms of change – and two in the public sector according to pro-activity: 'departmental' and 'ministerial', the former being initiated and led from within 'the department', whilst the latter occurred through interaction with the political arm of government, typically the minister. Each of these five approaches is described as holistic and requiring different styles and focus of leadership. The distinction between government-led and departmentally led innovation is important because it points to different drivers and policy levers for public sector innovation.

Five further observations from the Kay and Goldspink studies are relevant to this discussion:

- When 'the department' was in declared 'reactive' innovation mode, responding to externally imposed innovation by 'the minister', the chances of failure were massively increased (2012b pp 1 & 2). From this finding, the authors concluded that time taken to reduce uncertainty and the risk of failure was the most valuable asset for the department (time-to-market was the equivalent private sector asset, irrespective of accompanying failures).

- Whilst departmental innovation shared some common characteristics with private sector innovation, ministerial innovation was a substantially different category, the former thereby presenting the possibility for learning from private sector innovation practice but the latter leaving little such room (2012b).

- The public service's diminishing control over the innovation environment leads to a recommendation that the public service needed to work with the government to get back to an environment that allowed it to play to its strength, namely time.

- Both public and private sector leaders had no desire to innovate in and of itself: rather innovation was one of a number of tools used to solve problems (Kay & Goldspink 2012b p 7). Put another way, when viewed from a management perspective innovation was created, rather than naturally occurring.

- Every innovation is influenced by contextual factors.

Naming observed public sector innovation types 'ministerial' and 'departmental' reflects the data set derived from interviews with departmental heads and deputy heads. Whole-of-public-service innovation, however, is more important than this innovation dichotomy. If the broad direction of public sector management in Australia over the last 30 or so years has been integrative to address the fragmentation caused by the excesses of the New Public Management (NPM) reforms, then an important focus for change has been to 'join-up' the services of government. The literature on collaborative innovation and networks from the last decade or so has pursued this objective by seeking to put 'the public' back into 'public services' via processes of co-creation and co-production.

Beyond the pursuit of excellence in general, this is arguably where the major innovation challenge of government lies, namely within and across various parts of the public service and to third parties. The administrative arm of government needs to be allowed to develop strategic management capability within which cross-boundary management and accountability become 'natural'.[3] A central problem is that the field of public sector management, along with the dominant public service structures and operational models, remains framed around 'the department', 'the departmental head', and 'the minister responsible', as the fulcrum of public sector management. It is an outdated NPM-driven vertical management model that ignores the growing and dominant horizontal realities of public sector life.

Consequently, whilst whole-of-public-service activities generated by the leadership group in public administration – for example, the UK Civil Service Board and the Secretaries Board in Australia – are likely to be a (limited) source of public sector innovation today, they could well be the foundation for important public service innovation leadership tomorrow.

A further notable element of context is when the government is not simply the arbiter and deliverer of public policy interventions but a key player and beneficiary. In this case, serious divergences between the policy practised by the government of the day ('government policy'), and the policy that is in the community's best interest ('public policy'), may appear and be substantial.

---

3   It is arguable that much of the larger end of the private sector has the corporate mindset and access to the tools to deal with the horizontal and boundary issues that the public sector finds so difficult. The business literature sees the horizontal dimensions as a set of opportunities through which to create competitive advantage. See the discussion here in Chapter 8 and in Porter (1985).

9.2.1.3 A workable public service innovation typology

The development of a workable public sector innovation typology is important if we are to establish firm foundations for the promotion of a public policy–driven public service innovation capability. The starting point for this discussion of an effective public service innovation typology comprises the three core categories of 'ministerial', 'departmental', and 'whole-of-public-service'. Whereas the 'ministerial' category might reasonably be regarded as one, accounting essentially for those innovations imposed on the public service whether as a collective by the Prime Minister and Cabinet, or through individual departments by ministers within individual portfolio responsibilities, there is good reason to disaggregate the 'departmental' category through an assessment of the associated strategic intent. 'Departmental' innovation can be divided into three sub-categories.

The first two of these sub-categories are variants of 'top-down' departmental innovation. Consistent with Kay and Goldspink's observation from their study that neither public nor private sector leaders are 'natural innovators' and that innovation is typically a response to a crisis, the first type can be described in terms of crisis-driven projects. These projects might be in the form of information technology projects to integrate customer services, a change in service delivery focus from services to case management, a new regime of corporate governance, or a change from internal (departmental) service delivery to outsourcing. A team is built to deliver the project and effect the transition and is dismantled on its completion, leaving little or no legacy of organisational innovation capability. This projects approach to innovation lacks the benefits of ongoing efficiency and effectiveness.

The second of these 'top-down' sub-categories of departmental innovation is distinguishable from the crisis-driven approach, because its primary goal is to build such an organisational capability through a systemic approach to innovation. It is the real deal in terms of strategic intent, comprising what Bason describes as an innovation strategy focused on building organisation-wide innovation capability around an accommodating culture to shape the whole organisation as a serial innovator (Bason 2010). Bason describes this as 'choosing approaches and building skills and capacity internally in the organisation' (Bason 2010, p 73), and sees this strategy integrated with other functional and cross-organisational strategies into the whole-of-organisation strategic management framework.

The third sub-category of departmental innovation is of the 'bottom-up' variety, which Bason describes as 'self-directed' and occurring in organisations in the absence of innovative leadership. Indeed, based on Bason's observations, this form of innovation is likely to be the rule rather than the exception with public sector innovation today and the likely foundation of observed departmental innovation.[4] Bason describes this 'self-directed' innovation as random incrementalisation – in other quarters this might be described as marginal innovation (as opposed to radical). Important, however, is the absence of a strategic development framework and the consequent random and unsupported nature of the activities.

The third of the major categories of innovation is described as whole-of-public-service. It is the whole-of-public-service counterpart to the second of the departmental sub-categories of innovation strategy. Under this strategy, the centre leads and directs an integrated strategy in the same way as the department does in the earlier category. The resulting typology is presented in Table 9.1 with the various categories (and sub-categories) distinguished across a range of characteristics.[5]

A final taxonomic subtlety rests with the precursor to innovation, invention. For public sector organisations whose primary mission is the creation of knowledge and whose core activity is research and development, a steady stream of associated innovation activities will most likely follow. While there are many organisations that fit this picture – for example, in public health, education, agriculture, and transport research – the focus should be on the establishment of an operating environment within which innovation flourishes across all organisational functions.[6]

---

4   In practice it will of course be difficult – in the absence of suitable screening data – to distinguish random incrementalisation (i.e. departmental, bottom-up innovation), from departmental top-down process-driven innovation. Consideration of the existence and nature of an innovation strategy is a prerequisite for empirical research into an organisation.

5   The Kay and Goldspink studies do not readily recognise the second and third of the major categories because their innovation stories were derived from departmental secretaries and deputy secretaries who, as can be expected, related stories of projects they initiated, rather than those that emerged from the Secretaries Board or from the lower reaches of their organisations.

6   Whilst innovation may occur across all business functions proportionately to the bounds of possibility, the mix of management and governance models employed also imposes possibilities and constraints. For example, it is likely that organisational units operating within a 'joined-up' or networked philosophy will be more strategic in their approach to innovation, and more innovative than those operating under a traditional hierarchical model, if only because the 'joining-up' or networking of government (and non-government) activities is a fertile ground for public sector innovation.

Table 9.1 Types and characteristics of public sector innovation

Characteristics	Ministerial	Departmental		Random incrementalisation (bottom-up)	Whole-of-public-service
		Projects (top-down)	Innovation strategy (top-down)		
Originating source	Generated by the political arm of government and imposed on the public service*	Generated by departmental management project by project*	Across the organisation within an innovative culture	Self-directed middle/lower managers/staff	Strategic priorities directed from the centre
Impact	Likely to have major structural and operational impacts on public service	Important to departmental operations and future	Could be cumulatively large	A number of smaller activities with limited impact	Today focussed on workforce. High potential in wide range of areas
Content	Could range from new ideological beliefs and policies through structures to services and service delivery	Could range from rationalisation of diverse departmental IT systems to new CRM systems	Supportive internal resources added, along with ongoing budget allocations	All one-offs	Cross dept and sector boundaries. Could be IT, customer driven, personnel or efficiency driven
Political risk tolerance and activity management	Failure is not an option within tight timelines and little wriggle room but high risk	Projects are internal to department and time can be used to offset risk. High political risk	Projects are internal to department and time can be used to offset risk	Little risk and exposure	Variable

Characteristics	Ministerial	Departmental		Random incrementalisation (bottom-up)	Whole-of-public-service
		Projects (top-down)	Innovation strategy (top-down)		
External to government visibility	High	Limited unless failure	Limited	Negligible	Likely to be limited
Resource allocation	No business case ex ante or ex post	Business case likely to be built	Small budget subject to business case	No budget etc.	Project based allocations from department budgets
Innovation budget	Project allocations but minimal. No ongoing budget	Project allocations. No ongoing budget	Small but ongoing allocation to fund internal processes	Nil	Project allocations from departments
Supportive internal processes	Project teams built and dismantled	Project teams built and dismantled	An innovation strategy with staged internal process management	Nil	Strategic project teams built and dismantled across public service
Contribution to ongoing public sector innovation capability	Negligible	May be some legacies	Important objective	Limited	May be some

* Projects on which the department and minister work together, initiated by either or both, sit on the boundary of the two categories of 'top-down' innovation. These are distinguished from the standard category of 'ministerial' innovation by the time taken and, in some cases, from 'departmental' innovation, through their initiation by the minister. These projects are best classified as 'departmental' as they lend themselves to the tools of strategic management.

Two questions arising from this taxonomy are, firstly whether it establishes a pathway for government to elevate levels of public service innovation, and whether the public service is capable of delivering its part of the bargain; and, secondly, whether there is a public policy case for so doing on the basis of it being a beneficial use of public resources?

9.3 Public service innovation management

9.3.1 The public sector literature

The foundations of a useful public service strategic management framework, and of the necessary public policy framework, must explain how public sector innovation activity levels can be increased with government support/intervention, and in a manner that is beneficial in public-value terms.

The public innovators playbook (2009) by William D Eggers and Kumar Singh lays out a blueprint for the public sector to develop and sustain a culture of innovation – to make it 'part of public sector DNA'. The authors observe that government can and does innovate but that not enough public sector organisations accord the necessary sustained attention to the innovation process (Eggers & Singh 2009, p 17).[7] Their premise is that because governments cannot escape broad economic turmoil, they must innovate on a sustainable basis to meet community needs. To achieve this, they must learn to treat innovation like any other discipline, such as strategy, finance, planning and budgeting.

The authors argue that public sector organisations must be able to move beyond the two standard ways in which (they argue) innovation in government typically occurs – either in response to a crisis or the results of individual (or small group) endeavours, but in both cases with limited benefits or lasting capacity for innovation. They note that few organisations in the public sector cultivate change, let alone innovation: 'It requires a methodical view of the whole process linked to organisational structure, processes, and reward systems' (Eggers & Singh 2009, p 5). Their stated objective is to help government become a serial innovator,

---

7   While there is a tendency to treat the public sector as a whole and not distinguish between the 'government' and the public service, I argue that, in this case, the playbook is equally applicable to all arms of government.

moving beyond projects and big ideas. They describe the ideas in their 'playbook' as concentrating on processes organised around three aspects of the discipline of innovation:

- the innovation process (idea generation, selection, implementation, and diffusion)
- the five strategies of innovation (cultivate, replicate, partner, network, and open source)
- the innovation organisation (boundaries, porosity, capabilities, and structure)

The authors note that, with regard to the innovation process, governments are not short of ideas, but spend too much time on idea generation (or capture), and too little on the transformation of the ideas into successful innovations. Another drawback in the current public sector environment is that, because there are no established theoretical frameworks for cultivating innovation, the proposed strategies of innovation may conflict with the existing organisational structure and culture. And, in regard to the innovation organisation, they note the necessity for organisations trying to build new capacities and ways of doing business, to change the culture. In conclusion, they observe:

> Proper execution of innovation will require government organizations to move from hierarchy to inclusion; from ownership to collaboration; from invention to adaptation; and from a culture of acquiescence to a culture of performance. This transition may involve rethinking organizational boundaries, acquiring new capabilities to better manage the innovation process, and creating flatter, less siloed organizations with a culture focused on performance. (Eggers & Singh 2009, p 126)

The value of the playbook lies in its comprehensive and holistic nature, the emphasis on creating shared goals (a vision), and the recognition that organisations trying to devise and embed new capacities and new ways of conducting business may need to change the prevailing culture. In acknowledging the contributions of both the formal (e.g. structures) and informal (e.g. behaviours) to the outcomes, the authors provide a useful tool to assess the management models that lie behind innovation in the public sector, and how these differing strategies and models impact the outcomes delivered.

Geoff Mulgan's *The art of public strategy* (2009) is a book written from the perspective of someone who has been at the heart of government and understands how governments think and act – and who is primarily interested in achieving results for citizens. Like Eggers and Singh, Mulgan's book considers change in the public sector and how it can be used to make citizens' lives better. He also embraces the utility of the public-value criterion as a measure of success and his focus is the role that 'public strategy' plays in achieving this.

Mulgan sees much to despair in the public sector's inability to innovate, pointing to successful innovators succeeding despite, rather than because of, the 'dominant structures and systems'. As with Eggers and Singh, Mulgan records the slow emergence of the institutionalisation and formalisation of these routes to innovation within governments around the globe. He provides a number of UK examples of innovation and argues that all are small in scale and institutionally fragile and operate, as elsewhere, on tiny budgets. Mulgan then moves on to argue that, while there is no simple formula for making governments more creative or innovative, there are six essential elements to support and encourage innovation and creativity: leadership and culture; pulls and pushes; creativity and recombination; prototypes and pilots; scaling and diffusion; and sophisticated risk management. He highlights the interaction between risk management and funding, especially through the testing, early stage implementation, and scaling and diffusion phases of innovation, and recommends the use of private sector capital (where possible) and the removal of the testing phase from the immediate responsibility of government.

Bason's *Leading public sector innovation* (2010) aims to make the practices and tools of successful public sector organisations readily accessible. Built on the premise that there are a number of major driving forces shaping the acute need for public sector innovation, Bason acknowledges that there are numerous barriers to such innovation and that most public sector organisations are ill-suited to dealing with the problems of the day, resulting in random innovation rather than the strategic or systematic innovation that is required, but that it is possible to systematically apply the practices of successfully innovating public sector organisations 'to create radical new value'. He argues that public sector leaders must embed innovation as a core activity in their organisations, and describes leading public sector innovation as being 'the art and practice of balancing between inspiration and execution, between exploring mysteries and exploiting resources to generate results' and concludes that public sector innovation must become 'a natural discipline' based around a new paradigm at the heart of which must lay 'co-creation' (Bason 2010, p 253).

As with Mulgan, Bason takes a determinedly strategic management approach to his subject: he notes that strategy defines an organisation's objectives and the means of meeting them, and he defines three key terms: strategic management – as the means of linking the organisation's activities with its goals; strategic innovation – which he describes largely in project terms as the activity-level means of bridging the gap between strategic ambitions (the what of public sector innovation and the realisation of value); and innovation strategy – which he likens to any other functional or work unit strategy – for example, human resources or information technology. Bason describes his new paradigm in terms of 'an innovation ecosystem, encompassing the four C's of consciousness, capacity, co-creation and courage'.

In considering how possible the achievement of an innovative public sector might be, Bason argues that there are a number of barriers and missing enablers to innovation in the public sector, but that nonetheless it is possible to reorganise, shifting some of the public sector boxes around, establishing a centrally supported innovation unit to help staff bring good ideas to fruition, even employing leaders with 'the right' management styles, and still fail to change innovation performance. Bason observes that, even when these sorts of changes are made, 'not much permanent change will happen if the culture and everyday working habits of those working in government do not change' (2010, p 115). Bason further argues that innovation must be everybody's job, and that the challenge is to stimulate a culture and behaviour that enforces it.

Eggers and Singh, Mulgan, and Bason offer three different perspectives of public sector innovation and, whilst all would argue that there is no proven theory that enables the automation of the innovation process in public or private sectors, they highlight many common threads and a framework within which to view public sector innovation. The 'model' of public sector innovation that emerges is one of a strategically led and managed approach to innovation integrated with a whole-of-organisation strategy that systematises the innovation process.

9.3.2 The private sector literature

Private sector literature on innovation has a different emphasis to the public sector material and ranges over an extended period, commencing with the emergence of business strategy as the capstone organisational capability some 40 or more years ago, the evolution of its focus from the numerist-driven tools determining positioning, to the emergence of people and innovation as central to strategy. The literature of the last quarter of a century has focused on growth and disruptive competition, eschewing the path dependency of incremental adjustments to strategy. Gary Hamel and CK Prahalad's pioneering *Competing for the future* (1994) outlines their goal:

> Our goal in this book is to enlarge the concept of strategy so that it more fully encompasses the emerging competitive reality – a reality in which the goal is to transform industries, not just organisations; a reality in which being incrementally better is not enough; a reality in which any company that cannot imagine the future won't be around to enjoy it. (Hamel & Prahalad 1994, p xi)

The subsequent work of Christensen and Raynor (2003) examined the corporate history of successful companies only to discover that many of them could not escape the success of the past to build new growth platforms before it was too late. For his part, Roger Martin (2009) described the distinction between reliability and validity as being at the heart of the innovation dilemma, and the need to identify and explore 'mysteries' by detaching oneself from the logic train that identified the mystery to find the real answer. Rita McGrath (2013) argued that for business to win in a volatile environment, executives needed to learn how to exploit short-lived opportunities. Whether considering Christensen and Raynor, Martin or McGrath, the theme common to all these arguments is that the past is not a reliable guide to the future (or at least not a comforting one), and that organisations must find ways to live in the future and start to change the rules of competitive engagement now.

The particular value of the pointers in this private sector literature to the effective management of innovation in any setting lies in the design of structures and processes to balance established operations with the ongoing development of the business. The specific issues that arise for consideration in a public sector context are:

- the emphasis placed on organisational renewal through innovation from the discovery of new sources of value
- the allocation of formal responsibility for exploration, the development of capabilities, and choice of structures to execute it
- the focus it brings to resource-allocation processes to get the longer-term balance between exploitation and exploration 'right', and to integrate with day-to-day project and activity processes
- achieving the continuing release of resources into corporate renewal, given that in many organisations 'ownership' of resources is a measure of individual status
- the focus it places on an organisation's corporate strategy and its integration with the management of innovation.

This literature is most obviously applicable to large public sector organisations with a measure of independence comprising the various government business undertakings along with the service-delivery agencies. It should also be applicable to the individual government departments that comprise the inner budget sector of public administration, and more particularly for public policy purposes, to the collective of these departments, from whence change across the broader public sector can be driven.

9.3.3 Implications for a model of public sector innovation

It is possible to distil this collective wisdom into a suitable theory of change for public policy purposes, acknowledging that this theory of change must comprise two integrated parts: the first must identify the government interventions by which public sector innovation levels can be elevated – the public policy lever(s); whereas the second must identify the means by which the target organisation converts the intervention into the identified public policy outcomes.

The preceding models lie in the realm of the descriptive, listing the many key features thought to accompany productive public sector innovation rather than tightly determined theories of change. Nonetheless Bason, Eggers and Singh, and Mulgan go some way to establishing a suitable internal theory of change as they provide complementary 'cookbook' views of how to innovate successfully in the public sector. The model that emerges of a successfully innovating public service is one that sees innovation as part of its strategic management challenge (and the trigger point for public policy), that builds capability and culture by supporting processes and structures, and executes it along the lines of the Eggers and Singh's playbook.

I propose that a theory of change be no more nor less than the standard model of strategic management in the management literature as applied to the public service, one in which there is an integrated set of organisational goals that drives public service organisation, resource allocations and management, of which innovation is one. The innovation strategy then becomes the vehicle through which the Eggers and Singh, Mulgan, and Bason processes and activities are applied to the public service. The public policy levers become the incentives that the government can develop to induce more public service innovation outputs. This should include the allocation of dedicated resources to innovation processes, support for a wider range of innovation strategies, a more tolerant approach to risk management, and the development of suitable organisational structures to manage the processes, strategies and governance of the activity.

Ministerial innovation commonly (but not only) occurs as a consequence of elections, and may range across the full set of public service activities as described by Windrum, and will almost certainly impact broadly across the public service in efficiency, effectiveness and morale. It may produce change but its net positive impacts – on customers, the broader community, the public service, and third party service providers – is less certain. Departmental innovation creates a different picture in that it lends itself in prospect to the full array of private sector innovation management techniques and their public sector equivalents, which indicates that a substantial increase in output from this category could be achieved. Whole-of-public-service innovation could also add substantially to public service innovation levels through collective and systemic leadership, risk-spreading, active pursuit of cross-departmental and cross-sectoral synergies.

There are many different forms that public sector innovation might take, a number of different drivers of innovation, a resultant variety of different organisational contexts and levels within which innovation might take place, with each possibility placing different demands on the political/bureaucratic interface. This latter might range from the direct demands on the public service of a government wishing to pursue new ideological directions, new policy frameworks, new service delivery methods, and new methods of community engagement, through to the demands made of departmental risk management practices associated with a more systematic, whole-of-public-service approach to innovation. The question is whether innovation, if and when it occurs, will involve a beneficial use of public resources?

9.4 The public policy case for a more innovative public service

The consideration of whether net benefits can arise from additional public service innovation lies at the heart of any public policy consideration but, as Mulgan points out, the absence of documented experience and evidence makes it difficult to determine if this will be the case. Mulgan observes the slow institutionalisation and formalisation of new routes to innovation within governments around the globe (2009, p 157). He concludes:

> The basic argument for innovation hasn't yet been engaged with let alone won, in the great majority of OECD governments. Part of the reason is that there has been very little serious analysis of when innovation is a good thing – and when it is not … So innovation happens – but it happens as much by chance as by design, and public innovators are usually marginalised. (2009, pp 158, 161)[8]

Moreover, not only is the general case not made and prevailing budget allocations remain small, but also the public sector is 'not up to the job'. Mulgan and Bason both noted that the public sector was ill-prepared to meet the challenges it faced, cataloguing a long list of barriers to public sector innovation (long at least by comparison with the private sector), in Bason's case concluding that 'we have an almost perfect storm crashing down on any (public sector) innovation effort' (2010, p 15). Mulgan's conclusions include that 'Public sectors are often poor at innovation from within, and poor at learning from outside' and '[Public sector] innovators usually succeed despite, not because of, dominant structures and systems' (2009, pp 149, 170).[9]

---

8   To make his point about 'bad' innovation, Mulgan instances low community tolerance for experimentation with ambulance and nuclear power safety arrangements because the risk involves people's lives.

9   Bason identifies a range of barriers, including paying a price for politics – such as limited incentives to share and tight regulation of activities; anti-innovation DNA; fear of the new and the unknown; a focus on efficiency rather than customers; few or no formal processes; leading into a vacuum and spending little time in exploring the future; and an inability to scale up successful innovations (2010, p 15 ff). Mulgan's list is similar including: no one's job, risk aversion, too many rules, uncertain results, high walls and unsuitable structures (2009, p 159 ff).

This book argues for raising public sector innovation management beyond the realms of chance to a more strategically led and integrated state. A government policy to deliver this change should remove a number of the identified barriers and put associated enablers in place. A government-endorsed public service innovation management policy comprising the elements of process, strategy, structure, capability, and governance would address the majority of these issues, simultaneously removing barriers and putting in place key enablers, and lift innovation activity levels and improve effectiveness. The commitment of additional resources to public service innovation would be a further stimulus. And, whilst it is easy to be pessimistic as a consequence of existing innovation activity levels and the absence of government desire to change its policy towards the public service in this regard, there are many additional reasons for it to do so (see Bommert 2010).

There is anecdotal evidence that substantial net benefits can be generated through innovation, as Bason records, 'Real world cases show that cost savings of between 20 per cent and 60 per cent are possible while also increasing citizen satisfaction and generating better outcomes' (2010, p 4). And Mulgan notes that, 'Even today the caricature of public agencies as stagnant enemies of creativity is disproven by the innovation of thousands of public servants around the world' (2009, p 149).

More public service–specific arguments include the assertion by Kay and Goldspink that the public service often, but not always, has time, and should use this advantage in the public interest. This is so in relation to its own innovation because of limited competition, and is consistent with the notion that the public sector discount rate lies some way below the private sector rate. But it equally applies where the public service is the vehicle through which longer-term technology developments occur in conjunction with the private sector. This argument is reinforced by the observation of Kay and Goldspink along with the Auditor-General for Australia that where it does not have time it often performs poorly (Kay & Goldspink 2012b; McPhee 2015).

A further argument for (greater) public sector investment in innovation is the argument made by William Lazonick (2012). His private sector–focused argument, that the drivers of technological change in our economy are the large organisations with market power that can generate the surpluses required to invest in the development of new market and technical advances, applies equally to the public sector. Viewed in this light, the public sector should be a leader in scientific research and technological development and, indeed, in many democratic countries, including Australia, it is. Moreover, as the public sector accounts for over one quarter of national expenditure, it has a duty to contribute to rising living standards, rather than leaving such progress entirely to the private sector. There is no reason why this cannot happen; the public sector has the scale, the time, and the diversity of experience to make it happen.

The general case for a more innovative public service can be made based on the challenges inherent in public administration today and the need for catch-up, both in operating performance and in modern (i.e. private sector) leadership and management techniques. Time and scale arguments point to additional reasons why a government policy to build a more innovative public service should be in the public interest. Even if the public policy case for a more innovative public service can be made, there are at least two further sets of issues to consider, the first being the transition of the public service from its present position of being perceived as not yet up to the job to one of being more innovative, and the second being the government decision-making path to free up the public service to properly pursue this goal.

McGrath's discussion of the necessary changes to existing resource-allocation processes is based on her observation that the typical corporate processes reinforce the hold of the present over the future (2013). Indeed, to break this hold she suggests that leeway be built into the early stages of establishing organisational-innovation proficiency. Concessions might include a two- to three-year plan to get the innovation system in place because of the resistance of the established exploitation-orientated organisation, and an additional fixed allocation (share) of funds to develop organisational experience in innovation processes beyond the investment in the accompanying administrative support systems and resources.[10]

The *Public Service Act 1999* does not provide the necessary freedoms and protections for a public service that wants to become more innovative. The primary problem is that the immediate 'owner' of public policy – the

---

10   The challenges of breaking free from the stranglehold of the past should not be underestimated. This process must be consciously and centrally driven and recognise the need for such balance between exploitation and exploration. Not only does exploration involve a fundamental shift in the public service mindset away from a century-long focus on efficiency, which places cost above value, but there is the additional challenge of achieving the sort of flexibility in resource allocation demanded by this approach in public sector budgets that simply do not have the flexibility to cope.

government – has a direct stake in 'the game', which is based on power and who has it. Unfortunately, the government is likely to see this as a zero-sum game. Thus, the path to change – a loosening of the public service reins enabling it to become directly responsible for its successes and failures (and thereby absolving governments from some of the latter) – is difficult to envisage with a government most likely opposed to it and a community that does not understand the need to change this interface, despite it being in its best interests. The case for political change to embrace the necessary public policy change hinges heavily on demonstrating a 'win' for government.

Nonetheless, innovation must be the tool of choice for public service organisational adjustment to a changing environment because, (a) it can be systemically managed, (b) it focuses on change for the better, (c) it can be integrated with standard resource-allocation processes, (d) it is focused on outcomes, (e) its costs and benefits can be measured, (f) it is equally applicable to all parts of an organisation, (g) the necessary management and operational tools are available, and (h) it can be readily integrated with other environmental adjustment mechanisms. McGrath provides persuasive support for elevation of the role of innovation:

> Innovation is not optional in a world of fleeting advantages. Innovation is not a sideline. Innovation is not a senior executive hobby or a passing fad. Innovation is a competency that needs to be professionally built and managed. Where in the years past we often thought of strategy only with respect to the existing advantages, in a transient-advantage economy innovation can't be separated from effective strategy. (2013, p 134)

9.5 Conclusions

Arguments that make the case for a more innovative public sector reinforce the benefits of a more strategically managed public service and point to an important part of the public policy framework that needs to be considered. The focus must be placed on governments taking a step back and enabling the public administration arm to be publicly responsible for its own failures. This is how a more innovative public service will ultimately be established.

Ben Bommert's theoretical case in support of collaborative innovation asserts:

> Since the introduction of collaborative innovation entails a transfer of authority and possibly of accountability it concerns fundamental decisions about the distribution of power, accountability and control in society. These might need to be addressed in a more fundamental and normative way and not as a subject to a rather practical trade off with innovation assets. (2010, p 30)

It is arguable that not only are the barriers and missing enablers discussed in this chapter inherent in the existing relationship between government and public service, but that these are merely some of the manifestations of a flawed model of public administration.

Unfortunately, with the public service in legislated lockstep for the last three decades, there has been little opportunity, or incentive, for it to innovate, with successive governments on a path to privatisation of public assets along with key public service activities. The public service has been, and continues to be, under threat, with survival its main goal. There are two important consequences arising from the constraints imposed on public sector activity and the behaviours that come with such a close working relationship. The first is that successive governments have driven a wedge between their own interests and those of the community at large, thereby undermining the role that the community might reasonably expect the public service to play. The second is that systematic innovation from the public service has not been possible where such a close relationship between government and public service has existed.

Australia's public service organisational structures and accountabilities are based on a failed philosophy that is embedded in the Public Service Act, which is clearly designed to subsidiarise the Australian Public Service. Siloed structures and little in the way of strategic management capacity have led to a public service that is locked into the subservient siloed nature of departmentalism. Auditor-general reports and speeches by past and present public service leaders point to a lack of blue sky/ over the horizon thinking: too little attention paid to developing private sector management and leadership techniques, especially in the field of organisational design and planning; the wrong skills mix (too many economists and not enough engineers); and an inability to systematically demonstrate public service efficiency or government effectiveness at any of service, program, policy, department or whole-of-government levels.

There are, then, good reasons rooted in sound public policy why a more independent and innovative public service is needed. Having drawn the policymaking activities of government away from the public service and to itself, governments have essentially bankrupted the policy formation process. Equally, having substituted the various think tanks, lobby groups and industry associations for the public service in the policy formation process, the government has displaced 'the public' in public policy with a disparate group of rent-seekers (including itself). Having expanded the range of influential beneficiaries from the exercise of power, governments have largely forsaken community health and welfare for the opportunity to occupy government. This is a very poor bargain from a whole-of-community standpoint.

10

Public policy towards
the public service

10.1 Introduction

There are many important issues to consider in the process of public policy formation towards the public service, and its role in public administration. Two studies of government performance from different continents are useful here in framing a discussion of the complexity of public policy. The first, by Hood and Dixon (2015), is a study of UK Government experience with the New Public Management (NPM), focusing on the performance record for the 30 years from 1980 to 2010. The second is Donald Kettl's *The next government of the United States* (2008), which diagnoses the problems and proposes a radical solution for a government in crisis.

The Hood and Dixon book takes a high-level and historical view of the cost and quality of government, while Kettl homes in on outsourcing as the major problem and challenge of a dysfunctional US Government. The two studies focus on the public policy implications of their research as being radical. Both were delivered out of a number of years of research built on many conversations with government officials in the aftermath of Cyclone Katrina (Kettl) and data/research (Hood and Dixon), and respectively address why the US Government isn't working, and whether the UK Government is.

10.2 The complexities of public policy formation and delivery: The importance of the long view

10.2.1 Hood and Dixon: *A government that worked better and cost less?* (2015)

10.2.1.1 Were the New Public Management reforms worth it?

Hood and Dixon designed their study to fill a scholarly gap in research on what happened to running costs and the perceived consistency and fairness of government administration in the United Kingdom over the 30-year period 1980–2010, following the introduction of the NPM reforms. The authors note variation in the international recipes for public sector modernisation via the NPM reforms but observe two recurring themes – the first being the idea that poor public sector management was a problem that could be addressed through the adoption of common business practices, and the second, the belief in the capacity of new types of information technology to transform costly and user-unfriendly bureaucratic processes.

Hood and Dixon note the huge international academic field that grew up around the subsequent analysis of these reforms, focusing on their promises and processes but very little on the management, IT, and business-process reforms that promised to deliver more for less. They further note the ideology-driven and evidence-free nature of much of the associated public sector management literature and failure to adequately address the bottom-line question of the NPM reforms thus far. This is the premise for their detailed attempt to arrive at overall conclusions about the cost and performance of the UK Government.

Their analysis focuses on what happened to running costs (the 'cost less' part of the research) and on the incidence of formal complaints and judicial challenges to government (the 'worked better' bit). With regard to the former, the authors found that far from falling, (real) running costs rose substantially over the 30 years studied, driven up not by civil service wage costs but the outsourced running costs. Similarly, complaints and judicial challenges rose substantially. The authors' overarching conclusion was that the UK Government probably 'cost a bit more and worked a bit worse' (p 183), a conclusion they point to being strikingly at odds with the common academic view that the NPM reforms had major consequences (positive or negative!) for government performance.

In reaching this conclusion, Hood and Dixon examined motivation for the reforms and a number of alternative explanations for their apparent failure. Motivations included efficiency-seeking gains from the application of private sector management tools, rent-seeking behaviour of politicians, and a belief in spin rather than substance. Explanations for apparent failure included the agenda being obstructed by other parties, inexpert implementation, and weak leadership. Whilst conclusions are tentative, the analysis points to evidence of political rent-seeking behaviour in initiating the changes and rising information technology costs as the primary reasons for higher costs.

10.2.1.2 Relevance to Australia

The discussion and research presented in the preceding chapters supports the conclusion that a similar position has been reached in Australia, namely that the NPM reforms have somehow 'failed'. Firstly, as to motivation and based on the evidence considered to date, the NPM reforms were imposed on the Australian public service by a national government keen to wrest control of the goals and processes of government from the public service. Given that a mid-1980s federal Labor government led the reforms in Australia, it is reasonable to rule out an ideological reason for change and confirm the rent-seeking argument as the likely dominant reason for the NPM reforms.

Secondly, as to the results of these reforms, a range of academic research, auditor-general, and parliamentary committee reports present a similar description of the challenges facing government(s) and the public service across the two jurisdictions. The legacies of the NPM reforms are visible in both jurisdictions – including the fragmentation of the public service and growing questions of the use of markets to deliver public sector outcomes, which points to similar impacts and time frames.

Another common feature is the unrealised benefits from information technology. The evidence of rising information technology costs associated with outsourced activities contradicts expectations that accompanied what Kiechel described as having operated in the private sector in the 1990s, as 'the imperative to exploit the latest information technology turbocharged push for efficiency and competitiveness' (Kiechel 2012). The Hood and Dixon conclusion for the United Kingdom is matched by the Australian public sector's poor track record in the implementation of new 'transformative' information technology systems and facilities and its ongoing practice in contradiction of the private sector's scrapping of a 25-year-old management fad that Kiechel describes as 'discredited, to be later held up as a chief example of a management fad gone horribly wrong'.[1]

In the construction of their primary data series, Hood and Dixon noted a civil service commitment to management by numbers, but apparent ongoing destruction of data that would not enable that commitment to be met. They explain this in terms of the machinations of the bureaucracy, and point to the management consequences:

> On the practical side, the implication is that only very short-term evidence-based performance management is likely to be possible – and if the data on our volatility index is anything to go by, there are indications that the time-frame actually got shorter over the period considered here. (Hood & Dixon 2015, p 64)[2]

---

1   There are, however, positive signs that some of the present generation of public sector information technology projects may be different, at least in conception. In a speech to the National Press Club in Canberra on 20 September 2016, then Minister for Social Services Christian Porter outlined his department's latest research project. Impressively, it examines a mountain of data to sort out some of the wicked problems that the social services portfolio faces. The title of Porter's speech – 'The Australian priority approach to welfare investment' – points to a determination to identify, invest in, and enable the most dependent groups and individuals to become self-sufficient. Moreover, the background report prepared by PWC estimates the lifetime costs of the existing policies for the existing population at $4.8 trillion. This number confirms that investment in encouraging self-sufficiency in the groups more at risk of becoming system dependent provides wins for the individuals concerned and for taxpayers at large. The use of information technology systems to collect the data to enable this analysis, rather than simply serve the political need of downsizing the public service, is all too rare in government today (Porter 2016).

2   The problem with the public service use of data in management is, however, not just one of data generation, but the widespread problem with the use of data and supporting information in management. Where suitable information is available to support good management and appropriate governance in the public sector, it is not always properly used. This shortcoming can be observed in a number of public cases of maladministration where the availability of primary information should have triggered a course of action but was simply not acted upon. Indeed, many of the more public failures of state and national governments in Australia in recent decades have overlapping and common recurring elements relating to the failure:

- to recognise warning signs from data generated in the normal course of operations
- to recognise that other parties may have/should have an interest in this data
- to share this information with other parties either within or across organisational boundaries
- of the entity generating information to act on it where it falls within its jurisdiction
- to 'join the dots' from the information generated
- to elevate an issue within an organisation to a level at which appropriate action could be taken
- to develop the right skills.

Some or all of these elements can be seen to be present in the Lindt Café siege in Sydney (arguably the wrong skills); the national home insulation scheme (arguably inadequate skills and a failure to share information); the (Victorian) Country Fire Authority Training College at Fiskville (an apparent management failure to connect the dots and act); and the Bacchus Marsh, Victoria, baby deaths (a clear failure of governance). All four cases resulted in loss of life.

10.2.2 Donald Kettl: *The next government of the United States* (2008)

10.2.2.1 The case for recalibrating public institutions

In his examination of the institutions of government in the United States, and why they are failing so many Americans, Donald Kettl considers two case studies – one of the public healthcare system and the other of Cyclone Katrina – and concludes that many of the most important problems faced by Americans do not match the institutions created to govern them. He describes the growing complexity of service delivery systems; interlocking public–private–non-profit systems that lack adequate governance or a clear government role; and multiple systems, responsible for important issues over which no one has control.

Kettl argues that routinised services – for example, the processing of pension claims – should not be problematic but, where there is a requirement to determine the delivery of particular services and in what quantities, and oversee their combined impacts on a single customer, outsourcing becomes a potential (and serious) problem of effectiveness. Kettl points to a growing tendency throughout the three tiers of US government to rely on other parties to deliver government services – the private sector and non-profits – through a developing program of contractors. He points out that contracting-out processes and underlying policies are themselves being contracted out. He identifies the pressures behind arguments that just about anything can be privatised and should be and the resultant increase in privatisation. In a world of networked government, the engagement of agents with different goals and the multiple boundaries that these networks must cross magnifies the problem of ensuring responsible government. Since no one is in charge, no one is accountable. Kettl argues that without adapting the institutions to the problems, governance, accountability and effectiveness are the victims.

Kettl's solution to these challenges is akin to rocket science. He proposes the necessity of leveraged government across complex networks involving 'government leaders who can effectively align public private, non-profit, American, and global players across the messy boundaries of action' (Kettl 2008, p 178). He further argues that the puzzle is how to govern through two interconnected systems, one for routine policies managed by hierarchies, and the other for non-routine problems governed through networks. His answer is to make government managers into rocket scientists with a set of skills, indeed tenets, that comprises the following: focus on results, steer results through interrelated partnerships, use information to fuel communication, rely on bureaucracies as holding companies for expertise, create relationships of trust before the relationships are needed, steer resources, and lead by making the public interest drive complex partnerships. Kettl then notes that:

> With the rise of wicked problems that demand creative rocket science solutions, however, government faces a twin challenge; (1) helping to breed rocket scientists and (2) creating a governance system, focused on results that supports their work. (2008, p 214)

Kettl writes in this final chapter that, 'The central challenge of twenty-first century government is finding a way to match the governance needed for the problems at hand, to produce high quality results in an accountable way' and he focuses on developing a new strategy for accountability (2008, p 221). Kettl points to an evolution in governance models from the traditional public administration (when policymakers relied on hierarchy to hold administrative systems accountable) through the NPM (in which the accountability strategy focused on outputs) and finally to 'leveraged government' where the accountability strategy focuses on blended contributions to shared outcomes. Overall, he regards the public policy challenge as 'daunting'.

10.2.2.2 Relevance to Australia

There are at least three reasons why the US Government is several decades ahead of Australia in going down the path of leveraged government. Firstly, the United States is notable for its unbridled faith in a system of free enterprise. This ideology is underpinned by scale: there is very little that US private enterprise cannot manufacture or produce more efficiently (although not always more cheaply). Moreover, a wealth of experience to back this efficiency is hallmark of such a large economy.[3] At the level of the direct costs of service delivery, and especially in the general case of routinised service delivery, the private sector can almost certainly do more cheaply whatever it is that the public sector wants to do. Australia does not have the benefits of this scale to draw on, however the prevailing sentiment aspires to the same options existing here.

---

3   See Stern and Stalk (1998, pp 12–24) for some history of the experience-curve concept. See Alford and O'Flynn (2012, fn 1, Chapter 2) for a discussion of the concept in a public sector setting.

A second argument relates to the degree of outsourcing engaged in by US governments, resulting in a level of comfort with the process. Kettl traces this comfort to government reliance on the defence equipment manufacturing industry during the Second World War. Whilst arguably the comparative advantage that private sector defence industry manufacturing contractors have over equivalent public sector corporations is much greater in manufacturing than for service industry activities, the tools and practices of outsourcing based on this experience have been readily available to those in other arms of government. This necessity has, by default, become a necessity in the delivery of services. Australia does not have this history, or the military–industrial complex of the United States.

The third argument is based on the differences between the United States and Australian political systems. Changes to US governments result in a clearing out of the top echelons of the public administration. According to Kettl, this goes as far as the top four or five tiers of the administration, which leaves a large number of new players in the administration. Most come from the private sector and bring experience, knowledge and contacts with them. Equally, most know little about the capabilities of their career public sector colleagues. As a consequence, the pull to go to their existing networks in the private sector to meet their needs is strong. In Australia's case, there is no such natural pull to the private sector.

In his concluding chapters, Kettl warns against a piecemeal approach to outsourcing. He argues that it is relatively easy to make the case for outsourcing 'anything' in the United States. With a predisposition to outsource, governments may well find themselves progressively outsourcing parts of a service – he uses a health industry example – to the point where both the formation of policy itself has been outsourced and no one is responsible for the coordination of the parts of the service to the final customer. Each supplier has a contract with the government to manage their partial relationship with the final consumer but no one coordinates and manages any overlaps and externalities from the delivery of the separate services to the final customer.

Kettl's arguments are relevant to Australia. This is an avoidable future, but it is the current trajectory without taking action to avoid it. I recognise the existing and growing challenges of managing complex public policy problems, however, I have also considerable reservations about the manner in which the outsourcing of public sector services is occurring in Australia. There is a primary focus on short-term cost savings and the longer-term costs associated with organisational capital – knowledge and capabilities in particular – are being ignored.

Kettl points out that once governments start down this path, it is difficult to deny the momentum. Degradation of public service capability to deliver, indeed manage, anything, is insidious and a program of contestability quickly becomes an active outsourcing (everything) program because of its apparently inescapable logic (the private sector does everything better), and the appearance that it delivers smaller government (well, smaller public service numbers at least). A program of outsourcing can very quickly become a program of contracting out. Surely this is a future to avoid?

10.3 Public policy towards the Australian Public Service

10.3.1 Finding the right public policy balance

In the formation of public policy towards a particular industry, the questions asked consider why the government should intervene, what foundations there are for intervention, and what are the prospective costs and benefits. The arguments for intervention generally vary according to the external costs and benefits generated by different firms and industries, and the intervention is then shaped around the structural and product features of the industry and its markets, along with the nature of competition in that industry. The Australian Public Service (APS) competes in the industry of public administration with varying mandate (and market share) across its market segments.

The unique position of the APS in its industry is established by legislation, however, by virtue of the decisions of a succession of governments over the last 30 or more years, the competitive position of the public service has been eroded, and this in turn has diminished its capacity to provide the perspective and continuity that protection of the public interest demands. Moreover, a rapidly changing political, social, economic, or fiscal environment changes the game for both government and the public service and raises ongoing questions about the appropriateness of the role assigned to the APS and its capacity to deliver. The ongoing relevance of the *Public Service Act 1999*, along with the impact on the public service of related legislation and government policies, should be a matter for regular formal review.

One of the central issues in public policy towards the public service must be determination of the optimal balance between legislative and operational control. A guiding Act is a broad canvas that enables successive governments to paint their own picture of the public service and will require irregular change. A more prescriptive act will (should) require frequent change. The fact that there have been only two substantial rewrites of the guiding Act in over 100 years since Federation, the last in 1999, suggests that the 'broad canvas' option has been followed.

Yet, notwithstanding the relatively short amount of time that has elapsed since the last major redraft, I argue that there are now good reasons for changes to the Act. This is imperative because of the Act's flawed nature; continuing changes in the global, economic, societal and fiscal circumstances within which the Australian Government operates; and the fact that successive Australian governments are on an unjustified path of creeping replacement of the APS under the guise of productive efficiency through contestability of policy and service delivery functions. The last of these three is clearly a sham masquerading as an efficiency drive. This downsizing seems clearly focused on diminishing the role of the public service in government (a) for ideological reasons; (b) to enable the determination and manipulation of the advice that government receives (Public Service Act notwithstanding); and (c) to distance the government from maladministration in service delivery when it occurs.

The flawed nature of the Public Service Act is accompanied by weaknesses in the surrounding policy and institutional structure that dilute the management focus and directly impact on public service accountability and performance. Examples of this include the wrong charter for the auditor-general and the attachment of an abundance of commissioners to government departments. The changing domestic social and institutional context is a parallel influence with the ever widening integration of our globe in political, social, economic and security terms, and the cost to government of effective engagement with it, involving the need to contain new and expanding terrorism, border control, and cyber-security risks.

A recent and important arrival on this scene is the systemic misbehaviour of large organisations in public, private and non-profit sectors, over the last decade, along with the publicly reported behaviour of senior members of these organisations underpinned by a fundamental failure of a duty of care, financial and moral, towards their customers. This has led to a community wanting, through government, greater direct involvement in their operations. As a foundation for related changes it is arguable that much private sector misbehaviour brought to light in the last couple of years is linked to poor government behaviour, with successive governments expecting the private sector to attain standards of behaviour they will not contemplate for themselves. Reported cases of regulatory failure at the interface of the two are evidence of this failure of government leadership and encouragement for substandard private sector behaviour. Clearly, more responsible and accountable government underpinned by a reinvigorated public service that truly serves the Australian public is required *in the public interest*.

10.3.2 Application of private sector concepts and tools to the public service

One of the continuing puzzles in contemplating the path forward for the public service is the role that private sector management tools and markets should play in government. There are several overlapping elements at play here, including the efficacy of these tools in a public sector setting, and the use of markets (market efficiency) to best allocate (allocative efficiency) and utilise (productive efficiency) resources. Discussion of these issues is surrounded by a growing global view that the so-called neo-liberal experiment has failed. From a public policy standpoint, the unifying element in an integrated discussion is the important differences between public and private sectors.

I argue that, when it comes to the application of private sector management tools to public sector activities, there are underlying and case-specific differences reflecting the diversity of public service activities and the broader demands for a collegiate approach. Rather than representing outright barriers, however, such differences require a pragmatic approach with a light touch. In practice, the sorts of contextual differences that need to be observed are no more than those observed between businesses in different industries and countries in the private sector, even different sizes of businesses, where the basis of successful application of new tools lies in recognising that the differences are the building blocks of that success.

The two differences here relate to the collegiate nature of public service activity and the time frame embedded in the formation of all government policies, not just those towards the public service. The first of these two issues underlies public sector performance (wicked policy problems, interdepartmental and cross-sectoral coordination and the associated challenges of performance measurement and management, organisational structures and horizontal strategy). The policy formation challenge – especially the matter of time frame – is worthy of further consideration.

A substantial difference between the public and private sectors is the cost of capital. Governments are able to raise funds more cheaply than the private sector and therefore complete similar tasks at a lower cost, assuming similar physical efficiency levels as the private sector. Alternatively, this can be viewed as the public sector having more time at the same cost. This matter of time has arisen in two separate contexts in this book, both relating to the comparative advantage that the public sector has in innovation over the private sector – in studies by Kay and Goldspink (2012a, 2012b) and William Lazonick (2012).

A second point arises from the differences between the 'products' of the public and private sectors. The short-termism of governments, and the associated costs, result in policies that contain rather than resolve public policy problems; policies that fail to acknowledge longer-term consequences of their intent (for example, the loss and irrecoverability of public service strategic capabilities through outsourcing) and a lack of interest in the cumulative effects of individual actions within an 'acceptable' policy framework; for example, the loss of economic control from over-reliance on individual international trading partners.

Closely associated with these problems is the lack of a holistic approach to public administration, either as a matter of time (the cumulative effects) or breadth of coverage (inclusion of the right spread of parties). The unique capacity of the public service to provide this holistic approach with the right time perspective is another element that applies to public sector 'products' but does not apply to private sector products. Whilst, in a private sector context, the board may be assumed to be responsible for the health of the organisation, in the case of the public sector, no one owns this ultimate responsibility.

10.4 The policy implications

10.4.1 The policy issues

In *Rethinking public service delivery* (2012) John Alford and Janine O'Flynn point to the waves of reform occurring over the last 50 years, from postwar hierarchically managed service delivery with a focus on efficiency; to the 1980s mantra of better, cheaper government; to the turn-of-the-century collaborative and joined-up style. They observe that: 'Now there is an emerging trend to think expansively about ultimate purposes, and concomitantly about means of realising them. The key concern in this emerging trend is to optimise what is of value to the public' (Alford & O'Flynn 2012, p 255). Both Kettl and Hood and Dixon think expansively about the path being taken and, not liking what they see within their own analytical domains, point to the need for change. Kettl points to the problems with outsourcing, networked governance, and the mismatch between problems and institutions, whilst Hood and Dixon point to the ongoing legacies of a process of public sector reform initiated some 40 years ago in the United Kingdom.

These observations raise the question of what is really known about the past performance of government, which is a necessary foundation to deal with the question of future performance. If, as Hood and Dixon propose, three decades of reform efforts to cut the costs of government and make it work better for citizens have failed, not just in the United Kingdom but around the globe, then serious questions must be asked regarding the current foundations on which to build a better future. If the pace of economic and social change does not waver and the pace of political change continues, there is good reason to be concerned about the future of our governments (and citizens!).

Even in the face of an absence of historical evidence, the desirable future for the public service is different from the past. Kettl, and Alford and O'Flynn, point to the passing of the days of 'one best way' for the public sector and the consequent challenges for public sector managers. Kettl writes of blended systems of hierarchically driven routine-based systems with interlaced networks and Alford and O'Flynn describe finding new paths within a broader perspective. The management challenge is growing and the solution is a broader conception of the work of public servants and greater flexibility for those who might make these choices, matched by governance procedures that enable organisations to ensure that the bundle of relationships in which they are involved is not (unnecessarily) in conflict, or redundant. Alford and O'Flynn observe that, whilst there has been much of a taxonomic nature written about this 'constellation of relationships', there has been remarkably little written about how to go about doing this.

There are other missing pieces as well. Much of what is written is from the perspective of the individual manager who must choose the right model for the right problem and juggle this complex constellation of relationships. Little is written about the organisational context/perspective – both departmental and whole-of-public-service – either from an operational or strategic perspective. The organisational dimension must be considered alongside those of management and governance. Indeed, much of this book is about the role of organisational structures in determining the boundaries of the playing field and the rules of engagement for any game played out in an organisational context.

How, then, is such a brave new world to be conceived of on a whole-of-public-service basis? How are relationships between departments to be conceived in order to avoid conflicts and overlaps? How should the public service/individual departments be organised/structured to best enable them to meet this emerging challenge? How is the measurement challenge – for results measurement, performance management, governance and accountability – to be conceived? What are the organisational data architecture and the supporting administrative systems and information technology capabilities required to support these challenges? How is what Kettl refers to as the hierarchically managed routinised services vending machine model to be integrated with the network-driven rocket science driven model of government that he deems necessary to successfully tackle today's problems? And, most importantly of all, how is this new style of operation going to be developed and successfully embedded across the public service?

The operating dimensions of this challenge demand a top-down approach to integrate the management dimensions with operating protocols for a model of leveraged government in order that activities that cross departmental boundaries fit comfortably together as required, but also to enable similar cohesion when crossing sectoral boundaries. Yet the public service is ill-equipped to develop and bed down an integrated new operating style: it is not another project to be given to an interdepartmental committee sponsored by the committee of secretaries; rather it is a change of strategic direction that requires high-level leadership on an ongoing basis, an injection of outside experience, a board to oversee, and a dedicated corporate team to develop the detail and implement, while departmental heads get on with management.

Nowhere is this more obvious than in regard to the new administrative systems and supporting data architecture required for management and oversight (governance) of these activities. The more flexibility required in operations to meet varying market conditions, the more complex and demanding will be the supporting data and reporting requirements to meet both management and governance needs. This is the hard part and, unfortunately, the need for these basic but fundamental data requirements – for service, program, solution and program management, for reporting and governance, for resource allocation and accountability – tend to be noted as throwaway lines in much of the literature.

This is one reason why, after some 30 years of change in governance and management models, public service services and program-level reporting are still at a rudimentary level. These messy and hard bits are much less glamorous than discussions about choices between collaborative, hierarchical, and market-based innovation management models and models of governance. Such history provides little comfort that the existing and emerging data and systems requirements will be addressed during the next public sector management revolution, when it occurs. Kettl, in particular, acknowledges the size of this challenge. He notes that redefining information-driven accountability for complex, blended systems while retaining authority-based accountability for routine problems is a huge challenge for elected officials. He proposes a blend from a menu of accountability mechanisms comprising authority, contracts, regulation, private standard-setting, voluntary self-regulation, negotiated rule-making, markets, incentives and competition. But what and how?

10.5 Achieving change

10.5.1 Will the future look like the past?

Practical and academic concepts of public sector governance and administration have changed over the last 30 to 40 years. These have evolved from the Weberian hierarchical concept of government that has characterised the organisation of the APS (formerly the Commonwealth Public Service) for some 70 years. There has been a continuing progression from hierarchical government through the private sector–driven reforms of the 1980s to the joined-up government and networked government concepts of the present decade. This may, however, reasonably be described as a history of path-dependency, a path with severe limitations.

A linear view of history, extrapolating the recent past into the future, clearly reveals the future of government. It will almost certainly involve more networked government in the design and delivery of services, greater community participation in these processes along with the rise of 'community government', and, most likely, a growing role for the minor political parties. What is likely to mark out this future is the extended participation of the community in the processes of government, not just through established community-based organisations, but through the continuous formation and dissolution of coalitions of interest around particular issues – such as building a freeway extension, public access to a national park, the construction of a primary school in a new suburb or the location of safe injection facilities for drug users. This future might also be marked out by private monies – private sector, philanthropic, even crowd funded – used to resolve community issues with or without government funding. This is the future that beckons and indeed is already evident around the globe at the local government level. Academic literature on the United States suggests that it is already more broadly in evidence there.

This is an attractive future to many, with greater community participation in the decision-making processes of government and the prospect that private resources might be more readily available to address community problems. Others might focus on the downsides of the lobbying requirements to get things done, pointing to the replacement of regular election-based voting (every three or four years) with more frequent but irregular, issues-based 'voting' by a changeable feast of players and 'forums' – ranging from national summits, to citizens' juries to informal local coalitions. The concept of government governance would take on a whole new meaning. The challenge with this future lies with the almost certain diminution in the accompanying accountability for public sector resource use.

10.6 Conclusions

It is clear that the fragmentation of the public service in Australia some 30 years ago has left it ill equipped to confront the challenges of today. A fragmented public service is indeed many public services and, given the levels of intra-government coordination and external networking required to address today's complex policy problems, only a strongly and centrally driven public service will be able to deliver sound management and government accountability in future.

The Public Service Act provides the starting point for discussion of government and public policy towards the APS. This starting point must necessarily be complemented by consideration of a range of overlapping legislation, and government policies of the day. These policy foundations are importantly augmented by the behaviours of governments, to deliver the operative public policy. In response to an evaluation of the capacity of the Public Service Act to deliver good public policy, and these broader considerations, I have recommended a number of changes to the Public Service Act.

Underpinning such legislative change should be the provision of greater public service independence, enabling it to actively compete for influence and market share, and 'to win'. AG Lafley and Roger Martin describe the concept of 'winning' in terms of an organisation's winning aspiration. Whether described as a vision, winning aspiration, or mission statement, I cannot determine what it is that the public service would describe as 'winning'. I assume that it somehow relates to the quality of service it provides the government of the day, consistent in part with the objects of the Public Service Act. As described by Lafley and Martin, however, such an aspiration would be regarded as 'playing to play' rather than 'playing to win'. Moreover they argue:

> To play merely to participate is self-defeating. It is a recipe for mediocrity … When a company sets out to participate, rather than win, it will inevitably fail to make the tough choices and the significant investments that would make winning even a remote possibility. (Lafley & Martin 2013, p 36)

In recommending change to address the identified problems, my primary 'solutions' are derived from a comparison of public and private sector leadership and management structures, processes, and capabilities. What is missing in the public service is the specialised and dedicated skills and experience that an effective board, public service CEO and corporate office are designed to bring to enhance an organisation's capacity to meet shareholders' expectations. These skills and experience are all key contributors to what I described in Chapter 1 as the foundations of a high-performing public service, namely strategy, positioning, organisation and governance. Ultimately, it is from clear choices about what to do and how to do it that the integrated organisation of resources, sound governance, and 'high performance' emerge.

Looking below this model of organisational leadership down into the management of the APS, there is much that is widely respected amongst public administrations around the world. This is a strength and weakness of the APS. On the one hand, the idea of adopting public service best practice and doing it better than most is comforting, but it also confines the APS to the herd. The aim of being a high-performing public service sets an unnecessarily (and unmeasurable!) low benchmark.

My core public policy argument is not an unbridled case for imitating the private sector, but rather one of recognising that the present public sector mantras are not working for the community, that path-dependency is a poor strategy for the public service, and that step change is needed. Whilst the public service has been slow to grasp the importance of a strong focus on the customer as the driver of their business, the academic literature has moved on developing the notion of public value as the centrepiece of purpose. For example, Alford and O'Flynn, in a discussion of the purposes of public administration, point to an emerging trend to focus on what is of value to the public (Alford & O'Flynn 2012, p 255). The practical refocusing of any business on its customers and consumers, and at all levels of an organisation – what Lafley and Martin describe as 'making the consumer the boss' – opens up myriad possibilities for business improvement and of adding of value to the final consumer experience. Moreover, this approach has much corporate literature and experience to draw upon, enabling some short cuts in the trial and error process of building successful public service equivalents.

I started this book with the observation from Peter Hughes that the public service in New Zealand needed to move on from outputs, efficiency and managerialism to outcomes, effectiveness and leadership. I argue that the same refocusing is required in Australia and that a substantial change of direction is required to achieve it. With successive governments on a path to public service replacement, only a clear break with the past will achieve such change, in the public interest.

11

Reflections

11.1 The short-termism of governments

Over the three years or so since I started to write the pieces that have evolved into this book, there has been much of interest to observe in Australian politics and public administration. The most interesting feature has been the growing community dissatisfaction with our politicians and major political parties, arising from both the short-termism exhibited by our elected representatives and the venal and sloppy nature of their personal behaviour. The former has been a global feature whilst the latter is a particularly notable feature in Australia. The question is, if we continue to head down the present path, what will the future look like?

I have regularly used the word 'fragmentation' to describe the present state of government. Our political system is presently fragmenting into a large number of smaller parties; our public service has been fragmented and rendered ineffective; government policies are fragmented; our community is being fragmented by the politics of ethnicity and political survival, rather than being united by the politics of cohesion and national leadership; and we have lost sight of our national interests across societal and policy spectrums.

Table 11.1 A sad tale of fragmentation

Element	What we have	What we need
Political system	Decline of the major parties and rise of minor interests	Good policy!
The politics of compromise	Compromised policies	More leadership and less negotiation
Public service	An absence of the consciousness of the overall management function	Public service leadership and continuity in management
Government policies	Focused on the marginal voter in the marginal electorate	Integrated policy frameworks
Political leadership	An absence of vision; an attitude of divide and survive	The light on the hill and the path
Community activism	A trend towards localisation of policy and its ownership	Involvement of enough local groups and individuals to make this cohesive
Government governance	Low-level reporting and an absence of commitment	A commitment to report holistically and be judged accordingly

A continuation of these trends will mean an increasingly adversarial future at all levels – political, business, community. Indeed, this discussion points to the emergence of a more competitive, less equitable, and indeed combative, form of democracy and public administration. Ironically, perhaps, community activism at the local level represents a force for further fragmentation, but also an obvious source of change for the better, through growing community involvement in politics. This must be the foundation of our future, because change for the better at the highest level of politics (i.e. state and national parliaments) is unlikely to be originated therein. Perhaps our system of government needs to substantially break down before it can get better? There are a number of issues to consider in determining the role that the public service could play in better government, which must have regard to the past (where did we come from and how did we get here), the present (where are we), and the future (where would we like to go).

11.2 A subordinated public service: Looking for answers

In working from problem definition to prospective solutions it is important to be clear about the framing of the problem, both for what it offers and what it leaves out. A key challenge in addressing the quality of government is to recognise the many stakeholders and interested parties, and the respective roles that they can play in addressing difficulties. My starting point has been to isolate the role of the public service and its contribution and consider how this might change for the better.

In examining the contribution of the public service to better government, the analytical framework set out in Chapter 1 identifies the features that are most important to achieving the commonly stated public service goal – a high-performing public service. Those features are a strategically driven and well-governed public service that is competitively positioned and has supporting organisational architecture. That structure gives rise to this book's four foundational elements of strategy, competition, organisation, and governance. This is a pragmatic way of describing the integrated conception, organisation and management of the business of the public service.

Strategy defines the business choices made, competition defines how these choices are pursued, and organisation defines how the business is constructed to pursue these choices. Furthermore, governance describes how custodians account to the stakeholders for the business undertaken. When viewed from a public service (looking-out) standpoint, these features define a business competing in the industry of public administration: when viewed from a public policy (looking-in) standpoint, they define a business established to meet community needs. I have explored the importance of viewing the activities of the public service from the first vantage point in order to achieve the best outcome from the second. This distinction is important to avoid confusing the different roles played for the community by the public service and its elected officials. I also argue that the single best way to view public service activity is through the prism of governance because once we ask 'of what?' and 'for whom?', most of the other important questions fall out. This framing also draws attention to the critical nature of the interface between the three key participants – the government, the public service, and the Australian public.

The differences between the two noted vantage points – of public service strategy and public policy – can be seen through the four foundational elements. In the case of strategy, a public service vantage point considers the activity choices within the domain established for the public service by the government; from a public policy vantage point, the consideration is the rationale for the domain. In the case of competition, the primary interest is in the competition of the public service for the business of government for the former. In the case of the latter, the interest is in the competition between the various entities for the business of the government. In the case of governance, the focus is on public service governance in the first case and government governance in the second. In the case of organisation, for the former, the interest lies in the internal public service alignment of the organisational structures, administrative systems, and behaviours; whilst, in the latter, the focus is the alignment of the interests of the government, the public service and with the community at large.

This framing of the challenges of better government determinedly locates the public service in a competitive context, viewing it as a competitive enterprise, rather than as the monopoly that much discussion treats it to be. In fact, it already 'competes' for most of the business it conducts on behalf of government – in the central policy advisory and service delivery roles – although it has been accorded a monopoly over the management of service delivery – and a near-monopoly in the delivery of government governance in regard to public administration, but beyond that it must be seen to be competing for influence across the spectrum of government activities. Indeed, being influential within government is critical to its capacity to win government business, and being seen to be influential by external parties makes its role in stakeholder management that much easier. A public service treated as irrelevant by its government will be similarly treated by external parties. The public service must be enabled to compete and view itself as having an existence beyond the dictates of the government of the day, enduring, and looking over the horizon, if it is to perform a community value-adding role. If all it does is view its role as a series of tasks given it by successive governments – a purely transactional relationship – then there is, I suspect, little reason why all of its duties should not be outsourced.

In seeking solutions, incremental changes made through a strategy of path dependency readily emerge from analysis of public sector issues in public sector terms. Major governance challenges remain, however, and are not receiving the necessary attention for their resolution. 'Government without governance' remains a ready description of much of today's circumstances. Framing the problem in terms of the four pillars of strategy, competition, organisation, and governance, encourages us look outside the boundaries of the public sector and the field of public administration for possible solutions.

Consequently, I have looked to the private sector for some answers, knowing full well that many would like to see what happens in the private sector as irrelevant to the public service in principle, with others seeing it as the only way to go, and still others point to the Australian experience with the private sector–based New Public Management (NPM) reforms as a cautionary tale.

I subscribe to the view that the philosophy and tools of managerialism, which underpin the NPM reforms, have a place in the public service but that insufficient attention to differences between public and private sectors have led to ongoing consequences. For example, I have noted the negative impact of performance bonuses at the pointy end of public administration, whilst noting at the same time the potential destruction of public administration capability of advising governments in a holistic manner through a poorly designed contestability program. I have further pointed to the selective nature of organisational structures chosen, their importance to public service leadership and management and the establishment of a cohesive and effective public service pursuing the public interest. It is on the 'missing organisational bits' from the reforms of the 1980s and 1990s that I have particularly focused for solutions to the current predicament.

11.3 The fish rots from the head: The importance of organisational leadership[1]

A discussion of how the problem of achieving better government has been framed for consideration very quickly leads to a consideration of the role of leadership. In the early chapters of the book, I focused on defining the broader problem and the contribution of the public service,

---

1   Bob Garratt (2010) notes a dead fish rots first in the guts. His use of the metaphor reflects the common understanding that, when organisations fail, the cause is most likely at the top.

considering the respective roles of management and operations, whilst noting that many of the resulting challenges for the public service in these areas could be attributed to absent leadership. In particular, I focused on the shortcomings in government governance and the absence of systemic public service governance.

It is easy to attribute any or all organisational failure to inadequate leadership, and most organisations could benefit from more skilled leaders. One of the difficulties in having an informed discussion on this subject is that there is not common agreement about what constitutes a leader, and therefore how the presence or absence of leadership might best be assessed. And whilst there is no doubt that the qualities of individual leaders are important in determining organisational success, this is not the sort of leadership on which I focus in this book – what I have drawn attention to in the case of the Australian Public Service (APS) is what I can best describe as structural leadership. This is the important component of leadership that is determined by organisational structures and associated processes.

I compared alternative private sector organisational models with the structure of the public service and noted that the structure of the APS operating today is akin to a large private sector multi-divisional organisational form. However, by comparison with private sector models, the public service lacks a properly tasked board, a CEO, and a corporate office to provide strategic leadership and drive its constituent businesses. The public service also lacks much of the operational glue that is provided by active pursuit of corporate strategies and horizontal synergies, and the consequent cohesion that contributes to a stronger sense of self.

The absence of these structures and processes is clearly driven by the constraints of the *Public Service Act 1999* (derived from the decentralising philosophical foundations of this Act) and, to a lesser extent, by the APS's limited perception of its role. Successive APS commissioners (and heads of the Department of the Prime Minister and Cabinet (PM&C)) have noted the need for a more strategic and whole-of-government approach to be delivered by the APS, but the public service leaders appear, at best, prepared to treat the strategic management challenge as a series of projects rather than one requiring the establishment of a dedicated corporate capability; and this despite strategic capability, in their own assessment of APS capabilities, scoring amongst the lowest in their capability surveys.

Curiously, an important part of such a strategic role could have been played by PM&C, as it, and its counterpart state and territory departments, were until the mid-1980s essentially auditors of the agenda of the government of the day, overseeing service delivery roles and activities of other departments but without major service delivery responsibilities themselves. This position has changed substantially over the last two or three decades, however, as service delivery by PM&C has become a way of signalling the importance of particular programs to the government of the day (e.g. Indigenous disadvantage), addressing intractable whole-of-government coordination issues (ultimately collocating Indigenous policy programs and services from eight different departments and agencies in PM&C), and thereby attempting to internalise and eliminate the negative impacts of some of these challenges.[2] With this change of role – from auditor and coordinator to operator – an avenue was closed for the public service to develop a head office providing the sort of strategic leadership and oversight described by Terry Moran.

The other critical part of structural leadership that is absent from the public sector is associated with the board role. It is the role of the board to determine a clear strategy and goals for the organisation and ensure that there are companion governance processes to achieve those goals. Organisational structures are key contributors to organisational leadership and I argue that, critical to the establishment of an effective public service in Australia, are the establishment of both board and CEO/corporate office roles for the time, skills, experience, and perspective that these additional layers bring to organisational health. This is the missing piece and the philosophy that underlies it that is the source of the bulk of public administration difficulties today.

11.4 Playing to win or playing to play: The value of strategy

One theme that emerges in this book is present in a number of different concepts, namely: agility and stability, deliberate and emergent strategy, exploration and exploitation, ambidextrous organisations, design thinking, transient and sustainable competitive advantage, the learning organisation, and innovation. These concepts focus on environmental

---

2   See Watt (2013).

change and ways of enabling an organisation to systematically adjust to this change. And this adjustment to change should be integrated with an organisation's competitive positioning.

In looking for a way to present a simple management map of these concepts I proposed that it be viewed in two interrelated parts: the first is contained in the relationship *strategy = competitive positioning + innovation*; while the second is contained in the notion that *structure follows strategy*. There is nothing new or immutable about either of these relationships, but together they provide a useful framework within which to understand the value of important structures and processes missing from the public service kit of leadership and management tools. The former is designed to describe the important concept that an organisation must both determine its initial competitive position and build the means of change into its organisational processes. The second proposition – that structure follows strategy – is a reminder about the role that structures can play in aligning the various parts of the organisation behind its strategy. Both require systemic leadership to be effective.

11.5 Government without governance. Who's in charge?

I have used the concept of governance as a prism through which to view public service performance, arguing that many of the issues that arise in public service management can be identified from this standpoint. What is often overlooked in the public service is the close relationship between management information, performance reporting, and corporate governance. Indeed, if corporate governance systems are properly designed and responsibility similarly allocated, then any work unit's management information is also the foundation for its contribution to corporate governance because both are designed to provide information about organisational performance at the work-unit level. Good management information should enable programs to be managed in all of the efficient, effective, and innovative dimensions that the Public Service Act requires.

This exploration of the quality of public administration in Australia has focused on the program-level performance reporting of auditors-general, the evolving public sector management measurement philosophies – from inputs, to outputs, to impacts and outcomes, and more recently to public value – and the growing gap between this academic evolution and public administration practice.

Measurement of activities enables an organisation to set and communicate goals for improvement, and the larger and more diverse the organisation the more important is the latter of these two through its contribution to organisational cohesion. An ambitious journey of quantification, even if not entirely successful, will lead to a better understanding of the business, thereby enabling better decisions. Measurement enables future activities to be shaped and it lies at the heart of good government governance; it should also lie at the heart of good public service performance and governance. I argue that having a watchdog with ex post governance responsibilities as a substitute for agency responsibility merely dilutes real agency responsibility for performance measurement and governance.

When governance is examined as a top-down and bottom-up exercise, a bigger issue emerges, namely the added difficulty that providing accountability for public service expenditure associated with joined-up (services/programs/business units/departments) and networked (with a mixture of co-designers, co-producers and service deliverers) activities that government creates. When integrated with the existing inadequate performance measurement system, these developments point to a magnified set of problems in the future. Donald Kettl (2008) pointed to problems of responsibility for the citizen to whom multiple services may be delivered, even within the same program. The bigger problem, however, relates to the overall accountability for major blocks of resource use. The concept of 'government without governance' is an increasingly apt description of the path that government in Australia is on.

11.6 The identity of the public service. Whose public service is it?

It is clear that a different APS could emerge from the changes proposed in this book. There are a number of overlapping elements that could substantially change the public face of the public service, including the establishment of independent board and CEO leadership, more active stakeholder management, and the publishing of an annual public service performance report, all of which would raise the profile of the public service, with the important objective of raising public confidence in government. From a public service strategy point of view, these issues point to the establishment of an identity for the public service and, from a public policy standpoint, they point to the contribution of this identity to the legitimacy of government noting that there is an inverse relationship between legitimacy and the costs of governing.

Determining the elements of identity of the public service that should emerge in formal terms, can be no better characterised than in the terms contained in the Public Service Act, especially the values, code of conduct, and employment principles, embracing the goal expressed in objects clause 3(a) – to establish an apolitical public service that is efficient and effective in serving the government, the parliament and the Australian public. An APS of this nature would replace a largely colourless and invisible structure with a visible, self-confident, impartial and thoroughly professional contributor to the health and wealth of our community.

11.7 Coherence and cohesion: The importance of not getting 'lost in the weeds'

In his retiring speech Auditor-General Ian McPhee identified governance frameworks as among the strengths in Australian Government administration, and losing sight of the guiding principles, getting lost in the weeds, and taking a narrow view of responsibilities, as amongst the 'soft spots'. There are many ways of characterising a game played at too low a level, and the material covered in this book highlights a number of dimensions of this problem.

There are laudable high-level objectives contained in the Public Service Act and the *Public Governance, Performance and Accountability Act 2013* (PGPA Act), of the sort that reasonably enable the auditor-general to point to the strength of Australia's governance frameworks. Similarly, however, a lack of alignment of public service structures, resourcing, and desired organisational behaviours, leaves these objectives unattainable. More detail and suitable enforcement mechanisms are required to make the Public Service Act work in the public interest, in addition to changed philosophical underpinnings. It is equally likely that the PGPA Act, which builds on the Public Service Act in relation to departmental activities, will (substantially) under-deliver in this sphere for the same reason; 30 years of performance auditing has left the public service a long way from producing meaningful output data, and even further, now, from the publication of purposeful impact and outcome data.

Another perspective from which public service activity might be seen to be 'lost in the weeds' is the long history of management focus on only one half of the cost–benefit equation of government activity, efficiency, and at the expense of effectiveness. This focus on production and cost rather than customer value and net benefit is a longstanding public sector failure, and not a particular failure that should simply be attributed to the framing of the present Public Service Act nor to the APS. It is, however, a luxury that the community can no longer afford and could readily be addressed through changes to the Act. In all businesses the focus, indeed the unit of organisational integration, should be the customer and, viewed in a public sector context, once the focal point moves from program- and department-level efficiency to effectiveness, then the important additional view of efficiency emerges (that is, additional to productive efficiency), 'allocative' efficiency, built around community net benefit (public value). If the three Cs of strategy are costs, customers and competition, it is time for the public service to integrate notions of customers and competition with the present focus on costs.

11.8 Every business delivers a value proposition. What is the public service value proposition?

An important and relatively unexplored issue that emerges in this book regards who is the customer of the public service. I drew on the work of Michael Lanning (2000) and his foundation notion of a value proposition as the entire set of resulting experiences that a customer has from acquisition and consumption of a product, and the value-delivery system as a framework to define and manage the business relationship between an organisation and its customers. Lanning goes as far as to observe that a business *is* the delivery of a value proposition.

In analysing customer relationships, Lanning points to several common business mistakes, firstly of treating the relationship as if there were only two players in it, and secondly of placing too great an importance on the immediate customer. He goes on to describe the business challenge as deciding where in the chain to deliver what value propositions, and how to do so given the interacting and sometimes conflicting motivations of the various entities in that chain.

Much of the discussion in this book has been around the importance to the public service of rebalancing the present focus away from 'the government' towards the end consumers of its products, namely the general public and parliament. This argument has both public service strategy (creating a separate identity) and public policy (raising public confidence in government) foundations. What Lanning does is provide an analytical framework within which these overlaps might reasonably be considered. The public service also needs to find an analytical structure by which to properly rationalise and better manage its customer relationships, and adoption of the Lanning framework would be a step in this direction.

11.9 Where is the big picture? The cost of seeing everything in bits

Considerations of strategy and structure lie at the heart of this book, with their requirement to establish an integrated sense of purpose and organisational coherence. The Public Service Act only partly envisages and enables this sense of togetherness, placing both structural and process barriers in its way, and consequently the operations of the public service lack an underpinning sense of self. A number of important costs can arise from the practice of 'seeing everything in bits'.

The first relates to the continuing degradation of public service strategic capabilities. For example, to be effective in creating community value, contestability programs require that an understanding of the strategic capabilities of the public service be built into any associated program guidelines: such 'capabilities' may be expressed in varying functional and activity terms across programs, policy areas and agencies, and the whole of the public service. The need for a strategic case-by-case analysis is clear; a function or capability that is 'strategic' in one activity area may not be in another. The other dimension missing from these considerations is their impacts on policy and program effectiveness, especially the cumulative effects of individual decisions on the whole.

The second class of cost of not seeing the whole, goes back to the critical issue of service delivery coordination within the public service and across to other sectors. Porter (1985) stresses this as one of the key challenges and opportunities for diversified businesses – what he calls horizontal strategy – and has noted that it has traditionally received much less attention than its companion strategic question of the selection of industries (and activities). Pursuit of horizontal strategy should involve the active examination of opportunities to create synergies built around the notion of strong clusters of activities as an important basis for corporate competitive advantage, and the capture of efficiency and effectiveness gains at the level of the individual business units (departments).

The third cost arises from the blunting of efficient resource-allocation processes associated with the use of limiting fiscal management instruments such as efficiency dividends and the mantra of local savings to fund local initiatives; both are likely to see continued nibbling at policy and program funding and defer the necessary program and policy choices. Both Geoff Mulgan and Rita McGrath observe that effective organisational strategy requires that money be systematically liberated from the past, with McGrath (2013) pointing to a 'hostage' problem, and Mulgan (2009) observing that much of the machinery of government tends toward rigid allocations, leaving only a small margin of budget expenditure for funding new programs in any one year. These practices clearly point to a likely accumulation of under-performing activities over time.

Within a public administration context, effectiveness of the resource-allocation system can be achieved by asking cross-cutting allocative-efficiency questions that span departmental and portfolio activities. For example, it is clear that expenditure is made in life-saving activities across a range of government portfolios, from road authorities investing in so-called black spot road intersections; health authorities making decisions about hospital equipment funding for emergency wards, and investment in research to prevent deaths from particular diseases; social services departments making expenditure decisions about suicide and domestic violence prevention programs; border force decisions to allocate funds to programs to prevent illicit drugs entering the country; to the sort of equipment and protective clothing decisions that defence authorities make regarding our armed forces' activities in combat zones. A pertinent question that can highlight the need for broader consideration of these sorts of issues asks what investment government agencies are prepared to make to save a life. It is likely that there would be major differences both on average and at the margin, which lay beyond the (reasonable) explanation of 'other factors'.[3]

Another interesting, but somewhat more difficult, version of the same sort of question would ask how much the government is prepared to invest in particular classes of citizen to reduce/eliminate the drain on the public purse in future? This research could involve an examination of 'investments' in a variety of social, cultural, language and work-based skills in: (a) migrants, (b) the unemployed, (c) people in jail, and (d) those on a variety of welfare support payments. To do this effectively would require the viewing of recurrent expenditure as a mix of consumption and investment. The outcome of such research would indicate the effectiveness of resource-allocation within government. In this case, research would again, most likely, show great disparities and underinvestment in providing citizens with the capabilities to escape the public purse in future, once having entered the system.

The report *Counting the costs of lost opportunity in Australian education* (2017) is an example of the sort of research needed to underpin good policy in this regard. Focused on the costs of educational disadvantage in Australia, the report points to the lifetime cost of $334,600 for each individual aged 19 who will never achieve year 12 or equivalent, an annual cohort cost of some $315 million, and a lifetime cohort cost of $12.6 billion. The projected individual cost of $334,600 provides a ready 'fund' that should encourage governments to invest in these individuals to avoid part, indeed most, of this lifetime cost, and avoid merely passing on the problem to future generations.[4]

11.10 Creating a winning culture: Not enough or the wrong sort?

An important contributor to organisational cohesion and identity is the package of behaviours commonly associated with the notion of culture and the less formal organisational arrangements that contribute to these.

---

3   I suspect research would show that one of the important 'other factors' is different valuations of a death (life lost) under different circumstances. For example, that prevention of air accidents would most likely be valued more highly than road or sea accidents.
4   See Lamb and Huo (2017).

Because of the difficulties of measurement at the organisational level, discussions of organisational behaviour(s) and culture rarely deliver useful outcomes in a consistent manner that enables benchmarking. The star of 'culture' shone bright in the 1980s on the back of the Peters and Waterman book *In Search of Excellence*, but has faded since because of the absence of metrics and the subsequent failure of a number of the companies the authors highlighted as exemplars (Peters & Waterman 1982).

There is no doubt that the companion concept of 'the way things get done around here' is a useful one, but practitioners in the field have found concepts of values and, more particularly, the derived behaviours, more useful in that they lend themselves more readily to quantification and benchmarking. Quantification of behaviours also provides part of a useful framework for consideration of organisational alignment. Indeed, a problem more commonly noted in the public sector than the private sector is that formal organisational goals and behavioural incentive systems are poorly aligned (See Halvorsen et al. 2005).

An equally important and related problem is that there may be a whole-of-organisation code of conduct, set of values, and a set of employment principles, along with an objective of providing career-based employment, aligned with organisational goals, but if the behaviour of board members, senior managers and other influential stakeholders flies in the face of this framework, then behaviours at odds with the values and the code will quickly become the norm. The removal or transfer of staff every time there is a problem, ministerial advisers who are allowed to make work for departmental staff trying to promote their own careers, flexible use of departmental funds (ministerial offices are accounted for in departmental budgets), and sham recruitment processes – send clear messages to staff about the real rules of the game whether in public or private sectors.

The public service is likely to be more exposed to these sorts of distractions because of the servant–master relationship it shares with the government. Moreover, the only protection for the public service in the Public Service Act for the exercise of the powers normally held by a master – clause 19, which requires that a departmental secretary not be the subject of direction by any minister in regard to public service employment matters – is of little practical use in these circumstances as there are many ways around this direction. And, equally unfortunately, all such activities impact on the cohesion of individual work units, departments and the whole of the public service. In particular, if public servants know that their departmental head will readily throw them under a bus in the face of any ministerial 'difficulties', then the only sense of self evident in public service operations will be 'myself'.

11.11 The importance of boundary conditions: Leveraging for success

Boundary issues are the issues of overlap and coordination that pervade the effective design and operation of the public sector with their extent being a distinguishing characteristic of government activity. The associated strategic, management, and operational challenges of boundary issues include service delivery overlaps, the absence of institutional memory, the need to deliver solutions not services, the need for horizontal strategy, the absence of a strategic centre, different models of governance, the challenges of wicked problems, performance measurement and governance issues, accountability, skills issues (rocket scientists?), the challenges of collaboration, organisational issues (structure and behaviour), and the whole-of-public-service challenge.

Given the overlaps, it is unsurprisingly often difficult to consider any one issue without considering a number of the others. When considered simply in organisational design terms, Mulgan (2009) views this challenge in terms of the absence of self-contained fields of activity, and the undesirability of seeing government simply as a set of self-contained projects or horizontal activities. This necessitates recognition that the imposition of what may sometimes be seen as arbitrary boundaries and separations is necessary, and he posits the organisational-design challenge as minimising the number of critical boundaries whilst recognising that there are no ideal structures. The existence of critical boundaries creates further difficulties in leveraging the whole-of-public-service experience.

The concept of leveraging is not an easy one to practise, but is just as important, for example, in adding value to the grind of the daily news cycle from reflective policy research (e.g. bringing in other jurisdictional experience), as it is in building institutional memory to leverage organisational experience in order to avoid repeating past operational mistakes. To not do this systematically is to ignore the opportunities to learn from past mistakes at a local level, but also to miss out on the opportunity to learn more at a whole-of-organisational level by combining whole-of-organisation experience. Interestingly, one of the organisational forms canvassed in Chapter 5 – the meta-national – takes its rationale from globalising local experiences as opposed to localising global knowledge. A successful organisation will do a measure of both!

11.12 Alignment: Master–servant or partners?

Discussions about the reasons for the existence of the public service and its identity can also be couched in terms of the alignment of government and public service. This issue has arisen from a number of directions. The first of these – the realignment of the interests of the public service with governments in Australia in the 1980s through the NPM reforms – was considered in Chapter 2, with the conclusion being that these reforms as implemented fragmented the public service. The second arose from an examination of the Public Service Act and a requirement for the public service to serve three communities simultaneously.

The third issue arose from Simon Longstaff's (2015) observation that, while the public service was established under its own Act of parliament and a constitution and range of derivative Acts providing for the government of Australia, ultimately, government is undertaken by private enterprise through registered political parties.[5] In keeping with this position, there is no legislated code of conduct for parliamentarians and, overall, there is a level of freedom accorded our elected officials that is more in keeping with private rather than public sector employment. Our politicians legislate for the upright behaviour of public servants, but see no merit in imposing such constraints on themselves, their behaviour being 'regulated' largely on an exception basis by their own manner of choosing. The fourth reminder of the issue has arisen in discussion of whether the public service is in any way 'entitled' to see itself and act as an independent entity. Was the APS established simply to serve the government of the day? The answer to that question as per the Public Service Act is clearly, no.

---

5   Clause 123 of the *Commonwealth Electoral Act 1918* sets out the definition of an 'eligible political party' for the purposes of the Act as one that is either a parliamentary party (has at least one member of the parliament of the Commonwealth) or has at least 500 members, and is established on the basis of a written constitution.

11.13 Good policy: The holy grail!

In Chapter 1 I considered the absence of good policy from parliamentary consideration in terms of political fragmentation, the rise of the politocracy, and the emergence of the enabling fine-grained electronic polling and targeting tools. Looking beyond these environmental factors to the role of the public service in the formation and delivery of good policy reveals a number of points that have arisen through this book. At the highest level it is the openness of the policy formation process to corruption and the need for this to be the subject of systematic external scrutiny – under existing arrangements that responsibility should lie with the auditor-general. I describe this in terms of the need for good policy governance much as better governance of expenditure is needed.[6]

Then there is the content of policy itself, which can be considered in terms of complex problems, solutions and services, containment rather than resolution, and the dominant focus of investment in physical (inanimate) assets, rather than in human assets and individuals. In this light, it is necessary to distinguish between the focus of the public administration arm of government on government policies, including their discussion in terms of strategic policy, and the need for the public administration to be able to advise governments on public policy matters that relate to its own activities spanning the leadership, management and operations of the public service.

Then there are the policy and program-level measurement issues, the what, the how, and for whom – impacts, outcomes, and public value rather than outputs, noting the important link between good program-level management information and organisational performance measurement – and the central strategic management issue of allocative efficiency. McGrath (2013) points to a raft of such issues – hostage resources, the need for flexibility in the processes, the distinction between the accounting

---

6   The concerns expressed here about the opaque nature of the government's policy formation process are given voice by the Australian National Audit Office's (ANAO) recent release of a performance audit of PM&C's management of the Australian Government Register of Lobbyists (ANAO 2018b). In the ANAO's typically understated way, the report is critical of the low level at which the policy bar was set for the administration of the register (although the ANAO does not have a mandate to criticise government policy), and the accompanying lack of commitment of resources to the low-level of tasks set for the department in its administration. And, in reminding us that only third-party lobbyists are required to register, the ANAO further indicated the limitations of the register's initial objectives. This should be a matter of great concern for the community.

life of an asset and its competitive best-in-class life, and the central importance of the resource-allocation process in shaping organisational behaviour, all with the aim of balancing the exploitation of the present with the exploration of the future.

The final policy issue is that pointed to by Kettl (2008) in his discussion of outsourcing US Government activities, asking who is in charge. It is an interesting question because it indicates that a series of individually 'right' decisions – in this case to outsource the services required for the various parts of the American healthcare system – can become a cumulative problem. In Australia's case, the same question might be asked, for example, about foreign investment: at what point do many individual foreign investments become a cumulative and national problem? Or it might be asked in regard to the export of natural gas, or at what level of domination of national trade with one country do we risk becoming an economic, and political satellite of that country? Whole-of-policy-life considerations, and investment in solutions should be the starting point for all government policy considerations. An auditor-general assigned the responsibility to audit the policy formation process could readily be assigned a checklist including such elements of 'good policy'. These issues point to the need for good policy – clean processes, the right players, and the long view – as the cornerstone of effective government.

11.14 An opportunity for the public service?

Creating a different future invites a clear determination of where the public service's competitive advantage lies in a world of growing fiscal pressures and contestability. Given the trends in the operating environment – smaller government, declining public service numbers, expanding contestability, and the growing influence of community groups and professional lobbyists on both the processes and outcomes of government – the influence of the public service will continue to diminish. The role that is emerging is one of facilitation and administration replacing its influence over high-level policy and the shape of the nation.

Some see this process of transfer of the power of government to the community – from the parliament, government and the public service – as a desirable continuation of the process that saw power transferred from public servants to politicians through the NPM reforms. Such a future promises greater community involvement in the determination of the activities of government and their implementation – what might be called 'community government' – but also promises a future of greater fragmentation of government, and limited, certainly reduced, governance of these activities. It also promises a future where policy is fragmented, and made at a lower level. Ludwig von Mises' economic calculation regarding the foundation of democratic government will be lost to a new form of bureaucracy.

If community government is the future, then avoiding this breakdown in governance can be achieved by the public service and governments of the day together reoccupying the high ground of good policy and sound public administration. To deliver its part of such a bargain, the APS needs to reposition itself at the highest level across the spectrum of policy formation, service delivery, and good governance, built around the whole-of-government approach only it can deliver and on the foundations of a pre-eminent policy position. Yet there seems to have been little call on such a public service capability in recent decades.

11.15 The path ahead

Due to their complexity, the two overlapping themes of this book, the first about public service strategy and the second about public policy towards the activity of public administration, are touched on only lightly. Be that as it may, I hope that the conclusions are sufficiently interesting to invite closer inspection of the major proposition, namely that the Australian public would be better served by a more independent, active, competitive, visible, and strategically led public service and that governments prepared to see the big picture of public administration and readmit the public service to the game of governing would benefit as well.

References

Advisory Group on Reform of Australian Government Administration, *Ahead of the game: Blueprint for the reform of Australian Government administration*, Department of the Prime Minister and Cabinet, 2010.

Alford, J, 'The implications of "publicness" for strategic management theory', in G Johnson & K Scholes, eds, *Exploring public sector strategy*, Prentice-Hall. London, 2001, pp 1–13.

——, 'Corporate management', in J Shafritz, ed, *International encyclopedia of public policy and administration*, vol 1, Westview Press, Boulder, Colorado & Oxford, UK, 1998, pp 538–39.

Alford, John & Head, Brian W, 'Wicked and less wicked problems: A typology and a contingency framework', *Policy and Society*, vol 36, no 3, 2017, pp 397–413, doi.org/10.1080/14494035.2017.1361634

Alford, John & O'Flynn, Janine, *Rethinking public service delivery: Managing with external providers*, Palgrave Macmillan, 2012, doi.org/10.1007/978-1-137-00724-7

——, 'Making sense of public value: Concepts, critiques and emergent meanings', *International Journal Of Public Administration*, vol 32, 2009, pp 171–91, doi.org/10.1080/01900690902732731

——, 'Public value: A stocktake of a concept', conference paper, Twelfth Annual Conference of the International Research Society for Public Management, Brisbane, 26–28 Mar 2008.

Allison Jr, Graham T, 'Public and private management: Are they fundamentally alike in all unimportant respects?', in *Setting public management research agendas: Integrating the sponsor, producer and user*, Office of Personnel Management, Washington DC, 1980, pp 27–38.

Arundel, Anthony, Bloch, Carter, & Ferguson, Barry, 'Measuring innovation in the public sector', conference paper, OECD Blue Sky Forum, Ghent, Belgium, 21 Sept 2016.

Aulby, Hannah & Campbell, Rod, 'The cost of corruption: The growing perception of corruption and its cost to GDP', The Australia Institute, Canberra, 2018, www.tai.org.au/sites/default/files/P381%20Costs%20of%20corruption%20FINAL_0.pdf

Australian Banking Association, 'Banks set trust benchmarks', media release, 28 Aug 2017, www.ausbanking.org.au/media/media-releases/media-release-2017/banks-set-trust-benchmarks

Australian Broadcasting Corporation, 'Here's what we know about the banking royal commission', *ABC News*, 4 Dec 2017, www.abc.net.au/news/2017-12-04/banking-royal-commission-heres-what-we-know/9210214

——, *Vote Compass*, 2016. votecompass.abc.net.au/

Australian Competition and Consumer Commission, 'What measure of regulation', speech by chairman Rod Sims to Ports Australia Conference, Melbourne, 20 Oct 2016.

Australian National Audit Office (ANAO), *Efficiency through Contestability Programme*, report no 41, Commonwealth of Australia, Canberra, 2018a.

——, *Management of the Australian Government Register of Lobbyists*, report no 27, Commonwealth of Australia, Canberra, 2018b.

——, *Implementation of the annual performance statements requirement 2016–17*, report, no 33, Commonwealth of Australia, 2017–18.

——, *Australian Government procurement contract reporting*, report no 19, Commonwealth of Australia, Canberra, 2017a.

——, *Indigenous advancement strategy*, report no 35, Commonwealth of Australia, Canberra, 3 Feb 2017b.

——, *The Auditor-General annual report 2015–16*, Commonwealth of Australia, Canberra, Sept 2016.

——, *Public sector governance: Strengthening performance through good governance (Better practice guide)*, Commonwealth of Australia, Canberra, June 2014a.

——, *The Auditor-General annual report 2013–14*, Commonwealth of Australia, Canberra, 2014b.

Australian Public Service Commission (APSC), *Values and code of conduct in practice*, Commonwealth of Australia, Canberra, 2017a.

——, *State of the service report 2016–17*, Commonwealth of Australia, Canberra, 2017b. www.apsc.gov.au/state-service-report-2016-17

——, 'Why and how HR in the Australian public service must change', by Commissioner John Lloyd, conference paper, Australian Human Resources Institute Symposium 'HR in the Public Sector', Melbourne, 25 Aug 2015a.

——, 'Australia's public service is confident, not cowed', by Commissioner John Lloyd, *Financial Review*, 14 Dec 2015b.

——, *State of the service report 2013–14*, Commonwealth of Australia, Canberra, 2014a.

——, 'Delivering performance and accountability', Commonwealth of Australia, Canberra, 2014b, www.apsc.gov.au/delivering-performance-and-accountability

——, *A history in three acts*, Commonwealth of Australia, Canberra, 2013a.

——, *Foundations of governance*, Commonwealth of Australia, Canberra, 2013b, www.apsc.gov.au/foundations-governance

——, *Tackling wicked problems: A public policy perspective*, Commonwealth of Australia, Canberra, 2012 (2007).

——, *Chronology of changes in the Australian Public Service 1975–2010*, Commonwealth of Australia, Canberra, 2010.

——, *Building better governance*, Commonwealth of Australia, Canberra, 2007.

——, 'Thinking and acting strategically: Building the strategic capability of the Australian Public Service', by Commissioner Lynelle Briggs, address to the Australian Strategic Policy Institute, Sydney, 8 Dec 2005.

——, *A history in three acts: Evolution of the Public Service Act 1999*, 2004.

Australian Stock Exchange Ltd., Corporate Governance Council, *Board Charter*, Mar 2016.

——, Corporate Governance Council, *Corporate governance principles and recommendations*, 3rd edn, 2014.

Bason, Christian, *Leading public sector innovation: Co-creating for a better society*, Policy Press, Bristol, UK, 2010.

Bevir, Mark, *Key concepts in governance*, Sage Publications, London, 2009.

Bogdanor, Vernon, ed, *Joined-up government*, Oxford University Press, 2005, doi.org/10.5871/bacad/9780197263334.001.0001

Bommert, Ben, 'Collaborative innovation in the public sector', *International Public Management Review*, vol 11, no 1, 2010.

Börzel, Tanja A & Risse, Thomas, 'Governance without a state: Can it work?', *Regulation & Governance*, vol 4, no 2, 2010, pp 113–34, doi.org/10.1111/j.1748-5991.2010.01076.x

Boston, Jonathan & Gill, Derek, 'Working across organisational boundaries: The challenges for accountability', in B Ryan & D Gill, eds, *Future state: Directions for public management in New Zealand*, Victoria University Press, Wellington, New Zealand, 2011.

Bourgault, Jacques, 'The deputy minister's role in the government of Canada: His responsibility and his accountability', in J Gomery, ed, *Restoring accountability: Recommendations*, Privy Council Office (Canada), Ottawa, 2006, pp 253–96.

Bouvard, François, Carsouw, Robert, Labaye, Eric, Levy, Alastair, Mendonca, Lenny, Remes, Jaana, Roxburgh, Charles, & Test, Samantha, *Better for less: Improving public sector budget performance on a tight budget*, McKinsey & Co, 2011.

Bovaird, Tony & Löffler, Elke, 'Evaluating the quality of public governance: Indicators, models and methodologies', *International Review of Administrative Sciences*, vol 69, no 3, 2003, pp 313–28, doi.org/10.1177/0020852303693002

Bowen, S & Zwi, A., 'Pathways to "evidence-informed" policy and practice: A framework for action', PLOS Medicine, vol 2, no 7, 2005, e166, doi.org/10.1371/journal.pmed.0020166

Boyne, George A, 'Public and private management: What's the difference?', Journal of Management Studies, vol 39, no 1, 2002, pp 97–122, doi.org/10.1111/1467-6486.00284

Brown, Nicholas, 'The Seven Dwarfs: A Team of Rivals', in S Furphy, ed, *The Seven Dwarfs and the Age of the Mandarins: Australian Government Administration in the Post-War Reconstruction Era*, ANU Press, Canberra, 2015.

Burns, T & Stalker, GM, *The management of innovation*, Tavistock, London, 1961.

Byrne, John A, 'B-school Dean of the Year: Rotman's Roger Martin', *Fortune*, 27 Dec 2013, fortune.com/2013/12/27/b-school-dean-of-the-year-rotmans-roger-martin/

Cameron, Sarah & McAllister, Ian, *Trends in Australian political opinion: Results from the Australian Election Study 1987–2016*, School of Politics and International Relations, The Australian National University, Canberra, 2016.

Caves, Richard, *American industry: Structure, conduct, performance*, 2nd edn, Prentice-Hall, Englewood Cliffs, New Jersey, 1967.

Centre For Policy Development (CPD), 'What do Australians want? Active and effective government fit for the ages', discussion paper, Dec 2017a, cpd.org.au/2017/12/what-do-australians-want-discussion-paper-december-2017/

——, 'Australians want their democracy to be fit for the ages', media release, 12 Dec 2017b, cpd.org.au/wp-content/uploads/2017/12/Press-Release-What-do-Australians-Want.pdf

Chambers, Naomi & Cornforth, Chris, 'The role of corporate governance and boards in organisational performance', in K Walshe, G Harvey & P Jas, eds, *Connecting knowledge and performance in public services: From knowing to doing*. Cambridge University Press, 2010, doi.org/10.1017/CBO9780511762000.007

Chandler, Alfred D, *Strategy and structure*, MIT Press, Cambridge, 1962.

Christensen, Clayton M, *The innovator's dilemma: When new technologies cause great firms to fail*, Harvard Business Review Press, Boston, Massachusetts, 1997.

Christensen, Clayton M & Raynor, Michael E, *The innovator's solution: Creating and sustaining successful growth*, Harvard Business School Press, Boston, Massachusetts, 2003.

Christensen, Tom & Lægreid, Per, 'The whole-of-government approach to public sector reform', *Public Administration Review*, vol 60, no 6, 2007, pp 1059–66, doi.org/10.1111/j.1540-6210.2007.00797.x

Coase, RH, 'The nature of the firm', *Economica*, vol 4, no 16, 1937, pp 386–405, doi.org/10.1111/j.1468-0335.1937.tb00002.x

Dahlström, Carl, Peters, Guy, & Pierre, Jon, eds, *Steering from the centre: Strengthening political control in Western democracies*, University of Toronto Press, 2011, doi.org/10.3138/9781442687066

Delft University of Technology, 'Confronting Wicked Problems: Adapting Architectural Education to the New Situation in Europe', 1st Wicked Workshop on Architectural and Urban Sustainability, Delft, Netherlands, 19–25 April 2015. www.ace-cae.eu/fileadmin/New_Upload/_15_EU_Project/Wicked_Workshop_booklet_April_2015.compressed.pdf

Department of Finance, *Corporate plans for Commonwealth entities*, Resource Management Guide, no 132, Commonwealth of Australia, Jan 2017.

——, *Whole-of-government: Shared and common services programme*, discussion paper, Australian Government, Canberra, 2015, www.finance.gov.au/sites/default/files/discussion-paper-shared-common-services.pdf

Department of Industry, *Australian innovation system report*, Australian Government, Canberra, 2013.

Department of the Prime Minister and Cabinet, Corporate plan 2016–2020, Commonwealth of Australia, Canberra, 2016.

Department of Treasury & Finance, *Victorian public sector operating manual on machinery of government changes*, State of Victoria, Oct 2016.

Di Francesco, Michael & Eppel, Elizabeth, 'A public management heresy? Exploring the managerial role of ministers within public policy design', in B Ryan & D Gill, eds, *Future state: Directions for public management in New Zealand*, Victoria University Press, Wellington, New Zealand, 2011.

Doz, Yves L, Santos, José, & Williamson, Peter, *From global to metanational: How companies win in the knowledge economy*, Harvard Business School Press, Boston, Massachusetts, 2001.

Edelman Holdings, '2017 Edelman Trust Barometer', 2017, www.edelman.com/research/2017-edelman-trust-barometer

Edwards, Meredith, Halligan, John, Horrigan, Bryan, & Nicoll, Geoffrey, *Public sector governance in Australia*, ANU E Press, Canberra, 2012, doi.org/10.22459/PSGA.07.2012

Eggers, William D & Macmillan, Paul, *The solution revolution: How business, government, and social enterprises are teaming up to solve society's toughest problems*, Harvard Business Review Press, Boston, Massachusetts, 2013.

Eggers, William D & Singh, Shalabh Kumar, *The public innovator's playbook: Nurturing bold ideas in government*, Deloitte Research, 2009.

Esty, Daniel C & Caves, Richard E, 'Market structure and political influence', *Yale Faculty Scholarship Series*, paper 455, 1983.

Fagerberg, Jan, 'Innovation: A Guide to the Literature', in J Fagerberg, DC Mowery & RR Nelson, eds, *The Oxford handbook of innovation*, Oxford University Press, 2005.

Fagerberg, Jan, Mowery, David C, & Nelson, Richard R, eds, *The Oxford handbook of innovation*, Oxford University Press, 2005.

Fukuyama, Francis, 'What is governance?', *Governance: An International Journal of Policy, Administration, and Institutions*, vol 26, no 3, 2013, pp 347–68, doi.org/10.1111/gove.12035

Funnell, Warwick, Cooper, Kathie, & Lee, Janet, *Public sector accounting and accountability in Australia*, UNSW Press, 2012.

Furphy, Samuel, ed, *The seven dwarfs and the age of the mandarins: Australian government administration in the post-war reconstruction era*, ANU Press, Canberra, 2015, doi.org/10.22459/SDAM.07.2015

Garratt, Bob, *The fish rots from the head*, 3rd edn, Profile Books, London, 2010.

Goldsmith, Stephen & Eggers, William D, *Governing by network: The new shape of the public sector*, Brookings Institution Press, 2004.

Golub Harvey, Henry, Jane, Forbis, John L, Mehta, Nitin T, Lanning, Michael J, Michaels, Edward G & Ohmae, Kenichi. 'Delivering value to customers', *McKinsey Quarterly*, Jun 2000.

Grant, Robert M, *Contemporary strategy analysis*, Blackwell Publishers Inc, Oxford, UK, 1995.

Halligan, John, 'Central steering in Australia', in C Dahlström, G Peters, & J Pierre, eds, *Steering from the centre: Strengthening political control in Western democracies*, University of Toronto Press, 2011, doi.org/10.3138/9781442687066-007

Halvorsen, T, Hauknes, J, Miles, I, Røste, R, 'Innovation in the public sector: On the differences between public and private sector innovation', *Publin Report No D9*, Oslo, 2005.

Hamel, Gary & Prahalad, CK, *Competing for the future*, Harvard Business School Publishing, 1994.

——, 'The core competence of the corporation', *Harvard Business Review*, May–Jun 1990, pp 79–90.

Hanger, Ian, *Report of the Royal Commission into the Home Insulation Program*, Commonwealth of Australia, 2014.

Hansen, Jesper Rosenberg, 'Strategic management when profit isn't the end: Differences between public organizations', conference paper, National Public Management Research Conference, Elder College of Management, University of Arizona, Tucson, Oct 2007.

Hansen, Jesper Rosenberg & Ferlie, Ewan, 'Applying strategic management theories in public sector organizations: Developing a typology', *Public Management Review*, vol 18, no 1, 2014, pp 1–19, doi.org/10.1080/147190 37.2014.957339

Harris, Michael & Boyle, David, *The challenge of co-production: How equal partnerships between professionals and the public are crucial to improving public services*, NESTA, 2009.

Hartley, Jean, 'Innovation in governance and public services: Past and present', *Public Money & Management*, vol 25, no 1, 2005, pp 27–34.

Hartley, Jean, Sørensen, Eva, & Torfing, Jacob, 'Collaborative innovation: A viable alternative to market competition and organizational entrepreneurship', *Public Administration Review*, vol 73, no 6, 2013, pp 821–30, doi.org/10.1111/puar.12136

Head, Brian W, 'Wicked problems in public policy', *Public Policy*, vol 3, no 2, 2008, pp 101–18.

Head, Brian & Alford, John, 'Wicked problems: Implications for public policy and management', *Administration & Society*, vol 47, no 6, 2015, pp 711–39, doi.org/10.1177/0095399713481601

——, 'Wicked problems: The implications for public management', conference paper, International Research Society for Public Management 12th Annual Conference, Brisbane, 26–28 Mar 2008.

Hehir, Grant, 'A reflection on how far performance auditing has come from its roots in the 1970s to where we are today and where we are heading', speech to International Meeting of Performance Audit Critical Thinkers, Brisbane, 15 Mar 2016.

Ho, Tin Kam & Basu, Mitra, 'Measuring the complexity of classification problems', conference paper, 15th International Pattern Recognition Conference, Barcelona, Sept 2000.

Hobday, Liz '7-Eleven wage underpayment claims taking too long: Allan Fels', *ABC News*, 31 Aug 2016, www.abc.net.au/news/2016-08-31/7-eleven-wage-claims-taking-too-long-allan-fels/7803008

Hood, Christopher, 'A public management for all seasons?', *Public Administration*, vol 69, no 1, 1991, pp 3–19, doi.org/10.1111/j.1467-9299.1991.tb00779.x

Hood, Christopher & Dixon, Ruth, *A government that worked better and cost less? Evaluating three decades of reform and change in UK central government*, Oxford University Press, UK, 2015.

Hughes Peter, 'Preface', in B Ryan & D Gill, eds, *Future state: Directions for public management in New Zealand*, Victoria University Press, Wellington, New Zealand, 2011.

Hunter, Fergus, 'Cambridge Analytica, the "psychographic" data firm behind Donald Trump, eyes Australian move', *Sydney Morning Herald*, 12 Jan 2017, www.smh.com.au/politics/federal/cambridge-analyticathe-psychographic-data-firm-behind-donald-trump-eyes-australian-move-20161212-gt926e.html

Hyde, Jim, 'How to make the rhetoric of joined-up government really work', *Australia and New Zealand Health Policy*, 2008, vol 5, no 22, 2008, doi.org/10.1186/1743-8462-5-22

Independent Broad-based Anti-corruption Commission (IBAC), 'IBAC lays charges in relation to "banker schools" corruption', media release, 10 Jan 2017, www.ibac.vic.gov.au/media-releases/article/ibac-lays-charges-in-relation-to-banker-schools-corruption

Institute of Public Administration Australia (IPAA), *Twelve speeches 2016: A year of speeches from public service leaders*, Canberra, 2017.

Karp, Paul, 'Sussan Ley quits as health minister as Turnbull outlines reforms to expenses', *Guardian*, 13 Jan 2017, www.theguardian.com/australia-news/2017/jan/13/sussan-ley-quits-health-minister-turnbull-outlines-reform-expenses

Karre, Philip Marcel, van der Steen, Martijn, & van Twist, Mark, 'Joined-up government in the Netherlands: Experiences with program ministries', *International Journal of Public Administration*, vol 36, no 1, 2013, pp 63–73, doi.org/10.1080/01900692.2012.713295

Kay, Robert & Goldspink, Chris, 'What CEOs mean when they say they want to innovate', workshop presentation, 2012a, www.inceptlabs.com.au/publications

——, 'What public sector leaders mean when they say they want to innovate', workshop presentation, 2012b, www.companydirectors.com.au/~/media/resources/events/act/robert-kay.ashx

Kelly, G, Mulgan, G, & Muers, S, 'Creating public value: An analytical framework for public sector reform', Cabinet Office Strategy Unit, UK, 2002.

Kettl, Donald F, *The next government of the United States: Why our institutions fail us and how to fix them*, WW Norton and Company, New York, 2008.

Kiechel III, Walter, 'The management century', *Harvard Business Review*, vol 90, no 11, 2012, pp 62–75.

——, *The lords of strategy: The secret intellectual history of the new corporate world*, Harvard Business Review Press, Boston, 2010.

Kostyuk, A, Braendle, UC, & Apreda, A, *Corporate governance*, Virtus Interpress, Sumy, Ukraine, 2007.

Koziol, Michael, 'Distrustful nation: Australians lose faith in politics, media and business', *Sydney Morning Herald*, 21 Jan 2017, www.smh.com.au/politics/ federal/distrustful-nation-australians-lose-faith-in-politics-media-and-business-20170118-gttmpd.html

Lægreid, Per, Nordø, Åsta Dyrnes, & Rykkja, Lise, 'The quality of coordination in Norweigian central government: The importance of coordination arrangements and structural, cultural and demographic factors', COCOPS Working Paper, no 14, Dec 2013.

Lafley, AG & Martin, Roger L, 'Customer loyalty is overrated', *Harvard Business Review*, Jan–Feb 2017.

——, *Playing to win: How strategy really works*, Harvard Business Review Press, Boston, Massachusetts, 2013.

Lam, Alice, 'Organizational innovation', in J Fagerberg, DC Mowery, & RR Nelson, eds, *The Oxford handbook of innovation*, Oxford University Press, 2005.

Lamb, Stephen & Huo, Shuyan, 'Counting the costs of lost opportunity in Australian education', Mitchell Institute Report No. 2, Mitchell Institute, Melbourne, 2017.

Lanning, Michael J, *Delivering profitable value*, Perseus Books, Boulder, Colorado, 2000.

Lawrence, PR & Lorsch, JW, 'Differentiation and integration in complex organizations', *Administrative Science Quarterly*, vol 12, no 1, 1967, pp 1–47, doi.org/10.2307/2391211

Lazonick, William, 'Who needs a theory of innovative enterprise?', University of Massachusetts, Lowell, Aug 2012.

Levin, Kelly, Cashore, Benjamin, Bernstein, Steven, & Auld, Graeme, 'Overcoming the tragedy of super wicked problems: Constraining our future selves to ameliorate global climate change', *Policy Sciences*, vol 45, no 2, 2012, pp 123–52, doi.org/10.1007/s11077-012-9151-0

——, 'Playing it forward: Path dependency, progressive incrementalism, and the "super wicked" problem of global climate change', *IOP Conference Series: Earth and Environmental Science*, vol 6, no 50, 2009, doi.org/10.1088/1755-1307/6/0/502002

Longstaff, Simon, 'Democracy, trust and legitimacy', *Papers on Parliament*, no 63, Department of the Senate, Parliament House, Canberra, July 2015, pp 77–93.

Management Advisory Committee (MAC), *Empowering change: Fostering innovation in the Australian Public Service*, Commonwealth of Australia, Canberra, 2010.

——, 'Connecting government: whole of government responses to Australia's priority challenges', Commonwealth of Australia, 2004, www.apsc.gov.au/connecting-government-whole-government-responses-australias-priority-challenges

March, James G, 'Exploration and exploitation in organizational learning', *Organization Science*, vol 1, no 2, 1991, pp 71–87, doi.org/10.1287/orsc.2.1.71

Martin, Roger, 'The big lie of strategic planning', *Harvard Business Review*, Jan–Feb 2014.

——, 'Don't let strategy become planning', *Harvard Business Review*, 5 Feb 2013.

——, *The design of business: Why design thinking is the most competitive advantage*, Harvard Business School Press, Boston, Massachusetts, 2009.

McGrath, Rita Gunther, 'Old habits die hard but they do die', *Harvard Business Review*, Jan–Feb 2017.

——, *The end of competitive advantage*, Harvard Business Review Press, Boston, Massachusetts, 2013.

McGuire, Michael, 'Collaborative public management: Assessing what we know and how we know it', *Public Administration Review*, vol 66, no 1, 2006, pp 33–43, doi.org/10.1111/j.1540-6210.2006.00664.x

McKeown, Deidre, *Codes of conduct in Australian and selected overseas parliaments*, Parliament of Australia, 2012.

McKinsey & Company. *Better for less: Improving public sector budget performance on a tight budget*, The McKinsey Center for Government, 2011.

McPhee, Ian, 'Reflections on 10 years as Auditor-General for Australia', speech to Australasian Council of Public Accounts Committees, Adelaide, 16 Apr 2015.

Megalogenis, George, 'Balancing act: Australia between recession and renewal', *Quarterly Essay*, no 61, 2016.

Miles, Ian, 'Innovation in services', in J Fagerberg, DC Mowery, & RR Nelson, eds, *The Oxford handbook of innovation*, Oxford University Press, 2005.

Milliken, Robert, 'An incisive guide to Australia's think tanks', *Anne Summers Reports*, no 11, 2015, pp 35–45.

Mintzberg, Henry, *The fall and rise of strategic planning*, New York Free Press, 1994a.

——, 'The fall and rise of strategic planning', *Harvard Business Review*, Jan–Feb 1994b, pp 107–14.

——, *Structures in fives: Designing effective organizations*, Prentice-Hall, New Jersey, 1993.

——, *The structuring of organizations*, Prentice-Hall, Englewood Cliffs, New Jersey, 1979.

——, 'Patterns in strategy formation', *Management Science*, vol 24, no 9, 1978, pp 934–48, doi.org/10.1287/mnsc.24.9.934

Mintzberg, Henry & Waters, James A, 'Of strategies, deliberate and emergent', *Strategic Management Journal*, vol 6, no 3, 1985, pp 257–72, doi.org/10.1002/smj.4250060306

Mishan, EJ, *Cost-benefit analysis*, 4th edn, Routledge, London, 1988.

Moore, Bruce, ed, *The Australian Oxford Dictionary*, Oxford University Press, Melbourne, 1999.

Moore, Mark H, 'Managing for value: Organizational strategy in for-profit, nonprofit, and governmental organizations', *Nonprofit and Voluntary Sector Quarterly*, vol 29, no 1, 2000, pp 183–204, doi.org/10.1177/0899764000291S009

Moore, Mark, *Creating public value: Strategic management in government*, Harvard University Press, Cambridge, Massachusetts, 1995.

Moran, Terry, 'Who does what in government and will it change?', speech, Institute of Public Administration, Brisbane, 25 May 2015.

——, 'If I knew what I know now', speech, ANZSOG Conference. Canberra. 7 Aug 2014a.

——, 'How economists captured the policy process', *The Mandarin*, 2 Oct 2014b, www.themandarin.com.au/5190-terry-moran-economists-captured-australias-policy-debate

Mulgan, Geoff, *The art of public strategy: Mobilizing power and knowledge for the common good*, Oxford University Press, 2009.

Mulgan, Richard, *Politicising the Australian Public Service*, Research Paper no 3, Parliament of Australia, 1998–99.

Naschold, Frieder, *New frontiers in the public sector management: Trends and issues in state and local government in Europe*, Walter de Gruyter & Co, Berlin, 1996, doi.org/10.1515/9783110809626

National Audit Office (NAO UK), *The centre of government*, 2014.

——, *Reorganising central government*, Report by the Comptroller and Auditor-General, 18 Mar 2010.

National Commission of Audit (NCOA), *Towards responsible government: The report of the National Commission of Audit*, Phases One and Two, Commonwealth of Australia, 2014.

Nethercote, John, 'Unearthing the seven dwarfs', *Canberra Times*, 5 Oct 2010.

——, *The Australian experience of public sector reform*, APSC Occasional Paper 2, Commonwealth of Australia, 2003.

Netherlands Ministry of Finance, *Government governance: Corporate governance in the public sector, why and how?*, 2000.

Norman, Richard & Gill, Derek, 'Restructuring: An over-used lever for change in New Zealand's state sector?', in B Ryan & D Gill, eds, *Future state: Directions for public management in New Zealand*, Victoria University Press, Wellington, New Zealand, 2011.

Norris, Pippa, *Democratic deficit: Critical citizens revisited*, Cambridge University Press, New York, 2011, doi.org/10.1017/CBO9780511973383

O'Flynn, Janine, 'From New Public Management to public value: Paradigmatic change and managerial implications', *Australian Journal of Public Administration*, vol 66, no 3, 2006, pp 353–66, doi.org/10.1111/j.1467-8500.2007.00545.x

O'Flynn, Janine, Buck, Fiona, Blackman, Deborah, & Halligan, John, 'You win some, you lose some: Experiments in joined-up government', *International Journal of Public Administration*, vol 34, no 4, 2011, pp 244–54. doi.org/10.1080/01900692.2010.540703

O'Reilly III, Charles & Tushman, Michael L, 'Organizational ambidexterity: Past, present and future', *Academy of Management Perspective*, vol 27, no 4, 2013, pp 299–312, doi.org/10.5465/amp.2013.0025

Organisation for Economic Co-operation and Development (OECD), 'PISA 2015 – Results in Focus', 2015, www.oecd.org/pisa/pisa-2015-results-in-focus.pdf

Osborne, Stephen P & Brown, Louise, 'Innovation, public policy and public services delivery in the UK: The word that would be king?', *Public Administration*, vol 89, no 4, 2011, pp 1335–50, doi.org/10.1111/j.1467-9299.2011.01932.x

Pallot, June, '"Newer than new" public management: Financial management and collective strategizing', conference paper, 'The New Public Management in International Perspective', Institute of Public Finance and Fiscal Law conference, St Gallen, Switzerland, 11–13 July 1996.

Parliament of Victoria, *Inquiry into the CFA Training College at Fiskville*, final report, Environment, Natural Resources and Regional Development Committee, 2016a.

——, *Inquiry into machinery of government changes*, final report, Legal and Social Issues Committee, 2016b.

Patty, Anna, '7-Eleven compensation bill climbs over $110 million', *Sydney Morning Herald*, 13 Jun 2017, www.smh.com.au/business/workplace/7eleven-compensation-bill-climbs-over-110-million-20170612-gwpdfx.html

Peever, David, *First principles review, 'creating one Defence'*, Department of Defence, Canberra, Apr 2015.

Pegnato, Joseph A, 'Is a citizen a customer?', *Public Productivity and Management Review*, vol 20, no 4, Jun 1997, pp 397–404, doi.org/10.2307/3380680

Penrose, Edith, *The theory of the growth of the firm*, Oxford University Press, 2009 (1959).

Peters, B Guy, 'What is so wicked about wicked problems? A conceptual analysis and research program', *Policy and Society*, vol 36, no 3, 2017, pp 385–96, doi.org/10.1080/14494035.2017.1361633

Peters, B Guy & Pierre, John, 'Governance without government? Rethinking public administration', *Journal Of Public Administration Research & Theory*, vol 8, no 2, 1998, pp 223–43, doi.org/10.1093/oxfordjournals.jpart.a024379

Peters, Tom & Waterman, Robert, *In search of excellence: Lessons from America's best-run companies*, Harper Collins, Sydney, 1982.

Petrusma, Jacquie, 'Joined-up support services for Tasmanians', media release, 19 June 2014.

Pfeffer, Monica, 'Thriving in turbulent times', in *Hyper-government: Managing and thriving in turbulent times: Conference highlights*, 2016.

Piketty, Thomas, *Capital in the twenty-first century*, Harvard University Press, Harvard, 2014.

Poister, Theodore H & Streib, Gregory D, 'Strategic management in the public sector: Concepts, models and processes', *Public Productivity & Management Review*, vol 22, no 3, 1999, pp 308–25, doi.org/10.2307/3380706

Poister, Theodore H, Pitts, David W, & Edwards, Lauren Hamilton, 'Strategic management research in the public sector: A review, synthesis and future direction', *The American Review Of Public Administration*, vol 40, no 5, 2010, pp 522–45, doi.org/10.1177/0275074010370617

Porter, Christian, 'The Australian priority approach to welfare investment', speech, National Press Club, Canberra, 20 Sept 2016.

——, 'Address to Family and Relationship Services Australia Senior Executive Service Forum', speech, Parliament House, Canberra, 24 Feb 2016, formerministers.dss.gov.au/17495/family-and-relationship-services-australia-senior-executive-forum/

Porter, Michael, *The competitive advantage: Creating and sustaining superior performance*, The Free Press, New York, 1985.

——, *Competitive strategy: Techniques for analysing industries and competitors*, The Free Press, New York, 2004 (1980).

Potter, Ben, 'ACCC's Rod Sims "exasperated" as privatisations "increase prices"', *Australian Financial Review*, 27 Jul 2016, www.afr.com/news/economy/acccs-rod-sims-exasparated-as-privatisations-increase-prices-20160726-gqdyjv

Productivity Commission, *Report on government services 2018*, Commonwealth of Australia, Canberra, 2018, www.pc.gov.au/research/ongoing/report-on-government-services/2018

——, *Report on government services 2016*, Commonwealth of Australia, Canberra, 2016.

——, *Public Infrastructure*, Productivity Commission Inquiry Report no 1, Commonwealth of Australia, Canberra, 2014a.

——, *Overcoming Indigenous disadvantage: Key indicators 2014*, Commonwealth of Australia, Canberra, 2014b.

Provan, Keith G & Milward, H Brinton, 'Do networks really work? A framework for evaluating public sector organizational networks', *Public Administration Review*, vol 61, no 4, 2001, pp 414–23, doi.org/10.1111/0033-3352.00045

Pryor, Joshua, 'Governance without government', working paper, California State University, August 2014, doi.org/10.2139/ssrn.2308840

Rhodes, RAW, 'Understanding governance 20 years on', 2017, www.raw-rhodes.co.uk/wp-content/uploads/2017/07/National-Governance-Review.pdf

——, 'Understanding governance, ten years on', *Organization Studies*, vol 28, no 8, 2007, pp 1243–64, doi.org/10.1177/0170840607076586

——, 'The new governance: Governing without government', *Political Studies*, vol 44, no 4, 1996, pp 652–67, doi.org/10.1111/j.1467-9248.1996.tb01747.x

Rittel, Horst WJ & Webber, Melvin M, 'Dilemmas in a general theory of planning', *Policy Sciences*, vol 4, no 2, 1973, pp 155–69, doi.org/10.1007/BF01405730

Roberts, NC, 'Wicked problems and network approaches to resolution', *International Public Management Review*, vol 1, no 1, 2000, pp 1–19.

Royal Commission into the Home Insulation Program, 2014, Commonwealth of Australia, Canberra.

Royal Commission into Institutional Responses to Child Sexual Abuse, 2017, Commonwealth of Australia, Canberra.

Royal Commission into Misconduct in the Banking, Superannuation and Financial Services Industry, 2019, Commonwealth of Australia, Canberra.

Ryan, Bill, 'Thoughts after "Future State"', speech, Institute of Public Administration New Zealand (IPANZ), Wellington, 27 Mar 2012. ipanz.org.nz/Folder?Action=View%20File&Folder_id=84&File=Ryan%20Thoughts%20After%20Future%20State.pdf

Ryan, Bill & Gill, Derek, eds, *Future state: Directions for public management in New Zealand*, Victoria University Press, Wellington, New Zealand, 2011.

Schultz, Julianne & Tiernan, Anne, 'Fixing the system', *Griffith Review* 51, 2016.

Schumpeter, Joseph, *The theory of economic development: An inquiry into profits, capital, credits, interest, and the business cycle*, Transaction Publishers, Piscataway, 1934.

Schwartz, Peter, *The art of the long view*, Currency Doubleday, New York, 1991.

Scott, Patricia, 'Our custodial role for the quality of advisory relations at the centre of government', in J Wanna, S Vincent, & A Podger, *With the benefit of hindsight: valedictory reflections from departmental secretaries 2004–11*, ANU E Press, 2012, doi.org/10.22459/WBH.04.2012.12

Sørensen, Eva & Torfing, Jacob, 'Collaborative innovation in the public sector', *The Innovation Journal: The Public Sector Innovation Journal*, vol 17, no 1, 2012, pp 1–14.

——, 'Enhancing collaborative innovation in the public sector', *Administration & Society*, vol 43, no 8, 2011, pp 841–68, doi.org/10.1177/0095399711418768

Starbuck, WH, 'Learning by knowledge-intensive firms', *Journal of Management Studies*, vol 29, no 6, 1992, pp 713–40, doi.org/10.1111/j.1467-6486.1992. tb00686.x

Stern, Carl W & Stalk Jr, George, eds, *Perspectives on strategy from the Boston Consulting Group*, John Wiley & Sons, New York, 1998.

Stoker, Gerry, 'Governance as theory: Five propositions', *International Social Science Journal*, vol 50, no 155, 1998, pp 17–28, doi.org/10.1111/1468-2451.00106

Sweeney, Lucy, 'Sam Dastyari resigns from Parliament, says he is "detracting from Labor's mission" amid questions over Chinese links', *ABC News*, 13 Dec 2017, www.abc.net.au/news/2017-12-12/sam-dastyari-resigns-from-parliament/9247390

Tingle, Laura, 'Political amnesia: How we forgot how to govern', *Quarterly Essay*, no 60, 2015.

Transparency International, 'Corruption Perceptions Index 2016', 25 Jan 2017, www.transparency.org/news/feature/corruption_perceptions_index_2016

Tricker, Bob, *Corporate governance: Principles, policies and practices*, 3rd edn, Oxford University Press, 2015.

Turnbull, Malcolm, 'Royal Commission – Banks and Financial Services', media release, 30 Nov 2017, pmtranscripts.pmc.gov.au/release/transcript-41355

——, *PM Transcripts*, press conference, Sydney, 13 Jan 2017, pmtranscripts.pmc. gov.au/release/transcript-40682

Tushman, Michael L & O'Reilly III, Charles A, 'Ambidextrous organizations: Managing evolutionary and revolutionary change', *California Management Review*, vol 38, no 4, 1996, pp 29–44, doi.org/10.2307/41165852

UNDP Global Centre for Public Service Excellence, *From old public administration to the new public service*, Singapore, 2015.

Verspaandonk, Rose, Holland, Ian, & Horne, Nicholas, 'Chronology of changes in the Australian Public Service 1975-2010', Australian Government Parliamentary Papers, Oct 2010, www.aph.gov.au/About_Parliament/Parliam entary_Departments/Parliamentary_Library/pubs/BN/1011/APSChanges

Victorian Auditor-General's Office (VAGO), *Access to public sector information*, Dec 2015, www.audit.vic.gov.au/sites/default/files/20151210-Public-Sector-Info.pdf

——, 'Freedom of Information', 18 Apr 2012, www.audit.vic.gov.au/report/freedom-information?section=

von Mises, Ludwig, *Bureaucracy*, Dead Authors Society, Victoria BC, Canada, 2017 (1944).

Wachhaus, Aaron, 'Governance beyond government', *Administration & Society*, vol 46, no 5, 2014, pp 573–93, doi.org/10.1177/0095399713513140

Wanna, John, Vincent, Sam, & Podger, Andrew, *With the benefit of hindsight: Valedictory reflections from departmental secretaries 2004–11*, ANU E Press, 2012, doi.org/10.22459/WBH.04.2012

Watt, Ian, 'Address to the APS: The path forward for the APS', Department of the Prime Minister and Cabinet, 6 Dec 2013, www.pmc.gov.au/news-centre/pmc/address-aps-path-forward-aps

Weick, Karl E & Quinn, Robert E, 'Organizational change and development', *Annual Review Of Psychology*, 50, 1999, pp 361–86.

West, Jonathan & Bentley, Tom, *Time for a new consensus: Fostering Australia's comparative advantages*, e-book, *Griffith Review* 51, 2016, griffithreview.com/time-for-a-new-consensus-e-book/

Wheeler, Chris, 'The public interest revisited: We know it's important, but do we know what it means?', *AIAL Forum*, 72, 2013, pp 34–39.

Whelan, James, *The state of the Australian Public Service: An alternative report*, Centre For Policy Development, Aug 2011, cpd.org.au/wp-content/uploads/2011/08/CPD_OP12_2011_State_of_APS_Whelan.pdf

Williamson, Oliver E, 'Transaction cost economics: The natural progression', Nobel Prize Lecture, Aula Magna, Stockholm University, 8 Dec 2009.

——, 'Public and private bureaucracies: A transaction cost economics perspectives', *Journal of Law, Economics, & Organization*, vol 15, no 1, 1999, pp 306–42, doi.org/10.1093/jleo/15.1.306

——, 'Comparative economic organization: The analysis of discrete structural alternatives', *Administrative Science Quarterly*, vol 36, no 2, 1991, pp 269–96, doi.org/10.2307/2393356

——, *Corporate control and business behavior*, Prentice Hall Inc, Englewood Cliffs, New Jersey, 1970.

Windrum, P, 'Innovation and entrepreneurship in the public service', in P Windrum & P Koch, eds, *Innovation in public sector services*, Edward Elgar, Cheltenham, UK, 2008, doi.org/10.4337/9781848441545.00009

World Economic Forum (WEF), 'The global competitiveness index 2016–17', Geneva, September 2016.